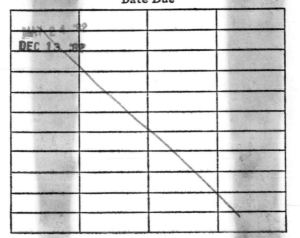

Confucius

THE MAN AND THE MYTH

The title opposite has very kindly been written by Mr. K'ung Tê-ch'êng, the direct descendant of Confucius in the seventy-seventh generation, who is charged by the Chinese government with the function of maintaining the sacrifices to Confucius. The large characters are K'UNG TZǓ—"Confucius"—written in the form which was used during Confucius' lifetime. The small characters on the left read, "Written by K'ung Tê-ch'êng." The seal bears the personal name of Mr. K'ung in the style of characters which were used during the Shang dynasty (?1766-1122? B.C.) This seal was carved for Mr. K'ung by Mr. Tung Tso-pin of the Academia Sinica, who directed the first scientific excavation of the Shang capital at Anyang.

孔子

孔德成題

Confucius

THE MAN AND THE MYTH

H. G. Creel

ASSOCIATE PROFESSOR OF EARLY CHINESE LITERATURE AND
INSTITUTIONS IN THE UNIVERSITY OF CHICAGO. AUTHOR OF
The Birth of China, Studies in Early Chinese Culture, etc.

GREENWOOD PRESS, PUBLISHERS
WESTPORT, CONNECTICUT

Library of Congress Cataloging in Publication Data

Creel, Herrlee Glessner, 1905-
Confucius, the man and the myth.

Bibliography: p.
1. Confucius. I. Title.
B128.C8C65 1972   299'.5126'4   72-7816
ISBN 0-8371-6531-8

Originally published in 1949 by The John Day Company, New York

Reprinted with the permission of the original publisher, The John Day Company, Inc.

Reprinted by Greenwood Press, a division of Williamhouse-Regency Inc.

First Greenwood Reprinting 1972
Second Greenwood Reprinting 1975

Library of Congress Catalog Card Number 72-7816

ISBN 0-8371-6531-8

Printed in the United States of America

CONTENTS

Contents

PREFACE

AMONG a large fraction of mankind, Confucius has for many centuries been considered the most important man that ever lived. His philosophy has played a part in the development of some of the most basic social and political conceptions of the modern West. In eastern Asia his name is still invoked in ideological struggles by the most conservative and by some of the most radical, who seek by means of varying interpretations to show that Confucius favored their views.

When we turn from his reputation to examine what tradition tells us of the man behind it, we are disappointed. He is described as completely unoriginal, intent solely upon reviving the usages of antiquity. The account of his life which is generally accepted depicts him as a man of little personal force, whose actions often failed signally to embody the ideals he preached to others. It is impossible not to feel that something must be wrong. This man, portrayed by tradition, seems an inadequate cause for the effects attested by history. A possible explanation is that tradition does not accurately portray the Confucius who lived. This book is an investigation of that possibility.

This is not, of course, the first attempt to find the real Confucius. It will not be the last. Its author will be well satisfied if it proves to be a step in the right direction.

Although this book has no footnotes, it is not undocumented. In addition to the notes in the back of the book, there is a special section of references, on pages 329-340, which lists the sources of all quotations and cites evidence for each major point. These references are so numerous that if a number had been included in the text for each of them, the page would have been difficult to read. They have therefore been placed where they will not bother the reader, but are available for consultation when desired. Thus, if one wishes to know the source of a quotation, or the evidence for a statement, appearing in the fourth line on page 127, he need only turn in the references to "Page 127, line 4," where the source or the evidence is cited. In a few cases the references for an entire paragraph have been combined.

Some of the individuals mentioned in this book are called by several names in the texts. To avoid confusion, I have arbitrarily called each person by only one name. For convenience, references are commonly given to translations of Chinese texts, but the original Chinese has been consulted in every instance. Some of the translations are new, either wholly or in part.

This book could never have been written without the generous advice, assistance, and criticism of many kind friends. The mere listing of their names here is nothing more than a token of my gratitude.

The contribution of my wife, Lorraine Creel, has been especially great. Her doctoral dissertation has been a source of important ideas. Each major point has been discussed with her, and many changes have been made at her suggestion.

The entire manuscript was read in draft form, and criticized, by Professor Adrienne Koch and Professor Earl H. Pritchard, to whom I am deeply indebted. For reading it in part, and making many valuable suggestions, my thanks are due to Professor Louis Gottschalk, Professor S. William Halperin, Professor Jerome G. Kerwin, Professor Edward A. Kracke, Jr., and Professor Donald F. Lach. For much valuable advice I wish to thank Professor Nabia Abbott, Mr. Edwin G. Beal, Jr., Professor Herman Finer, Professor Alan Gewirth, Professor William A. Irwin, Professor Richard P. McKeon, Dr. Charles Morris, Dr. H. I. Poleman, Professor G. K. Strodach, Professor T'ang Yung-t'ung, Professor Têng Ssŭ-yü, Professor Tung Tso-pin, and Professor John A. Wilson. I am indebted to Mr. T. H. Tsien not only for advice on bibliography, but also for writing the Chinese characters. For one year this research was carried on at the Library of Congress; I wish to express my appreciation to Dr. Arthur W. Hummel and his staff in the Division of Orientalia, for their great helpfulness in matters both of bibliography and of content. To the Rockefeller Foundation, my thanks are due for a fellowship which made it possible to devote my full time to this research during the year 1945–1946.

Mr. Richard J. Walsh has made a number of excellent editorial suggestions which I have gladly incorporated. The map has been prepared by Miss Susan T. Richert. Miss June Work has had a large part in the preparation of the book, from the gathering of material through the reading of proofs and the preparation of the index. She has eliminated many errors, and deserves a large share of credit for any good qualities it may possess.

The responsibility for any inaccuracies which remain must rest upon myself alone. Because the subject is a large and complex one, there is no doubt that the mistakes are many. My position is that of the man mentioned in *Analects* 14.26, who "wished to make his faults few, but had not yet succeeded."

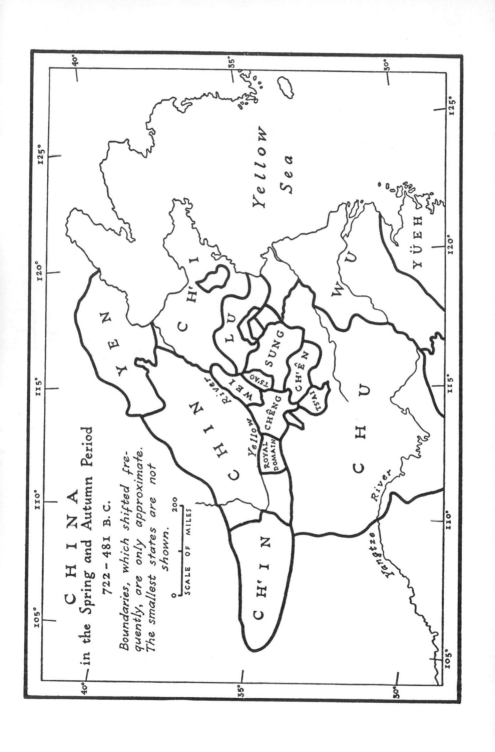

CHINA
in the Spring and Autumn Period
722-481 B.C.

Boundaries, which shifted frequently, are only approximate.
The smallest states are not
shown.

SCALE OF MILES
0   200

Yellow Sea

YÜEH

WU

CHU

CH'I

YEN

CHIN

CH'IN

LU

SUNG

TS'AO

CH'ÊN

TSAI

WEI

CHÊNG

ROYAL DOMAIN

Yellow River

Yangtze River

Confucius

THE MAN AND THE MYTH

BACKGROUND

CHAPTER I

TRADITION AND TRUTH

TWENTY-FIVE hundred years ago there was born in China a child whose life was to influence human history as few have done. Tradition says that he came of noble ancestry and was the descendant of kings. At his birth, it is related, dragons and "spirit maidens" hovered in the air. But Confucius himself said, "When young, I was without rank and in humble circumstances."

Tradition paints him as a strict pedant, laying down precise rules for men to follow in their conduct and their thinking. The truth is that he carefully avoided laying down rules, because he believed that no creed formulated by another person can excuse any man from the duty of thinking for himself.

He is often called a reactionary, whose primary aim was to restore the ways of antiquity and to bolster the authority of the hereditary aristocracy. In fact, he advocated and helped to bring about such sweeping social and political reforms that he must be counted among the great revolutionaries. Within a few centuries after his death hereditary aristocracy had virtually ceased to exist in China, and Confucius had contributed more than any other man to its destruction.

As a young man he had to earn his living at tasks that bor-

1

dered on the menial. From this he gained, and never lost, a deep sympathy for the common people. Their problems and sufferings were many. Centralized government had broken down. The feudal lords acknowledged only nominal allegiance to the king. Yet they could not be called independent, for some of them were no more than puppets in the hands of their own swashbuckling underlings. Public and private wars raged unchecked. There was very little law and order save what each man could enforce by his own right arm, his armed followers, or his powers of intrigue. Even the greatest noble could not be sure that he would not be ruined and perhaps assassinated. The position of the common people was tragic. Whoever won the wars, they lost. Even when there was peace they had no security, for they had no power. They were virtual pawns of the aristocrats, whose principal interests had come to be hunting, war, and extravagant living. To pay for these pastimes they taxed the people beyond what the traffic could bear, and suppressed all protest ruthlessly.

To the young Confucius these conditions seemed intolerable, and he resolved to devote his life to trying to right them. He talked to others about the way in which the world might be made a better place to live in. Gradually he gathered about himself a group of young men to study his doctrines, and so he became known as a teacher.

The essentials of his teaching were simple. Everywhere about him he saw men struggling against each other, but he refused to believe that that was the natural state of society. He thought it was normal for men to cooperate; to strive, not to get the better of each other, but to promote the common welfare. In his opinion a ruler's success should be measured by his ability, not to amass wealth and power for himself, but to bring about the welfare and happiness of his people.

Confucius realized that the world of which he dreamed would never exist so long as the kind of rulers who occupied the thrones were directing government. There is reason to believe that if it had been possible he would gladly have dispensed with hereditary rulers,[1] but that was out of the question. Instead, he tried to persuade the rulers to turn over their administrative functions to ministers who were virtuous, capable, and properly trained. He tried to educate young men to be such ministers. For such education he accepted the poor and humble on exactly the same basis as the rich and well born. He demanded only two qualifications: intelligence and industry.

He was trying to produce a bloodless revolution. He wanted to take the actual power from rulers who inherited thrones and give it to ministers chosen on the basis of merit, and to change the aim of government from the aggrandizement of a few to the welfare and happiness of the whole people. He knew that mere intellectual conviction is not enough for revolution, and he tried to kindle in his disciples a veritable passion for the cause to which his life was dedicated. In this he had a large measure of success. This group of "Knights of the Way" (to borrow Arthur Waley's felicitous phrase) was inspired by a measure of devotion not less than that later found in Christian chivalry.

Yet for Confucius it was not enough to be a teacher. He wanted to direct the government of a state and to see the world of which he dreamed come to life under his hand. It is clear, however, that the rulers of the day cannot have seriously considered putting real power into his hands. At best they must have thought him a harmless eccentric, but one who could become dangerous if given power. They did, however, give rather high posts to some of his disciples. It was doubtless at the insistence of these students that Confucius was finally given an office, in his native state of Lu, that carried a respectable title but probably involved no real authority.

When he saw that he could accomplish nothing he resigned his post, and set off on travels which took him to a number of states, in search of a ruler who would use his Way. He never found one. These journeyings lasted a decade or more. They accomplished little, but they did prove that he was willing to undergo great hardship and abuse for his principles.

Returning to Lu he resumed his teaching. Five years later he died. His life had had about it very little of the dramatic. There was no climax and no martyrdom. None of his chief ambitions had been fulfilled. There is little doubt that when he died everyone considered him a failure. Certainly he himself did.

After his death, as his teachings were handed down from one generation of disciples to another, the Confucian group gradually grew in size and influence. The doctrine was changed and elaborated until Confucius himself would scarcely have recognized it, yet two principles remained: the insistence that those who govern should be chosen not for their birth but for their virtue and ability, and that the true end of government is the welfare and happiness of the people. This latter principle made Confucianism popular with the common people, as war and oppression increased and life became more and more difficult.

In 221 B.C. the relatively barbarous state of Ch'in overran China and converted it into a totalitarian empire. The Confucians refused to collaborate. Circulation of their books and teachings was forbidden, and some of them were put to death. Within less than two decades Ch'in was destroyed by a revolution in which the Confucians took a prominent part.

The Han dynasty, which succeeded, was on the whole much more favorable to the Confucians. A number of them came into conflict, however, with its sixth emperor, Wu, who had totalitarian ambitions. He was far too clever to oppose Confucianism openly; instead he posed as its patron and subsidized it. By putting large numbers of Confucians on the government payroll, and personally manipulating the examinations by which officials were beginning to be selected, he exercised considerable influence over the development of Confucian doctrine. From about this time there dates the misuse of Confucianism to justify despotism. This was a perversion of everything that Confucius stood for, against which enlightened and courageous Confucians have never ceased to protest.

Most of the information about Confucius that is current today derives from the Han period or later. This is true of his biography and of those commentaries that seek to put flesh and blood on the dry bones of the classical books. Confucius was scarcely dead before the embroidering of traditions about him began. It seemed unthinkable that one whose ideas were so important could have been unappreciated in his own day; his biography was so written as to make him a powerful statesman. Rival schools of thought at first attacked and ridiculed him; later, they adopted him. Even the totalitarian Legalists converted Confucius to totalitarianism. Most effective of all, they put totalitarian sentiments into his mouth, in passages written into the most venerated scriptures of Confucianism.

All this was useful to those who found the democratic sentiments of Confucius embarrassing and wished to represent him as a supporter of unlimited imperial authority. They needed only to stress these false additions to his supposed sayings, to interpret others, and to forget the rest. Thus they built up a façade behind which it has been very hard, for two thousand years, to find the real Confucius.

There were almost always a few scholars, however, who were capable of discernment. So were a number of the Jesuit missionaries who entered China and became scholars and even officials at the Chinese court in the seventeenth and eighteenth centuries. They brushed aside as so much chaff the accumulation of recent interpretation, and sought to go back to Confucius himself. In letter after letter to Europe they told of the wonderful new philosopher they had discovered.

Thus Confucius became known to Europe just at the beginning of the philosophic movement known as the Enlightenment. A large number of philosophers, including Leibniz, Wolff, and Voltaire, as well as statesmen and men of letters, used his name and his ideas to further their arguments, and they themselves were influenced in the process. Both in France and in England the fact that China, under the impulsion of Confucianism, had long since virtually abolished hereditary aristocracy, was used as a weapon in the attack on hereditary privilege. The philosophy of Confucius played a role of some importance in the development of democratic ideals in Europe and in the background of the French Revolution. Through French thought it indirectly influenced the development of democracy in America. It is of interest that Thomas Jefferson proposed, as "the key-stone of the arch of our government," an educational system that shows remarkable similarities to the Chinese examination system. The extent to which Confucianism contributed to the development of Western democracy is often forgotten, for rather curious reasons that we must examine in their proper place.

In China the story was similar. Confucius was an important intellectual ancestor of the Chinese Revolution. Sun Yat-sen declared that "both Confucius and Mencius were exponents of

democracy," and gave to the Republic of China a constitution
that bears the deep impress of Confucian principles. Yet some
of his countrymen today think of Confucius as a reactionary
who helped to forge the chains of despotism, and regard him
with hostility or indifference.

In a book concerned only with Europe, W. E. H. Lecky wrote
a description that applies to Confucius with remarkable aptness:

> There arise from time to time men who bear to the moral
> condition of their age much the same relations as men of genius
> bear to its intellectual condition. They anticipate the moral
> standard of a later age, cast abroad conceptions of disinterested
> virtue, of philanthropy, or of self-denial that seem to have no
> relation to the spirit of their time, inculcate duties and suggest
> motives of action that appear to most men altogether chimerical.
> Yet the magnetism of their perfection tells powerfully upon their
> contemporaries. An enthusiasm is kindled, a group of adherents
> is formed, and many are emancipated from the moral condition
> of their age. Yet the full effects of such a movement are but
> transient. The first enthusiasm dies away, surrounding circum-
> stances resume their ascendancy, the pure faith is materialised,
> encrusted with conceptions that are alien to its nature, dislocated,
> and distorted, till its first features have almost disappeared. The
> moral teaching, being unsuited to the time, becomes inoperative
> until its appropriate civilization has dawned; or at most it faintly
> and imperfectly filters through an accumulation of dogmas, and
> thus accelerates in some measure the arrival of the condition it
> requires.*

All of this is true of Confucius. It helps to explain why, as he
himself said, no one fully understood him even in his own day,
and why later generations have often seriously misunderstood
him. It helps to explain the fact that this man, who lived so
long ago and was so obscure in his lifetime, left behind him an
influence that continues to affect men's thoughts and actions
even in our own day.

---

* The source of this, and of all other quotations, is given in the References,
pages 329 to 340. For such references, and for routine citations of evidence,
figures are not inserted in the text; they may be located, however, in the References under the appropriate page and line.

CHAPTER II

THE EVIDENCE

It has long been recognized that the traditions about Confucius, which are accepted even by many scholars, are of questionable accuracy. More than eleven hundred years ago one of the most famous of Confucians, Han Yü, complained that his contemporaries repeated the most utter nonsense about Confucius. Thus, he asked, if one wishes to learn the truth, "from whom can he seek it?"

Almost every account of Confucius is based upon the biography included in the *Historical Records*, which was written around 100 B.C. Indeed, a Western scholar has written that it "will form the basis of the biographies of Confucius for all time." Yet at the beginning of the nineteenth century the great critic Ts'ui Shu pointed out that in fact this biography is, as he pungently put it, "seventy or eighty per cent slander." A Chinese scholar of our own day, who has studied this problem exhaustively, asserts that the biography contained in the *Historical Records* is so "utterly confused and disordered" that it could not have been written, in its present form, by its supposed author. Nevertheless, this is the foundation upon which are erected accounts of the sage that we are asked to believe.

If we are to arrive at something closer to the truth, we must

7

Since the only full

approach the problem from a new direction. Since the only full accounts of Confucius that exist were written centuries after his death, it is customary to begin with them, but to seek to eliminate from them that which appears legendary or improbable. After this has been done, however, we have no assurance whatever that what remains is the truth. Once a man has become, as Confucius became, the hero of a culture, his name is used in countless stories that are based far more upon the beliefs and aspirations of those who tell them than upon any actual events of his life.

Let us consider an example from Christian tradition. Most of the early Christians were, as Paul has reminded us, humble folk, often despised and persecuted. When their children were mistreated by their playfellows, some of them consoled themselves with the thought that the boy Jesus, with his divine powers, could not have been so used with impunity. Thus in two of the Apocryphal Gospels it is related that when other children offended the young Jesus he used his supernatural powers to strike them dead on the spot.

How should we interpret these stories, as history? Should we say that they are exaggerated and reduce the number of children killed to one? Shall we eliminate the supernatural element and say that this child was killed by purely natural means? Shall we go further and say that Jesus did not intentionally kill a child at all, but that this incident is no doubt based upon the fact that he had killed one accidentally? Obviously, all these suppositions are nonsense. And the more we alter the stories, trying to make them credible, the less chance we have of understanding their origin at all. For they grew out of the daydreams of miserable and oppressed people, and as such they have meaning and considerable historical value. But if we try to derive facts about the life of Jesus from such tales, we shall be misled, for they have almost nothing to do with Jesus at all.

No more do most of the stories about Confucius have anything to do with him. If we place them in their setting and study them carefully, they will tell us a great deal about the people of the period in which they originated, whether the Han dynasty or another. But it is quite hopeless to take the mass of legend about Confucius, as it existed when he had been dead for three centuries and more, and try to sort out the truth. It is too utterly confused, and there is no satisfactory standard by which the true may be distinguished from the false.

Instead, we shall try to find the real Confucius by means of two other kinds of material. First, while we shall not ignore the traditions that have been current in relatively recent times, we shall regard them as of secondary value, and shall place our chief reliance on records about Confucius that were written down as near to his own time as possible. We shall take as our basic materials books written within two centuries of his death. Second, we shall pay careful attention, as regards each major point, to the works that describe the situation which existed before the time of Confucius.

The importance of studying the pre-Confucian materials is sometimes overlooked. But if we are really to understand what sort of person Confucius was, it is essential. To use a modern example, it means little to say that John Smith advocated a forty-eight-hour working week unless we know under what circumstances he did so. If he did it in the middle of the twentieth century, in one of those countries where a forty-hour week is regarded by many people as standard, then he was proposing to lengthen the week and was what some would call a "reactionary." But if he did it under the conditions prevailing in many countries at the beginning of the nineteenth century, he was advocating a drastic shortening of the week and would certainly at the time have been called a "dangerous radical."

Similarly, there is little significance to the fact that Confucius said that one of his disciples might properly occupy the position of a ruler, unless we know all of the circumstances; but when we do, it is very important. For this disciple was not the heir of a ruler, and it was even intimated that his heredity was in some manner tainted.[1] That Confucius nevertheless said that he might properly occupy a throne, because of his virtue and abilities, would have been a commonplace in Han times. But in the literature and bronze inscriptions dating from any time earlier than that of Confucius, inheritance seems to have been the only claim to such a place that was ever considered.[2] In the light of this fact it is clear that Confucius' remark was not a casual compliment, but the statement of a revolutionary political principle of the greatest importance.

For our picture of pre-Confucian China we shall draw upon the classic known as the *Book of Poetry,* the genuinely early portions of the *Book of Changes* [3] and the *Book of History,* [4] the *Spring and Autumn Annals,* and inscriptions cast on bronze vessels that have come down to us. We shall also make use of the historical work known as the *Tso Chuan,* but since it does not seem to have been written in anything like its present form until around 300 B.C., it must be utilized with considerable caution. [5]

For the foundation of our understanding of the life and thought of Confucius we shall use the *Analects.* This book consists chiefly of sayings of Confucius and his disciples. Not all of it is genuine, but those portions that have been added later often betray themselves in several ways at once. Not infrequently they differ so greatly from the genuinely early sections in style, in vocabulary, and in ideas simultaneously that there is no question that they are false. Many scholars have worked on these problems; their results are summarized and the authenticity of various portions of the *Analects* is discussed in detail in the Appendix.

The book named after the philosopher Mo Tzǔ makes some mention of Confucius. At first glance it would seem that it should be a good source since Mo Tzǔ lived immediately after Confucius; unfortunately, however, as critics have pointed out, most of the discussion of Confucius personally is found in passages that are obviously late additions to the *Mo Tzǔ.* [6]

The book called *Mencius* is, on the other hand, a very valuable source. The Confucian philosopher Mencius was born about a century after Confucius died. The work that bears his name records the tradition about Confucius in some detail and in a very early form, which is in general quite similar to that found in the early portions of the *Analects.* The *Tso Chuan* records, in much detail, the history of Confucius' native state during the period of his lifetime. On the whole, however, it tells us remarkably little about the life of Confucius. This is one of the many facts which make it clear that in reality Confucius was not, in his lifetime, the important political figure that later tradition has represented him. The *Tso Chuan* also contains some stories about Confucius that disagree with the earlier accounts and in some cases even involve the weird or supernatural. Since this is true, and since the *Tso Chuan* was not written in its present form until around 300 B.C., only a part of what it has to say about Confucius can be accepted as trustworthy. This part, however, is valuable in helping to fill out the picture.

Works written after Confucius had been dead for centuries give much more detailed information about him than those written near his lifetime. This is the reverse of what we should expect, and it is clear that much of the added information was derived from imagination rather than from knowledge. We shall look at a number of these later works when we come to examine the growth of the Confucian legend.[7]

CHAPTER III

THE CHINA OF CONFUCIUS

To understand Confucius it is necessary to realize what sort of world he lived in. He is criticized as having been too much interested in the orderly arrangement of affairs, so that his ideas seem dry and unexciting. But it must be remembered that he was trying to bring order out of something close to chaos. He had no need to seek ways to make life interesting. To hold his revolutionary ideas and to talk about them as freely as he did in a world where that was extremely dangerous gave life adventure enough. Confucius is frequently quoted as addressing what sound like pedantic little homilies to various nobles and rulers. Yet when we understand their background it is clear that some of these remarks are pointed denunciations of weaknesses, not to say crimes, made directly to men who would have felt as much compunction about having Confucius tortured to death as about crushing a fly.

In Confucius' day, China stood at the crossroads. Let us look briefly at the process by which she arrived there.

Archaeology indicates that human beings related to the modern Chinese have occupied China for a very long time. Our actual knowledge of Chinese history begins, however, with the Shang state in the fourteenth century B.C. Although we know this state, which had its capital in what is now northern Honan Province, only from excavations and brief inscriptions, it is evident that it had a remarkably advanced civilization. Many of its productions show a high degree of sophistication, and its bronze vessels rank among the finest artistic productions of the human race. This civilization was not destroyed, but it suffered a setback when, in 1122 B.C. according to the traditional chronology, the Shang were conquered by a coalition of relatively rude tribesmen who came from what is now Shensi Province, to the west. The conquerors were led by the Chou people, who established the Chou dynasty. These invaders pushed their conquests to cover a considerable portion of North China, but it was impossible for them to administer this territory as a strongly centralized state. For this they would have needed good communications, an effective monetary system, and great political experience, all of which they lacked.

Of necessity they parceled out most of their territories to relatives of the Chou ruler and to the principal chiefs of other tribes that had assisted in the conquest. Thus there grew up a feudal system in which each vassal was free to rule his own territory much as he pleased, so long as it did not disturb the peace of the realm. He was expected to pay to the king certain tribute and to lead his army to fight in the king's service when required.

In the time of Confucius, and later, the early Chou period was pictured as an almost ideal time of Chinese unity, peace, and justice. The truer picture, which we get from inscriptions on bronzes cast at the time, shows that this is gross exaggeration. Nevertheless there probably was a considerable degree of political morality, relatively speaking, if only from compulsion. For the Chou vassals in the east were surrounded by strange and hostile people. On the one hand, this compelled them to obey the king and cooperate between themselves. On the other, it restrained them from treating the subject population too oppressively. In fact, if the Chou were to maintain themselves as rulers, they had to conciliate the people.

Important among the means by which they did so was a propaganda campaign, which represented the Chou conquest as an altruistic crusade designed only to liberate the people of the east from their "wicked" and oppressive rulers. In order to gain ac-

ceptance for this fiction the Chou brought forth what seems to
have been a new version of Chinese history.¹ They alleged that
both the Hsia and the Shang states, which preceded Chou, had
had good rulers at first but wicked ones at the end. In this situation the principal deity, "Heaven," looked about for a virtuous
noble to whom to give "the decree," a mandate to rebel and set
up a new dynasty. Thus there grew up the theory of the "right
of revolution," according to which it is not only a right but a
sacred duty to overthrow a wicked ruler. If it is asked how one is
to tell a mere rebel from a successor appointed by Heaven, the
answer is that the people will adhere to the cause of the latter
and give him victory. Clearly, although the Chou propagandists
had no such intention, they laid an excellent foundation for the
later development of democratic ideas.

As the Chou dynasty became older, the descendants of the
first feudal lords were no longer under the same necessity of
mutual cooperation. Gradually they paid less and less attention
to the orders of the king. They fought among themselves more
and more frequently, and large and powerful states swallowed up
the territory of their weaker neighbors. In 771 B.C., 220 years before Confucius was born, a coalition of feudal lords and "barbarian" tribes attacked the Chou capital in the west. The king
was killed, and the "Western Chou" period came to an end. The
later kings had their capital to the east, at Loyang in what is now
Honan Province; for this reason the later period is known as
"Eastern Chou." They were established at Loyang under the
protection of certain of the feudal lords, and from this time forward the kings were little more than puppets in the hands of
their chief vassals.

The "barbarian" tribes by whom the Chinese states were surrounded were not necessarily men of different race; the distinction was that they did not practice Chinese culture. Over the
centuries most of these people were gradually Sinicized and became Chinese, but before this had happened they were a constant menace, poised on the borders to pillage and even to annex
Chinese territory at any sign of weakness. As political disunity
made the Chinese states less and less capable of concerted defense, it became evident that they must have a leader if Chinese
culture were not to perish. But the Chou kings were weak and

incapable, and while a number of the feudal lords would have liked to become king, if any one of them threatened to become too powerful the rest banded together to pull him down. Beginning in 679 B.C. a makeshift variety of leadership was developed. A sort of league composed of the eastern Chou states was formed, and the most powerful noble in the league took the title of *Pa*, First Noble. During the following two centuries several feudal lords held or claimed this title. When they were effective, they collected tribute from those states that recognized their leadership, supervised the common defense, and replaced the king in everything but his religious functions.

In the two centuries between the beginning of the Eastern Chou period (770 B.C.) and the birth of Confucius (551 B.C.), the boundaries of states were shifting, but the situation can be described in a general, schematic way (see map, p. xii). Toward the center of the Chinese world, near the Yellow River, were the states that, in general, preserved Chinese culture nearest to its traditional purity. Especially important in this respect were the royal domain of the Chou kings, the state of Sung (ruled by descendants of the Shang kings), and to the northeast the native state of Confucius, Lu. These and the other small states of the center were more cultured but less powerful and less extensive than the peripheral states. The central states produced thinkers who tended to emphasize peace and human happiness, while many of those who extolled force and "discipline" were men of the peripheral states.

Although the great southern state of Ch'u dominated almost the entire Yangtze Valley, its tremendous potential power was diminished by frequent altercations among its noble families. Culturally, it held somewhat aloof from the Chinese states. Ch'u was originally a "barbarian" state, which only gradually came into the fold of Chinese culture.

The same is probably true to some extent of the great western state of Ch'in, which had its capital in what is now Shensi, near the present Sian. This was the ancient seat of the Chou, but there are indications that the culture of the state of Ch'in differed in significant respects from that of the thoroughly Chinese central states. It seems probable that these differences later facilitated the growth of totalitarianism in Ch'in.

There were two other large and powerful states. Chin had its capital in what is now Shansi Province, and Ch'i included much of what is now Shantung. Ch'i was rich and powerful, and its Duke Huan was the first to seize the place of First Noble, superseding the Chou king in almost everything but name and religious functions. But in defending his title, Duke Huan wore Ch'i out with military expeditions, and after his death in 643 his sons contended for the throne in civil war. Ch'i was so weakened that it never again held the preeminent power.

It is unnecessary to recount in detail the almost constant wars of this period. Not only were the Chinese states always fighting with each other, and with the semibarbarian state of Ch'u, but the northern barbarians known as Ti were also an active menace at this time. At one point the reigning Chou king asked the Ti to help him against a Chinese enemy and ended by being temporarily ousted from his capital by the barbarians. A regular pattern developed of almost continuous warfare between the great peripheral states. The smaller states of the center would have been glad to remain neutral, but they could not; they were compelled to adhere to one side or the other and to change sides as new pressure was exerted. What was most unfortunate for them was the fact that, lying between the great states, they formed a predestined field of combat in which their powerful neighbors met for their battles, sometimes annually. Thus the great peripheral states were spared many of the horrors of war, but the central states got far more than their share. This is undoubtedly one reason why the philosophers of the central states were in general strong advocates of peace, while those of the peripheral areas tended to extol the glories of war.

Sometimes the armies of the great states did not fight each other but were content merely to punish the vacillation of the central states, and force them to swear new covenants of allegiance. The making of covenants was a solemn religious ceremony. A sacrificial animal was slain, and its blood was used to smear each copy of the agreement. Each of the rulers or officers subscribing to the treaty then read it aloud and smeared his lips with the blood of the victim. Finally, a copy of the treaty was buried along with the victim, so that the spirits might enforce its terms. Such a treaty made a few years before the birth of Confucius, forced upon the central state of Chêng and subscribed to by a group of states, ended as follows: "If any should fail to do as is enjoined by this agreement, may those who preside over men's sincerity and watch over covenants, [the spirits of] the famous mountains and rivers, the multitude of spirits and all those who are sacrificed to, and all the ancesters of our seven surnames and twelve states—may all these bright spirits punish him, so that he shall lose his people, his appointment shall fall to the ground, his family shall perish, and his state and his clan shall be utterly overthrown." A fearful oath. Yet within two months Chêng was compelled, under military pressure, to transfer its allegiance again.

Other states as well suffered in this manner. But the regularity with which Chêng was forced to swear eternal fealty to a new master became so farcical that at one point Chêng said frankly that the whole thing was meaningless, and asked that it be permitted to swear to be loyal, not to any particular state, but to whatever one acted as it ought to act.

This state of affairs had two important effects on men's thinking. First, it was quite obvious that states were constantly entering covenants with fearful sanctions and breaking them as soon as it was expedient, without suffering the penalties that the spirits were supposed to inflict. Indeed, it was those who tried to remain true to their undertakings even in the face of superior force who were made to regret it. It is quite natural, then, that in this period there was a growing scepticism as to even the existence of the spirits, not to mention their power. Second, not only religion but even ethics was shaken to its very foundations. Might seemed everywhere to be right, and the only right to which anyone but a fool would pay any attention.

Confucius' native state, Lu, was relatively small and weak. The wonder is that it was not destroyed and annexed by one of the large states. That it nevertheless persisted until the very end of the Chou dynasty is probably due in part to the fact that Lu was founded by the famous Duke of Chou, a brother of the founder of the dynasty, and was considered a repository of the ancient culture and ceremonies. It would have been easy for a powerful state to extinguish Lu, but it would not have looked well. This does not mean that the state had an easy time. It was constantly beset by troubles, from within and from without. As compared with the more central states, however, Lu suffered much less from war. James Legge has calculated that during the years covered by the *Spring and Autumn Annals*, 722–481 B.C., Lu was invaded only twenty-one times. While this is often enough, it is little for the period.

The great state of Ch'i bordered Lu on the northeast and was its principal cross. War with Ch'i was frequent. Ch'i constantly nibbled away pieces of territory from Lu's boundary, and Lu was constantly trying, sometimes with success, to get them back. Lu could resist Ch'i only by calling another powerful state to its aid. As early as 634 Lu asked and received aid against Ch'i from the southern barbarian state of Ch'u. In 609 Ch'i supported a minister of Lu who murdered two rightful heirs to the throne and set up the son of a secondary wife as duke of Lu. As long as this duke lived Ch'i dominated the government of Lu, and Lu finally had to ask aid of Chin to regain its independence. Thus it went, with Lu as the pawn of whatever state was powerful at the moment. Yet it is not to be supposed that Lu was a poor suffering innocent. Trembling before the great states, Lu lorded it over smaller ones, invading, looting, extinguishing, and annexing them whenever it was able to do so.

The internal politics of Lu presented an aspect that was common to other states as well. In China as a whole, the various feudal states had grown in power at the expense of the king until he was reduced to a puppet. Now, within the feudal states, there was a tendency for the clans of the principal ministers to usurp power at the expense of the ruler of the state.

Any reader of the Confucian *Analects* has encountered the term "the three families." These three clans were descended from three of the sons of Duke Huan of Lu, who reigned from 711 to 697. The families were named Mêng,[2] Shu, and Chi, literally Eldest, Third, and Youngest, after the three brothers. Just as in a European fairy tale, it was the youngest son who proved the most successful. This son, the founder of the Chi family, opposed the schemes of his murderous brother, founder of the

Eldest family, who sought the throne for himself. Chi Yu saved the life of the rightful heir to the throne of Lu; as his reward he became prime minister and had great power in Lu. From this time through that of Confucius the position of prime minister of Lu seems to have been held successively by the heads of the Chi family, with only slight intermission when one of the other families became more powerful.

For the century and a half before the birth of Confucius, the power of the dukes of Lu was largely in the hands of these three families, which gradually tightened their grip. The heads of two of the families took part in the murder of two ducal heirs, in 609, to set a more acceptable one on the throne. In 562 they divided the state, its army, and most of its revenues between themselves, leaving the Duke of Lu little but his ceremonial prerogatives. In 537, when Confucius was fifteen, the Chi family took over half of the state, leaving a fourth each to the Mêng and Shu families; the Duke was then dependent for revenues on such contributions as the families were pleased to give him.

It is not to be supposed that the dukes made no effort to free themselves of this domination. When Confucius was thirty-four, Duke Chao led a group that attempted to kill the head of the Chi family, who had a narrow escape. But the Shu family rescued him, and Duke Chao was compelled to flee to Ch'i, where he lived in exile. The Chi family regularly sent horses, clothing, and shoes for the Duke and his followers but would not allow him to return to Lu, and he died abroad after seven years. This was the most spectacular of numerous attempts by the dukes to assert their independence.

Quite naturally noble families other than the powerful three were jealous of them. Quarrels developed over such matters as illicit intrigues with women and in one case even over a cock-fight in which one of the parties equipped his cock with metal spurs. These quarrels commonly led to violence, frequently under the guise of an attempt to regain for the duke his usurped prerogatives. But the three families stayed in power. Sometimes they quarreled among themselves, but they were usually wise enough to realize that they must cooperate, however unwillingly, or face destruction.

The process by which the power of the emperor was usurped

by the rulers of the states, and their power was usurped by their chief ministers, did not stop there. The officers of the ministers also encroached on the power of their superiors as much as they were able. When these officers were put in charge of towns, as governors, they sometimes closed the city gates and renounced their allegiance, holding their cities in a state of insurrection. Towns and districts on the border sometimes transferred their allegiance from one state to another in this way.

When Confucius was forty-seven the chief officer of the Chi family, named Yang Hu, attacked the head of the family and imprisoned him, forcing him to subscribe and swear to a covenant. The next year he forced the chiefs of all three families, as well as others in the state, to swear to another covenant. At this time Lu was actually ruled neither by the Duke, nor by the three families, but by Yang Hu. Two years later Yang, with some other officers, plotted to murder the heads of all three families; Yang expected to replace the chief of the Chi family himself. The plan almost carried, but when it was discovered at the last moment Yang had to flee the state.

Not merely in Lu, but in the other states as well, there was almost no basis of authority and order, save the constantly shifting balance of brute force. The forms of religion were widely practiced, as witnessed by the ceremonies with which treaties were constantly being solemnized, but an officer of Ch'u struck the keynote of the age when he said, "If we can gain the advantage over our enemies, we must advance without any consideration of covenants." Nor was there our concept of the law, which stands over all alike. Human life was cheap. When a ruler of Wu did not wish bad news he had received to spread, he cut, with his own hand, the throats of seven men who happened to be in his tent. Food suspected of being poisoned was tested on a dog and a servant. The ruler of one small state was a collector of swords and tried out new acquisitions on his subjects. Duke Ling of the great state of Chin enjoyed shooting at the passers-by from a tower, to watch them try to dodge his missiles; when his cook did not prepare bears' paws to his taste, he had the cook killed. Such rulers were unusual, but it was not unusual for nobles to threaten subordinates who dared to advise against their conduct and to kill those who continued to remonstrate. Hired murderers were sometimes used. Punishments were severe and common; in Ch'i mutilation of the feet was so usual that special footgear was sold in the shops for those who had suffered it. Bribery at all levels was common, from the perversion of justice in favor of individuals to bribes demanded and received by ministers of great states, from other states, to insure a favorable foreign policy.

Even relatives could not trust each other. An idea of the degree of confidence that existed between members of the ruling group may be gained from the account of a banquet which one of his relatives gave for the ruler of Wu, when Confucius was about thirty. This relative, named Hê Lu, intended to kill the ruler at this banquet and to succeed him. He concealed his assassins in an underground chamber beneath the banquet hall. The ruler suspected the plot but went anyway, taking due precautions. He had his soldiers line the road all the way from his palace to the place of entertainment and posted his friends, well armed, all over the banquet hall. These friends met each waiter bringing food, at the door, stripped him and made him change clothes, and then made him crawl in with the food on hands and knees; even then two of them accompanied him, with drawn swords. The precautions seemed more than ample. But one of Hê Lu's bravos placed a dagger inside a fish, crawled to set the fish before the ruler, then suddenly drew the dagger and stabbed the king to death. At the same moment, says the chronicler, "two swords met in the assassin's breast."

Two powerful families in Ch'i were inimical toward two other families and heard that their enemies were coming to attack them. Immediately they assembled their followers and gave them arms. This done, they inquired into what their enemies were doing and found that the whole story had been false. Concluding, nevertheless, that as soon as their adversaries heard that they had armed their followers they *would* attack, they took the initiative themselves.

If it be true, as sometimes alleged, that Confucius was puritanical in his ethics, the same charge cannot be made against many of his contemporaries. Adultery and even incest were rather common among the nobles. Women, even the wives of other nobles, were sometimes appropriated without ceremony by those who had the desire and the power.

There were, of course, some cases of great fidelity and chivalry, of men dying for their lords and for their principles, and of men refusing unjust gain. But they are far less numerous in the records than the reverse, and many of them are far less convincing as history. Some idea of the disordered and precarious nature of the times may be gained from the fact that some nobles, far from wanting more territory, deliberately turned some of their lands back to their overlords, hoping that the lack of great possessions might enable them to escape catastrophe.

Relations between states were characterized by as great a lack of ethics as those between individuals. An envoy had to be a brave man, for if the state to which he was sent became annoyed at his own state he might be killed. Even rulers were not immune from detention when they made friendly visits to other states; such detention might be in preparation for attacking their states, or for other reasons. The rulers of two small states were held in Ch'u for three years each, because they refused to give its prime minister certain jewelry, furs, and horses that he wanted. Once when the Duke of Lu visited Ch'i, he was held until he agreed to marry his second daughter to a minister of Ch'i. One ruler of Ch'u, hearing that the wife of the ruler of the small state of Hsi was beautiful, went there (as he said) to give a feast for Hsi's ruler. Having arrived he killed him, extinguished his state, and carried his wife off to his harem in Ch'u.

Aristocrats had little enough security. The people had none. They were chiefly farmers, commonly virtual serfs. They had few if any rights as against the nobility; in practice they were taxed, worked, expropriated, scourged, and killed by the aristocrats, with almost no check save the fact that, if goaded too far, they might rebel. The penalty for unsuccessful rebellion, however, was death by torture.

Nobles traveling, even outside of their own domains, went through the land like a plague of locusts, cutting down trees for fuel, denuding the fields, damaging the houses in which they lodged, and backing "requests" for contributions with violence. These were the commonplaces of peace. The frequent wars brought more dramatic sufferings. In 593 B.C., for instance, the capital of the state of Sung was besieged so long that the inhabitants were reduced to eating the flesh of the children. Since they could not bear to eat their own, they exchanged children before killing them.

The gradual breakdown of centralized governmental authority increased the difficulties of the people in more ways than one. As time went on the number of aristocrats increased greatly, thanks in part to the institution of polygamy, and at the same time the standard of living of even minor aristocrats became more and more luxurious. China could easily support one royal court in lavish style, but when a score of heads of feudal states tried to live like kings, there was a strain on the economy. When in turn their vassals and the vassals of their vassals tried to adopt the ways of their superiors, abject poverty for the masses was unavoidable. When there is added the fact that in order to maintain their dignity these aristocrats felt compelled to wage a multiplicity of interstate, interclan, and even private wars, it is not surprising that the situation became insupportable.

This disease within the body of society produced its own antitoxin. In theory all the sons of aristocrats should have received fiefs and posts in the government, but the time soon came when there were so many men of noble ancestry that this was impossible. The result was that even some who were near relatives of rulers were reduced to penury. Thus there came into being a large group of men who by ancestry and sometimes by education were aristocrats, but who in poverty and in position came near to sharing the lot of the common people.

It was such reduced scions of the aristocracy who made up, in the first instance at least, the class of impoverished *shih* (士), which played such an important role during the latter part of the Chou dynasty. Some of them were warriors, bravos with swords for hire. Others were officers or clerks at the various courts. Still others were philosophers. Without exception they were discontented. Having known better things, or at least feeling entitled to them, they were not inclined to accept the *status quo.* They were not ignorant peasants, willing to suffer mistreatment without protest. All of them were resentful of such oppression as bore upon themselves, and a few were so altruistic as to espouse the cause of the whole people. Confucius was the most famous of their number.

CHAPTER IV

BIOGRAPHY

Of Confucius' ancestry we have no certain knowledge. It is true that the *Tso Chuan* gives his genealogy in detail, but the very fact that it supplies so many particulars on a matter of which earlier works say nothing is suspicious. Other circumstances as well throw doubt on this account, particularly the fact that it makes Confucius a direct descendant of the Shang royal house.[1]

He was born in the state of Lu, in a town, Tsou, located near the modern city of Ch'ü-fu in southwestern Shantung Province. The traditional date given for his birth, 551 B.C., is at least approximately correct.[2] No early work names either his father or his mother;[3] this supports the tradition that he was orphaned at an early age. All we know about his family is that he had an elder brother and a niece, while he himself fathered a son and a daughter. We know that his son died while Confucius was still living, but of his wife not a word is said. All this refers only to the early sources; later tradition supplied the sage with all of the appurtenances of a gentleman, including a divorce.

It is hard to determine what was the social position of his family.[4] He himself said that as a young man he was "of humble status," and it is clear that he did not own any considerable property. In so far as we can judge from the *Tso*

25

Chuan he was the only person of the K'ung surname to attain
prominence in the state of Lu, though the name was celebrated
in several other states. One of these was Sung, from which,
tradition states, his ancestors had emigrated some three generations earlier; this tradition, however, is none too surely based.
Nevertheless, it is probable that Confucius' ancestors had been
aristocrats, however minor. In China at that time the descent
from noble rank to "humble status" was swift; scions of great
families could be found tilling the fields. This is not to say that
Confucius was a peasant. He was educated and had some leisure
for such pursuits as archery and music. This is best explained on
the ground that he was, as tradition says, a man of aristocratic
ancestry, even though impoverished.

As to the way in which Confucius secured his education, the
records leave us almost wholly in the dark. The disciple Tzŭ-
kung stated that his Master had had no "regular teacher," [5] but
it does not necessarily follow that he was wholly self-taught. He
probably got the rudiments of his education as a young appren-
tice official doing clerical work. Mencius wrote, "Confucius was
once keeper of stores, and he said, 'It is only necessary that my
accounts be correct.' He was once in charge of pastures, and
said, 'It is my duty only to see that the oxen and sheep are well-
grown and strong.' "

Although Confucius never tried to hide his humble past, he
was a little ashamed of it when he grew older. Yet without these
early vicissitudes it is unlikely that he would have been so great
a man; indeed, they influenced the whole subsequent history of
Chinese culture. For his own early struggles gave him a touch
with and a sympathy for the common people that never left
him, and have colored Confucianism ever since. They made him
resolve that in so far as he could effect it every young man of
ability, no matter how humble, should have his chance. When
he later declared that he had never turned away an aspiring
student no matter how poor, and asserted that every youth
should be treated with respect until he has a chance to prove
himself, he was both stating the magnanimous principles of a
great man and (unconsciously no doubt) vindicating the cause
of his own younger self.

Confucius was ambitious. Since he had inherited no position

of influence he had to win one by his own efforts. Yet it was by no means clear that he was fitted for any of the careers which might lead to that end. One of the most promising might have been political intrigue, but for this he had neither the talent nor the character; he was never able to stoop to intrigue, even in a righteous cause. Nor did he care for war as a vocation. This left, of the orthodox paths to fame, only one; that of the official who achieved high place by winning and holding the favor of his prince. But for this Confucius was woefully unfitted.

He was constitutionally unable to flatter. Rather, it would appear that whenever some of his friends had managed with great difficulty to get one of the mighty into a favorable frame of mind toward Confucius, and arranged an interview, Confucius seized upon this as a golden opportunity to explain to his prospective patron the errors and excesses of his ways. This may or may not have contributed to the moral health of the government, but its effect upon Confucius' political career was most unsalutary. Furthermore, Confucius was not very skillful in talking to "practical" men; he did not care, and he probably did not know how, to conceal the barb inside a worm. Some of his disciples were far better at this, and it is not surprising that a man like Tzǔ-kung was better liked by the rulers and far more successful. Confucius condemned eloquence so frequently that one cannot but suspect that he unconsciously envied those who possessed it.

He was temperamentally unfitted for a successful role in practical politics. His gifts were rather those (in many ways diametrically opposite) of the born philosopher and teacher. As a young man Confucius could not know this, however, and if anyone had told him so, he would have denied it hotly. Even if he had recognized the fact, his proper course of action would have been far from clear. For Confucius wanted two things. Like any ambitious young man he wanted to make a name for himself. Even more, he wanted to alleviate the appalling human misery that he saw all about him. It was not at all clear how philosophy and teaching could attain to either goal.

In his day the path both to fame and to practical effectiveness led through public office. Scholarship and teaching were almost, if not entirely, activities carried on by officials as subordinate

and incidental aspects of their work. As a result they were undoubtedly done but poorly. Officials who had to supervise court
ceremonies studied ritual, and others consulted the historical
archives for particular purposes. But men engaged in the daily
conduct of public business had not the leisure to make all of
learning their province, nor the intellectual repose that is essential to the philosopher's quest for the meaning which underlies
the ever-changing phenomena of the universe.

Confucius did. His very failure to attain the sort of responsible position that he coveted left him the leisure for study and
contemplation. His repeated rebuffs at the hands of the "practical men," whom he believed (and in one sense correctly) to
be far less capable than himself, must have spurred him to study
harder and harder, in order to excel in one field in which he was
without serious rival. Bitterly as he lamented the failure of his
practical career, it is quite clear that study (and later, teaching)
were what he really enjoyed. In the halls of state he remained
ineffective, a fish out of water, to the end of his life; among his
students he was in his element.

Confucius was probably one of the most learned Chinese of
his day, but this does not necessarily mean that he had read a
very great number of books. For one thing, many of the classical
works later proclaimed as originating from high antiquity had
not yet been written. And while there were others that have
since been lost, copies were few and difficult of access. The
typical manuscript of his day was written on strips of bamboo
held together by cords, resembling a miniature picket fence;
such "books" were both bulky and clumsy. Confucius was familiar with a number of historical documents, and he probably
committed to memory the anthology of about three hundred
poems that we know as the *Book of Poetry*. He also made a
close study of ritual (we would say both religious and secular,
but the distinction is one that was foreign to his world). To
what extent ritual was merely a matter of tradition in his time
and how much of it had been written down is not entirely clear.

While books provided the background for his thinking, they
were by no means the sole source of his ideas. In fact, he sometimes did not hesitate to interpret books in a manner that can
only be called careless, in order to make a point.[6] For he was

not, basically, a scholar, but a reformer, seeking a way out of the near chaos of his world. He believed that government should be administered for the benefit of the whole people. And he reached the conclusion (which has been fundamental to Confucianism ever since) that no sovereign formula, however glittering, could guarantee this. This goal, he believed, could only be reached if the government were continuously administered by men of the highest personal integrity, trained for government service and so devoted to the cause of the public welfare that they would die, if necessary, rather than betray it.

It is not remarkable that he came to think of himself as the person best qualified, by this standard, to run the government. He became convinced that it was his mission to save the world, and he undertook to do so in the only way that appeared possible, by trying to win a commanding place in the administration. Failing in this, he turned, just how we can only conjecture, to teaching. It has been said that he was the first private teacher; the point is hard to prove, but if there was an earlier his fame has been blotted from history by that of Confucius. It is clear from the *Analects* that as yet teaching was not even recognized as a vocation.

Probably the first students were simply a group of friends; [7] what became the "Confucian school" may well have started as an informal debating society. This is borne out by the fact that some of the disciples were only a little younger than Confucius. [8] Yet it cannot have been long before the quality of his mind and the force of his personality made him the recognized Master. His preeminence was obvious; it is still obvious to any reader of the *Analects*. His students became disciples, bound to him with a loyalty and devotion that are altogether remarkable. He told them his dream, of a world in which war and hatred and misery would be replaced by peace, good will, and happiness. He offered them little, save the chance to work to make the dream come true. He drove them unmercifully, insisting that only by intense study and self-cultivation could they become worthy to be officials in the new kind of administration. He chided them for laziness, ridiculed them for stupidity, and lashed them with scorn if they betrayed his principles.

The number of Confucius' disciples has been greatly exaggerated. The *Analects* mentions twenty-two men who were probably disciples, and the *Mencius* adds two more. Undoubtedly there were others whose names we do not know. Traditions that are probably trustworthy tell us that while most of them came from Lu, others were from several adjoining states. The early records, which give little detail on such matters, indicate that Tzŭ-kung was from Wei, while Ssŭ-Ma Niu was a scion of one of the principal families of Sung.

Ssŭ-Ma Niu was the most "blue-blooded" of the disciples. His family hereditarily held high office in Sung, and one of his brothers was long the favorite of the Duke. When this situation eventuated in disaster, and (through no fault of his own) Ssŭ-Ma Niu had to go into exile from Sung, his noble status was such that the state of Ch'i gave him a city as his fief. Yet there is no indication that, when this aristocrat was his student, Confucius gave him special consideration. He was kind to him, but his attitude was more one of pity (Ssŭ-Ma Niu's life was not happy) than of awe. Confucius' favorite disciple, Yen Hui, was perhaps the most impoverished of them all.

In the early sources we have little or no data concerning the family background of most of the disciples. A little more than half of them had surnames that figure in the *Tso Chuan* as those of important aristocratic families, but in most cases we have no way of knowing whether they were closely related to persons of consequence. Confucius emphasized that he received all aspiring students, only demanding that they be intelligent and willing to work; he expressly declared that neither poverty nor heredity should be allowed to stand in the way of the capable and industrious. Once in the group, all were on an equal footing, distinguished only by their attainments.

Why did students go to Confucius? One of the foremost reasons was certainly his personality. It is still magnetic; even his pale and distorted shadow, reflected dimly in the *Analects* across the gap of twenty-five hundred years, kindles enthusiasm and evokes something close to reverence in men of many lands and various religions. In the flesh, he must have been a powerful "fisher of men." As a teacher he must have appealed, also, to the sober intellectual interests of those with a taste for scholarship; we know of no other teacher in his time who was able to offer the opportunity for advanced study in literature, history, and philosophy. Finally, and perhaps (since human nature has changed but little) we must say most importantly, he trained men for political careers. The training he offered and his recommendation seem to have been of considerable help to them in getting positions.

There is no indication that Confucius used this economic argument to recruit students, as his imitator Mo Tzǔ later did quite openly. On the contrary, he repeatedly denounced those who pretended to be men of principle yet were concerned with wealth and physical comfort; he declared that if a state were badly governed it was shameful, not cause for pride, to hold an administrative post. Nevertheless the *Analects* tells us that at least one of his disciples was studying "with salary as his objective," and the Master himself lamented that "it is hard to find one who is willing to study for three years without thinking of material reward."

The hope of material reward on the part of Confucius' first students was probably slight, but in time it undoubtedly came to be known as a wise practical move to study with him, for a number of his disciples got very good jobs. The *Analects* mentions twenty-two disciples. One of them, Ssǔ-Ma Niu, had a fief. It is only incidentally and almost accidentally that the early sources tell us what positions these men held; nevertheless it is clear that of the remaining twenty-one at least nine became officials of some importance, while a tenth refused a place he was offered. Two of the nine held office successively in Lu and in Wei. The lowest of these positions was that of governor of a town. The highest, held successively by three of Confucius' disciples, was that of steward to the Chi family; [9] this was the most important post in Lu that could normally be attained in any manner other than inheritance, since the real power lay with the Chi family and their steward had great influence in affairs of state. While some of the disciples might have been able to get posts for themselves, the most important of these appointments seem to have been arranged for by Confucius. [10]

Thus it is not hard to understand why young men studied with Confucius, but it may seem a little surprising that the aristocrats, whose practices he denounced, should have been willing to take his students into their service. There were good reasons, however, why the rulers were attracted by the idea of engaging subordinates who had had sound moral training. Edward Gibbon has pointed out that "whatever latitude an absolute monarch may assume in his own conduct, whatever indulgence he may claim for his own passions, it is undoubtedly his interest that all his subjects should respect the natural and civil obligations of society."

The conditions of the time emphasized the desirability of trustworthy officers. From 505 to 502 B.C. the government of Lu was dominated, and in fact terrorized, by a nominal subordinate of the Chi family named Yang Hu. In the latter year he plotted with five others to kill and replace the heads of the "three families"; it was only by a narrow margin that the plan miscarried, and Yang was forced to flee.[11] Such an experience was enough to make even the most dissolute courtier desire retainers of dependable moral character. While Confucius advocated loyalty to principle rather than to individuals, he preached reform by persuasion rather than by violence. Rulers could be fairly certain that if they entrusted power to disciples of Confucius the affair would not end in bloody revolution; indeed, Tzŭ-lu died defending his ruler in Wei. It is probably no accident that it is shortly after the abortive coup of Yang Hu that we first see Confucius' disciples given governmental posts.

Furthermore, Confucius educated his students in the principles and some of the techniques of government; they had skills that were useful. This must have given them a great advantage over their contemporaries since we know of no other educational institution like his at that time. The disciples were a picked group; Confucius would tolerate neither dullards nor sluggards. Their wits were sharpened by discussion and debate both with the Master and among themselves. Their minds were furnished by the study of history, poetry, and ritual. It is not surprising that a man like Tzŭ-kung was more than a match in diplomacy for the adversaries of Lu, so that when the head of the Chi family went to a conference with another state without Tzŭ-kung he regretted it. By long study of the principles of government and discussion of the situations likely to arise, the disciples knew what to do. Thus, when the ruler of Wu unexpectedly made a ceremonial gift to the head of the Shu family (who had, as it happens, a low opinion of Confucius) and that worthy found himself tongue-tied, it was Tzŭ-kung who stepped up behind him and helped him out of an embarrassing situation. Even the renegade disciple Tzŭ-kao, whose education was cut short, was able to advise the head of the Mêng family on diplomatic protocol. Thus we need not suppose that it was from love of virtue, or because they believed in Confucius' principles, that the rulers employed his disciples. They were useful.

The prestige of Confucius himself must also have played a part in winning places for his students. His intellect and personality cannot be neglected in this connection. Coupled with his learning, they won him a unique place even in his own lifetime. There was not, of course, the reverence for scholarship that developed in China later; nevertheless, tradition was highly regarded centuries before he was born, and he was an earnest student of tradition. In some aspects of the Confucian legend as it developed later he appears almost exclusively as a wise man who is sought out by the great to answer their questions. This is an exaggeration, but there is no doubt that he had many acquaintances in high places and that his opinions were accorded a respect which can not be explained on the basis of his birth or rank.

It is clear from the *Analects*, however, that he was most successful, not with his contemporaries, but with younger men. That is not remarkable. The somewhat impractical idealism of the reformer and the slightly pontifical manner of one who feels himself to have a mission repel the seasoned man of the world, but are likely to compel the admiration of the young. There is nothing like a gray beard to add conviction to the message of a prophet. Significantly, it is not until after Confucius was fifty that we hear of his disciples playing a part in the history of Lu.

The Chi family, as we have seen, had usurped the power in Lu from the Duke and did a great many things of which Confucius did not approve. Nevertheless, it was the Chi family that gave his disciples most, if not all, of their opportunities for employment in Lu. He urged the disciples to remain true to their principles and eventually renounced Jan Ch'iu for carrying out orders to collect excessive taxes, but he did not forbid them to take office with the Chi family. To do so would have been quixotic. Instead, he tried to move the Chi in the direction he wished them to go and criticized them openly and fearlessly.

Chi K'ang Tzŭ, who became head of the Chi family in 492 B.C., seems to have been the principal patron of the Confucian group. The career of this noble, who was the actual ruler of Lu, reveals little of outstanding vice or virtue, with the exception of one incident. He owed his succession as head of the Chi family to the mysterious murder of his infant half brother. There is no evidence that he was the murderer, but as the principal beneficiary he is the logical suspect. In general, however, his administration was just what we should expect of a man in his position. He waged aggressive war, and used bribery to prevent the Duke from becoming too powerful; but on the other hand he defended the state capably and seems to have treated his duke fairly well even though he did not like him. He was very possibly a better administrator of the state than the Duke would have been.

The relationship between Confucius and Chi K'ang Tzŭ is rather interesting. Although he did not become head of the Chi family until 492, his acquaintance with Confucius began at least six years earlier.[12] He is mentioned in the *Analects* more often than any other individual except the disciples of Confucius; he seems not to have merely asked questions, as do most of the persons who figure in the *Analects*, but to have taken some part in discussion. It is recorded that he sent a present of medicine to Confucius, who made the wise comment, "Not knowing what it is, I dare not taste it." Almost every time he asked a question, Confucius put the answer in the form of a combined homily and rebuke. On one occasion, being worried about the great number of thieves, K'ang Tzŭ asked for advice and was told, "If *you*, sir, had no improper desires, they wouldn't steal if you paid them to." When he asked how to govern the state, Confucius told him he had better first learn to govern himself.

These pungent rejoinders do not seem to have alienated him, quite the contrary. He must have appreciated the teacher's sincerity, and he probably found his idealism admirable if impracticable. He once asked whether the disciples Tzŭ-lu,

Tzŭ-kung, and Jan Ch'iu would make good officials. Confucius said they would, and K'ang Tzŭ evidently recommended them to his father, Chi Huan Tzŭ. For although we have no record that Confucius ever talked with Chi Huan Tzŭ, the *Tso Chuan* tells us that in 498, six years before K'ang Tzŭ came to power, Tzŭ-lu was steward to the Chi family. After he succeeded his father, K'ang Tzŭ used a number of the disciples in his government.

The mention of Tzŭ-lu as steward of the Chi family, in 498, gives us what is probably the first reliable date in the history of the Confucian group. Here, when Confucius was fifty-three, we see evidence that he was beginning to win some recognition. We cannot tell how long Tzŭ-lu had been holding this position, but it is improbable that his tenure began before 502. That was the year of the attempted rebellion led by Yang Hu; the detailed account of that affair does not mention Tzŭ-lu.

In this attempted coup there was also involved another subordinate of the Chi family, named Kung-Shan Fu-jao, who had charge of the fortified city of Pi, which was the principal seat of the Chi. Kung-Shan was disaffected toward the Chi, for what reason it is not known. He was not, however, an utterly self-seeking swashbuckler like Yang Hu; indeed, Kung-Shan mildly opposed Yang Hu at one point, defending the interests of the ducal house. It is quite probable that Yang Hu secured Kung-Shan's adherence to the plot by representing that it was a move to restore the power in the state to the Duke. While Kung-Shan may have been misguided, he was nevertheless a man of principle. He proved this when, even after he ultimately had to flee from Lu, he remained loyal to the state and helped it against its enemies. This conduct contrasted markedly with that of Yang Hu, who tried to get Ch'i to invade Lu.

When Yang Hu's coup failed, Kung-Shan did not at once leave Lu. Instead, he held the city of Pi in rebellion against his nominal overlords, the Chi family. His position against the Chi, who commanded the resources of the state of Lu, was obviously untenable over a long period unless he could enlarge the basis of his support. It is possible that he dreamed of restoring the power of the Duke, under his own protection rather than that

of the Chi family. At this juncture he asked Confucius to join
his "government."

It is understandable that Confucius was sorely tempted. His
vocation, as he saw it, was government; his mission, to save the
world. Yet he would soon be an old man, and if he did not act
quickly he would reach feeble senility without ever once having
the opportunity to test his ideas in actual practice. Pi was, to be
sure, a small place, and Confucius disapproved in principle of
violent revolution. But the Chi family had exiled the previous
duke and had dominated the state by force for generations; was
the use of force not justified to right this wrong?

Tzŭ-lu was horrified that the Master should consider going.
Tzŭ-lu was one of those terrifyingly sincere people who believe
that "right is right and wrong is wrong," who operate on a few
simple principles and consider the slightest modification to be
wicked. He would have been at home as a knight of the Round
Table. Confucius had taught him that it was wrong to use force
against one's superiors; Kung-Shan had used force against his
superiors; therefore Kung-Shan should be shunned like the
plague. Without impugning Tzŭ-lu's motives, which seem always to have been appallingly pure, we may also note that at
this time he was probably already steward of the Chi family; it
was therefore his duty to eliminate the threat from Kung-Shan
(which he later did).

Confucius gave up the idea of joining Kung-Shan. But he
said to Tzŭ-lu, "Certainly he did not call me for nothing. If
anyone were to use me, might I not make a new Chou here in
the east?" He dreamed, in other words, of setting up a new
dynasty that would rival the former glories of the sadly declined
Chou empire.[13]

What had Confucius been doing up to this time, aside from
teaching? We simply do not know. As a young man he held
various very minor posts. Later he may well have been supported
by his disciples. We know that he accepted gifts from them,
and he may have charged tuition of those who were able to pay;
he was relatively poor and had to live. It is quite possible that
he was given some sort of pension by the state, particularly

after he had attracted the favorable attention of K'ang Tzŭ of the Chi family.

Tradition has insisted that Confucius occupied high office in Lu and played a leading role in its affairs. The *Tso Chuan* relates that in 500 B.C. he seconded Duke Ting of Lu at a diplomatic meeting with Ch'i, where, by his courage and cleverness, he thwarted a plan to kidnap the duke and forced Ch'i to restore lands it had taken from Lu. Many things are wrong with this story, and a number of Chinese scholars have long since rejected it as false. If this incident had really occurred, it would have been the high point of Confucius' political effectiveness. Yet neither the *Analects* nor the *Mencius* says a word about it. It is a little melodrama that has been added to the text, which has nothing to do with the life of Confucius.[14]

More persistent is the idea that he was once minister of crime in Lu. At first sight it seems well authenticated, since three relatively early works, the *Mo Tzŭ*, the *Mencius,* and the *Tso Chuan,* all aver that he held that office. On examination, however, the testimony of two of them breaks down. Although the statement is made in the *Mo Tzŭ*, it occurs in a section of the work that is well recognized to be a late addition.[15] The case of the *Tso Chuan* is very strange. This work records the history of the state of Lu in considerable detail, and it is dominated by a strong interest in Confucius. Certainly, if Confucius was minister of crime of Lu, the *Tso Chuan* should describe his official acts with some thoroughness. Yet its only indication that he ever held the office, entered under the year 509, is this statement: "Later when Confucius was minister of crime, he united the tombs [of the various dukes of Lu] by means of a ditch."

This is an odd way to dismiss the matter. It is evident that no one knew what, if anything, Confucius had done when he was minister of crime; Mencius only explained why he had resigned the office. Later, when chroniclers felt obliged to give their readers the full details of Confucius' life, they filled this vacuum with absurdities, relating that he practiced summary execution and prescribed the death penalty for a strange catalogue of such crimes as "inventing unusual clothing." These things are completely at variance with everything we know about Confucius from earlier and more reliable sources.[16]

It is inherently improbable that Confucius would have been made minister of crime. This was an important office such as was normally held only by the chief of a prominent noble clan. We know that the head of the powerful Tsêng family, related to the ducal house, was minister of crime in the year before Confucius was born, and it is probable that the office remained a hereditary perquisite of the Tsêng, as Henri Maspero has supposed.[17] The disciples of Confucius coveted recognition for their Master, and if he had succeeded in attaining such an office, it is hard to conceive that the *Analects* would not have recorded the triumph. Yet it never suggests that he held any high post. The fact that Mencius said Confucius had been minister of crime merely shows that, after a hundred years, the Confucian legend was beginning to grow.

After several of his disciples had posts in the government of Lu it must have become increasingly awkward for all concerned that Confucius, who desired one so fervently, had none. Shortly after 500 B.C. it is probable that not only Tzŭ-lu, who was their steward, but also Tzŭ-kung and Jan Ch'iu were in the service of the Chi family.[18] The *Analects* tells us that "someone said to Confucius, 'Sir, why are you not in the government?'" He evaded the question, pointing out that by merely being a good citizen one made a contribution to government; he may have been as embarrassed for his disciples as for himself.

Yet there is little question that Confucius could have had a position if he had been willing to accept one on any terms. This he would not do. Tzŭ-kung once reproached him for remaining aloof from affairs, comparing his talent for government to a precious jewel and saying, "Suppose I have a beautiful gem here; should I just keep it stored away in a case, or should I seek a good price and sell it?" "Sell it," Confucius replied, "sell it by all means. I, you see, am just waiting for the price."

The price he wanted for participation was a voice as well as a place in the government, and a real opportunity to correct what he regarded as crying abuses. That those in charge of the government hesitated to give him such power is understandable. Chi K'ang Tzŭ regarded his ideas with toleration and even with interest, but at the same time he must have looked with some trepidation on one who not only held radical views but was perfectly capable of trying to put them into practice. Furthermore, there is some question as to just how effective Confucius would have been as a practical administrator. When Chi K'ang Tzŭ asked him how to deal with thieves, and he replied that all would be well if K'ang Tzŭ merely regulated his own desires, he preached an excellent sermon. As practical advice for dealing with a crime wave, however, this is scarcely adequate. One may say, of course, that it was not Confucius' purpose at the moment to give practical advice, but in fact we have little indication that he could have given it if he had wanted to. Confucius was very successful as the chief architect of his nation's culture, but if he had been put in charge of the practical operation of a state in his own day he might well have bungled the job.

Nevertheless he was at length given a post, though it is not easy to say exactly what post or when. The time can be fixed, however, with a good deal of probability, as somewhere in the period between 502 and 492.[19] The *Analects* never tells us directly what office he held; it merely gives us hints, like the clues to a riddle. It makes it clear that Confucius believed that his position was such that he would be consulted on any important governmental decisions; at the same time it strongly suggests that he was not so consulted. It tells us that at court when he talked with officials *(tai fu)* of superior rank he was restrained and formal, while with the lower *tai fu* he was informal and direct.[20] Finally, Confucius himself says twice in the *Analects* that he "follows in the rear of the *tai fu.*"

This last expression would seem to mean that Confucius was himself one of the lower *tai fu*; he says that he "follows after" the *tai fu* as a matter of conventional modesty.[21] He can scarcely have been a colleague of the upper *tai fu* since his manner with them was "restrained and formal"; and if he had been less than a *tai fu* he could scarcely have expected to be consulted on matters of state. For the lower *tai fu* were the lowest grade of officials who had standing at the ducal court.

We do not know, but it is not hard to guess, how Confucius came to be given such a position. His disciples must have worked hard to get him such an appointment, and even a man like Chi K'ang Tzŭ must have realized that it was unsuitable for Confucius to have no position while his disciples were becoming increasingly important figures. The Chinese have always been sensitive to the necessity of maintaining appearances, and it was probably decided that, in order to do so, Confucius should be given a position with an impressive title but with no "burdensome responsibilities" and no authority to do anything that might embarrass his superiors. There are such posts in every administration, designed to divert the energies of individuals who might make trouble for the government if they remained outside it. The fact that Confucius dallied with the idea of supporting Kung-Shan Fu-jao in his rebellion against the Chi family may have helped convince those gentlemen that they could not afford to leave so well known a person as Confucius was coming to be unattached. They gave him a title that was perhaps equivalent to Member of the Council of State.

Such evidence as we have makes it almost certain that his office was a virtual sinecure. Naturally this has caused later Confucians acute embarrassment. They have wished to believe that he was a figure of the highest importance, the principal adviser to the Duke of Lu. The fact is, however, that the *Analects* records only two conversations between Confucius and Duke Ting, who probably reigned when he took office.[22] On these occasions the Duke merely asked the sort of questions he would put to a man reputed to be wise; these are not the sort of discussions we should expect between a ruler and his minister.

Some Confucians have been still more disturbed by the fact that Mencius says Confucius took office, not under the Duke of Lu, but under Chi Huan Tzŭ, the current head of the Chi family. They have considered it beneath Confucius' dignity to have served this usurper of power. In fact, however, it is probable that Confucius' position was technically under the Duke, but that since the Duke was a puppet Mencius was merely speaking realistically. In all likelihood it was Confucius' friend Chi K'ang Tzŭ, the son of Chi Huan Tzŭ, who actually arranged the appointment.[23]

That Confucius should have accepted an appointment that was in fact designed merely to keep him quiet may seem to reflect upon his integrity. Certainly it did not accord with his repeated assertions that the man of honor will accept rank and salary only if he is able to contribute effectively to good government. But he did hope, at any rate, that he would have this opportunity. Mencius says that Confucius "took office under Chi Huan Tzŭ because he saw that there was a possibility that his doctrines might be practiced." Some of his disciples undoubtedly urged him to accept a post in order to test out the possibility. He was probably the more willing to do so because of his age. Since he was now around fifty, he could no longer look forward to an indefinite future of further opportunities.

For decades the peace of Lu had been disturbed by intermittent insurrections centering in one or another of the cities that were the principal seats of the three families. The families had fortified these places strongly. After they controlled Lu, they moved to the capital and left governors in charge of them. Possession of such fortified cities was a constant temptation to the governors to rebel, and from time to time they did so. In 498 Tzŭ-lu, as steward of the Chi family, suggested that the fortifications of all three seats be demolished in order to remove this danger.[24] The plan was agreed to and at first was successful. Military opposition developed,[25] however, and its final phase could not be carried through.

This failure may have been the beginning of the fall from favor of Tzŭ-lu. It is remarkable, indeed, that he was ever able to succeed in politics at all. Confucius was uncompromising enough, but it is hard to see how Tzŭ-lu, whose code was as rigid as that of the most inflexible puritan, could ever have got along with the Chi. He did not continue to do so indefinitely. The *Analects* tells us that another courtier spoke against Tzŭ-lu to the head of the Chi family, who came to have doubts about him. His influence probably went down as that of Jan Ch'iu rose. Although Jan Ch'iu was also Confucius' disciple, he was less hampered, in public life, by the Master's teachings; he "knew which side his bread was buttered on." We do not know how much longer Tzŭ-lu continued in the service of the Chi family, but it seems likely that he either was discharged or quit in disgust before Confucius set out on his travels.

Confucius was not happy. It seems reasonable to assign to this time the passage in the *Analects* in which, one day when Jan

Ch'iu returned from the court, the Master asked him why he
was so late and Jan replied that there had been affairs of state.
Confucius, nettled, replied, "They must have been minor matters.[26] If there had been anything important enough to be called
'affairs of state' I would certainly have been consulted, even
though they do not give me any real responsibilities."[27] But he
soon lost even this illusion and realized that there was no prospect that he would be able to accomplish anything in Lu. Mencius says that it was because Confucius was "not used" that he
resolved to leave the state. Although he was nearing the age of
sixty, he set off on his travels, determined to seek a prince who
would give him a real opportunity to put his principles into
practice.[28]

Concerning his years of journeying, we have only occasional and disconnected bits of information. The *Historical
Records*, written in Han times, has a complete and detailed
itinerary, of the utmost complexity, but we cannot use this late
and at many points clearly erroneous fabrication as our guide.
From the *Analects*, the *Mencius*, and the *Tso Chuan* it is possible to derive a list of the states visited and an itinerary on which
these sources are in general agreement; even the Taoist work,
Chuang Tzŭ, corroborates it.

Only one portion of Confucius' travels is very difficult to
place. The *Mencius* tells us that he visited Ch'i, and both the
Analects and the *Mo Tzŭ* say that while there he saw Duke
Ching. We have no clear indication that he visited Ch'i in his
later travels, and it is doubtful that he did, since Duke Ching
died in 490. It seems probable therefore that, as the *Historical
Records* states, the trip to Ch'i had been made at some previous
time. Those who later elaborated the Confucian tradition told
a number of tales about Confucius' visit to that state that are
quite evidently false.[29]

The date at which Confucius left Lu on his long journey has
been debated endlessly. The *Historical Records* offers a liberal
choice; in different chapters it places this event in 498, 497, and
496. In any case, it was not later than 493, for in Wei he saw
Duke Ling who died in that year.

It is impossible to tell by what disciples Confucius was accompanied on his travels or how long each stayed with him.

Tradition gives him a large retinue, but it is probably influenced by the practice of the traveling teachers of later times. When Mencius traveled about a century later, he is said to have been "followed by several tens of carriages and attended by several hundred men"; posterity probably felt that the dignity of Confucius required that he be endowed (if only by anecdote) with a comparable entourage. There is little doubt that tradition has exaggerated the number of his traveling companions.[30] In fact, there are only two disciples concerning whom there is definite evidence that they were with the Master while he was abroad; these are Tzŭ-lu and Yen Hui.

He went first to Wei. There, Mencius relates, Tzŭ-lu's wife had a brother-in-law who was in favor with the Duke. This noble told Tzŭ-lu that if Confucius would stay with him, he could become one of the highest officers of Wei. Confucius seems to have refused the offer. Nevertheless, he was well received by the Duke, and Mencius says that he took office. This probably means nothing more, however, than that he was treated as a guest of the state and given a stipend for his support from the public treasury. It is probable, as Mencius seems to indicate, that Confucius received such support in several states; as he was not a wealthy man, he could hardly have traveled otherwise. But that he became an active official is most unlikely. Since Confucius' disciples were eager for him to obtain office and felt that the world neglected him, we should expect that the *Analects* would celebrate the fact if he had held any real administrative post on his travels; this is never suggested.[31]

The wife of Duke Ling of Wei, known as Nan Tzŭ, was a lady of considerable notoriety. She is accused of having had an incestuous relationship with her brother and of continuing it after her marriage; she seems also to have dabbled in political intrigue. According to *Analects* 6.26 Confucius had an audience with Nan Tzŭ, probably at her command, but Tzŭ-lu was considerably disturbed that he should have done so. Later Confucians have been disturbed too, and some of them have wished to expunge this passage as libelous.

The situation Confucius found in Wei was much like the one he had left in Lu; he was treated with respect and supported, but had no opportunity to put his principles into practice.[32] We do not know how long he stayed there, but he seems to have left not later than 492.

He set out to go southward to Ch'ên. As he was passing through Sung, Huan T'ui, a high noble of that state, tried to waylay and assassinate him. No reason is given for this attempt on his life, even in the biography in the *Historical Records*. There is evidence, however, which, though purely circumstantial, provides a plausible if not quite certain motive. To develop it we must digress.

This Huan T'ui was a member of a powerful family in Sung and a spoiled aristocrat of the worst sort. He was a favorite of Duke Ching of Sung, and exploited this fact to extort from others property he wanted. When this resulted in his being soundly thrashed, he did not have the courage either to defend himself or to retaliate. Nevertheless he remained in favor, even though his arrogance alienated other high officers from the Duke and caused some of them to rebel. Not until 484 did he begin to fall from grace. In 481 the Duke tried to kill him, and Huan and all the other members of his family had to flee from Sung.

Huan T'ui's younger brother was the Ssŭ-Ma Niu who was a disciple of Confucius. We have no evidence as to when or for how long he studied with Confucius; it is possible though not certain that he was a disciple for a time before the Master left Lu.[33] There is no direct proof that his study with Confucius turned him against Huan T'ui. It is quite clear, however, that he had a low opinion of that gentleman. After the whole family had to leave Sung, Ssŭ-Ma Niu refused to live in the same state with Huan T'ui. On one occasion he lamented that he "had no brothers," though in fact Huan T'ui and yet another of his brothers were still living.

As a disciple of Confucius, Ssŭ-Ma Niu must have learned to despise those who believed that noble birth entitled them to plumb the depths of degradation. On the contrary, as Tzŭ-hsia told him, the Confucians believed that the true gentlemen are those who act toward all men with respect and courtesy, and such men, throughout all the world, are brothers. Confucius taught Ssŭ-Ma Niu, as the Confucians eventually taught all China, that nobility depends on the mind and the spirit, not the pedigree, and that a man's worth depends on what he is, not on what his grandfather was. Yet the new set of values clashed strongly with the conduct of Ssŭ-Ma Niu's relatives, and he could not suppress a sense of foreboding and anxiety. For this reason Confucius once told him, "If, when you look into *your own* heart, you find nothing wrong there, then you have nothing to worry about and nothing to fear."

It is easy to see that Confucius would have been guilty, in the eyes of Huan T'ui, of the crime for which Socrates was executed: corrupting the young. And it may well be for this reason that he tried to assassinate him. It must be emphasized, however, that we cannot be sure that this was his grievance, for we have no way of being certain of the date at which Ssŭ-Ma Niu studied with Confucius.

In any case, Confucius conducted himself with fortitude; he declared himself to be charged by Heaven with a mission, which Huan T'ui was powerless to obstruct. Mencius says that Confucius took the precaution of donning "inconspicuous clothing" before completing his journey across Sung. The *Analects* also contains an account of a very similar adventure that befell Confucius and his party at a place called K'uang; it seems probable that this is another report of the same event. On that occasion Yen Hui became separated from the others and Confucius feared that he had been killed, but at length they were reunited.

It is possibly owing to this incident that Confucius and his companions found themselves in straitened circumstances when they reached Ch'ên; in fact, it is said that they became weak from lack of food. Eventually, however, they reached the capital of Ch'ên, where Confucius was received as a guest by an officer of the ducal court.[34]

The *Tso Chuan* says that Confucius was in Ch'ên in 492. Time was running out for that unhappy state. It, like the small state of Ts'ai to the west, represented a southward projection into the territory of the great state of Ch'u. Both states had become pawns in the struggle between the "barbarian" states of Ch'u and Wu. Ts'ai sided with Wu; in retaliation, Ch'u conquered Ts'ai in 494 and ordered its people to remove from the territory. Ch'ên refused to aid Wu in attacking Ch'u at a time when that state was prostrate, but the attempt to remain neutral proved futile and Ch'ên was invaded periodically, first by Wu and later by Ch'u, until Ch'u extinguished the state and annexed its territory a dozen years after Confucius' visit.

He may still have been in Ch'ên when one of the invasions took place. In any case, its duke can have had but little leisure for the discussion of philosophy; he must have been very difficult to convince that virtue leads to peace, prosperity, and happiness. In fact we have no evidence that Confucius ever saw the Duke, and while it is recorded that he had an audience with the Minister of Crime, that dignitary was not sympathetic. Confucius seems to have made few friends in this part of the world. He became homesick for Lu and declared his intention to return, asserting that the disciples he had left there were getting out of hand. But in fact he did not yet give up his quest.

We are informed of only one occurrence of real interest in this period. That is a meeting between two remarkable men. One was Confucius; the other was a noble of Ch'u known as the Duke of Shê. "Duke" is commonly used to translate the character *kung*, and this officer had this title; it is necessary to understand, however, that in Ch'u where the ruler called himself *wang*, king, the *kung* were only rulers of small districts.[35] Nevertheless the Duke of Shê was a person of consequence, said to be related to the ruling family of Ch'u, a power in the state, and (what is far more unusual) a man of principle. He was at one time marshal of the left and was prominent in numerous military actions. The *Tso Chuan* quotes him as having, on a number of occasions, uttered sentiments remarkably like those of Confucius, urging the importance of virtue rather than force, advocating liberal treatment of the people, and criticizing aristocratic bravos who delighted in daring to the detriment of the state. Such speeches in the *Tso Chuan* are not always credible; sometimes we find them put into the mouths of men whose actions make it clear they could never have uttered them. For the Duke of Shê, however, we have deeds as well as words. It is attested that he was popular with the people, and when (long after his meeting with Confucius) a rebel murdered the Prime Minister of Ch'u and got control of the state, the Duke of Shê led an army to put down the rebellion. Having done so, he administered the government only long enough to restore order.

This done, he installed the son of the former Prime Minister and returned to Shê.

It was natural that Confucius should have wanted to meet such a man, and that he should have been interested in the ideas of Confucius. At about this time the Duke of Shê was in the small adjoining state of Ts'ai, helping to consolidate its annexation by Ch'u; Confucius probably went there to see him.[36]

We have only snatches of their conversation. The Duke asked Confucius how he thought government should be conducted and was told that a really good government would care for its subjects so well that not only would they be pleased, but men of other states also would wish to come under its jurisdiction. If we can believe the *Tso Chuan*, this agreed with the Duke's views. They also discussed that ethical problem, vexing in any culture but especially in China, of whether one's first loyalty is to his family or to the state. The Duke held for the state, Confucius for the family, and the two venerable gentlemen seem to have agreed to disagree. The Duke did not know what to make of this wandering philosopher and would-be statesman. He asked Tzŭ-lu what manner of man his Master was, but Tzŭ-lu did not know what to reply. Tzŭ-lu related this incident to Confucius, who said, "Why didn't you tell him, 'He is this sort of man: so intent upon enlightening those eager for knowledge that he forgets to eat, and so happy in doing so that he forgets his sorrows and does not realize that old age is creeping up on him'?"

He was growing old, but he did not yet give up and return to Lu. It was probably at about this time that he was again tempted with the offer of the one thing he most wanted, an administrative post, but under circumstances that complicated the issue. The invitation came from a city in Chin. That state, which had once controlled most of the Chinese world, was now torn by civil war between two factions among its great noble families, which treated the Duke as their pawn. The situation is obscure, but it appears that first one group and later the other was able to control the person of the Duke and issue orders in his name. A subordinate of one of these groups, who controlled a city, asked Confucius to join him, and Confucius would have liked to go. However, since at that time the opposing group had control of the Duke, this official was technically in rebellion.[37]

The ever meticulous Tzŭ-lu was quick to point this out, and insist that the Master must not soil himself by association with one whose conduct was not irreproachable. Confucius' reply marks the high point of pathos in his long series of disappointments. He said, "There may be something in what you say. But is it not also said that there are some things 'so hard that no grinding will wear them down' and 'so white that no steeping will dye them'? Am I a bitter gourd, fit only to hang up out of the way, not good enough to eat?" He was becoming very impatient with the world for making no use of him. In the end, however, he did not go to Chin.[38]

This and the very similar incident described earlier, which is mentioned in *Analects* 17.5, are the only two occasions on which the *Analects* ever suggests that Confucius was tendered a position of administrative authority. In both cases the offers came from petty functionaries who controlled nothing more than small towns, yet in each case Confucius was strongly inclined to accept. This fact in itself indicates how completely Confucius was denied such recognition in his own day and makes manifest the absurdity of the later stories to the effect that he was a high official. It is not surprising that a number of Confucian scholars, jealous of the dignity of their Master, have felt obliged to prove these passages in the *Analects* false, and have sometimes resorted to very dubious arguments to do so.[39]

We do not know how long Confucius remained in Ch'ên; there is a stretch here of several years concerning which we have even less information than is usual. When we next hear of him, in 484, he is back in Wei.

At this time Wei was in a most unhappy condition, governed by a group of contending (and sometimes warring) rulers and ministers, some of whom stand out even in that wayward age. We have seen that the Duchess, Nan Tzŭ, who is accused of incest, was so notorious that Tzŭ-lu was disturbed merely because Confucius had an interview with her. Her son, the heir-apparent K'uai-wai, plotted to assassinate her, supposedly because of shame. Whether matricide is justifiable under such circumstances might be debated; in any case the conduct of K'uai-wai was scarcely admirable. Instead of acting as his own executioner, he ordered a subordinate to be the assassin, but the man's nerve failed at the last moment. The Duchess, realizing that she was about to be murdered, screamed and ran to the Duke. Although K'uai-wai tried to throw the blame on his retainer, he and all his adherents had to flee from Wei. As a result, when Duke Ling died in 493, K'uai-wai was in exile in Chin, and it was the son of K'uai-wai who succeeded; this was Duke Ch'u. In Chin, one of the contending groups of nobles espoused the cause of K'uai-wai and installed him, by force, in a city in Wei.

Thus at the time of Confucius' second visit to Wei the son was in the ducal palace while his father held an outlying city by force of arms, awaiting his opportunity to seize the throne. The real power in the state was neither prince, but a minister named K'ung Yü.

Mencius says that Confucius was given a stipend by the Duke of Wei at this time,[40] but we have no indication that Confucius ever saw Duke Ch'u, perhaps because the Duke was too young. Confucius was honored and deferred to, however, by the minister, K'ung Yü. (Despite the identity of family name, there is no indication that he was related to Confucius.)

We know very little about K'ung Yü but quite enough to prove that he was far from being a saint. Because this is true, some Chinese scholars have been disturbed by the fact that Confucius associated with him. In this, however, they misunderstand Confucius. He would have liked to be able to associate only with those who conformed to his ideal of conduct, and he wished very much that such men might occupy the seats of power. But in fact they did not, and since Confucius wished to influence the practical operation of government, he had no choice but to associate with, and try to temper the conduct of, those whose standards were not his own. This does not mean that he was utterly indiscriminate but that he used common sense and judgment. His disciples (like children censuring the conduct of a parent) expected him to follow a rigid rule. On one occasion he told them, "When I talk with a man I am not answerable for what he may do afterward. Why be so severe? . . . Neither am I thereby assuming responsibility for his past conduct."

It is uncertain whether Confucius actually held an official

post or was merely a more or less permanent guest of K'ung Yü. It is clear enough, however, why Confucius stayed. K'ung was the actual ruler of Wei; it was through him, if at all, that the conduct of the government must be influenced. Furthermore, K'ung sought the advice of Confucius, and on occasion even acted upon it; he is perhaps the only ruler of whom this can be said with assurance. Finally, whatever his shortcomings, he seems to have been a sincere seeker after knowledge. Confucius said of him that he was "diligent and fond of study, not ashamed to ask questions of those below him in rank."

Notwithstanding his virtues, he overtried the patience of Confucius. K'ung married a daughter of Duke Ling and thought so highly of alliance by marriage as a means of cementing his power that he compelled another noble of Wei to divorce his wives and marry one of K'ung's daughters instead. When the noble continued seeing a favorite former concubine, K'ung wanted to lead some soldiers to attack him and asked Confucius for advice on how to go about this. Confucius was disgusted by the whole affair and told K'ung to drop the plan. He did so, but Confucius ordered his carriage, intending to leave Wei.[41] Thereupon K'ung apologized and Confucius reconsidered, but at that point messengers came from Lu to invite him to return to his native state.

While Confucius had been absent, some of his disciples had been busy in Lu. As early as 495 Tzǔ-kung had attended an important diplomatic conference. At another conference in 488 a high official of the powerful state of Wu summoned Chi K'ang Tzǔ (the real ruler of Lu) to his presence. K'ang Tzǔ was afraid to go and in his place sent Tzǔ-kung, who talked well enough to carry off the incident without an immediate rupture. Thereafter Tzǔ-kung continued to prove himself useful.

Concerning the career of the disciple Jan Ch'iu we have no information until 484, but by that time he occupied the commanding position of steward of the Chi family. In that year an army of Ch'i invaded Lu; Jan Ch'iu planned the measures for defending the state and goaded the heads of the three families into action. Jan also led the "army of the left," with Fan Ch'ih (who later was himself a disciple of Confucius) as his lieutenant. In the battle one of Lu's armies was defeated and fled, but

Jan Ch'iu used his troops so effectively that the invaders had to retire.

It was in this same year that Confucius was invited back to Lu, and it may well be that the prestige which Jan Ch'iu had acquired had much to do with this. Their old teacher had now been wandering about for something like a decade, and the disciples who remained in Lu must have wished very much for him to return. They were genuinely affectionate toward him, and the reception with which he had met in his travels can have contributed little either to their peace of mind or to their self-esteem as his protégés. The *Tso Chuan* tells us that "messengers from Lu came to Wei with presents to invite him." It was usual to send such presents when asking a man to assume office; probably he was asked to resume his old, almost meaningless, position. By this time Confucius can have had few illusions about the opportunity that awaited him in Lu, but after all, he had been disappointed everywhere else too. He was now sixty-seven, and in Lu at least his friends and disciples awaited him. He returned.

It would be easy to liken the travels of Confucius, which on the surface accomplished little or nothing, to those of the celebrated knight of La Mancha who tilted at windmills. But there are significant differences. Don Quixote was an echo of the past, imitating the knight-errantry that was at its last gasp. Confucius was a prophet of the future; his philosophical journey, which apparently accomplished so little, became a pattern for several succeeding centuries. The travels of Don Quixote, by ridiculing chivalry, sounded the death knell of the knighthood he admired. Confucius, through the doctrines he vainly sought to practice in his wanderings, assured that later travelers in his footsteps would utterly destroy the oppressive hereditary aristocracy which he detested.

If Confucius' travels had no outward result, it is nonetheless true that if he had stayed in Lu he would have been a different man. Assuredly his proper realm was that of ideas and of teaching them to others; he was incapable of the compromises necessary to put them into practice. But it was extremely important that he should *try*. The difference is that which distinguishes an officer who says, "Follow me!" from one who says "Advance!"

If Confucius had stayed in Lu, enjoying a sinecure and strolling about with his pupils, he would have remained a preacher; by setting off on his hopeless quest he became a prophet. The picture of this venerable gentleman, in some respects still unsophisticated, setting off in his fifties to save the world by persuading the hard-bitten rulers of his day that they should not oppress their subjects, is in some ways ridiculous. But it is a magnificent kind of ridiculousness, found only in the great.

The fact that Confucius had been invited back to Lu should by no means be interpreted as betokening a change of heart on the part of the Chi family or its head, Chi K'ang Tzŭ. In fact, Confucius had scarcely become settled before that luxury-loving noble devised a plan to increase his revenues by raising (Mencius says doubling) the taxes assessed against his already poverty-stricken subjects. The *Tso Chuan* says that he sent Jan Ch'iu to ask the advice of Confucius concerning this plan. It is hard to understand this unless he hoped, by gaining the sanction of Confucius who was known as a champion of the people, to lessen the popular reaction against the imposition of the new levies. Perhaps he thought that it was time he received some *quid pro quo* for the salary that had been paid to Confucius for some years. What he got, however, was a denunciation.[42]

Undeterred, Chi K'ang Tzŭ put the new taxes in force, and Jan Ch'iu collected them for him. This brought to a head the question that had been developing for some time: was Jan Ch'iu the man of the Chi family, or of Confucius? Confucius expected his disciples to be loyal to their superiors, but their highest duty, he believed, was to principle; when they could not obey the commands of their superiors and still remain true to principle, it was their duty to resign. Jan Ch'iu was not the man, however, to abandon a promising career for a few scruples. He had given cause for doubt before, and now he tried the Master's patience too far. Confucius told his disciples, "He is no follower of mine. Beat the drum, my children, and set upon him; I give you leave."

This seems to be the only recorded instance in which Confucius definitively repudiated a disciple, and even this proscription appears to have had little effect. Jan Ch'iu seems to have continued as a member of the Confucian group; whether he was at all chastened we cannot tell.

Of Confucius' activities in these closing years of his life we know very little. On his travels he had no doubt collected certain manuscripts and information, and he probably spent some time in putting these in order. He may have rearranged the order of some of the pieces in the anthology of poetry, which we know as the *Book of Poetry*, at this time. Undoubtedly, however, his major energies were applied to teaching, and he seems to have had a number of students at this period. Through his disciples who were in public life he also exercised a certain influence on public affairs. For instance, when Duke Ch'u of Wei had to flee from that state to Lu, Jan Ch'iu and Tzǔ-kung consulted Confucius concerning the attitude to be taken toward that ruler.[43] He seems, too, to have remained on terms of polite social intercourse, at least, with the head of the Chi family. Yet we are informed of only one instance in which Confucius tried personally to intervene in the conduct of the government. This was in connection with the murder of the Duke of Ch'i.

Two centuries earlier a son of a duke of Ch'ên had fled from that state to Ch'i. There the ruler received him kindly and gave him office; he founded, in Ch'i, the family known as "Ch'ên," the name of his native state. The Ch'ên family continued prominent in Ch'i, and for some generations its scions were men of ability and character. Their position in the state was still not a commanding one, however. The *Tso Chuan* tells us that when Confucius was a small boy the Ch'ên family installed itself in popular favor by handing out largesse to the people. Its members also became adept at intrigue; by deceit, treachery, and violence they removed one after another of the more powerful families that stood between the Ch'ên and the control of Ch'i. In 489 they were deeply implicated in the murder of a duke of Ch'i who was a mere child. In his place they set up Duke Tao; Tao proved less tractable than they had hoped and was mysteriously murdered (history does not say by whom) four years later. His son was made Duke Chien. Chien's supporters planned to expel the Ch'ên from the state, but in 481 the Ch'ên forestalled this by revolting and killing the Duke.

At this juncture Confucius proposed intervention. Ch'i was the great northern neighbor of Lu, which had alternately kept the smaller state in subjection and made war upon it, for many years. For Ch'i to be ruled by the ruthless and unscrupulous Ch'ên could help neither its own people nor the state of Lu.

When Confucius heard the news of the rebellion and murder in Ch'i, he fasted (as befitted one about to make a solemn proposal), then went to court and proposed to the Duke of Lu that Ch'i be invaded. The Duke said, "Lu has been kept in a weakened condition by Ch'i for a long time. If we attempted such an invasion, what could it accomplish?" Confucius replied, "Ch'ên Hêng has murdered his ruler; half of the people are against him. If the army of Lu be added to one half of that of Ch'i, we can conquer." The Duke then said, "Inform the chiefs of the three families of it." Confucius did so, but they were unwilling to take action.[44]

Death was taking its toll of Confucius' circle. His son, whose lack of outstanding abilities had been a disappointment to him, died during his father's later years. An even more grievous blow was the death of his favorite disciple, Yen Hui. In 481 Ssŭ-Ma Niu, the disciple most exalted in rank, died in tragic circumstances. The year 480 saw the end of the intrepid Tzŭ-lu; he died, as was fitting, with his boots on, trying vainly to rescue his chief during a rebellion in Wei.

These losses must have told on Confucius. As he looked back on his life, he must have felt that he had accomplished very little. He had scarcely succeeded in improving the government of Lu, and he had never achieved the control of a state as he desired. His best disciple was dead, and those who were left to him were not exceedingly promising. He could neither hope that his ideas would be transmitted to posterity with clarity nor that their realization in practice would be pushed with energy. It is no wonder that he said to Tzŭ-kung, "Alas, there is no one who understands me!"

Yet except for such rare lapses he made no complaint, and there is no indication that he ever indulged in that cheapest and most universal of luxuries, self-pity. To a man of his ambitions and vision, failure must have been a bitter pill, and fail he had, to all outward appearances. Calumny was added to his other trials. The *Analects* tells us that he was reviled by the powerful head of the Shu family, and Mencius speaks of Confucius as "harassed by the herd of small men." The sphinx of history gave no sign that one day the names of all the proud rulers of his day would be forgotten while that of Confucius would be famous to the ends of the earth. He did not dream of this, but neither did he weep.

Of Confucius' death we have no trustworthy account.[45] We know how he faced death, however, for we have a story of a previous illness that promised to be fatal. The well-meaning Tzŭ-lu, grieved that the Master had never been able to win high office, had the disciples attire themselves as if they had been ministers in attendance upon a high dignitary. Confucius, regaining consciousness and seeing this play-acting going on about him, scolded Tzŭ-lu and asked, "By making this pretence of having ministers when I have none, whom do you think I am going to deceive? Shall I deceive Heaven? Furthermore, is it not better that I should die in the hands of you, my friends, than in the hands of ministers?"

Tzŭ-lu requested permission to pray for him, and the Master asked, "Is it done?" Tzŭ-lu assured him that it was customary, but Confucius only smiled and said, "My kind of praying was done long ago."

Confucius died in 479. Mencius indicates that the disciples spent three years in mourning near Confucius' grave and that Tzŭ-kung remained there three years longer. While Mencius does not specify which disciples were there, from the context it is probable that he meant to include all of the surviving disciples of any importance. This sounds like one of the "miracles" that have been added to Confucius' biography by later generations. To a Western mind it is almost inconceivable that these men, some young and some in their prime, some beginning and some at the height of successful careers, could have taken three years out of their lives to be spent in the almost complete inactivity of mourning at Confucius' grave. This would be a "living sacrifice" indeed. And for whom? Not for a parent, or a ruler, or even a man of high station. But for a self-made man, who never rose very high or accomplished very much—their old teacher.

Can we, then, believe this story? When we remember that in the *Tso Chuan* Confucius' disciples suddenly drop out of sight for a period of years after his death (with the significant exception of the renegade disciple Tzŭ-kao); [46] when we see how the disciples revered him, so that Tzŭ-kung compared him to the sun and the moon and Yu Jo said, "From the birth of mankind until now, there has never been the equal of Confucius"; when we consider these things we can believe that perhaps this miracle did, after all, take place. And we can understand how this simple teacher came to be known to later generations as "the uncrowned king."

CHAPTER V

THE MAN

WHAT sort of person was Confucius? What would he have been like to meet, to talk with, to know? To answer this question we should not depend, of course, only upon the testimony of his disciples and friends; we should also consult the opinions of his enemies and (even better) of those whose feelings toward him were neutral. Unfortunately, however, we have almost nothing from the latter sorts of people that can be considered reliable. Later in this book we shall consider the attacks that were made upon Confucius by partisans of rival philosophies, and we shall see that there is almost nothing which seems to relate to the real Confucius who lived. Rather, these enemies are criticizing the head of a powerful and hated group, and attributing to him whatever characteristics they think will be most damaging; commonly these attacks include details which make it at once apparent that their content can not be historical. We are therefore compelled again to base our study chiefly upon the *Analects*, as the most reliable source available.[1]

Even the attacks of enemies rarely contradict the impression, which we get from the *Analects*, that Confucius was a pleasant person. "When at leisure," that work tells us, "the Master's manner was informal and cheerful." Elsewhere it states that he was "affable yet firm, commanding yet not austere, dignified yet pleasant." He was respectful, though not obsequious, where respect was due. In return, he expected due respect from others, and felt that he had a certain position to maintain. Yet he did not for all that remain aloof from his fellow men, even the humble; he not only preached but practiced a democratic attitude.

On the other hand, it is doubtful that he was the sort of person who is always the center of a large and eager group of acquaintances. He had many fast friends, but he was not the kind of man to be extremely popular. He was too thoughtful and too frank. He said, "To conceal resentment, and remain on friendly terms with those toward whom one feels it . . . I should be ashamed of such conduct." He seems to have followed, for the most part, the practice of criticizing men to their faces and praising them behind their backs. This makes for respect but not for popularity. On the whole he was somewhat reserved. This reserve seems to have extended even to his attitude toward his own son, in whose abilities, as he frankly admitted, he was disappointed.

While he was almost always courteous, he considered it beneath him to curry favor with the mighty. When he talked with rulers and powerful hereditary nobles, he seems to have made little if any effort to ingratiate himself and was commonly quite critical. The practical wisdom of this course is debatable, but it did accord with his precept of strict sincerity. His dislike of eloquence was part of the same attitude. He distrusted loquacity in others, and if we may judge from the *Analects*, he did not practice it himself. Mencius quotes Confucius as having said, "I have no talent for making speeches." While his statements were sometimes both moving and noble, they were seldom either wordy or flowery. In other respects as well, he had a native hostility toward outward show that would be less surprising in a rustic than in so polished a man of the world. Physical comfort and wealth were not, he believed, objects for which the true gentleman might strive. "The Master said, 'If wealth were a proper object of my search, I would do whatever were necessary to get it, even if I had to become a groom holding a whip. But since it is not a proper object, I shall follow after that which I love.' "

From all of this we might easily conclude that Confucius was an ascetic, but we would be mistaken.[2] For the true ascetic commonly thinks of pleasure as in itself evil and may even consider pain to be good. There was none of this in Confucius. Indeed, Confucianism as a philosophy has never opposed the pleasures of the flesh in moderation, and Confucius personally did not disapprove of enjoyment unless it was incompatible with virtue and integrity, quite the contrary. He lauded study as being a source of pleasure, and his delight in music as a source of sheer enjoyment seems to have been exceptional. He was keenly interested in orchestral music, and he himself played a kind of lute and took part in informal group singing.

In recognizing the profound psychological truth that pleasure is not merely a desirable but even a necessary part of life, Confucianism was unique among the principal philosophies of ancient China. Each of the others, having in different ways some tendency toward totalitarianism, tended to frown upon enjoyment, at least for the common people. Mo Tzǔ and his school decried every adornment of life and every activity that did not strictly contribute to economic production; they even advocated eliminating the emotions. Similarly the Taoist work, *Lao Tzǔ*, condemned adornment and wished the people to be "without desire."[3] The Legalists, full-fledged totalitarians, believed that men should be nothing but organs of the state, having no personal thoughts or feelings; one of them asserted that the people's normal life should be made so unpleasant that they would welcome war as a release from it.

Confucius, on the other hand, did not consider a government worthy of the name unless it made its people happy, and specifically told his students to plan their lives so as to include relaxation. The *Records on Ceremonial* (*Li Chi*), compiled in the Han dynasty, includes a story that, while no doubt apocryphal, seems to be based on a correct understanding of Confucius' attitude. It relates that the disciple Tzǔ-kung, having gone to an agricultural sacrifice at the end of the year and seen the people making merry, complained that they seemed to be quite mad. Confucius told him, however (according to this story), that he should understand that they were only taking necessary relaxation after their long months of toil, and to remember that even a bow cannot be kept forever taut and yet retain its resiliency.

This sympathy with the feelings and the needs of ordinary men and women is much of the secret of the appeal of Confucianism. The balance that it represents, avoiding sheer abandonment to pleasure on the one hand and meaningless austerity on the other, is typical of Confucius' character. For a genius (which he surely was) and a great creative leader, he seems to have been remarkably well balanced.

He was supremely self-confident, to the point of feeling that the whole destiny of civilization depended upon himself. His assurance was so genuine that he was not disturbed even by unfair criticism but could accept it with a smile. Nevertheless he made no pretense to omniscience; he knew the words most essential for any scholar's vocabulary: "I don't know." He sought information by asking questions and did not care if this caused people to think him ignorant. His dignity was not offended if his students disagreed with him, and he was capable of admitting that they were right.

Despite his conviction that he was charged with a tremendous mission, he seems to have been truly modest. Although he constantly insisted that one should be concerned about one's merit, rather than about one's reputation, he had enough regard for the opinions of mankind to lament sometimes, to his intimate disciples, that no one seemed to understand him.

Neither his conviction of his own importance nor his lack of success caused him to feel bitterly toward his fellow men or to try to make others seem small that he might appear great by contrast. He seems to have been both kindly and thoughtful. It is recorded that when entertaining a blind man he was careful to make sure to acquaint his guest with each of the persons present and to inform him of everything about which he might be curious but could not see. He was humane enough to care more for the welfare of human beings than for his property. "When the stable burned down the Master, returning from court, asked, 'Was anyone hurt?' He did not ask about the horses." In the field, he was sporting: "The Master angled, but he did not use a net; he shot, but not at sitting birds."

His dictum concerning the young should win Confucius the gratitude of all young people everywhere. "A young person," he said, "should be treated with the utmost respect. How do you know that he will not, one day, be fully the equal of what you are now? It is the man who has reached the age of forty or fifty without having done anything to distinguish himself, who is not worthy of respect."

Perhaps the most remarkable fact about this unusual man is this: he was a zealot with a sense of humor (which is almost a contradiction in terms). He did not often, in so far as we know, tell jokes, but there must frequently have been a twinkle in his eye; many of the things he said have a humorous point which is not at once obvious. His humor has given pious commentators many bad moments, for some of them have been perfectly certain that it is beneath the dignity of a sage to jest.

One of his contemporaries once remarked, with heavy sarcasm, "Great indeed is Confucius! He is vastly learned, and yet—he has not made a name for himself in any profession." When Confucius heard this he did not defend himself by pointing out that he had gained some considerable repute as a teacher. Instead he readily acknowledged that this was a grave criticism and said to his disciples, "Now let me see, what shall I take up? Shall it be charioteering, or archery? I have it! I'll take up charioteering." Most of the commentators have been quite unwilling to see that Confucius was making an ironical reply to an absurd criticism. They treat the whole occurrence with the utmost seriousness and assert that he was giving "a modest reply to praise." The opening words of this passage, "Great indeed is Confucius!," are still hung on walls, written in large characters, as mottos designed to laud the sage. Even where, in the *Analects*, Confucius specifically said that he was joking, some commentators have refused to believe it.

Yet Confucius was no saint, nor was he perfect. He conformed, as most of us do, to the conventions of social intercourse of the society in which he lived. This necessarily involves telling an occasional untruth that is designed less to deceive than to respect the dignity of the hearer. On one occasion he made his disapproval very clear to a man who asked for an interview. "Ju Pei wished to see Confucius. Confucius declined, on the ground that he was ill, but as the messenger was going out the door Confucius took his lute and sang, making sure that he was heard."

The self-control of Confucius was great but not preternatural. Although he believed that the emotions should be regulated, on the death of his favorite disciple, Yen Hui, he grieved without restraint. The other disciples told him, "You are grieving excessively," whereupon Confucius replied, "Am I indeed? And if I am not to mourn excessively for this man, for whom am I to do so?"

It is recorded that he once lost his temper with a rude acquaintance to such an extent that he "struck him on the shank with his staff." Deplorable conduct on the part of Confucius, beyond doubt; but we would not have it expunged from the *Analects*. It makes him human.

CHAPTER VI

THE DISCIPLES

IF we are to understand Confucius as a teacher, we must first know something about the sort of students he had to work with. As we have already noted, the number of his disciples has been grossly exaggerated, even up to the number of three thousand. But the *Mencius* and a number of other works give their number as seventy, and it is probable that this is a maximum. In order even to approximate this number of names, almost every individual who has been mentioned as being associated with Confucius must be represented as a disciple; thus the *Historical Records* includes among the disciples one Kung-Po Liao, of whom it is known only that the *Analects* says that he was a political enemy of Tzŭ-lu.

Even when men are cited in the *Analects* as having asked questions of Confucius, it is not easy to be certain whether or not they were disciples. That work mentions some twenty-two persons who, it seems reasonable to believe, were disciples, but of these only a few stand forth as distinct individuals.

A contemporary Chinese scholar, Ch'ien Mu, has pointed out that the disciples fall into two large groups, namely (1) the early ones who studied with Confucius before he left Lu on his travels, and (2) the later students who were taught by the Mas-

63

ter after he returned to Lu. It is not easy, however, to define these groups with precision. Some who seem to belong in the later category may well have studied with Confucius, if only briefly, before he set off on his travels, while some of the early disciples continued to consult him in the later years. We have almost no information on the ages of the disciples; the *Historical Records* gives birth dates for more than a score, but as Ts'ui Shu has shown these are of very doubtful validity.

It is nevertheless quite probable that, as tradition holds, Tzŭ-lu was the oldest of the disciples. Sometimes he appears less as Confucius' student than as his "best friend and severest critic." We have seen that he was scandalized by the Master's interview with the Duchess Nan Tzŭ, and that he twice protested when Confucius considered entering the service of men holding cities in revolt. Tzŭ-lu was just as strict with himself. It was said that he "never slept over a promise," and Mencius related that "when anyone pointed out to Tzŭ-lu that he had a fault, he rejoiced."

Yet despite all this earnestness and uprightness, Tzŭ-lu is the most warm and human figure among the disciples. He would seem to have been formed by nature to be a soldier. Confucius recommended him as capable of managing an army and once declared that "a man like Tzŭ-lu will never die a natural death." His simple directness and impetuosity made him quite out of place among the courtly manners and scholarly tastes of the other disciples. His realization of this gave him a feeling of inadequacy, which heightened his natural tendency to boast of those qualities he knew he did possess. Thus on one occasion when Confucius praised the capacities of his favorite disciple, Yen Hui, Tzŭ-lu spoke up and said, "Well, if you were leading a great army, whom would you want with you then?" Confucius replied, "I would *not* have with me the sort of man who (as the poem says) 'would attack a tiger with his bare hands, or cross a river without a boat.' I would want someone who approached difficulties with caution, and preferred to succeed by careful planning." Poor Tzŭ-lu was always being rebuked for his boldness. Sometimes Confucius deliberately laid traps for him, and he was always taken in. One day Confucius said, "My doctrines make no progress. I shall get upon a raft and float out to sea. Tzŭ-lu, I am sure, will come with me." This pleased Tzŭ-lu greatly, whereupon Confucius added dryly, "Tzŭ-lu is more fond of daring than I; he does not use judgment."

Inevitably Tzŭ-lu attracted to himself a great deal of criticism; for all his virtues of straightforwardness, he was far from achieving Confucius' ideal of conduct for his disciples. But the Master was careful, too, to soften his criticism so that it might not cut too deeply. Despite (or perhaps even because of) the great difference in their temperaments, there was a strong bond of affection between Confucius and Tzŭ-lu. While the Master constantly tried to curb his excessive enthusiasm, he fully appreciated the sterling qualities of his stalwart follower. Tzŭ-lu, like Yen Hui, shared the hardships of Confucius' travels. And it is a question whether the Master felt the deeper attachment toward Yen Hui, whom he always praised, or Tzŭ-lu, whom he nearly always criticized. It was Confucius who asked, "Does not love always lead to strictness with its object?"

In 481, after Confucius and Tzŭ-lu had returned to Lu, there was an occurrence that brought out sharply the difference between Tzŭ-lu and Jan Ch'iu. An officer who controlled a city in a neighboring state called Little Chu came to Lu, offering to annex his city to Lu in return for certain guarantees to himself. This was usual enough; such agreements were commonly cemented with sworn treaties. The unusual feature was that he would have no sworn treaty; instead, he demanded merely a gentleman's agreement with Tzŭ-lu. Whether Tzŭ-lu had again gone into government service in Lu is uncertain; in any case, he refused to see the man from Little Chu. Thereupon Chi K'ang Tzŭ sent Jan Ch'iu to persuade him. Jan asked, "How can this be a disgrace to you, since he will not trust the sworn covenant of a great state, yet puts faith in your mere word?" Tzŭ-lu replied, "If Lu should go to war with Little Chu, I would willingly die before its capital without asking the reason for the hostilities. But this man is a traitor to his ruler; to act as he desires, and treat him as an honest man, is that of which I am incapable."

Soon afterwards, Tzŭ-lu went to Wei, taking along his protégé Tzŭ-kao. They both entered the service of the K'ung family, with which Confucius had been associated in Wei. When rebellion brought serious danger to the K'ung, Tzŭ-kao fled and tried to persuade Tzŭ-lu to do likewise. "I have eaten their pay," Tzŭ-lu replied, "and will not flee from their misfortunes." Trying to save his chief, he was struck down with dagger-axes and killed.

Jan Ch'iu, also prominent among the early disciples, was almost the opposite of Tzŭ-lu. He did not suffer from the fault of overenthusiasm; on the contrary, Confucius once commented that it was necessary to urge him, because he was backward. On one occasion Jan Ch'iu told the Master, "It is not that I do not delight in your Way, but that my strength is insufficient." Confucius replied, "Those whose strength is insufficient go as far as they can before stopping, but you do not even do that."

Jan Ch'iu seems to have coldly weighed the probable profit of every course before embarking upon it. He was a capable man, as Confucius somewhat grudgingly admitted. He was a suave talker, a good administrator, and even an able general. His shrewdness in selecting the profitable course aided his political career, for he quickly saw that once Confucius had secured him a place with the Chi family it was they, and ñot Confucius, who could help him most from that point onward. He set himself, therefore, to further their policies rather than the doctrines of the Master. As a natural result he rose in favor, while the uncompromising Tzŭ-lu declined. Confucius became increasingly dissatisfied with Jan Ch'iu. As we have seen, when Jan helped the Chi to increase their already oppressive taxation the Master disowned him as a disciple. It does not appear, however, that he was in fact excluded from the Confucian circle, at least for very long.

As we have seen, Tzŭ-lu lost his life because he refused to desert his post even when the odds against him were hopeless. Jan Ch'iu, when we last see him some years later, is still flourishing and in high favor. The moral we must leave to moralists.

More of a happy medium in temperament was struck by the disciple Tzŭ-kung. He seems to have had the fortunate faculty of being able to please those for whom he worked without toadying and to prosper without deserting his principles. He was probably what would be called a well-adjusted person, combining something of both the introvert and the extrovert; he was something of a philosopher in his own right, yet so pleasant in manner that everybody seems to have liked him. In speech he was eloquent; as a diplomat he was so able that the head of the Chi family once regretted his rashness in going to a diplomatic conference without him. His judgment on political affairs was eagerly consulted, and he seems even to have prospered financially.

The *Analects* clearly shows that Tzŭ-kung was on very intimate terms with the Master. It is probably this fact, as well as his seniority and abilities, which caused him to be looked to as the leader in the mourning ceremonies after Confucius' death. At all times his loyalty to Confucius was unswerving. On two occasions others (once the disciple Tzŭ-ch'in) asserted that Tzŭ-kung was quite the equal of the Master. On both occasions Tzŭ-kung explained, with complete calm, that such an assertion merely showed the lack of understanding of the speaker; he warned Tzŭ-ch'in that he had better be careful not to get himself a reputation as a fool. Never in human history, Tzŭ-kung declared, had there been the equal of Confucius.

The Master praised Tzŭ-kung for his intelligence and recommended him to the Chi family as a man of penetration. But he was mildly irritated by Tzŭ-kung, too. Confucius was always suspicious of eloquence, in which Tzŭ-kung excelled. And he would probably have had to be more than human not to be slightly annoyed at the easy manner in which success came to this urbane disciple, with his wealth of natural charm. It is not surprising that Confucius could not resist the impulse to take occasional sly digs designed to puncture Tzŭ-kung's aplomb. In particular, Confucius was distressed that Yen Hui, whom he considered by far the most capable of all the disciples, remained obscure and in poverty while Tzŭ-kung and others won easy success. He once asked Tzŭ-kung, "Whom do you consider the better man, yourself or Yen Hui?" Tzŭ-kung replied that he did not dare to compare himself with Yen Hui.

This favorite disciple, Yen Hui, is hard to appraise. A great deal is said about him, but when we add it up it comes to little more than a catalogue of virtues. Confucius himself admitted that "it is not until one knows a man's faults that one can truly judge whether he is virtuous." If we read between the lines, however, it is easy to suspect Yen Hui of serious shortcomings.

Unlike a number of the other disciples, we almost never find
Yen Hui saying anything; usually he just agrees with Confucius,
or accepts his pronouncements without comment. One cannot
help wondering if he is merely stupid, having no mind of his
own.

Almost never does Yen Hui make a warm and human gesture.
Once when he and Tzŭ-lu were with Confucius, the Master
said, "Why don't each of you tell me what you'd like to do?"
Tzŭ-lu at once replied, "I'd like to have carriages and horses
and fur clothing, and I'd share them with my friends and not
care even if they ruined them." Yen Hui said, "My wish is not
to boast of my excellence, nor make a display of what I do for
others." Tzŭ-lu was so embarrassed that he quickly asked the
Master what were *his* wishes. Nevertheless, the impression that
Yen Hui was a totally unsympathetic person may well be erroneous. Tzŭ-lu was a lovable character, but his perennially
boyish boastfulness and eagerness for praise must have been
hard, at times, to live with.

Confucius himself wondered what to make of the unusual
docility of Yen Hui. He said, "I can talk with him the whole
day and he never disagrees with me, as if he were stupid. But
when I inquire into what he does when he is away from me, I
find that his conduct fully demonstrates what I have taught
him. No, Hui is not stupid." Not only the Master but other
disciples as well lauded Yen Hui both for his outstanding intelligence and for his virtue. Confucius praised him as far superior
to all the others, both as a diligent student and as one who
could hold, unvaryingly, to the ideal of conduct.

Nevertheless, it appears that Yen Hui never attained the goal
of public office.[1] It is true that he died relatively young, but this
is not the whole explanation. None of the rulers of the day seem
to have taken an interest in Yen Hui, as they did in other disciples,[2] and the Master spoke of Yen Hui as being, like himself,
unemployed.

If the reason lay in a defect it was not of intellect but of personality. All his life he was very poor; this fact, and a natural
reserve, probably caused him to withdraw into himself. Confucius declared that in the face of privations that other men could
not have borne Yen Hui "maintained an unvarying cheerful-

ness." But after a time such cheerfulness becomes a bit mechanical. This is especially true if one must endure the supreme trial of the human spirit: seeing those who are one's inferiors, in intellect and ability, preferred over oneself, time after time. This was the fate of Yen Hui. It was also that of Confucius, but Confucius was able to rise almost completely superior to it; this is one of the reasons why he is one of the great men of all time. If Yen Hui, being more like the rest of us, was slightly soured, we can hardly blame him.

Confucius looked upon Yen Hui as if he had been his own son. When he died, the Master cried out, "Heaven is destroying me!" and mourned as on no other occasion. Since Yen's family was poor, they could not afford to give him a great funeral. The other disciples joined forces to bury him in style (Confucius protested that this was in poor taste). The disciples followed Yen Hui to the grave with profound respect and also, perhaps, with a sense of relief. The post of teacher's pet is a most difficult one.

By no means all of the disciples were as able as these few outstanding ones we have discussed. Tsai Yü distinguished himself for sheer recalcitrance. He not only differed with but even poked thinly veiled fun at Confucius' precepts. This might have been all right if he had been extremely able, but he was not. He was a good talker, but that seems to have been his only virtue. The Master said, "I used merely to listen to men's words, and assume that they would carry them out. But now I listen to what they say and also look into their conduct. My experience with Tsai Yü has brought about this change." He was also lazy, to the point of trying Confucius' patience severely.[3] Nevertheless we find Tsai Yü in conversation with the Duke of Lu; no such distinction ever came to Yen Hui.[4]

The later disciples are extremely important because it is through them that the teachings of Confucius were transmitted to later generations. None of them reached high political posts like those held by Tzŭ-lu, Jan Ch'iu, and Tzŭ-kung. But Confucius did not significantly influence the world either by his own political activity or by that of his disciples. He did so, rather, by his teaching. His teaching was effective only as it was propagated by his disciples, and it seems to have been the later disciples who were most important in this role. As we should expect, what they taught was not wholly identical with what they learned. These men shaped and gave its first direction to the Confucian doctrine and the Confucian tradition; we must therefore consider what sort of men they were.

It is not easy to be sure just which of the disciples were teachers on any considerable scale; the traditions in this regard seem to be rather faulty.[5] Ts'ui Shu, who probably knew the evidence as well as anyone ever will, considered the chief propagators to be Tzŭ-yu, Tzŭ-chang, Tzŭ-hsia, and Tsêng Shên.

Still another of the later disciples must be mentioned, if only because of a curious story about him which Mencius tells. After the death of Confucius, he says, Tzŭ-hsia, Tzŭ-chang, and Tzŭ-yu "considered Yu Jo to resemble the sage" and wished to serve him as they had served Confucius. They urged Tsêng Shên to join them, but he refused, declaring that no one was worthy to be compared with the Master; apparently the plan was dropped. Yu Jo may have had students of his own, for in the *Analects* he is three times referred to as Master Yu. But we know very little about him.

We have only a little more information about Tzŭ-yu. He was lauded for his accomplishments in literary studies, and like others of the later disciples he seems to have been particularly interested in ritual. The *Analects* records that when Confucius approached the town of which Tzŭ-yu was governor he heard the sound of stringed instruments and singing. Inquiring into the source, he found that Tzŭ-yu was teaching his townspeople the music and ceremonies usually reserved for the use of gentlemen at court; in this manner, he explained, he was teaching them the Way of Confucius. This would seem to make Tzŭ-yu one of the earliest practitioners of mass education.[6]

Tzŭ-chang seems to have been the most energetic among the later disciples; in fact Confucius once said that he erred on the side of "going too far." He frankly studied with a view to winning a position and a salary and hoped to become famous. He had no patience with those who pursued the Way halfheartedly, and declared that one should be prepared to die for his principles if necessary. This energetic disciple was not entirely popular with his fellows. Tsêng Shên called him self-important, and Tzŭ-yu said, "My friend Chang can do difficult things, but he is not completely virtuous." The *Analects* does not say directly that Tzŭ-chang had students of his own, but both the *Han Fei Tzŭ* and the *Historical Records* name Tzŭ-chang among the disciples who taught after Confucius' death; the former work makes him the founder of a school within Confucianism.

The *Analects* does state specifically that Tzŭ-hsia had disciples and tells us something about his teaching. A conversation is reported, in the book of *Mo Tzŭ*, between Mo Tzŭ and a disciple of Tzŭ-hsia. The *Historical Records* tells us of four men who studied with Tzŭ-hsia and afterward "became the instructors of kings." Tzŭ-hsia himself, at the end of his life, was tutor to the Marquis Wên of Wei. Undoubtedly he is very important among those who transmitted and formed the Confucian doctrines.

Tzŭ-hsia seems to have been somewhat pedantic.[7] In the *Analects* he is lauded as a student of literature. Confucius contrasted his temperament with that of Tzŭ-chang, saying that while Tzŭ-chang went too far Tzŭ-hsia did not go far enough. The difference between these two reached the point of verbal conflict. On one occasion a disciple of Tzŭ-hsia asked Tzŭ-chang what principles should guide one's association with others. Tzŭ-chang asked, "What does Tzŭ-hsia tell you?" The disciple replied, "'Tzŭ-hsia says, 'Associate with those who act properly; keep the improper at a distance.'" Tzŭ-chang said, "That is different from what I have been told. The gentleman honors the virtuous and talented, but is indulgent toward all."

Arguments of this sort flourished after the death of Confucius. As the *Han Fei Tzŭ* says, each of the disciples who taught declared himself to have "the true Confucian doctrine," and since Confucius "could not come back to life, who could render a decision?"

Tzŭ-yu said, "The disciples of Tzŭ-hsia do well enough when it is only a question of sprinkling and sweeping the ground, answering summonses and replying to questions, coming forward and retiring. But these things are superficial; concerning more fundamental matters they are quite at a loss." Tzŭ-hsia defended himself by declaring that students cannot be introduced to the whole of truth at one time, but that it must be taught to them gradually.

It would be a mistake, however, to suppose that Tzŭ-hsia was nothing but a pedant. He held office as governor of a town, the range of his interests was wide, and some of his sayings remind one of those of Confucius. Nevertheless, there was a certain pedestrian quality about Tzŭ-hsia. This appears, for instance, in his statement that "so long as one does not overstep the boundary-line in matters of great moral import, he may pass and repass it in matters of small moral import." Here it is evident that he is thinking of morality in authoritarian terms, as a matter of certain hard and fast rules, rather than, in the manner of Confucius, as a positive program to attain certain desirable ends. It is perhaps such tendencies that caused Confucius to admonish Tzŭ-hsia to conduct himself "in the manner of the gentleman, not of the small man."

As in the case of other disciples, there are a great many anecdotes about Tzŭ-hsia in the books that date from a period later than those which we are using as our principal sources. Thus the Legalist work *Han Fei Tzŭ* quotes Tzŭ-hsia as having made a thoroughly Legalist speech which would throw doubt on him as a loyal Confucian. This variety of posthumous conversion is a familiar device in ideological struggles. The later Confucian works also contain a great many stories about the various disciples, some of which may be true and some of which are certainly fanciful. In the last analysis it is almost impossible to distinguish the genuine from the false materials in these later works; for this reason we can only continue to seek for the truth in the less voluminous, but more reliable, early records.

Another disciple of great influence was Tsêng Shên.[8] In the *Analects* he is usually called Tsêng Tzŭ, Master Tsêng; since this is the way in which his disciples would have referred to him, it has plausibly been argued that the school of Tsêng Shên had a considerable hand in putting together the *Analects*. Mencius calls him a teacher and says that at one time he had as many as seventy students.

Mencius also states that Tsêng Shên was fearless, but in a story Mencius tells about him this does not appear. Mencius says that when a town in which he was living was raided by troops from a neighboring state, Tsêng Shên was the first to run away, for which he was criticized. Mencius defends him against the charge of cowardice, of which he may perhaps be acquitted since he was not a soldier. More important is the complete lack of humanity with which Tsêng told the caretaker of his house, as he left the city before the invasion, "Don't let people lodge in my house; they might injure the plants and trees." One cannot imagine Confucius saying this.

It would be a great mistake to suppose, however, that Tsêng Shên attached no importance to virtuous conduct. In fact, he paid attention to little else. Among his many sayings in the *Analects* one finds very little concern with the state of the world or the conduct of government, but an intense preoccupation with the manner in which the individual may cultivate his virtue. When he was very ill and the head of the Mêng family visited him, Tsêng said, "When a man is about to die, his words are good. A gentleman, in following the Way, values three things above all others: from every attitude and every gesture he removes all trace of violence or arrogance; every expression of his face must betoken good faith; from every word that he utters he must eliminate all trace of uncouthness and impropriety." Facing death, Tsêng seems to have been relieved that he would soon be beyond the danger of committing an impropriety.

Tsêng Shên is celebrated in Confucian lore for his filial piety.[9] He discourses on this subject in several passages in the *Analects*, and Mencius describes his unusually filial conduct at some length. It is an interesting fact that, with almost no exception, it is the later disciples rather than the early ones who give special attention to filial piety.

Obviously, there is a considerable difference between the interests and the activities of the early and the late disciples, considered as two groups. Part of the reason certainly lies in the personal history of Confucius. Up until the time when he was finally disillusioned by his travels, he always hoped to be able to practice, as an official, what he preached. He was teaching only temporarily, while waiting for his great opportunity to remake the world. In the interval he was glad to tell like-minded young men how they, too, might do what he was planning. And those he taught caught the enthusiasm. But after he had to face the fact that his opportunity was not to come he naturally turned more to books and teaching; if he could not rescue the world from its misery, he must teach others how to do so. The early disciples tried to be like the Master in his earlier years; they wished, and some of them were able, to take part significantly in government. The later disciples seem to have tried, for the most part, not to be what Confucius hoped his disciples would be but to be like the Master himself in his later years. This helps to explain their greater interest in teaching, in ceremonial, and in the implanting of virtue in the individual rather than in society as a whole. It is one of the reasons why Confucianism, as compared with Confucius, was marked less by the zeal of the crusader than by the formality of the pedant.

CHAPTER VII

THE TEACHER

UNCOUNTED millions have been teachers. But the number of teachers who have changed the course of human history, as individuals and solely by their instruction of the young, is small indeed. The fact that Confucius did so gives peculiar interest to the methods and content of his teaching.

There was education in China before the time of Confucius, but we do not know very much about it. There are, to be sure, books which assert that there was a veritable system of schools in operation thousands of years before Confucius' time, but most of these books were written centuries after he lived, and their reliability is doubtful.[1] Mencius, it is true, lived only a century after Confucius, and Mencius did assert that each of the two previous dynasties had established schools. But Mencius cannot be absolved of the suspicion of having attributed to the past what he wished to be done in the future. When we turn to the literature that actually comes from pre-Confucian times, we find no reference to any schools except those established to teach archery; these are mentioned in inscriptions on bronze vessels.[2]

It is evident, however, that there was a good deal of study with private tutors. It is probable that all prospective rulers, and perhaps all sons of high nobles, had tutors. Young men in minor offices were trained by their official superiors. But this was not the same thing as the educational program of Confucius. This had been training by teachers who were in fact government officials, of men who were already in the government or were destined by heredity to rule; it was designed to implement the conduct of government according to the existing pattern.

Confucius did something altogether different. Acting as a private individual, he took as his students men of every condition who seemed to be good material. He trained them with the intention of bringing about a different and, as he believed, a very much better kind of government.

His objective in education was, therefore, a practical one. But it was by no means narrowly practical. Although the end of education was to bring about good government, this did not mean that the end product of education should be an efficient administrator and nothing more. Far from it, he should, in fact, be as nearly as possible the ideal man, from every point of view. He definitely should not be a mere specialist in some particular technique. The Master once defined the complete man as one possessing wisdom, free from covetousness, brave, accomplished, and well versed in courtesy, ceremonial, and music. This was undoubtedly a model that he held before his students.

Some of the qualities that Confucius wished his students to possess, such for instance as bravery and sincerity, are not prerequisites for success in politics. But Confucius' object was not successful careers but good government, and this he believed to be possible only when the government was administered by men who, in addition to being educated in the ordinary sense, were also endowed with integrity and poise. "What," he asked, "has one who is not able to govern himself to do with governing others?" He believed, in fact, that heads of state and all officers of the government should provide an example of the highest type of conduct, and he believed that by doing so they could accomplish more than by any amount of either preaching or punishment.

In this respect Confucius has often been misunderstood. Considerably later than his time (we see it with special clarity in the

Han period) there came into vogue a type of metaphysical, or
perhaps it should be called pseudoscientific theory, that held
every part of the universe to be linked with every other part in
an intimate and remarkable manner. The smallest actions of
the emperor were believed to affect the cosmic mechanism.
Thus the *Records on Ceremonial* (which was compiled in Han
times) informs us that if the emperor were, in the last month of
summer, to wear white clothing instead of red, "even high
ground would be flooded, the grain in the fields would not ripen,
and there would be many miscarriages among women." Many
students have interpreted Confucius in the light of this metaphysical theory and supposed that when he spoke of the transforming influence of the ruler's virtue he was speaking of this
kind of almost magical compulsion.[3] The present writer formerly held this view.[4] But if we study the genuinely early literature carefully, we see that this type of thinking is foreign to the
pre-Confucian period and does not occur even in works somewhat later than Confucius. It is not that there was no superstition in the early period. There was a great deal, but it was of a
different kind, concerned with spirits and ghosts so substantial
that they could sometimes beget children, rather than with
mysterious and complex "influences." In the early literature
generally, and for Confucius, it was not by magical compulsion but by the power of virtuous example that rulers influenced
their people for good.[5]

Confucius, as we have seen, was trying to make his students,
some of whom were of humble condition, into men fit to rule in
every sense of the word. It is perhaps for this reason that he
called the ideal type of man, whom they were to strive to become, by the term *chün tzŭ*. Literally this means "ruler's son,"
that is, a relative of a ruler, and therefore a member of the nobility. In this sense it is contrasted with *hsiao jên*, "little man,"
plebeian. As referring to a hereditary noble the term *chün tzŭ*
is very common in the early literature; it seldom if ever has any
other sense in the literature earlier than Confucius.[6] Confucius
sometimes uses it in this older sense, but for him this is exceptional. Usually, when he speaks of the *chün tzŭ*, he is referring to a man who has those qualities that an aristocrat ought
ideally to possess, a man of true (rather than merely hereditary)

nobility. This change in meaning is quite similar to that of the English word "gentleman," which originally denoted a man born to a superior social station but is now commonly used to refer to one of correct deportment and cultivation, without regard to birth. For this reason we shall follow the practice of translating *chün tzŭ* as "gentleman."

As the new rather than the old meanings for *chün tzŭ* came to be current, rulers who did not conform to the Confucian standard of conduct automatically classed themselves as "no gentlemen." Thus the Confucians could point out that they, and not the hereditary rulers, were the true aristocrats and should, therefore, administer the government.

Confucius' aim was to make his students into gentlemen. On whom did he undertake to perform this operation? He himself declared that he had never refused to teach anyone, even though he might be so poor that he came with nothing more than a bundle of dried meat as a present. That this was no mere boast and that such hospitality to the humble persisted in Confucianism is indicated by an amusing story in the *Mencius*. Mencius traveled in considerable style; he was deeply offended, therefore, when the custodian of a palace in which he was lodged as a visitor accused his disciples of stealing a single shoe that was missing. The custodian justified his suspicion, however, by declaring that it was well known that Mencius accepted, without investigation, anyone who wanted to study with him.

Neither poverty nor humble birth acted as a bar to study with Confucius, but there were other considerations that did. He himself said that he refused to teach dullards and declared that he would instruct "only those who were bursting with eagerness" for enlightenment. He probably tried, too, to avoid wasting his time with students whose aim was merely to achieve wealth and position; men who pretended to be concerned with higher things, yet were ashamed of shabby clothes and coarse food, he dismissed as "not worth talking with." He lamented, however, that it was "hard to find one willing to study for three years without thought of material reward."

Those of his students who did not have homes nearby probably lived in Confucius' house.[7] His method of instruction seems to have been completely informal. There is no mention of classes or set examinations. Instead, Confucius conversed with one or a few of them at a time, sometimes talking himself and sometimes questioning them. Books, it would seem, they were expected to study for themselves, but the Master suggested what they should study and discussed particular passages with them. Although this individual method of teaching is not widely used at the present time (because it is too expensive), it closely resembles the tutorial method that is employed in some of the best colleges and universities.

This was the only method that Confucius could have used successfully. For he was not merely teaching scholars, but producing gentlemen capable of playing decisive roles in the world. He was not teaching certain subjects, but certain students. Therefore his methods were intensely individual, different for each student since each student presented a different problem.[8]

Thus the first task was to take the measure of each pupil. Confucius was, as every good teacher must be, a careful student of character. One of his devices, reminiscent of modern psychiatry, was to put his students at ease and then ask them to state their ambitions, freely and without reserve. On such occasions he could be a good listener, hearing them out with no interruption or comment, smiling, if he did so, only to himself. But all the time they talked he was storing away impressions, studying how to take advantage of their good points and overcome their weaknesses.

Once having made his analysis of the individual, the Master shaped his instruction accordingly. He sometimes gave different students entirely different answers to the same question. On one occasion Tzŭ-lu asked him whether, when he was taught anything, he should at once put it into practice. Confucius told him no, that he should consult his father and his elder brothers. A little later Jan Ch'iu asked the same question, and the Master told him yes, he should practice what he was taught immediately. The disciple Kung-Hsi Hua, knowing of the two answers, was puzzled and asked the reason for the difference. Confucius told him, "Jan Ch'iu is lacking in zeal, so I urged him on; Tzŭ-lu has more than his own share of energy, so I held him back." As we have seen, this did in fact correspond to the characters of the two men.

Confucius was not informal in his teaching methods alone. A little later, Chinese teachers stood very much on their dignity and expected their students to accept what they said without question. Confucius, however, treated his students with an easy informality and a lack of strict discipline that such later teachers would have found shocking. This was not accidental. It corresponded, as we shall see, with his philosophy of government and his philosophy of knowledge. In every sphere his emphasis was not on punishment for wrongdoing but on stimulus toward right-doing, not on coercion but on persuasion; consistently his emphasis was positive rather than negative.

We find, therefore, nothing comparable to the practice of Mo Tzŭ, one of whose disciples complained that Mo Tzŭ compelled him, as a neophyte, to wear short jackets and eat only coarse vegetable soup. Instead, Confucius concentrated on gaining the complete confidence of his students. This was the easier because he had a genuine liking and respect for the young; he retained a lively memory of his own difficulties as a young man. His attitude was that of a father, an older brother, or an older friend. He made no attempt to impress his disciples with mystification and declared that he had no secrets from them. Rather than constantly demanding loyalty from them, he gave the much more effective lesson of being loyal *to* them; he would very seldom "let them down" by criticizing them to those outside his circle.

The authority of the teacher very soon became proverbial in China and in Confucianism. Mo Tzŭ, born just after Confucius died, whose philosophy was an offshoot from Confucianism, declared, "My words are an adequate guide. To abandon my words and think for oneself is like throwing away the harvest and merely picking up grains. Trying to refute my words with one's own words is like throwing eggs at a boulder; one might use up all the eggs in the world without injuring the boulder." Hsün Tzŭ, the celebrated and influential Confucian who flourished around 300 B.C., said, "Not to consider right the ways of one's teacher, but to prefer one's own ways, may be compared to using a blind man to distinguish colors, or a deaf man to distinguish sounds; there is no way to get rid of confusion and error."

Confucius demanded no such blind faith. Indeed, he could not, since he had no such sublime certainty that he was in possession of absolute truth himself. And he was wise enough to know that if students are to be something more than phonograph records they must learn to think for themselves. They cannot do this while at the same time regarding the teacher's every word as sacrosanct. Confucius did not become angry if his students disagreed with him; sometimes he said frankly that they were right and he was wrong. Even when he was convinced that they were in error, he did not attempt to bludgeon them with the authority of a book, of antiquity, or of himself as a teacher. He tried to convince them by reason and, if he could not, let the matter drop.

All this does not mean that he was an easy teacher in the sense that he expected little of his students. On the contrary, it is clear that he expected a great deal. He was in position to demand the more because he made it clear to them that the ultimate responsibility for what they should make of themselves was theirs. Nor would it be correct to suppose that he never reproved his disciples. We have already seen that he went so far as to disown Jan Ch'iu because he had assisted the rich and powerful Chi family to increase its exactions from the people. Usually, however, his reproof was mild, and he was careful not to go so far as to injure the self-respect of the student at whom it was aimed. Often he used a dry and gentle humor to make his point; thus we read, "Tzǔ-kung was constantly criticizing others. The Master said, 'Obviously Tzǔ-kung has become quite perfect himself, to have time to spare for this; I do not have this much leisure.' "

The result of this light-reined discipline was not, as might be supposed, to leave the disciples unruly and recalcitrant. They did not always obey the Master, especially after they had gone out to take responsible places in the world, but their loyalty and affection for him are altogether remarkable and surely cannot have been duplicated often in human history. Mencius tells us that even Tsai Yü, the disciple whom Confucius was always scolding and whom he once said it was useless to reprove, declared that the Master was the greatest man who had ever lived.

What was the curriculum by means of which Confucius

undertook to transform all comers (provided they were intelligent and industrious) into "gentlemen"? While it was different from any modern curriculum, it was also different from the usual training of the young aristocrat of that day. A principal difference was its exclusion of archery and charioteering. These exercises, useful in war, were studied as polite arts, just as fencing was, until recently, a usual accomplishment of the European aristocrat. Confucius himself shot with the bow, and at least some of his students were adept at both archery and charioteering. Confucius did not decry these skills, but he did not teach them because they were not necessary to a "gentleman" in his sense of the word. Here again we see a symptom of the shift away from a hereditary and basically military aristocracy to an aristocracy of merit, of virtue, and of primarily administrative achievement.

Another of the traditional arts of the Chinese aristocrat was precisely suited to Confucius' purpose. He took it over, gave it his own particular emphasis, and developed it into what became almost the hallmark of the Confucian. This was the art known as *li*. *Li* has been translated by a variety of terms, including "ceremonial," "ritual," and "the rules of propriety." In some passages such translation not only fails to convey the sense of the Chinese, but even quite obscures its true meaning.

The Chinese character for *li* is a pictograph representing a sacrificial vessel in which precious objects have been placed as a sacrifice to the spirits. There seems no doubt that the earliest meaning of this character was "sacrifice"; it still retains this sense. By a simple extension of meaning it came also to signify the ritual used in sacrifice.

The pattern of its further development is more complex. To understand it we must realize, first of all, that what we call "religious" and "secular" activities were not widely separated in ancient China; in fact, they were almost inextricably mingled. The dividing line between the dead and the living was not sharp. Bronze ritual vessels were commonly made for presenting offerings to ancestors, but the inscriptions on a number of them tell us that they were made both for sacrificing to spirits and "to feast my friends." Divine honors were paid to Roman emperors, it will be recalled, while they were still living; similarly, in the early Chinese records we sometimes find sacrifices to the dead and ceremonies honoring living rulers described in almost identical terms. If a ruler who had dispatched a diplomatic mission died while it was abroad, the chief of the mission went, on his return, to the hall where the body of the ruler lay in state and "made his report to the corpse."

Religious usages touched almost every aspect of life. Sacrifices were not presided over by a professional priesthood, but by the head of the family or, in the case of state sacrifices, by the ruler. Military expeditions were inaugurated in the ancestral temple (where, it appears, weapons were sometimes stored) and at the *shê chi*, "altar of land and grain"; when concluded, their success was reported, and victorious generals were rewarded, in the ancestral temple. Diplomatic negotiations were carried on in the ancestral temple, in the veritable presence, it was believed, of the ancestors; diplomatic banquets were given there, also. Even a proposal of marriage was received by the father of the prospective bride in his ancestral temple, in the presence of the spirits.

Since the scope of religious observances was so wide it is not very surprising that the term *li*, which denoted the code and the manner of their proper conduct, was sometimes used more broadly to denote proper conduct in general. The character *li* is not exceedingly common in literature that can plausibly be held to be earlier than Confucius, yet even in moderately early works it has not only the sense of "sacrificial ritual" but also, in three instances, this broader sense.[9] Confucius did not, then, originate the concept of *li* as a norm of conduct, but as he employs and discusses the term it is developed far beyond anything that was suggested earlier.

It has been held that Confucius attached a "magic" efficacy to conduct in accordance with *li*.[10] The question of Confucius' attitude toward religion is a difficult one, which will be discussed in a later chapter. Certainly he proclaimed no scepticism concerning the religious ceremonial that was an important part of *li*, but when he discusses *li* in connection with his teaching he is usually talking in terms of very sound and common-sense social psychology. His world, we must remember, was one in which there was a nearly complete breakdown of moral stand-

ards. It is related, for instance, that a duke of Ch'ên and two of
his ministers simultaneously carried on an affair with the same
widow; each of them wore a piece of her underclothing, and
made jokes about the intrigue in open court. A minister who
protested against this public display of lewdness was murdered.

Only in the performance of religious ceremonies could there
still be found, consistently, a type of conduct regulated by a socially accepted norm of behavior, in which men's actions were
motivated by a pattern of cooperative action, rather than swayed
by the greed and passions of the moment. Then, said Confucius,
let this pattern be universalized! In all of your intercourse with
others, he told Jan Yung, "behave as if you were receiving a
highly honored guest"; and if you are so fortunate as to find
yourself in a position of authority over the people, discharge
that trust with solemn care, "as if you were assisting at a great
sacrifice."

Li included the forms of ritual practice, but these were of
value only if they were "the outward and visible sign of an inward and spiritual grace." A man who is not truly virtuous has
nothing to do with *li*. "I cannot bear," the Master said, "to
see the forms of *li* gone through by those who have no reverence
in their hearts." In mourning for the dead it is more important,
he declared, that there be sincere grief, than that every rite be
fulfilled meticulously. Mere outward show disgusted him. " 'It
is *li*,' they say, 'it is *li*.' Does *li* mean nothing more than a display of jade and silk?"

On the contrary, true *li* was incompatible with vulgar display.
A later treatise says, "Acts of the greatest reverence admit of no
ornament" and again, "The grand symbol of jade has a plain,
uncarved surface." Confucius said, "In *li*, rather than being too
lavish it is better to err on the side of restraint." If one had to
give a two-word definition of *li*, it might perhaps be "good
taste."

Good taste consists, of course, in doing in every situation
what is suitable. So did *li*. The *Records on Ceremonial* states:
"*Li* is the embodied expression of what is fitting. Any practice
which stands the test of being judged by its fitness may be
adopted on this ground, even though it may not have been
among the practices of the former kings." Confucius stated his

views on this point very clearly. Ritual required that a certain kind of cap, made of hemp thread and relatively costly, be worn by those taking part in sacrifice. Confucius said, "The hemp thread cap is prescribed by *li*, but nowadays people wear silk; this is more economical, and I follow the common practice." The matter was merely one of expense, and he saw nothing unsuitable in this departure from the letter of ritual. But in the very next sentence he tells us in what sort of situation he did consider it important to carry out the prescribed observance to the full. When a subject had an interview with a ruler, he ascended a flight of steps to the hall of state. Court etiquette required that he bow before mounting the steps, but the practice had grown up of omitting this bow. "This," Confucius said, "is presumptuous, and though it is contrary to the common practice I make a point of bowing while still down below."

This was not, it should be noted, a matter of currying favor by cringing reverence, far from it. Confucius believed that a subject should show full and proper respect for the ruler's position, in approaching his person, and that in talking with the ruler he should express his deepest convictions sincerely and truthfully, even if this must involve giving offense. This, too, was *li!*

Clearly, then, *li* was no simple matter of rules of propriety; a wooden adherence to rules might cause one to violate true *li* outrageously. Yet on the other hand it was not enough merely to feel sincere emotion; *li* was a vehicle for the *expression* of emotion, and that expression must be in a socially sanctioned manner. The need for this is obvious. In certain circles today the raising of a clenched fist is a friendly greeting, while in others it is a gesture of enmity. If one is to function as a social being he must employ, though he need not be enslaved by, the conventions recognized by those around him. The practice of *li* in the Confucian sense involved, therefore, a knowledge of the traditional practices of society plus the ability to modify them as the circumstances and common sense might require.

In relation to the individual the function of *li* was to conduct behavior into socially accepted and socially useful channels. *Li* distinguished the civilized man from the rude barbarian who gave immediate and undisciplined vent to his feelings. The naïve reactions to death, for instance, are grief at one's loss and at the same time revulsion from the corpse. *Li* provided a means of dealing smoothly with the disposal of the corpse and of beautifying with appropriate ceremonies what might otherwise have been disgusting. In the mourning customs it made available an accepted manner of expressing and thus assuaging grief. Not to mourn at all would have been to weaken the family ties that knit the fabric of society; to give oneself up to wild and interminable grief would have been to disrupt one's own life and that of those about one. *Li,* asserting the claims of society, prescribed a course according with the due mean.[11]

Li was in fact a kind of balance wheel of conduct, tending to prevent either deficiency or excess, guiding toward the middle path of socially beneficial conduct. Confucius stated it thus: "Courtesy, if not regulated by *li,* becomes labored effort; caution, if not regulated by *li,* becomes mere timidity; courage, if not regulated by *li,* becomes mere unruliness; frankness, if not regulated by *li,* becomes mere effrontery."

Li was extremely important as a method of guiding and facilitating human intercourse, which is of course indispensable to the existence of society. We tend to feel that ceremony is out of place between friends, yet we also recognize that to be excessively casual destroys friendship. Confucius said, "Yen P'ing Chung knew well how to maintain friendship; though the acquaintance might be long, he was still respectful." James F. Byrnes has described an excellent instance of American *li.* He writes that in the United States Supreme Court "each Justice, upon entering the conference room from which the group marches into the Court, shakes hands with every other Justice present. It seemed to me, when I first became a member of the Court, that this was absurd because I had often just concluded talking with one or more of the Justices. I learned, however, that many years ago a Chief Justice established the custom on the theory that no matter how heated the arguments of the Justices might have been the previous day, they would be able to reconcile their differences if they started the day with a handshake and on speaking terms."

The importance of *li* for education is obvious. Since Confucius wished to equip men of humble origin to take effective roles in the government, he had to teach them the forms of polite intercourse between gentlemen and of court ceremonial; this was *li* at the purely external level. But there was always the danger that emphasis on polished conduct might make them into nothing more than courtly fops, punctilious in manner but lacking in any personal force. This did in fact happen in later Confucianism too often. Confucius was fully aware of this danger and warned against it very explicitly. He made it clear that true *li*, as opposed to mere manners, was a way of expressing good character, not a concealment of nor a substitute for character. "The basic stuff of the character of a gentleman," he said, "is Right; he carries it out by means of *li*." And on another occasion: "If a man's natural qualities exceed his training he is uncultivated; if his training exceeds his natural qualities he is little more than an educated lackey. It is only when the natural qualities and the training harmoniously complement each other that we have the gentleman." *Li* was not, then, a basic quality of character, but a means of establishing and adorning the right kind of character.

We cannot be certain, from the *Analects*, whether Confucius actually rehearsed his students in the performance of *li*, as his disciple Tzŭ-hsia apparently did. But whether he used this physical method of establishing habits or not, it is clear that he considered *li* to be a means of disciplining the emotions (an aspect of man that is sadly neglected in modern Western education) and assuring, by establishing balance and rhythm, that the individual would not be surprised by any crisis into regrettable action. This function of emotional control superimposed on intellectual culture was repeatedly emphasized. "The Master said, 'The gentleman who studies extensively in literature, and who disciplines his learning with *li*, is very unlikely to overstep the bounds.' " The *Analects* relates that on one occasion during Confucius' travels he and those with him were reduced to such straits that they became weak from hunger. Tzŭ-lu asked indignantly if it were fitting that gentlemen should endure such hardships. Confucius told him, "It is only a gentleman who is able to stand firm in the face of hardship; the ordinary man, finding himself in want, is swept off his feet." [12]

The concept of *li*, as imparting a certain rhythm and decorum to life and poise to the individual, has been important in Chinese culture ever since the time of Confucius. Lin Yutang has called it "that principle which has been the objective of the Chinese national life, which has done the work of social organization and control. . . ." It has given the Chinese people some of their most distinguishing characteristics. Only with the current substitution of Western for Chinese ways has it begun to disappear.

Music was another art of the aristocrat that Confucius stressed. A great many ceremonies were accompanied by music. This, plus the fact that music consists of a rhythmical and harmonious system of relationships between sounds, caused music and *li* to be constantly associated together. The Chinese did not conceive the educational value of music, as we do, to be merely that of a polite accomplishment. More like the Chinese attitude is that of classical Greece, where "the primary role of music is a pedagogical one, which, in the meaning of the antique world, implied the building up of character and morals." Aristotle stated that "music has a power of forming the character, and should therefore be introduced into the education of the young," while Plato wrote that "musical training is a more potent instrument than any other, because rhythm and harmony find their way into the inward places of the soul. . . ."

Confucius was deeply interested in music. One passage in the *Analects* may indicate that he had some hand in fixing the arrangement of the works in the *Book of Poetry*, which anciently had musical accompaniments. He played on the *sê*, a stringed instrument resembling the lute, and was fond of singing. Like Plato, he believed that music was a matter of concern not only to the individual but even to the state, since some sorts of music were beneficial and other sorts harmful to the character and thus to society. Both philosophers believed that certain kinds of music should be encouraged and other sorts eliminated, in the ideal state. Mencius quoted the disciple Tzŭ-kung as declaring that "by hearing the music sanctioned by a ruler one may judge of his virtue."

Whether Confucius personally taught music is not clear. From purely accidental reference we learn that two of his pupils (including the stalwart Tzŭ-lu) played the *sê*; it is not improbable that all of them did. Certainly he talked to them about music, but he may have expected them to study it in detail with other teachers. He once said that the complete man must become versed in *li* and music as the final adornments of his character. On another occasion he said that the student's character should be "stimulated by the study of poetry, established by the study of *li*, and given its finish by the study of music." Clearly, he associated music with *li* as a teacher, not merely of the intellect, but also of the emotions and the spirit.

It is curious that in modern Occidental culture, where music has doubtless been raised to its highest point of complexity, relatively little attention has been paid to its deeper implications. The undeniable fact that music affects the emotions and even the thoughts of those who hear it has been recognized from ancient times, but surprisingly little advance seems to have been made upon this naïve observation. Such research as has been carried on has indicated that music has "the property of influencing the blood pressure, the heartbeat, respiration, basal metabolism, and the glands of internal secretion." It has also been observed that under certain conditions musical tones have exerted a definite influence upon the waves in the cerebral cortex. Undoubtedly there is a great deal in the Chinese theories concerning the educational and moral significance of music that would not stand the test of scientific investigation, but it is rather surprising that there has been so little real research on the subject. It is interesting to note, however, that while we pay little heed to the influence of music upon "normal" persons, a number of psychiatrists have for some time been studying, and experimenting with, the use of music in the treatment of the mentally ill.

It cannot be too strongly emphasized that Confucius did not consider such accomplishments as *li* and music to be primary. The basic point that he pounded at his students, again and again and again, was sincerity, sincerity, sincerity. "If a man lacks sincerity," he told them, "I don't know how he can get on, any more than a wagon could without a yoke for attaching the horses."[13] The disciple Tzŭ-chang asked how one should conduct himself. The Master told him, "In everything you say be sincere and truthful, in all your actions be honorable and careful, and you will get along very well even among the barbarians." He praised those who were not ashamed to seek enlightenment from those inferior to them in rank, and honest enough to cause their meritorious inferiors to be raised to rank on a par with their own. He was scornful of hypocrisy; he would be ashamed, he said, to stoop to "clever talk, meretricious manners, and simulated respect." The man who covers his inner weakness with a harsh and overbearing manner is no better, he declared, than a thief.

Yet even sincerity, admirable and indispensable as it is, is not enough. One may be completely sincere and equally mistaken. Confucius told his disciples that while something may be said for the man who is determined to stand by his word at all costs, and to finish whatever he starts regardless of the circumstances, this was not his ideal of conduct. The gentleman, he said, while he might have faults, must always be ready to correct them.

Furthermore, he told them, it is not enough to be sincere merely in thought and in speech. True sincerity calls for action. One who enters government service should give his whole thought and effort to the task to be accomplished, while regarding the salary or other reward that he may gain as purely secondary. To see what is right yet not do it is cowardice. If necessary, one should be prepared to give up his life for the sake of his principles.

One method by which Confucius stimulated such conduct was to hold up before his students the ideal of the *shih* ±. It is probable that originally this term merely denoted a young man; [14] it also came to mean "soldier" and, by a process that is very common in history, "aristocrat." In this sense *shih* was quite similar to the European term "knight"; both denoted a member of the lowest order of the nobility, usually a military man. But here again Confucius gives a different sense to the term. More than a millennium later, in medieval Europe, the Christian church undertook "the task of taming the measureless ferocity of knighthood," and tried by various means and with some success to get the knights to espouse the virtues and the cause of the church. Confucius, somewhat similarly, declared that no man was worthy to be called a *shih* who did not act as a true gentleman should act, and that any man (regardless of birth) who exemplified the Confucian virtues was a *shih* in the highest sense.

The Christian church tried to utilize the traditional knightly virtues of courage, loyalty, and devotion for its own ends, causing young noblemen to swear to "defend to the uttermost the downtrodden, the widow, and the orphan," and diverting their bellicose energies into the holy war of the Crusades. In what Confucius says of the *shih* it is also possible to see an allusion to the zeal and devotion to be expected of the true knight. "A *shih*," he said, "who thinks only of sitting quietly at home is not worthy to be considered a *shih*." The disciple Tsêng Shên said, "The *shih* must be large of spirit and stout of heart, for his burden is heavy and his course is long. Perfect virtue is the burden he has taken up; is it not heavy indeed? His course ends only with death; is it not truly long?"

It is necessary, however, to emphasize that whereas the Christian knight was still a knight, and still a member of the nobility, the Confucian "gentleman" was ordinarily not a warrior at all. Commonly, he was not even a hereditary aristocrat. Confucius tried to instill into his disciples the virtues of the aristocracy without its vices, and to borrow its prestige for them without teaching them war. Ultimately the attempt was so successful that the warrior could no longer vie with the scholar in Chinese esteem.

Confucius made his students feel that theirs was the highest of all callings. Its rewards, in so far as he set them forth, consisted only of the inner peace and exaltation that come from the assurance that one is trying (whether successfully or not is unimportant) to do that which is, above all other things, worth while. Its duties were many and onerous.

Constantly he urged upon them the importance of self-cultivation. The responsibility must rest upon themselves alone. If they made any advance, however small, the credit was theirs; if they stopped short of the goal, however near, they must bear the blame for failure. Remember, he told them, that "even the general of a great army may be kidnaped, but no force can steal the determination of even the humblest man." Self-reliance and independence were favorite themes. "The gentleman seeks

within himself; the small man seeks from others." "Do not be
concerned because you are not in office, but with making yourself qualified for office; do not be concerned that you are unknown, but with being worthy of reputation."

They should be critical of moral defects, but of their own
rather than those of others. "One who is strict with himself
yet indulgent with others avoids resentment." "Even when
merely walking with two others," Confucius said, "I can always
learn from them. I select their good qualities to imitate, and
their bad qualities to avoid." "When you see an admirable
person, think of emulating him; when you see one who is not so,
turn inward and examine yourself!"

The disciples were expected to be modest and were ridiculed
when they were not. Confucius told them, "Mêng Chih-fan is
no boaster. When the army was routed he was the last to flee;
but when he neared the gate of the city he whipped up his
horses, saying, 'It was not courage that kept me behind; my
horses wouldn't go.'" "A gentleman," the Master said, "is
ashamed to let his words outrun his deeds." "He acts first, and
talks about it afterward."

Not only boastful talk but undue talkativeness of any sort
was frowned upon by Confucius. He fully recognized the great
importance of language and its pivotal role in, for instance,
diplomacy. But he believed that, within the limits set by the
occasion, it should be as simple, direct, and functional as possible. "Language," he said, "should be such as fully to convey
one's meaning, but no more." [15] Loquacity he considered blam-
able. He told his students that if they immediately repeated
to others whatever they heard, they could derive little benefit
from it. "The gentleman," he said, "is slow to speak." He
regarded eloquence, as we have already seen, with something
close to loathing. Among the great principles that he laid down
to Yen Hui, to be followed in governing a state, was: "Stay far
from clever talkers, for they are dangerous."

This aversion to eloquence may seem excessive or even
ridiculous. But in fact there are sound reasons for it. We have
seen that Confucius did not try to convince those with whom
he argued by any claims of, or appeal to, final authority. Instead he tried to reason things out and discuss them on their

merits. But the moment eloquence or the language of debate enters, true reasoning becomes impossible. For the purpose of the debater is not to find the truth but to win the argument, and to this end he will often stay as far as possible from the real issues. Eloquence and debate are designed, not to decide issues, but to sway people; for this reason they lean heavily on appeals to emotion and prejudice, and make use of neat, clever, and sometimes humorous turns of phrase rather than profound analysis of ideas. Of all this Confucius was contemptuous.

In the political sphere, eloquence can be very dangerous. In a democracy, it misleads the people; in a monarchy, it is turned by the unscrupulous to the purpose of swaying the ruler. Confucius lamented that in his time it was very difficult to escape calamity unless one were eloquent.

Intrigue, as we have already seen, was the order of the day. Confucius declared, "I hate to see sharp mouths overturning states and clans." Intrigue might have rewarded the Confucian group handsomely in the short run, though in the end it would have discredited their movement; Confucius was wise enough to realize that "he who constantly seeks for small advantages never achieves great things." It is to his credit that he himself eschewed intrigue and that he taught his disciples to depend on courtesy and sincerity to recommend their cause, but to avoid clever speech like the plague. This insistence on the part of Confucius is probably one of the reasons why we find oratory playing a very small part in Chinese history, as compared with that of many other countries.

Since the Confucian was a man with a mission, it was his duty to maintain a certain dignity of bearing, so as not to discredit himself and the group. Although zealous in the cause, he should be too proud to wrangle. He should not strive for quick results but should act only after careful consideration has convinced him of the proper course.

To act from selfish motives was beneath him. "The gentleman in eating does not seek repletion, nor does he seek comfort in his dwelling." His concern was with the right; motives of profit he left to lesser men. Even reputation (especially if it were gained in an unworthy manner) was of less importance to him than self-respect. "What do you say," Tzŭ-kung asked, "of a man who is liked by all of his fellow-citizens?" "That is not enough," the Master told him. "Then what about one who is disliked by all of them?" "That is still not enough to judge from. The best thing would be for him to be liked by the good, and disliked by the bad." Yet despite his scorn for mere fame, the gentleman disliked, Confucius said, to feel that his life had been so completely without achievement that he would be forgotten the moment he was dead.

The ideal of the true gentleman that Confucius held up to his students may perhaps be summed up as a certain nobility, not to say loftiness, of spirit. When we reflect upon the kind of world in which he lived, surrounded by pettiness, greed, and violence, we realize how necessary it was that he and his disciples withdraw, intellectually, from their environment. Yet it must have been a very difficult thing to do. When we consider that they did this while continuing to live in the world and even to take part in its business, and that this withdrawal was not based on metaphysics nor materially aided by religion, we must grant that it was one of the major achievements of the human spirit.

The gentleman, Confucius believed, should be too proud to be arrogant. He is easy to serve, because he expects of men only what is reasonable in view of their capacities, but he is difficult to please, for his favor cannot be won by acts designed to please him unless they accord with the highest principle. He is normally cooperative and agreeable, but he is not a partisan and does not form cliques. Because his character is firmly grounded, he remains composed even in the face of emergencies. Though he never knows when his life may end in death by torture, he is unafraid. "The Master said, 'If, looking within, he finds nothing for which to reproach himself, why should he worry, what should he fear?' "

All of this sounds very much like preaching. Yet Confucius did not make the mistake of supposing that men could be made good by words alone. He attributed far more importance, as we see repeatedly in the *Analects*, to the power of example. He believed in a veritable "contagion of character." Of a man of Lu he said, "Such a man is a gentleman indeed. If there were no real gentlemen in Lu, how could he have acquired this character?" He warned his disciples that they must be most careful in their associations. Just as an artisan must sharpen his tools in order to do good work, so they must develop character by taking office only with worthy superiors and cultivating the friendship only of the virtuous. One should, he said, have kindly feelings toward all but be intimate only with those who are truly virtuous. He warned repeatedly against persisting, from a mistaken sense of loyalty, in the friendship of those whose conduct is unworthy and who refuse to change.

The power of his own example undoubtedly played a principal role in Confucius' teaching. Its informal nature and his close association with the disciples facilitated this. As we have seen, there were few instances in which he can be said to have failed to practice what he preached. On two occasions, when he was asked to ally himself with rebels and Tzǔ-lu protested, he did not do so in the end even though he felt that he would have been justified; undoubtedly, his responsibility to provide an unexceptionable example to the young influenced his decision.

It may seem surprising that, thus far, there has been scarcely any mention of books, especially in view of the fact that the term Confucian is sometimes considered almost synonymous with bookworm. We shall see later that the Confucians did, within a few centuries after the death of Confucius, become too much preoccupied with books. Still later the government examinations, and the education for them, became too exclusively literary, so that the reformer Wang An-shih complained, in the year 1058 A.D., that the instruction given in his day consisted chiefly of "explanations of the texts of the Classics, analyzed into sections and sentences." But that, he added, "was not the ancient method."

It certainly was not the method of Confucius. He considered the study of literature a part, but only a part, of the education of a gentleman. More basic was the cultivation of character, and learning to live as a social being with his relatives and his fellow men. To learn the contents of books was highly desirable if he gained real understanding from them, or if he could make practical application of his learning; but if this were not the case, Confucius declared it was useless merely to memorize them. A passage in the *Analects* says that "the Master taught four things." Exactly how the characters representing the four subjects should be translated is something of a problem; perhaps they mean "literature, conduct, loyalty, and good faith." In any case it is clear that books figured only as one aspect of the curriculum.

The only book that is frequently mentioned in the *Analects* is the anthology called the *Book of Poetry*, which Confucius referred to merely as the *Poetry* (*Shih*). This is a collection of poems, of various sorts and by various authors, which seem to have been composed between the beginning of the Chou dynasty and about 600 B.C. Our present *Book of Poetry* contains three hundred and eleven pieces, and Confucius indicated that the work he knew had, in round numbers, three hundred. It seems to have been almost but not quite identical with the work we now have. We shall leave until the next chapter the question of whether Confucius had any hand in the composition or editing of this and other books; here we shall concern ourselves with his use of them in teaching.

He told his son that if he did not study the *Poetry* he would be "like a man standing with his face to a wall." To a group of disciples he once said, "My children, why do you not study the *Poetry?* Poetry will stimulate your emotions, help you to be more observant, enlarge your sympathies, and moderate your resentment of injustice. It is useful at home in the service of one's father, abroad in the service of one's prince. Furthermore, it will widen your acquaintance with the names of birds, beasts, plants, and trees."

All this is quite true and quite understandable. There was another use of poetry in ancient China, however, that was much less simple. The poems were supposed (quite mistakenly, in most cases at least) to have been written to convey an allegorical meaning. They were then quoted, with reference to this allegorical sense, by diplomats in their official speeches. Thus, at a conference or a banquet the representatives of two or more states would plead their cases and make their points in a veiled manner, by quoting verses containing (or supposed to contain) subtle allusions. Their adversaries were expected to be able to identify the quotations and understand the intention immediately. If possible, they replied with quotations still more apt, designed to refute the contention; if they could not, they were bested.[16] For this reason an intimate knowledge of the *Poetry* was essential to one who would rise high in official circles. Confucius was probably referring to this use of poetry when he told his son, "If you do not study the *Poetry* you will have nothing to use in speaking," and when he said, "A man may be able to repeat all the three hundred pieces in the *Poetry*, but if when entrusted with office he is ineffective, and when sent on a diplomatic mission he cannot make his replies unassisted [that is, without prompting], although his learning is extensive, of what use is it?"

With us, somewhat similarly, quotation is a stock device of the orator. But we try, at least, to be critical of the way in which quotations are used and consider it to be a flaw if they do too much violence to the original intention. In the orthodox interpretation of the *Poetry*, however, the interpreters seem to ignore the obvious intention of the poems rather more frequently than they recognize it; this is the opinion of many contemporary Chinese, as well as Western, scholars.

There is, for instance, a poem called "The Cock Crows," which seems clearly to be a conversation between a young woman and her lover, in the lady's bedroom. She tells him the cock has crowed and the dawn is breaking. But he says no, it wasn't the cock but the buzzing of the blue flies, and it isn't the dawn but the rising moon; it would be sweet to share another dream. At that, she loses patience with him and tells him to go home quickly lest she have cause to hate him. The orthodox interpretation, however, makes the lady a "virtuous wife" who is urging her slothful husband to get up and attend to his duties at court.

Confucius does not, in any of the materials we have from him, perpetrate this kind of absurdity in connection with the poems, but he does on two occasions discuss them with his disciples in terms of analogies that are quite divorced from the meaning of the poems themselves. And we must probably agree with Ku Chieh-kang that Confucius, by making such use of the poems himself, was very largely responsible for the exceedingly fanciful use to which they were put by later Confucians.

As we have seen, there is no indication that Confucius gave any regular lectures on books or gave his students systematic guidance in their study. He told them to study certain subjects, and then discussed these with them. In the case of the *Poetry*, he was recommending a book. But whether when he advocated the study of music he was also referring to a book is a difficult question. Some scholars have believed that there was an ancient book on this subject, while others deny this. In any case there is no clear evidence that Confucius used such a book.

We are in somewhat similar case concerning *li*. While there are three works on *li* among the Thirteen Classics, it is doubtful that any one of them existed in precisely its present form in Confucius' day. Two of them are very clearly later; [17] the third work, the *Book of Etiquette and Ceremonial* (*I Li*), seems in part at least to be somewhat older than the other two, but it is very difficult to date. Some of traditional opinion has assigned it a date as early as the beginning of the Chou dynasty, ascribing it to the Duke of Chou; others have believed that it consists of the teachings of Confucius on *li*.

Nevertheless, it seems certain that, at the very least, this text underwent some editing and some interpolation after the time of Confucius. Thus we cannot point with assurance to any text on *li* and say that it certainly existed in its present form in Confucius' day. Nevertheless, there are indications that there were writings on *li*, of some sort. It is probable, therefore, that when Confucius told his disciples to study *li* he meant that they should read certain documents, as well as practice their precepts, but what those documents were we cannot tell.

Finally, there is reference in the *Analects* to certain documents known as *shu*. Literally this means simply "document," but it came to be used especially to refer to government documents, such as would be kept in the archives. At a time that we cannot fix definitely, but almost certainly later than Confucius, such documents were gathered into the corpus which we know as the *Book of History*.[18] Thus when Confucius is quoted in the *Analects* as having stated, "*Shu* says," this is ordinarily translated as "The *Book of History* says," but in fact Confucius probably meant merely, "There is a document which says."

The *Book of History* is one of the Five Classics, which composed the earliest Confucian canon. It is remarkable, therefore, that we find so few references to *shu* in the *Analects*. There are only three.[19] Nowhere is there any admonition by Confucius, to his students, to study these documents.

In the teaching of Confucius himself, we must conclude from the evidence, the place of books was relatively small. This stands in the sharpest contrast to the practice of later Confucianism, which has led to the usage of translating "Confucians" as "literati." When we examine the history of Confucianism after Confucius, we shall see that the increasing emphasis on books was a significant symptom of the shift of interest away from practical reform, in the direction of greater preoccupation with abstract scholarship.

CHAPTER VIII

THE SCHOLAR

The Master said, "To study, and when the occasion arises to put what one has learned into practice—is this not deeply satisfying?" [1] These famous words, with which the *Analects* opens, at once tell us that Confucius was a scholar, and that the aim of his scholarship was practical.

Confucius was curious, asking all sorts of questions about things he considered important and not caring whether or not this got him the reputation of being ignorant. Although it cannot be claimed that he was always as careful as the most scientific standards would demand, he did advocate a critical attitude toward information. He advised a disciple to see and hear much but "suspend judgment concerning what is doubtful." [2] He regretted that copyists, instead of leaving a blank when they could not be sure of a character in a text they were copying, filled the gap by guessing. The following statement is attributed to him in a late passage, and he may well have uttered its substance: "Love of wisdom, without the love of study, leads to superficial generalization."

He is quoted as saying that his "will was set on study" from the age of fifteen, and although he was very modest in most respects he avowed that he could say that he was more "fond of study" than most men. Others agreed with this self-appraisal. Both in his own day and later he was considered an exceptionally studious person. Indeed, as the traditions concerning Confucius developed he came, in books written long after his death, to be regarded as supernaturally wise and to be depicted as one versed in all sorts of ancient and strange lore. Thus it was said that whenever unusual objects were found, even in other states, he was asked, and was able, to explain them. This is legend, but legend is sometimes a distorted version of the truth, and it may well be that, as these stories would suggest, Confucius was the most learned man of his day.

We have seen, however, that when Confucius instructed his disciples he did not do so chiefly in terms of books. It is equally true that when he spoke of study he was not merely talking of reading books; the cultivation of character, too, came under this heading. Yet it is perfectly clear that he did study books. Not only do we have the testimony of the *Analects* on this point; even Mo Tzŭ, who always disparaged Confucius, seems to have assented grudgingly to the statement that he "had an extensive knowledge of the *Book of Poetry* and of historical documents, and clear understanding of *li* and music."

Everyone agrees that Confucius studied books. But when we ask whether he also wrote, or even edited books, we find ourselves in the midst of a controversy that has long divided Chinese scholarship.

Probably the most extreme partisan of the theory that Confucius was a prolific author was the famous political theorist and reformer, K'ang Yu-wei, who died in 1927. In 1897 K'ang published a book called *Confucius as a Reformer (K'ung Tzŭ Kai Chih K'ao)* in which he asserted that Confucius had deliberately effected a sweeping alteration of China's culture. In order to make his reforms palatable, K'ang declared, Confucius represented that all of his innovations were revivals of ancient customs. Although this was not true, it was right, K'ang said, just as it is right for a loving mother to use stories about ghosts to make her children be good. In order to make his stories believed, Confucius (according to K'ang) wrote all of the early classics; he composed, in other words, all of Chinese literature that is preserved from any period earlier than his own time.[3]

In support of this proposition, K'ang not only cites a great deal of evidence from Han times (which is too late to be convincing) but also tries to prove his point by passages from earlier works. The evidence is most feeble. His first "proof" is more or less typical; he quotes Mo Tzŭ as saying that the Confucians recited the *Book of Poetry* and declares that this makes it "most clear" that Confucius composed that work. One can hardly understand, from this evidence, why K'ang espouses his theory so vehemently. But a glance at his career is more illuminating. K'ang Yu-wei was one of the small group of Chinese scholars who realized, at the end of the nineteenth century, that China must adopt many Western techniques or be overrun. They were balked in their attempt at modernization by conservatism, the same conservatism that forced K'ang to flee for his life to Japan in 1898. The core of this resistance was orthodox Confucianism. It was therefore a shrewd (though undoubtedly quite sincere) move for him to attempt, in 1897, to popularize the idea that Confucius had himself been one who broke with the past. K'ang was trying to establish a precedent for violating precedent.

This recent event may seem irrelevant to our inquiry. But it is a perfect example of the way in which Confucius and his works have time after time become the playthings of politics and policy, to the detriment of the truth. And it indicates clearly that we must go back of all the disputes of scholars and statesmen, to the early sources, in order to determine what Confucius did or did not write.

The *Analects* has only one passage that bears on the general question. In a rather obscure context Confucius refers to himself as "a transmitter and not a maker, believing in and loving the ancients." This has commonly been taken to be a denial, by Confucius, that he wrote anything. But since we do not know the circumstances under which it was said, or the time at which it was said, it really proves very little.

The *Historical Records* states that the *Book of Poetry* had previously consisted of three thousand pieces, but that Confucius reduced them to three hundred and five, selecting the best.[4] We must regard this statement with caution, for the *Historical Records* is not always reliable concerning Confucius. Scholars ancient and modern have questioned that Confucius reduced the size of the *Book of Poetry,* pointing out that very few poems outside this corpus are quoted in early literature. Confucius himself twice refers to "the three hundred poems" as an established corpus; this would be rather arbitrary if he had determined the number. Moreover, he quotes one poem that is not in our *Book of Poetry* and twice condemns (once calling them licentious) a whole group of verses that *is* included; this is strange if he edited the book.

Confucius does say, however, that after he returned from Wei to Lu certain categories of the poems "found their proper places." This may mean that he made some sort of rearrangement of the pieces, but that is probably the most that he did to the *Poetry.*

Similar stories to the effect that Confucius edited the *Book of History,* or even selected its chapters from an original group of 3,240 documents, and that he wrote a preface to it, occur in various late works. It would be a waste of time, however, to examine them. As we have seen, it is not definitely established that government documents of this sort had been gathered into a fixed corpus in Confucius' day. If Confucius had edited such a fixed group of documents, Mencius would hardly have said of them, as he did a century later, that "rather than to believe in them entirely, it would be better not to have them at all."

Confucius has also been held to have edited the *Spring and Autumn Annals.* This allegation cannot, unfortunately, be dismissed so shortly. This work is a brief and unadorned chronicle, kept in the state of Lu, of events between 722 and 479 B.C. It gives the dry bones of political events, state marriages, important deaths, and wars; occasionally it records such significant items as "this spring there was no ice," "mynahs came and nested in trees," and "six fish-hawks flew backward past the capital of Sung." It appears to be just a chronicle of isolated events set down by court scribes as they occurred or became known.[5] Probably no one would ever have supposed that it were anything else if it were not for certain passages in the book of *Mencius.*

These indicate that Confucius wrote a work called *Spring and Autumn Annals* and that after it was completed "rebellious ministers and villainous sons were struck with terror." Yet there is nothing in the *Spring and Autumn Annals* that we know which appears designed to produce any such effect. Putting these facts together, later Confucian scholars decided that the work must have "hidden meanings." As a result, great numbers of them have burned midnight oil in what is perhaps the most extensive attempt to solve a cryptogram in all history. Efforts have been made to show, for instance, that the expressions used to record the deaths of various persons differ slightly in such manner as to express "praise or blame." Such principles have not been found, however, that can be applied throughout the work. The same interpreter will, in one place, describe as condemnatory the very language that he elsewhere interprets as praise. Legge, who studied these attempts at great length, wrote that "the whole Book is a collection of riddles, to which there are as many answers as there are guessers." If there were a cryptogram, these intensive efforts should have solved it. It seems clear that the work is, after all, a simple chronicle.

What, then, of the testimony of Mencius? The answer seems to be that the *Spring and Autumn Annals* which, according to his statement, Confucius wrote, was not the work we now have. There were various books by that name in ancient China, and the description Mencius gives fails to fit our present work in more than one respect.[6] Indeed, it may be questioned whether Confucius wrote any work called the *Spring and Autumn Annals* at all. Mencius says Confucius considered it his chief claim to fame; if that is true, it is very remarkable that the *Analects* says not one word to indicate that Confucius ever wrote this book or any other. We cannot lose sight of the fact that by Mencius' day the Confucian legend had grown hugely, so that, for instance, Mencius found it necessary to explain why Confucius had not been emperor.

Confucius has also been considered the fountainhead of *li*, and the *Records on Ceremonial* credits him with inspiring if not writing part of the earliest work on *li* that we have.[7] This is doubtful, but it is evident that Confucius did do a great deal to stimulate interest in *li* and thus, indirectly at least, to promote writing on the subject. The *Analects* not only attests Confucius' interest in *li* but indicates that he did historical research on it. In fact, he seems even to have believed that he could predict the manner in which *li* would change far into the future. There seems, however, to be no early evidence to justify the statement of the *Historical Records* that Confucius "put in order" the *li*, if by this it is meant that he either wrote or edited a book on the subject.

The same statement covers the case for music. Confucius was interested in it, and he studied it, but there is no indication that he wrote anything about it.[8] As we have seen, it is not even clear that there was a specific book on music in early China.

The last of the works we must consider in this connection is the *Book of Changes*. It is in effect a fortuneteller's manual, by means of which one who knows how to use it may, it is alleged, predict future events. This book consists of two quite different parts, an original text and a series of appendices. Almost all scholars have agreed in assigning the original text to a date earlier than that of Confucius, but persistent tradition has attributed the appendices to his authorship. Even today there are a few critical scholars who still believe that Confucius wrote or edited some or all of these appendices and who base their discussion of his philosophy upon an analysis of them.

It is probably correct to say, however, that most critical scholars now believe that Confucius had nothing whatever to do with the *Book of Changes*. There is a great deal of evidence that this is the case. Although divination had been practiced in China for at least a thousand years and probably much longer,[9] and was in common use in his own day, no early source indicates that Confucius ever divined. There is good reason to believe, indeed, that Confucius and the early Confucians frowned on divination.

Later, however, the *Book of Changes* was taken up and studied enthusiastically by some Confucian scholars, so that it came to be listed as the first of the Five Classics. It was such later Confucians who produced the appendices and who also attributed their authorship to Confucius. However, the fact that Confucius not only had never divined but had never even mentioned the *Book of Changes* was disturbing. For this reason *Analects* 7.16 seems to have been interpolated, in order that Confucius might appear to have given some sanction to the study of this book. When we come to examine later Confucianism we shall consider this development in some detail, and full evidence will be presented (see pages 198–202). This evidence makes it abundantly clear that Confucius neither wrote nor edited any part of the *Book of Changes*.

This completes our examination of the various books Confucius is supposed to have written, and leaves us with the conclusion that we have no convincing evidence that he wrote or even edited anything at all. This is not an original verdict; an increasing number of scholars have reached this same conclusion in recent years.

If he did not write books, he nevertheless read them and used them in his teaching. What function, it is pertinent to inquire, did they perform in connection with his thinking? To help us in finding an answer to this question, let us examine the way in which Confucius quoted from books, as this is recorded in the *Analects*.

In the *Analects* the *Poetry* is quoted more than any other work; Confucius personally quotes from or alludes to it seven times. In three of these cases the quotation is a straightforward application of the quoted lines in a sense that does no violence to the original. But in the remaining four cases this is by no means true; in all of these instances the original sense is stretched, twisted, or completely altered. The most glaring instance is a line that he quotes as meaning, "Let there be no evil in your thoughts." The words representing these ideas are there, all right. But, as Waley has pointed out, the character rendered as "thoughts" is here only an exclamation, "Oh." The poem is about horse breeding, and this line means, "Oh, may it be without mishap!" [10]

Documents of the sort that came to make up the *Book of History* seem to be quoted in the *Analects* only twice, and by Confucius only once. This is remarkable, in view of the degree to which he has been alleged to have derived his ideas from such works. Furthermore, in the one instance in which he does say, "A document says," he seems to twist the passage he quotes to suit his own purposes. [11]

We have already noted that it is uncertain to what extent actual treatises on *li* were known to Confucius. It is never clear that he quotes from them in the *Analects*; he never says, "The *li* says." There is one brief passage in the *Book of Etiquette and Ceremonial* and there are four scattered sentences in the *Records on Ceremonial* that are identical with or very similar to passages in the *Analects*.[12] But in some cases it is certain, and in all quite possible, that the works on *li* quoted the *Analects* (or the Confucian traditions on which it is based) rather than vice versa.

Confucius quotes one passage, eight characters in length, that appears in the *Book of Changes*. In the following quotation, this passage is italicized to distinguish it. "The Master said, 'The people of the south have a saying, "A man without constancy will not even make a good wizard or physician." Good! *"Inconstant in his virtue, he is likely to incur disgrace."* It is not sufficient merely to divine.' " [13] It is worthy of note that this passage (the only one in which he refers to divination in the *Analects*) indicates that Confucius did not have much faith in oracles.

Undoubtedly Confucius was much more widely read than the amount of direct quotation from books in the *Analects* would suggest. It would appear, however, that he had assimilated the results of his reading to a coherent system of thought that was his own; he was not the kind of scholar whose utterances consist chiefly of a patchwork of quotations. Nor did he, in discussion, have constant recourse to written authority to bolster his arguments; he was far more interested in whether an argument was reasonable than in whether it could be found in a book. Not infrequently his originality predominated to such an extent that he used quotations in a way that paid little heed to the meaning of the original work.

Confucius was not primarily a scholar, any more than he had intended primarily to be a teacher. He was a man who found the world about him full of misery and wanted to exchange it for happiness. In working for this end he used many tools, among them books. But his interest was not in knowledge for its own sake. When a disciple asked to be taught agriculture, Confucius declared that such a study was unworthy of a gentleman. He believed that the crying ills of his world centered in the related fields of ethics and government, and it was toward these subjects that he focused both his teaching and his study. He explicitly deplored extensive learning that could not be turned to some practical use, not because it was bad in itself but because it was a luxury which the state of the world could not afford.

CHAPTER IX

THE PHILOSOPHER

THE number of books that have been written about the ideas of Confucius is staggering. Probably no other philosopher has been the subject of more discussion. Yet our reliable knowledge of his philosophy remains regrettably meager. For this there are several reasons. Very important is the fact that his type of thinking was an extremely evanescent phenomenon. Indeed, it was almost necessarily so.

What happened in Confucius' day has occurred more than once. Old religious beliefs and old social, economic, and political patterns had persisted for many centuries. But then, as the political pattern of early Chou feudalism gradually broke down, every one of the other spheres was affected. The ties that had long held men together failed, bringing relative freedom to the individual and near chaos to society. A very similar crisis occurred in Egypt, around 2100 B.C. Something comparable happened in ancient Greece. As Windelband describes it: "The more the luxuriant development of individualism loosened the old bonds of the common consciousness, of faith, and of morals, and threatened the youthful civilization of Greece with the danger of anarchy, the more pressing did individual men, prominent by their position in life, their insight, and their character, find the duty of recovering in their own reflection the measure that was becoming lost." In Greece, such conditions gave us the philosophy of Socrates. In China, they gave us that of Confucius.

In times of such moral and political crisis, men are thrown back upon their essential humanity. It is no longer enough merely to conjure by the old gods and quote the old authorities, for they command but a dubious respect. It is necessary to get down to fundamentals, to deal with things that all men can understand. Those who dare to pioneer in such times do not win easy acceptance of their ideas. The need constantly to contend with sceptical criticism keeps their philosophy lean and hard.

Such philosophies have a universal quality. They may employ some terms that have little meaning for us. Confucius may speak of "Heaven" as the guarantor of his mission; Socrates may talk of "beauty" as a thing existing in itself apart from any beautiful object;[1] and we may not agree with them. Yet despite the difference in time and culture they seem to speak our language. We feel that they are dealing with real problems and that what they say may make some contribution toward a solution.

Such philosophies cannot last. If they are successful, their very success leads to their perversion. Those who inherit them elaborate their concepts far beyond their original forms. The crisis passes, and society is stabilized. New institutions replace the old, and philosophy conforms to the existing order. In Egypt, according to John A. Wilson, the crisis attending the collapse of the Old Kingdom brought "social-moral advances" under the Middle Kingdom, which were gradually lost under the Empire; thus the earlier individualism was replaced by a sense of man's helplessness, and the pattern became "conforming and formalistic." The philosophical ideas of Socrates, elaborated by Plato, eventuated in the complex mystical Neo-Platonism of Plotinus and Porphyry. Similarly, the predominantly ethical and rational teachings of Confucius were so altered within three hundred years that the famous Han Confucianist, Tung Chung-shu, preached to his emperor a doctrine in which morality was inextricably mingled with an elaborate technique for the reading of omens and the practice of magic on a cosmic scale. In each of these cases, the later philosophy flourished centuries nearer to our own day, yet intellectually they seem incomparably more remote from us than the earlier.

For the philosophy of Confucius we have two principal kinds of sources. On the one hand there is the *Analects,* not written by him but in the main composed near his own time and on the basis of traditions preserved by his disciples. On the other, we have a variety of later works (some falsely attributed to his authorship) that interpret his thought in terms of the later Confucianism. For the Socratic tradition the case is in some degree comparable since there are on the one hand the works of Plato and Xenophon, who knew him, while on the other we have the elaborations of the philosophy he founded in Neo-Platonism. Yet few would try to work back from the Neo-Platonists to reconstruct the philosophy of Socrates; the usual practice is rather to study such testimony as that of Plato and Xenophon, to determine how much of it may be believed. For Confucius, however, the common practice has been the opposite, and the most prodigious efforts have been directed toward bringing his thought into line with the later Confucian metaphysics. In reversing this approach and limiting our study to the early sources alone, we must resign ourselves in advance to a relatively meager harvest. But though what we learn may not be extensive it will (if we interpret our materials correctly) be true.

Our first problem concerns the source of Confucius' ideas. He has often been represented as one who was merely attempting to revive the glories of a real or fancied golden age of antiquity. The disciple Tzŭ-kung declared that Confucius needed no teacher in the ordinary sense since he was able to learn of the doctrines of the early Chou rulers, King Wên and King Wu. Mencius said that Confucius transmitted a teaching handed down from the mythical early emperors, Yao and Shun. One contemporary Chinese scholar has asserted that Confucius was not merely a reactionary but in fact a "counter-revolutionary" since (in this scholar's opinion) his whole desire was to undo the changes that had taken place in Chinese life and restore the past.

We shall defer until the following chapter a thorough investigation of the degree of Confucius' dependence upon antiquity. Here it may be predicted, however, that when we have examined the evidence we shall conclude that, on the one hand, Confucius did indeed talk about antiquity and derive some of his important ideas from that source, but on the other he did not even pretend that he was trying to revive antiquity, and he could not well have found some of his most basic conceptions there. In important respects he was, in fact, a revolutionary, albeit a discreet one.

We have already seen that Confucius was born in a period of great political and social change. This is a phenomenon of which we still know altogether too little, despite the excellent work that various Chinese scholars have done on it in recent years. Even in art this was a time of change, and it was a time in which art (like Confucius) looked to the great days of the past for some of its inspiration. Bernhard Karlgren has pointed out that "during the 7th-3rd centuries B.C. the Chinese world was already advanced enough to allow of a conscious artistic renaissance movement, which incorporated elements now already ancient and venerated. . . ." In art, however, as in thought, the old was so transmuted that the result was altogether new in character.

What, we must ask, was the particular role of Confucius in this cultural revolution? He was not its instigator, since it was an upheaval caused by forces beyond his control and was already under way before he was born. Some students have suggested that Confucius somehow happened to get the credit for ideas that were in fact developed by far more capable men before his time. In various works, especially the *Tso Chuan*, there appear several statesmen who, living shortly before Confucius, are quoted as having expressed ideas remarkably like his; in fact, their language is sometimes virtually identical with what we find in the *Analects*. This fact has long been noted by Chinese scholars; one has praised these statesmen as being far more advanced in their thinking than was Confucius. He noted admiringly that they figure in the *Tso Chuan* as veritable walking encyclopedias, informed on every subject. He failed to add, however, that the knowledge of such men was so extensive that they were able (according to the *Tso Chuan*) to predict political events even as much as a century in the future, with the most uncanny accuracy.[2]

It is obvious that most if not all of such prophecies were written long after the event, rather than having been spoken by the men to whom they are attributed. It also seems quite certain that many, if not all, of the fine "Confucian" speeches that the *Tso Chuan* puts into the mouths of its various characters were written, when the *Tso Chuan* itself was written, long after the death of Confucius, at a time when such ideas had become common currency.

This does not mean that the men themselves did not exist. They did, and they were undoubtedly able and wise. They may have had ideas very like those of Confucius, and have greatly influenced his thinking; this is quite possible. But we cannot tell whether it is true because we do not have expositions of their ideas in early and unimpeachable works. Yet one point is clear: if Confucius did take over, in significant degree, the ideas of some recent predecessor, that fact is never revealed in the *Analects* nor even in the writings of his enemies. On the contrary, tradition emphasizes his uniqueness. It seems clear that his role, in the changing world in which he found himself, was that of one who articulated and rationalized those changes which he found desirable, tried to suppress those of which he disapproved, and attempted to guide the course of Chinese culture in the way he believed it should go.

As background for our inquiry into his philosophy, let us consider the views of Confucius on religion. Religion is usually conservative, and in so far as we can tell there had been no major change in religion for centuries. In the Shang period, before 1122 B.C., the kings and presumably others had sacrificed elaborately to their ancestors and to other spirits; especially important was a powerful spirit called Ti. They believed that the spirits, and especially their ancestors, supervised human destinies; if pleased they bestowed success, if displeased they scourged mankind with various ills, from defeat in war to toothaches. The Shang people sacrificed to avert disaster and obtain felicity, and they constantly consulted the wishes of their gods through divination.

The Chou, who conquered the Shang, took over some phases of Shang religion and combined them with their own. The principal deity of the Chou was called 天 T'ien; the early form of this character was 大, simply a drawing of a large and therefore important man. From a variety of evidence, we can reconstruct its probable history. It came to refer to the most important men of all, the former kings who had died and taken up their abode in the heavens. As a sort of "council of the gods" they controlled human destinies. Then, because Chinese does not distinguish singular and plural, T'ien came to be thought of as singular, an overruling Providence located in the sky. The same word also came to be used for the material heavens. Thus there was derived the concept of Heaven as a rather impersonal intelligence. When the Chou conquered the Shang, they equated their Heaven with Ti, the Shang deity, as the Romans identified some of their gods with those of the Greeks.

Religion occupied a central place in the culture. The king was called the "Son of Heaven," and ruled by virtue of the help of his great ancestors. Lesser aristocrats were what they were because they had powerful ancestors. Sacrifices to these and other powerful deities were state ceremonies, more important for a good harvest than weeding, for victory than drilling troops. With increased sophistication, however, the rise of scepticism was inevitable. Improved communications brought men into contact with varying beliefs and customs. Treaties were constantly made which were supposed to be guaranteed by the spirits, and as constantly broken; but he who suffered was usually not the breaker but he who had the weaker army. Noble families fell into disgrace and penury, casting doubt on the power of their ancestral spirits. We know little of the details of the rise of scepticism since we have virtually no literature that stems from the period immediately preceding the time of Confucius, but that it did arise is clear. Mo Tzŭ, who was born about the time Confucius died, charged that the Confucians considered "Heaven to be without intelligence, and the spirits of the dead to be without consciousness."

The attitude of Confucius himself toward religion was complex. Some aspects of the traditional religion he approved and emphasized. Others he disapproved and tried either to transform or suppress. In general, however, he refrained from raising fundamental religious issues. This may be interpreted either as cowardice or as wisdom. The fact is that he was attempting to make what he considered vital reforms, of a political and social nature, on bases which were for the most part not metaphysical. It would not have served and might have hindered his purpose to argue metaphysics. He did not do so, and we are sometimes left in doubt as to what he did believe.

Quite clearly, Confucius took an almost childlike pleasure in religious ritual as such. Yet this tells us little about his belief; many sceptical intellectuals delight in "High Church" ceremonial. Confucius also emphasized the duty of children to spend three years in mourning for their parents.[3] To Western minds this seems an excessive measure of devotion, yet it does not conclusively prove a belief in life after death; Confucius could have insisted upon it merely as an aspect of family solidarity.

We have few statements from Confucius about spirits. In fact, it is said specifically that "the Master did not speak about strange phenomena [such as omens], feats of strength, disorders, or spirits." He is quoted, it is true, as having praised the mythical ruler, Yü, for being "extremely filial toward the spirits." However, when Tzŭ-lu asked him how to serve the spirits he replied, "You are not yet able to serve men; how can you serve spirits?" Tzŭ-lu then asked about death, and was told, "You do not yet understand life; how can you understand death?" The disciple Fan Ch'ih asked about wisdom; Confucius told him, "It is to attend diligently to those concerns which are proper to the people; and to respect the spirits and maintain the proper distance from them."

This last passage has been translated as "while respecting spiritual beings, to keep aloof from them," and considered to be clear evidence of agnosticism. But this does not accord with the understanding of most Chinese commentators,[4] and its usefulness as evidence is doubtful. Immanuel Kant has pointed out that men are directed by the principle of respect "to preserve a certain distance from each other," and we can scarcely hold that less is due to spirits. Confucius' view seems to have been that one should do for them all that was proper but should not fawn upon them with excessive attentions, any more than one should upon a ruler or an official superior.

Although there are several passages on sacrifice in the *Analects,* they do not (with one exception, which we shall discuss later) tell us clearly whether Confucius believed there was actual efficacy in the ceremony, or valued it merely as a social act. It is significant, however, that among the activities which he positively advocated for remedying the world's ills, neither sacrifice nor any other religious activity seems to have been included. As for prayer, we have already seen that he declined to have it made in his behalf even though he was very ill, declaring that he had "done his praying long ago," presumably with deeds rather than words.

If we look for a firm and frankly stated conviction on the part of Confucius as to things religious, we shall find it most clearly in connection with T'ien, Heaven. It is an interesting fact that nowhere in the *Analects* does he mention the name of the more personally conceived aspect of the same deity, Ti.[5] He looked upon Heaven, however, as the author of his power, which had entrusted him with a sacred mission as the champion of China's culture. In danger, he dismissed his enemies as powerless against him in the face of Heaven. In despondency, he took comfort in the fact that Heaven, at least, understood him. When accused of wrongdoing, he called upon Heaven to witness his innocence. Upon the death of his favorite disciple, Yen Hui, he declared, "Heaven is destroying me!"

This last passage is best understood as a simple cry of anguish, not as meaning that Confucius considered Heaven to be taking special and malevolent action against him. For we have no indication that Confucius conceived of Heaven in this manner. Anciently it had been so conceived. Thus we read repeatedly in the *Book of History* and the *Book of Poetry,* and in inscriptions on early bronzes, that Heaven supervised the change of dynasties, punishing vice by extinguishing the line of the oppressive ruler and rewarding virtue by setting up the good as his successor. Such works spoke of Heaven as "waiting for five years" to see whether an evil king would change his ways, and as "sending down destruction" and becoming "angry." King Ch'êng, the son of the founder of the Chou dynasty, was quoted as saying, on his deathbed, "Heaven has sent down illness upon me."

All of this seems to hark back to the origin of "Heaven" as a collective name for the great ancestors, who lived above and constantly watched the conduct of their descendants, rewarding or punishing as they pleased. For Confucius, however, Heaven was far less personal. He tells us little of how he did conceive it; the disciple Tzŭ-kung said that the Master did not talk about "the way of Heaven." Yet it seems clear that Confucius thought of Heaven as an impersonal ethical force, a cosmic counterpart of the ethical sense in man, a guarantee that somehow there is sympathy with man's sense of right in the very nature of the universe.

This did not mean, however, that justice must triumph or that virtue must certainly lead to success. If Confucius had ever supposed that this were true his own career, as well as history, must have disillusioned him. We never find him promising success as the reward for virtue. He does say that it tends toward success, just as oppressive conduct on the part of a ruler tends to bring about his downfall, but there is no simple and certain correlation between these things. Rather, the greatest rewards of virtue are the peace of mind it brings, and the satisfaction which comes from helping others. One's reasons for acting as one ought have nothing directly to do with prosperity or its reverse. "The Master said, 'A gentleman, in making his plans, thinks of the Way; he does not think of making a living. Even if one tills the soil, he may sometimes suffer hunger; and if one studies, he may be able to earn a high salary. But the concern of the gentleman is about the progress of the Way; he does not worry about poverty.'"

This is very different from what we commonly find in the earlier literature and bronze inscriptions. There, religious observances and especially sacrifice are regarded as something almost resembling a barter transaction. In the *Book of Poetry* a king, whose realm is devastated by drought, asks why Heaven and his ancestors are thus afflicting him, saying, "There is no spirit to whom I have not sacrificed and no victim that I have grudged. . . . Why am I not heard?" Time after time we read in this work and in the *Book of History* that the purpose of sacrifice is to secure blessings. The inscriptions on scores if not hundreds of bronze sacrificial vessels tell us quite frankly that they were made for the purpose of seeking blessings such as long life, long enjoyment of office, many sons and grandsons, and so on. A bronze bell cast in the state of Ch'i, at about the time when Confucius was born, recounts at particular length and in special detail the benefits its maker expected from his ancestors in return for his piety. Mo Tzŭ, who lived just after Confucius, condemned the practice of "offering one pig and asking for a hundred blessings"; but he seems to have been bothered chiefly by the inequity of this bargain, for he clearly believed that the spirits were influenced, in their bestowal of blessings, by the quantity and quality of the offerings they received.

From all such thinking Confucius stood wholly apart. It is quite true that one can also find, in literature from a time much earlier than his, occasional statements to the effect that virtue as well as sacrifice is pleasing to Heaven. But if Confucius derived his ideas from these works, he must have selected only this aspect, for his emphasis was almost exclusively ethical.

He also rejected certain elements of the traditional religion that had been very important, such as, for instance, human sacrifice. In the Shang period great numbers of human beings were sacrificed. The practice continued under the Chou and is referred to at least twice in the *Book of Poetry* and some eleven times in the *Tso Chuan*. Of the instances of human sacrifice mentioned in the latter work, three took place during Confucius' lifetime, one in the state of Lu itself. Mo Tzŭ, just after Confucius, declared that those who advocated elaborate burial wanted large numbers of men, as many as hundreds in the case of an emperor, killed to attend important persons in death. When the "First Emperor" of the Ch'in dynasty was buried in 210 B.C., a large number of the women of his harem are reported to have been killed to follow him in death. As late as the first century B.C. a prince of the house of Han ordered that his slave musicians should follow him in death, and sixteen of them were forced to commit suicide when he died.

In the *Analects*, however, there is no mention of human sacrifice. Mencius quotes Confucius as having condemned even the burying of images of men with the dead, presumably because this might tend to suggest the burial of actual men.[6] The

Records on Ceremonial recounts an incident in which Confucius' disciple Tzǔ-ch'in is supposed to have prevented the killing of some persons at the funeral of his brother. Confucians in general opposed human sacrifice, ultimately with great success. Thus the last instance of human sacrifice mentioned in the preceding paragraph was severely punished. Even though the prince whose slaves were killed was descended from a Han emperor, his son was not allowed to succeed him, and his fief was abolished. The language of the criminal charge against him shows clearly that it was made on Confucian grounds. The Confucians not only reduced the practice of human sacrifice; they all but abolished the mention of it in the literature. Thus when it is mentioned in the *Tso Chuan* it is commonly censured, and several times is said not to have been practiced "in antiquity," which is far from true. Even in the twentieth century a number of archeologists refused to believe that the Shang had practiced human sacrifice, until the discovery of the skeletons of hundreds of decapitated victims proved it. The Confucians were so successful that they almost destroyed the traces of their own success.

Another important Confucian innovation in religion has gone almost unnoticed. Before Confucius the most important possession of a ruler was his ancestors. They not only gave him legitimate title to rule but provided the powerful help of the gods that he must have for success in peace and victory in war. The *Book of Poetry* tells us that the house of Chou had "three rulers in Heaven, and the king is their counterpart in the capital." A lesser ruler boasted, in an inscription on a bronze vessel, that his illustrious ancestors above "grandly open up a path for their descendant below."

Confucius ignored all this. He went further and declared that it was not heredity but the qualities of the man himself that were important. Something, it is not clear what, seems to have been wrong with the heredity of the disciple Jan Yung. Confucius declared, however, that this should in no way be held against him.[7] Furthermore, he said of Jan Yung alone among the disciples that he might properly occupy the place of a ruler. This statement, concerning a man who seems to have been without eminent ancestors, is revolutionary; it quietly abolishes much that had been central in the earlier religion.

This was, in effect, to say that a man's fitness to rule depended on his own virtue and ability, which greatly reinforced the incentive to ethical conduct. This transition from ritual to ethical thinking has occurred, of course, in many religions. It has been remarked in ancient Egypt and in Mesopotamia; the instance that comes most readily to mind is that of the Hebrew prophets. The factor that makes Confucius unusual, if not unique, is the degree to which he divorced ethics from dependence upon anything outside of the ordinary understanding of all intelligent men. Max Weber has said, "In the absence of all metaphysics and almost all residues of religious anchorage, Confucianism is rationalist to such a far-going extent that it stands at the extreme boundary of what one might possibly call a 'religious' ethic. At the same time, Confucianism is more rationalist and sober, in the sense of the absence and the rejection of all non-utilitarian yardsticks, than any other ethical system, with the possible exception of J. Bentham's." [8]

It should be noted that Weber was speaking of Confucianism, not of Confucius. Nevertheless, these remarks will apply to Confucius himself if we note that Weber speaks of the absence of "*almost* all residues of religious anchorage." We have already seen that Confucius did retain, in the idea of Heaven, a sense of an impersonal ethical Providence. He seems also to have had a sense of an ideal cosmic harmony. This is probably the purport of the following passage: "Someone asked the meaning of the *ti* sacrifice. The Master replied, 'I do not know. He who knew its meaning would be able to deal with all things under heaven as easily as I show you this'—pointing to his palm." In this, and in some other passages, it is possible to see reference to a vaguely conceived universal order having some connection with religion. Yet even this is not stressed. It is there, but it is (to use Weber's term) a residue, a pale surviving counterpart of the ancient dominion of the all-powerful spirits.

Closely allied with this conception is that of *ming* 命, "decree," often translated as "fate." Used in this way, "decree" is an abbreviation of "decree of Heaven," although Confucius seldom used the latter expression.[9] The book of *Mo Tzŭ* accuses the Confucians of saying that all things are determined by a fate that human effort cannot change. For some later Confucians this may have been true, but it was not the doctrine of Confucius. He used the term "decree" as a synonym for "life" or "life span"; but it is perfectly clear that he did not think that this was fixed and beyond any control by the individual, for he speaks of one who "in view of danger is prepared to give up his life" (literally "decree") rather than his principles. This would be nonsense if the span of life were fixed, so that the individual could do nothing about it.

There is one (and only one) passage that at first glance makes Confucius seem a fatalist. At one time while Tzŭ-lu held office with the Chi, a friend and colleague of Tzŭ-lu told Confucius that another of his colleagues was slandering Tzŭ-lu to the head of the Chi family. The friend offered to use his influence to have the slanderer put to death. But Confucius told him, "If the Way is to prevail, it is so decreed. If the Way is to be rejected, it is so decreed." What, he asked, could the slanderer have to do with this decree (*ming*)?

Why did Confucius answer in this way? Let us consider the possibilities. He could have agreed to have the enemy executed, but this would have been opposed to his principles, for he did not believe that forming cliques and fomenting intrigue were even good policy in the long run. In refusing he could have said, "The course that you propose is unworthy," but this would have been gratuitously to insult and alienate a well-meaning friend. Instead, he fell back on reference to the common concept of what was "decreed," and handled the situation without injuring any feelings.

It is quite clear, however, that Confucius did not himself rely on destiny nor advise others to do so. On the contrary, he repeatedly insisted upon the importance of effort by the individual, the moral responsibility to do one's best, and the efficacy of striving. There is, nevertheless, still another passage in the *Analects* that has undoubtedly contributed to the development of fatalism in some circles within Confucianism. It begins, "Tzŭ-hsia said, 'There is a saying which I have heard . . .' "; from this it is commonly supposed that Tzŭ-hsia was quoting Confucius himself. The passage reads, "Death and life are as decreed,

wealth and rank depend upon Heaven; the gentleman is serious
and does not fail in his duties, he behaves courteously to others
and accords with *li*." [10] Those who quote this passage commonly
stop with "Heaven," but this is to miss its point. Life and death
are matters about which one can do relatively little; he does his
best, but when death comes after all one must simply resign
himself and say, "It is fate." That is what Confucius did, and we
today can do no better. About wealth and rank one *could* do
something, but a gentleman *would* not. As ends to be striven
for, they were beneath his notice. "The concern of the gentleman is about the progress of the Way; he does not worry about
poverty." About such matters, then, one did nothing, but dismissed them as "depending on Heaven." What one did do (and
this is the importance of the second half of the quotation) was
to attend to his own character and his relations with his fellow
men.

Here is the key, then, to Confucius' attitude toward religion.
He believed in it, apparently, but he was not much interested
in it. It had to do with the realm of forces beyond man's control. But Confucius was interested in making over an intolerable
world into a good world; what nothing could be done about
did not concern him very much. He was occupied with the very
practical problem of how best to utilize such ability as we have
to act effectively.

The central conception in the philosophy of Confucius is
that of the Way, to which we have often referred without
describing it. This has come to be, in much of Chinese thinking,
a metaphysical conception, but it was not so for Confucius.

The character commonly translated as "Way" is *tao*. It does
not seem to occur on the oracle bones of the Shang period. [11]
In bronze inscriptions from a time earlier than that of Confucius
it seems to be used seldom, and only in two ways: in its original
sense of "road," and as a proper name. In all of the pre-Confucian literature put together it is used only some forty-four times,
which is only half as many times as it appears in the *Analects*.
In this earlier literature its most frequent meaning is "road";
rarely it has the related meanings of "to conduct" and "to tell"

(developed from "to guide"); six times it has the sense of "a course of action." [12]

In the *Analects, tao* occurs with all of these meanings. Almost always, however, it refers to a "way of action"; in any other sense it is rare. We find it used of ways that are bad as well as those that are good; Confucius speaks of a way which is inadequate. Thus far, we have nothing new. But what does appear to have no precedent in the pre-Confucian literature is the use of *tao* to mean "*the* way" above all other ways; what we may conveniently write as "the Way." It is only with this sense in mind that Confucius could have said that "a great minister is one who serves his ruler in accord with the Way." It is with this new significance that the character *tao* is used most frequently in the *Analects.*

The Way is the way in which Confucius thought that individuals, states, and the world should conduct themselves and be conducted. If "all under heaven [*i.e.,* the Chinese world] has the Way," or a particular state "has the Way," this means that they are governed as they should be and that moral principles prevail. If an individual "has the Way" he acts as he should act, and is a person of high moral character. The conception is not, however, as colorless as this description might suggest.

Confucius once said, "My Way is pervaded by [literally, "is strung upon"] a single principle." What the principle was we are never told. But if we study the *Analects* closely, in its historical setting, we can see it plainly enough. It was a vision of a cooperative world. It was the conviction that antagonism and suspicion, strife and suffering, were largely unnecessary. It was a profound faith that men's true interests did not conflict but complemented each other, that war and injustice and exploitation injured those who profited by them as well as those they caused to suffer. This was, indeed, a thread which "ran through" all of Confucius' thinking, and from which much of his philosophy can be derived by logical deduction. The conception of the Way, as *the* way in which this vision of a better world could be made into reality was thus no sterile moral code of not doing wrong, but a body of principle that demanded positive and sometimes dangerous action.

In a recent study Lorraine Creel has analyzed the significance of the idea of the Way (*tao*), from the sociological point of view, as follows:

Tao . . . is what Confucius considered to be the ideal way of life for the individual and the state. It is a way of life which includes all the virtues, sincerity, respectfulness, justice, kindness, and the like. It pays full attention to the rules of propriety [*li*] and to music. Like the human body however, it is more than the sum of its parts; for by a kind of "emergent synthesis" it attains a character and a power of its own. . . .

While law provides a standard of action more constant and enduring than a virtuous ruler, *tao* provides a standard of action more constant and enduring than law. Law is dependent on the vagaries of a governing body and derives its authority from that body. *Tao*, on the other hand is completely independent of any government; it derives its authority from itself. It is, therefore, of especial value in periods of such disorganization and chaos as were the Ch'un Ch'iu (722–481 B.C.) and the Chan Kuo (468–221 B.C.). For it could provide a common standard and bond for men, over whom there was no central authority. The *chün tzŭ* [gentleman] in Ch'i and the *chün tzŭ* in Lu could both look to *tao* for their standard.

Tao is also superior to law in that it calls for more than a minimum standard of conduct . . . *tao* not only prohibits one from killing or injuring a neighbor, it also requires that one have a friendly and helpful attitude toward him. This is probably connected with the fact that *tao* does not operate by the use of sanctions. If punishments are invoked as a result of failure to conform to a standard, it is not possible to have such a high standard that the mass of the people are unable to conform to it. . . . Also related to the fact that *tao* has no sanctions is the fact that its stimulus to virtue is not based on an appeal to self-interest. Because it does not encourage the individual to be good by the promise of reward or punishment, it does not turn the attention of the individual back on himself and on what is profitable or unprofitable for himself. This is important because once the individual comes to assume that his own interest and profit are the ultimate end of action, he will do what is morally right only so long as the advantages outweigh the disadvantages.

If the individual strives to follow *tao*, the self and its interests cease to be the focus of attention. His criterion of action becomes conformity to *tao* rather than profit to himself. At the same time, his actions cease to be separate and meaningful only in themselves, for they are now related through a common focusing on *tao*. Likewise, the individual is able to place himself in a historical perspective, for he is able to view himself as a member of a group of men who may be distant in time and space, but who are all interested in the progress of the *tao*.

When Confucius speaks of a man or a state as "having" the Way, this sounds as if he conceived of it as a thing, perhaps as a metaphysical entity. Clearly, the idea was well adapted to being so conceived, and in later Chinese thought this was done. For Confucius, however, it remained a way, or better *the* way, of conduct. This is evident when he says, "Who can go out of a house except by the door? Why are there none who follow this Way?" Yet it is clear that he considered it of the highest importance, as shown by the famous passage, "The Master said, 'If one hear the Way in the morning, he may die in the evening without regret.' "

Precisely because the Way summed up the totality of his philosophy, Confucius never clearly defined it; to understand it we must look at his philosophy as a whole. We can, however, learn something of the source of its central conception, the idea of a cooperative world. It is probable that it was essentially based on the relationship which existed between the members of a family.

The family has been important in many cultures, but it is doubtful that it has anywhere been more important, for a longer time, than in China. Certain aspects of its importance, especially nepotism, have been deplorable, yet it has probably done more than any other institution to make possible the remarkable survival of Chinese culture. It has dealt with many social problems in their nascent stages. By virtue of it, China has consisted of a vast number of almost self-contained social cells, whose functioning has been little affected even by national catastrophe. It has been the incubator of morality and a microcosm of the state. From one point of view, Confucianism might be defined as the philosophy of the Chinese family system.

As regards the family, Confucius seems to have added little that was new. From what light the oracle bones give us (which is not very much), it seems to have been important even in

Shang times. In Chou literature the basic importance of the
family is constantly emphasized. It must be borne in mind,
however, that from the early literature we learn very little about
the common people. For the aristocrats the family was essential;
their status depended upon their ancestors. Furthermore the
Chou empire, won in battle, was cemented by a network of
feudal and familial ties, which were inextricably mingled
through intermarriage and the enfeoffment of royal relatives.
The early Chou rulers were fully aware of the basic role of the
family in the maintenance of order in their dominions. One of
the sections of the *Book of History* is a charge given to his
brother by the Duke of Chou (to whom Confucius looked as an
early precursor in the Way). The Duke instructs his brother in
the way in which he should govern the territory he is to rule
and adjures him to be especially cautious in the regulation of his
own family. He further declares that if his subjects do not respect family ties, "the principles [of morality] given to the people by Heaven will be thrown into disorder." The unfilial and
unbrotherly are, the Duke declares, worse than thieves and murderers and must be punished without leniency. But—and this is
of the first importance—not only the unfilial son but also the
hard-hearted father, not only the unruly younger brother but
also the overbearing elder brother, are condemned as deserving
punishment.

The duty of filial piety was constantly urged in the early literature. Its importance was obvious when the dead ancestors
controlled one's destiny. Confucius interpreted filial piety as
a social duty, but he still emphasized it. There was a potential
conflict, of course, between the idea that one should obey his
father and the idea that one should act in accordance with the
Way; what if they disagreed? Confucius says very little about
this. In one case, however, he does say that one may "remonstrate with his father and mother, but gently."

In another passage the conflict between the state and the
family appears sharply. "The Duke of Shê said to Confucius,
'Among us there are those who are upright; if his father steals a
sheep, the son will testify against him.' Confucius replied,
'Among us the upright act quite differently. The son shields the
father, and the father shields the son; we see this as upright-

ness.'" This conflict still exists, even in the Occident; if you knew that your father had committed a murder, would you inform the authorities? Confucius was not unaware of the claims of society, but he put the family first. It seems doubtful, however, that he enjoined the taking of "blood revenge" against the slayer of one's relatives, as later books have claimed.[13] He did not believe that the interests of family and state were fundamentally opposed; quite the reverse. It was in the family, as he saw it, that the individual learned those attitudes of obedience and cooperation, and gained the experience in socialized activity, which made it possible for him to be a useful citizen or official.

Confucius was not the first person in China to see some analogy between the family and the state; two early poems refer to rulers as "the father and mother of the people." Such expressions are common enough in many lands, but the important question is, what do they mean in attitudes and actions? Too often paternalism is a near synonym for despotism. There is little evidence that such ideas ever greatly mitigated the lot of the Chinese common people in the early period. In the Confucian application of this conception, however, it became a potent force for reform.

It is undoubtedly true that Confucius was attracted, in the analogy of the family with the state, by the fact that it was a pattern of orderly subordination to authority. But it is probable that another aspect attracted him still more strongly. The Chinese family was an organization in which every member was inherently "as good as" every other member. This does not mean that there was no subordination. The children were subject to the authority of their parents, but in time they would come in their turn to be parents. A younger son would never, under normal circumstances, be head of the family, but no stigma attached to this fact. He would have his voice in the family councils. Economic advantages were shared with considerable equity. If any member of the family were treated unfairly he could protest, with a considerable chance of success. In theory, the head of the family could be a despot; in practice it was difficult for him long to resist the disapproval of a majority of those with whom he lived every day. The Chinese family seems always to have been monarchic in theory, and largely democratic in practice. The result was that its members were, as some sociologists would put it, members of the "we group"; they were treated as ends, not as means. There was subordination among them, but each had his place, his functions, and his dignity.

It was into such status, and to such a community, that Confucius wished to welcome all men everywhere. This is the significance of the statement by Tzǔ-hsia that he had heard (almost certainly from the Master) that "within the four seas, all men are brothers." It is worthy of note that Confucius betrays no chauvinistic bias against the non-Chinese "barbarians"; Waley even attributes to him "a certain idealization of the 'noble savage.'" Certainly Confucius would have liked them to become "civilized" according to Chinese standards. His ideal state, however, was the world. It is of interest that, at the time when the League of Nations was being projected, K'ang Yu-wei submitted his understanding of Confucius' views on the world state, at the request of President Wilson.

Even more revolutionary, in his day, was Confucius' insistence that men of all classes possessed worth in themselves, and must be treated not merely as the means *by* which the state accomplished its purposes, but as the ends *for* which the state existed. That he held this is clear, for instance, from the fact that he said that the end of government was that it should make the people happy. The idea that the state was a mutual enterprise, in the good or bad fortunes of which all, high and low, should share, was stated by the disciple Yu Jo. Duke Ai of Lu declared that since the harvest was poor he did not know how he was to raise sufficient revenues, and asked what Yu Jo advised. Yu suggested that he levy a tax of one tenth. "With two tenths I have not enough," the duke replied. "How could I possibly get along with one · tenth?" Confucius' disciple answered, "When the people have plenty, with whom will you be obliged to share want? But when your people are in want, with whom can their ruler share abundance?"

In a cooperative world made up of agents who are (within limits) free, as opposed to a world dominated by coercion, the individual is paramount. The world can be no better than the sum of the individuals who compose it, and if a significant pro-portion of them are wanting in morality, the world is in danger. Thus Confucius begins with the individual. He emphasizes the necessity of self-examination, of the cultivation of virtue, and of education. He himself concentrated on the education of men who were, he hoped, to govern; there was a tremendous job of education to do, and this seemed the most important place to begin. But it has not been sufficiently noted that several passages in the *Analects* make it clear that his goal included at least some education for all the people. This was logically necessary; the totally ignorant may blindly obey, but they cannot cooperate for they do not know how. Thus Confucius said, "When the common people study the Way, they are easily directed." They are easily caused, that is, to do what is for the common good, since they have some understanding of the orders issued to them, their purpose, and how to carry them out.[14] Recent dis-cussions of military training have emphasized the importance of political indoctrination, the theory being that soldiers who know what they are fighting for will fight better. Confucius expressed the same idea in this way: "To lead an uneducated people to war is to throw them away."[15]

He conceived education, as we have noted, as being largely directed toward the cultivation of character. It was designed to develop such virtues as loyalty, sincerity, good faith, justice, kindness, accord with *li*, and so forth.[16] Concerning loyalty it should be noted, however, that this was not mere loyalty to an individual. Confucius specifically denounced blind personal loy-alty, of the feudal variety. His ideal retainer served his lord with all his strength as long as he could do so in accord with the Way, but when he had to choose between them he held to the Way and left the ruler's service.

This allegiance to principle rather than to persons is essential to democracy; without it, the state is constantly at the mercy of any general or politician who may accumulate a following. By providing such allegiance, Confucianism established one of the essential conditions for democratic government. It was this loy-alty to principle which later made possible the Censorate, that body in the Chinese government which has been charged, dur-ing the past two thousand years, with the function of criticizing derelictions of duty by any official or even by the emperor himself. It was this loyalty which caused some members of that body to do their duty fearlessly even when they knew that exile or death would reward their temerity. It may be that legend has exaggerated the frequency with which censors opposed the emperor, but the very existence of the legend is significant.

What reward did Confucius promise those who should be loyal to principle and cleave to duty, forsaking all others? Wealth, rank, and power? Not at all. Not only are they uncertain, but he considered it beneath the dignity of a gentleman to make such private gain his controlling object. Immortality, happiness after death? Confucius never mentions them. Then what in the world is it that men can want so much that they will be willing, "seeing danger, to sacrifice their lives?"

It is this: The man who cultivates and *practices* virtue, who loves the Way and does his best to *try* to realize it in the world, has fulfilled the whole duty of man. Poverty cannot touch him; Confucius declared, "With coarse food to eat, water to drink, and my bended arm for a pillow, I still have joy in the midst of these things." If one who practices the Way fails to gain high office, that is unfortunate since he might otherwise have been able to do much good; but it is cause for reproach, not to the virtuous individual, but only to the government that fails to employ him. "The Master said, 'Do not be concerned that you are not in office, but only about making yourself fit for one. Do not be concerned if you win no recognition; only seek to make yourself worthy of it.' " It was in this sense that it could truly be said of Confucius that he was "one who knows that what he is trying to do is impossible, and yet goes on trying." A nice calculation of one's chances of success was irrelevant. "If upon looking into my heart I find that I am right," Confucius is quoted as having said, "I will go forward though those that op‑pose me number thousands and tens of thousands." It was only necessary that one determine what he *ought* to do and then do his best.

Thus Confucius offered that most priceless possession, peace of mind. "If, looking within his own heart, one finds no cause for self-reproach, why should he worry, what shall he fear?" He put peace of mind within the reach of each individual, without regard to the vagaries of the external world. "Is virtue a distant thing?" he asked. "If I really want virtue, then it is here." Thus the individual possessed a kind of majestic autonomy; his heart was his castle. "Even the general of a great army may be kid-naped, but no force can steal the determination of even the humblest man." Historically this was very important. It enabled the Confucian "when the state had the Way, to take office; when the state lacked the Way, to roll up his principles and preserve them in his bosom." It made possible the continuance of Confucianism as a doctrine of the private scholar, biding its time, with little public recognition, until the Han dynasty.

Self-sufficiency for the individual is, within reason, good. But if it goes too far it cuts him off from all contact with his fellows. Shall one then relax his principles, become one of the crowd, and be a "good fellow"? No! says Confucius. "Do not choose your friends among those who are not your [moral] equals." This raises the familiar problem of whether equality is to be achieved by reducing everyone to a common level, or rather by raising the level of the masses. Confucius stood firmly for the latter course. Yet this did not mean that he held himself entirely aloof; we have seen that he was freer in his associations than some of the disciples would have liked. Confucius and Kant ex-pressed themselves on this matter very similarly. Kant wrote that "it is the duty of man . . . to construct for himself an im-pregnable center of principle, yet to regard this circle which he draws around himself as also being one part of an all-inclusive circle of cosmopolitan sympathy." Confucius said that one should "feel kindly toward everyone, but be intimate only with the virtuous."

Yet mere kindly feeling is not enough; we must do something for others if we are truly virtuous. The disciple Tsêng Shên once declared that his Master's doctrine consisted of nothing more than "integrity and reciprocity." Legge translates this more freely, but with a fine sense of its true meaning, as "to be true to the principles of our nature and the benevolent exercise of them to others." Confucius said that "reciprocity" was a principle which should be practiced always, and explained it as meaning that "what one does not want done to himself, he should not do to others." This has sometimes been criticized as being merely a negative conception. Whether that is true or not, Confucius certainly did not conceive of duty as merely negative. "The truly virtuous man," he said, "desiring to be established himself, seeks to establish others; desiring success for himself, he strives to help others succeed. To find in the wishes of one's own heart the principle for his conduct toward others is the method of true virtue."

The reader will at once have been reminded of Kant's famous categorical imperative: "Act as if by your will the maxim of your act were about to be made into a universal law of nature." This dictum is, as one would expect, much more sophisticated, yet its principle is similar. Both Kant and Confucius, being individualists, saw the world as consisting, from the individual's point of view, of two great aspects: one's self and the world. As regards himself, one's control and thus his responsibility are virtually unlimited. He must therefore, with unremitting diligence, cultivate his character. Having done so, and attained a knowledge of what is good, he must then do his utmost to realize this good for all other men. Thus Kant asserts that there are two ends toward which we are morally obliged to strive: "our own perfection—the happiness of others." This might serve to summarize the moral lessons of the *Analects*.

This is an austere and rational doctrine, yet it implies considerable optimism concerning human nature. If it is one's duty to act toward others with reciprocity, there should be that in them which can respond. Indeed, this is the necessary condition for a cooperative world. That Confucius did believe in this capacity for response is very clear. He declared that the influence of the example of a true gentleman was so powerful that even if he went among the barbarians he would find no rudeness, for it would disappear upon his advent. He told the head of the Chi family in Lu that he should not employ capital punishment since if his own desires were as they should be the people would be good.

We need not, however, take these fine phrases too seriously. The last statement was very much in order, as addressed to a despot who had just proposed the policy of killing off all those with the "wrong" ideas. But Confucius knew that perfection could not be attained overnight, and elsewhere we find him agreeing that if good men were to govern the state it would require a century before capital punishment could be eliminated. Likewise we cannot lay too much stress on such a statement as the following: "The Master said, 'Man's very life is uprightness; without it, he is lucky to escape with his life.' " If this be true, the world was full of lucky people in his own day, as Confucius well knew.

Clearly enough, Confucius thought that men have certain tendencies toward good and tremendous capacity to be influenced by education. "It is only the wisest and the most stupid," he said, "who cannot be changed." He also thought that there were some so perverse that it was futile to waste one's time with them. But he seems to have taken no stand on the question of whether men are naturally good or bad, though he did say that "men are by nature very similar, but by practice come to be very different." It is highly improbable that, as has often been supposed, he believed that some men were "born wise," endowed with knowledge from birth.[17]

How then do men acquire knowledge? More important, when they have acquired it how can they evaluate it; how does one distinguish the true from the false? And what is virtue? It is said that one should practice the Way, but how does one find out what the Way is? What is the great standard by which all things are to be measured? This is perhaps the most searching question that can be asked of any philosophy. And when we ask it of Confucius, we receive our greatest surprise.

He has no such standard.

He did not say that one need only imitate the ancients, such as the mythical emperors Yao and Shun. Mencius said this, and it has been supposed that Confucius believed it, but there is no such statement in the *Analects*. Nor did he say that the standard of truth was to be found in any book, or any set of books. We have seen that he himself did not depend on books as the sole source of his ideas, and there is no indication that he advised others to do so. Although Confucianism did in time come to regard certain books (the Classics) with the utmost veneration, there are indications that this tendency arose late, as part of what was in reality a reaction against the essence of Confucius' own teachings.[18] Finally, he did not set up his own words as an ultimate authority; on the contrary, as we have seen, he made no claim to infallibility and permitted his disciples to differ with him unrebuked.

Nevertheless, the mere fact that he never states in the *Analects* that antiquity or certain books provide the ultimate basis of truth, does not prove that he did not think they did. Such proof comes, rather, from the fact that even when tightly pressed in argument he makes no appeal to them.

That he had no such standard is stated in the *Analects* again and again. "There were four qualities from which the Master was entirely free: he had no foregone conclusions, he was not over-positive, not obstinate, and never saw things from his own point of view alone." He himself said that he hated obstinacy. His reputation for flexibility, acting always in accord with a careful consideration of all the circumstances, was so great that Mencius discussed it in detail a century later and called Confucius "the timely sage." Confucius' own best statement of this principle is the following: "The true gentleman, in the world, is neither predisposed for anything nor against anything; he will side with whatever is right."

What is here translated as "right" is the character 義, *i*. This is another conception that is very important. Its sense is not simply that of what is "right" or "righteous" in the ordinary meaning of these words.[19] It means rather that which is fitting and suitable. Thus when the disciple Yu Jo said, "If in making promises one stays close to *i*, his words can be fulfilled," he meant that before one agrees to do something one should consider all the circumstances and promise only what is proper and suitable. It was with a similar intent that Confucius approved the conduct of one who "seeing an opportunity for gain, thinks of *i*." Such a man reflects upon whether, by taking the profit which is possible, he will violate a trust, wrong another person, or in any respect act in a way which is unsuitable under the given circumstances.

Obviously this concept of *i* is an extremely important moral force. It is a regulator of conduct similar to *li* and the Way; and one that constantly places his own responsibility squarely before the individual. For whereas the Way is general, and one may look to others for some guidance concerning it, the question of what is suitable in each given situation is one that the individual must decide for himself. We have already seen instances in which Confucius was guided by this criterion of suitability.[20]

Yet the question still pursues us: how is one to determine what is suitable? By meditation? "The Master said, 'I once spent a whole day without food and a whole night without sleep, in order to meditate. It was no use. It is better to study.'" But study alone is not the answer. "The Master said, 'Study without thought is labor lost; thought without study is dangerous.'"

There are several statements in the *Analects* that describe the way in which Confucius thought that truth might be attained. "The Master said, 'I am not one who was born with knowledge; rather, I love the past, and am diligent in investigating it.'" [21] Investigation of the past is still one of our chief sources of knowledge. But it must be done methodically. "The Master said, 'I can say something about the *li* of the Hsia dynasty, but the state of Ch'i [a small state supposed to be ruled by the descendants of the Hsia kings] has no adequate evidence concerning it. I can say something about the *li* of the Yin [Shang] dynasty, but the state of Sung likewise lacks such evidence. . . . If the evidence were sufficient, I could then give descriptions for which there would be real proof.'" [22]

Not everything is equally reliable as evidence, however. To a student who wanted to know how to conduct himself in practical politics Confucius said, "Hear much, but leave to one side that which is doubtful, and speak with due caution concerning the remainder; in this way you will seldom incur blame. See much, but leave to one side that of which the meaning is not clear, and act carefully with regard to the rest; thus you will have few occasions for regret." [23] We must always keep our eyes open, learning all we can from experience. Yet we cannot expect to understand everything; we must understand what we can, and concerning the rest maintain suspended judgment. Thus he commended the practice of copyists who, instead of guessing when a word is illegible, "leave a blank in the text." He described his own way of acquiring knowledge in these words: "To hear much, select what is good, and follow it; to see much and remember it; these are the steps by which knowledge [or, wisdom] is attained." [24]

So far Confucius sounds very much like what philosophers call an empiricist, relying wholly on experience for his knowledge. Another time, however, he asked the disciple Tzŭ-kung, "Do you think that my way of acquiring knowledge is simply to study many things and remember them?" "Yes," Tzŭ-kung replied, "Isn't that the case?" "No," was the reply, "I have one principle which I use like a thread, upon which to string them all." Here he sounds like a rationalist, seeking to arrange the world's phenomena according to the principle of his own mind. In fact, as we have already seen, he was partly the one and partly the other.

Yet we still have not found the answer to our question: what is the standard for truth? And we will get no answer to this question from Confucius. If we could put it to him, he would undoubtedly reply that every man must find it for himself. *That is the only answer possible in a truly cooperative world.* A machine is operated, but it cannot cooperate. And in a world in which there is a fixed standard of truth and authority, the role of the individual is no more creative than that of a machine. He may refuse to conform, or he may conform, but he cannot truly contribute. If men have responsibility for the achievements of society, they must also have the opportunity to help in the choice of its ends, which means in the discovery (not merely the unveiling) of truth. Thus Kant saw clearly that it is impossible for anyone to achieve a fully developed personality unless "he has the power to determine his own ends for himself, according to his own ideas of duty."

Here again we are back to the individual. Are we to conclude, then, that one man is just as capable of judging what is right and true as any other? In one sense, yes. We are dealing here with a type of thinking which is similar to that of science. The scientist, like Confucius, looks to experience for his data and tries to link it all with one pervasive hypothesis, or series of hypotheses. The scientist also believes that essentially one normal man is *potentially* as good a judge of truth as another; royal birth or the possession of a billion dollars will not increase the respect accorded to a man's opinions as a scientist. The only things that will increase that respect are education, experience, and demonstrated competence.

Confucius judged similarly. He believed that all men were potentially equal; he was not awed by rank nor contemptuous of poverty. But those whose opinions were entitled to respect were those who realized their potentialities by study and by the cultivation of virtue. Thus the opinions of one enlightened man might count for more than those of a multitude of. the unthinking crowd.

To prevent misunderstanding, let it be stated clearly that there is no intention to claim here that Confucius "anticipated the methods of modern science." In some respects his thinking fell far short of the scientific ideal; [25] that is in no way surprising. But his thinking was characterized by an absence of dogma, a clear realization of the necessity of suspended judgment, and an espousal of intellectual democracy that, in its forthright acceptance of the minimal philosophic conditions of scientific thinking, is altogether remarkable. It may be asked whether, if this be true, the Chinese should not then have developed scientific method long ago. This may or may not be the case, but as we shall see these aspects of Confucius' thinking were soon lost, in large degree, from Confucianism.

Science, like Confucius, has no unalterable standard for truth; it is searching for truth, not deducing it from a prearranged formula. Yet this is not to say that it gives us no help toward finding the truth. It does not tell us *what* truth is, but it gives us a great deal of advice as to *how* to look for it. So does Confucius.

Surely few philosophers, or at any rate few prescientific philosphers, have laid such emphasis on flexibility as did Confucius. In the Occident we have tended to think of truth as being immutable, and to think that a god or a very wise man must partake of the unbending character of absolute truth. The ancient Mesopotamians (who are, through the Hebrews, among our intellectual ancestors) considered inflexibility to be an attribute of godliness; "The king's word is right; his utterance, like that of a god, cannot be changed!" We have commonly felt that it infringes the dignity of a man of position to change his mind and admit himself at fault; this shows that he was not, as he should have been, in possession of the immutable truth.

Confucius argued differently: "To be mistaken, and yet not to change; this is indeed to be in error." "If you have made a mistake, do not be afraid to admit the fact and amend your ways." He stressed this theme repeatedly. The disciple Tzŭ-kung said, "The mistakes of a gentleman may be compared to the eclipses of the sun or the moon. When he makes a mistake, all men see.it; when he corrects it, all men look up to him."

This readiness at all times to change is, of course, merely one necessary aspect of living in a state of suspended judgment. However noble such a state may be, it is not wholly comfortable. One walks on the sidewalk in front of one's dwelling every day and expects it to be there. Yet if one morning a gaping hole appears in it, one will (let us hope!) respond to the new situation and stay out of trouble. The fact is, however, that some circumstance *could* undermine that sidewalk so that, although it still appeared solid, it would in fact be a trap, only waiting for one to put his weight on it to collapse. Is one therefore to walk in the street—where the danger will probably be still greater? If one carried such fears far enough he would have, of course, to stop eating. No one (except a few of the mentally deranged) does any such thing. What we do is to estimate the probabilities of success or failure, safety or danger, in any given situation, and act in the light of this judgment. We do this all the time; it is the way we live. These judgments are personal, conditioned by all our previous training and experience, and they are *practical*. One may bring to them all the theory that he knows, but in the end there comes a time when he has to make a choice between two or more possible courses and hope it is correct.

Similarly one must draw a practical line in the matter of suspended judgment. To say, for instance, that since I know nothing with absolute certainty, I do not know that it is my duty to feed my neighbor when he is starving, is not true. Confucius recognized the need for drawing a practical line in the matter of knowledge; he defined wisdom as "when you know a thing, to recognize that you know it, and when you do not know a thing, to recognize that you do not know it." From what has gone before it is clear, of course, that Confucius was not using the word know in an absolute sense. Rather he was insisting upon the necessity of striking a reasonable and proper balance between unwarrantable scepticism and all-embracing dogmatic certainty.

This idea of striking a balance, of keeping to the middle path, was very important for Confucius. Mencius tells us that "Confucius did not go to extremes." In the *Analects* we read that "the Master said, 'Since I cannot get men who pursue the middle course with whom to practice my principles, I must take the impetuous and the over-cautious.'" He considered one kind of failing as bad as the other; "to go too far is as bad as to fall short." "The Master said, 'The middle course is indeed the way of the highest virtue; but its practice has long been rare among the people.'"

We have here essentially a philosophy of compromise. In Western thought there has been some tendency to look upon compromise with disfavor. This stems from our idea that truth and virtue are somehow fixed and absolute things with which the wise and good man has established communion; this being so, he should hold to the strict path of rectitude. Confucius, too, believed that one must draw a line beyond which he would not compromise his principles though death be the cost. But while he never expressed himself as to whether truth may or may not change, he quite clearly believed that our understanding of it must always be changing, just as long as we continue to be thinking and moral beings. Furthermore, no person has the right to regard himself as the sole anointed guardian of the truth. If your opinion differs from mine, we must discuss the matter; perhaps there is some truth in both our views, and something nearer the truth *may* lie between them. The necessity for such compromise follows logically, of course, from the conception of the world as cooperative, and it is essential to democracy.

Furthermore, even if I did know the truth, this would not tell me how to apply it in a concrete situation. We saw, for instance, that when rebellious vassals invited Confucius to direct their governments he was tempted to do so. He did not wholly approve of their actions; but did the desire to maintain his personal purity justify him in refusing an opportunity that might have led to alleviating the sufferings of the people? This was a real problem. Max Weber has pointed out that "no ethics in the world can dodge the fact that in numerous instances the attainment of 'good' ends is bound to the fact that one must be willing to pay the price of using morally dubious means or at least dangerous ones—and facing the possibility or even the probability of evil ramifications. From no ethics in the world can it be concluded when and to what extent the ethically good purpose 'justifies' the ethically dangerous means and ramifications."

Confucius recognized that the individual is constantly faced with such problems, which are in each case to some degree unique, for the circumstances are never twice the same. This recognition persists in Chinese law, to our own day. The French jurist, Jean Escarra, has pointed out in his book *Le Droit Chinois* that Chinese legal procedure remains basically Confucian. Thus the Chinese authorities "are preoccupied," he says, "with tempering the nominal severity of [the legally prescribed] punishments by an application which we may describe as rather humane, rather 'individualized.' And this explains the veritable genius of Chinese writers on criminal law for creating, with the utmost subtlety and refinement, all varieties of penal theory, from the casuistic analysis of the intent to . . . complicity, excuses, extenuating circumstances, recidivism, the accumulation of offences, etc." In China, even the courts know that morality is not, for the individual, a simple matter of keeping his conduct in accord with a set of hard and fast rules.

Since, in Confucius' philosophy, so much responsibility is left to the individual, little can be done for him except to educate his mind and strengthen his character for his tasks. In the training of character, the ideal of the mean has an important function. Like *li*, the Way, and *i*, it is another principle which can assist one in his self-discipline. One who is moderate may err, but he is unlikely to go so far wrong as the man who goes to extremes. Even in cultivation, Confucius held, one should not become so over-refined as to obscure one's basic manhood, which is the true foundation of character.

Even one's benevolence should be tempered with reason. The recalcitrant disciple Tsai Yü once said to Confucius, "If a man is really virtuous, I suppose that even if you told him that there was a man in the well he would go right in after him." "Why do you think so?" Confucius replied. "You could, in that way, get a gentleman to go to the well, but not to jump in; he can be deceived, but not made an utter fool."

Thus virtue and truth are not, for Confucius, snug havens in which we may rest in complacent security. Rather they are goals toward which we must continually make our way. "Study," he said, "as if you were following someone you could not overtake, and were afraid of losing." This does not mean that life must always be hectic and one's mind harassed. On the contrary, the race is not always to the swift, nor does the most impatient seeker always find the object of his search. Through education and self-discipline, and by keeping to the middle path, we may achieve poise and freedom from confusion. But so long as we live, our very possession of moral faculties imposes a corresponding obligation to exercise them, and to choose in each new situation between the various courses of action open to us. Confucius made this very clear; "If a man does not constantly ask himself, 'What is the right thing to do?' I really don't know what is to be done about him."

ꟋꟋꟋꟋꟋꟋꟋꟋꟋꟋꟋꟋꟋꟋꟋꟋꟋꟋꟋꟋ

CHAPTER X

THE REFORMER

AMONG thinkers roughly contemporary with Confucius, who have treated at length of politics, the most celebrated are Plato and Aristotle. It is natural, therefore, for Western students to take their ideas as something of a standard with which to compare the political philosophy of Confucius as it is stated in the *Analects*. The first result of such comparison is likely to be the impression that the ideas of Confucius are relatively simple and unorganized. There is some truth to this, but in fairness we must bear in mind some important differences.

The most obvious is that Plato and Aristotle have left us detailed treatises on politics, while from Confucius we have only an assortment of random sentences or paragraphs. No less important is the fact that Plato and Aristotle conceived the state as a small city-state; in the *Laws* Plato would limit it to 5,040 houses. Confucius conceived the state as embracing at least all of China, which at once imposes a far less neat and more difficult problem. Again, the political diversity of Greece allowed its thinkers to draw on a wide variety of political experience, including monarchy, oligarchy, democracy, and dictatorship; Confucius knew only the Chinese feudal state and the phenomena developed by its decay. Finally and perhaps most significant, both Plato and Aristotle discussed not only the actual and the practicable but also the ideal state. From Confucius, on the other hand, we have little discussion of theory. Almost always he talked of reforms which he believed it would be possible to put into operation in the near future.

We have seen what were the conditions he wished to reform. The common people were severely oppressed and almost without any rights; their rulers might use them as they would, subject only to the check of infrequent and ineffectual rebellion. Members of the ruling class were themselves the victims of the general lawlessness and frequent wars of the time. The rulers and their powerful ministers were scions of hereditary noble houses. With rare exceptions, they were prey to the degeneration usually suffered by families in which power and luxury are bequeathed from father to son for many generations. They needed two virtues, prowess in war and skill in intrigue, and these they cultivated to the utmost. The result was a world that no man who cared for human dignity and human happiness could contemplate with equanimity.

Confucius was such a man, and he was profoundly disturbed. He dedicated his life to the attempt to make a better world. Why? What was the source of his ideals, which were at variance with those of his environment, and of the ideas by means of which he hoped to transform it?

It has commonly been held, from ancient times to the present, that Confucius was seeking merely to revive the ways of antiquity, and that he advised men to go back to the ways of the virtuous "former kings." It is certainly true that he twice indicated that he considered antiquity to be the source of his ideas and that he frequently disparaged the present in comparing it with the past. Yet we must remember that when he spoke scornfully of those who ran the government in his own day he was in part merely blaming the men who would not permit him to carry out his reforms.

Confucius was not unique in his emphasis on tradition. Plato, whose innovations included the proposition that men should hold property, children, and women in common, nevertheless declared that "any change whatever except from evil is the most dangerous of all things," and said that the legislator must find a way of implanting "reverence for antiquity." In ancient China, such reverence was common. Tung Tso-pin has shown, by his researches on the Shang oracle bones, that the practice of conscious imitation of the past was already in existence more than half a millennium before Confucius was born. Later, when the relatively barbarous Chou tribesmen overran the Shang state and supplanted its rule, they explicitly declared their intention of following the regulations of its "former wise kings," and they asserted that the Shang state had perished because it had ceased to "use the old ways." The importance of following tradition was emphasized again and again in the *Book of History*, the *Book of Poetry*, and bronze inscriptions. In ancient China, it was fashionable to be old-fashioned.

Seen against this background, Confucius does not appear slavishly devoted to tradition. On the contrary he recognized that human institutions change and develop, and was quite ready to make or accept changes recommended by their suitability and approved by common sense; that he did so was recognized by Confucians as late as Han times. He said, "Chou had the advantage of being able to review the experience of the two previous dynasties. How rich is its culture! I follow Chou." It was very seldom that Confucius recommended a course solely on the ground that it was traditional. Eleven times he was asked how government should be conducted; he replied in terms of traditional usage only once. On this occasion he said, "Use the calendar of Hsia, the state carriage of Yin, and the ceremonial hat of Chou." Even here he did not simply counsel following antiquity but made a choice of what usages were to be followed from each period. This was characteristic; he was not an indiscriminate but a selective traditionalist.

So are we all; when we long for the good old days we are thinking of the good aspects of the old days. This raises the question of whether Confucius did indeed, as K'ang Yu-wei held, attribute his new ideas to antiquity as conscious deception. This is very doubtful, for the real Confucius of the *Analects* talks far less about antiquity than he is made to do in later and dubious works. And he seems to have made no attempt to find traditional support for his own most revolutionary ideas. Yet it cannot be denied that in one case he called ancient an idea which, it seems very probable, was relatively new.[1] Nevertheless, there seems to be no evidence of conscious fraud, which would have violated his clearly stated principles.

Mencius said that the doctrines of Confucius had been handed down from the ancient emperors Yao, Shun, and Yü, who are alleged to have reigned some twenty-two centuries before the Christian era. This became the orthodox doctrine, and it has commonly been held that Confucius was trying to restore the "golden age" of these early emperors. There is little in the *Analects*, however, to support this. Confucius does speak of these early emperors with high praise, but he never suggests, as Mencius and later writers do, that it is only necessary to imitate them in order to achieve perfect government. In fact, they are mentioned very little in the *Analects*, as compared with works of slightly later date.

There is good reason for this. During the present century Chinese scholars have discovered that Yao, Shun, and Yü are to all appearances wholly legendary. Neither Yao nor Shun seems to be mentioned in any book or any bronze inscription earlier than the time of Confucius. Yü is mentioned in the *Book of Poetry*, the *Book of History*,[2] and bronze inscriptions as a culture hero, who dredged out the great rivers, drained the land, and made it habitable and cultivable. As such he is linked with Hou Chi, the "Ruler of Millet," mythical founder of the Chou royal house. But as an emperor he seems to be mentioned earliest in the *Analects*, where the names of Yao and Shun are seen for the first time.

Their story got most of its growth after the time of Confucius; gradually these legendary emperors were made the very archetypes of all the Confucian virtues. It is extremely doubtful that Confucius invented these figures; if he had, we should expect him to have had more to say about them. But their legend was not very old in his day. Thus, he could not possibly have obtained his ideas from Yao, Shun, and Yü; it would be much nearer the truth, in fact, to say that they got their ideas from him.[3]

Confucius himself said that he was the intellectual heir of King Wên, the father of the founder of the Chou dynasty. He also implied, in a passage which is somewhat vague, that he looked upon the Duke of Chou, a son of Wên, as his inspiration. Chinese tradition, from a very early time, has regarded the Duke of Chou as a source of Confucian ideas and sometimes even as the founder of Confucianism, notwithstanding the fact that he lived more than five hundred years before Confucius. We have a good deal of information about the early Chou rulers in the *Book of Poetry*, in bronze inscriptions, and especially in the *Book of History*; some sections of the latter work seem to be from the hand of the Duke of Chou himself. In some respects these documents show a similarity to the ideas of Confucius that is quite surprising.

It is surprising because we know that the Chou were relatively rude barbarians who overran their more cultivated Shang neighbors and consolidated a large portion of North China under a rule that was necessarily rather harsh. The earliest Chou rulers had to be extremely capable men to succeed in their audacious enterprise of far-flung conquest. Especially able was the Duke of Chou, who seized the power as regent when the newly won territories threatened to fall to pieces, and turned over a well-knit empire to his royal nephew after seven years. These men were enlightened; yet, while giving them their due, we need not ascribe all of their humanitarian utterances to sheer sentiment.

The chiefs of the Chou tribe had neither the experience nor the facilities (communications and a monetary system) necessary for highly centralized government. They parceled out most of their territories to their relatives and to the chiefs of tribes that had assisted in the conquest, who were permitted to govern very much as they saw fit provided they kept the peace in their domains and assisted the king in war; they were also expected to render certain tribute. This was in effect a feudal system. Its result was to place Chou vassals in charge of garrisons scattered strategically through the empire.

The early Chou kings were wise enough, however, to realize that they could not hold China as they had conquered it, by force alone. A major rebellion by the Shang people underlined this fact. The Chou therefore promulgated an elaborate justification of their conquest and their rule. Like most conquerors they decried the use of force once it had served their purpose and declared that they had been very reluctant to take up arms.

Heaven, however, had commanded it. It was the practice of Heaven, they said, constantly to inspect the conduct of the ruler, and if he were incorrigibly wicked to give its mandate, the decree, to one whom it charged to set up a new dynasty. It was in response to this command, as the servant of Heaven, that the Chou ruler conquered Shang.

What "wickedness" was it, on the part of a king, that merited his downfall? The Chou placed special emphasis on failure to sacrifice properly to the gods and on drunkenness. The Duke of Chou also listed, among such crimes, failure to treat the people well.

The Chou rulers, we are told repeatedly, were very "virtuous." This does not tell us much, however, unless we know what it means. A Roman who was considered the very model of antique virtue, whom Cicero praised as "the brave and venerable Marcus Cato," made it his practice (according to Plutarch) after each time he entertained to go among his slaves with a leather thong and personally "scourge those who had waited or dressed the meat carelessly." Undoubtedly many "virtuous" aristocrats among the early Chou were very oppressive toward the common people. It is an important fact, however, that their position as recent conquerors was so precarious that they had some incentive for ingratiating themselves, as a protective measure. The Duke of Chou in particular seems to have recognized this, for in documents that he probably composed which have come down to us, he repeatedly insisted on the importance of justice and even mercy in deciding criminal cases, of treating the people indulgently, and of not oppressing the helpless and solitary.

This is reminiscent of the oath that Charlemagne required of his subjects, which bound them "to do no violence nor treason toward the holy Church, or to widows, or orphans, or strangers, seeing that the lord Emperor has been appointed . . . the protector and defender of all such." Like the Duke of Chou, Charlemagne was trying to consolidate his rule over a large and loose-knit territory; in each case, their motives combined humanitarianism and policy. Both men became legends, profoundly affecting subsequent history.

In China, the effect was to leave an ideal of kingship as a form of stewardship, in which the test of a good king was whether or not he brought about the welfare of the people. Since the Chou legitimized their title by the claim that they had replaced an oppressive sovereign, justice and kindness became the duty of every later ruler. The accepted theory was that every person in authority must regard his office as a sacred and difficult trust. As we have abundantly seen, it was almost universally honored in the breach rather than the observance. Yet the mere fact that such a code existed was of the highest importance. In it Confucius found ready to his hand much that was very useful for his undertaking. The fact that (like the teachings of Jesus) it was almost universally acknowledged to be right, though considered impracticable, gave to his doctrines a support they could have obtained in no other way.

Confucius has commonly been considered an advocate of feudalism; many scholars have believed that he was seeking to restore the feudal institutions of early Chou times. This belief seems to be principally associated with a speech made by a scholar who is presumed to be a Confucian, 266 years after Confucius died, blaming the Ch'in Emperor for not having given fiefs to his relatives and meritorious subjects. But this scholar was far from the teachings of Confucius when he advocated giving men governmental office merely because they belonged to a noble family. In fact, in all of those portions of the *Analects* that critical scholarship considers genuine, there is no advocacy of feudalism.[4] On the other hand, Confucius never directly denounced feudalism. But he wished to make, in the practice of government, changes so sweeping that what was left would have had little resemblance to a feudal order.

It is easy to know what sort of governments Plato and Aristotle advocated. We have only to turn to the *Republic*, the *Laws*, and the *Politics*, where they tell us in their own words. For Confucius we have no such documents, but only assorted scraps in the *Analects*. If he ever drew, for his disciples, a picture of his ideal state, it has not survived. We are compelled, therefore, to piece the scraps together and make a picture as best we can.

Since his own world was far from ideal, it is natural that he thought of the best state as one that had those things in which his own was conspicuously lacking; in which, that is, the whole people should enjoy peace, security, and plenty. When we speak of peace, it is not to be supposed that Confucius was a pacifist; clearly he was not. But needless war was against his principles, and since most of the war in his day was internecine and an aspect of the general lawlessness, the governmental reforms he advocated would, if successful, have automatically eliminated it.

"Tzŭ-kung asked about government. The Master replied, 'An effective government must have sufficient food, sufficient weapons, and the confidence of the common people.' 'Suppose,' Tzŭ-kung said, 'that one of these three had to be dispensed with; which should it be?' The Master said, 'Weapons.' 'And what if one of the remaining two must be let go?' 'Then,' replied the Master, 'let the food go. For, from of old, death has been the lot of all men; but if the people have no confidence in the government, the state cannot stand.'"

This last statement is extremely important. It does not mean that a government should starve its people to death in order to maintain itself; that would be absurd and very un-Confucian. What it does mean is that rulers should not drive and exploit their people unmercifully for the sake of economic gain, while giving the excuse that it is "for the people's own good" although they are too stupid to realize it. Even more important, it is an assertion that a state is a cooperative enterprise in which all, rulers and ruled alike, must share in the understanding of its purposes and the enjoyment of its benefits.

To us this seems commonplace and obvious. In Confucius' day, however, this was by no means the case, as history abundantly shows. In his time, the hereditary aristocrats rarely stated their creed; it was only after the "subversive" doctrines of Confucianism put them on the defensive that they were compelled to develop an articulate philosophy. In the third century B.C. we find Han Fei Tzŭ, a scion of the ruling house of the state of Han, eloquently denouncing the idea that rulers and subjects have basically identical interests. It is foolish, he declares, to liken a ruler to a father. A father wishes to protect his son, but a ruler "in time of war makes his people die, and in peace exhausts their strength." The people are stupid; their good will need not be striven for. The intelligent ruler has no need of benevolence and justice, which in truth lead to disorder; he will do far more good by keeping himself rich and powerful, for it is the nature of all subjects to wish to kill their rulers and supplant them. Therefore the ruler should trust no one but keep a stern watch on all; even his principal ministers should not be given too much power but made to stand in awe of their sovereign. Only in this way, Han Fei Tzǔ held, could there be brought about the order and good government necessary for the welfare of the people.

It was a good theory, in support of which much evidence could be cited. But Confucius thought otherwise. He refused to accept as inevitable a condition in which every man's hand was against every other's; on the contrary, he thought of men as related in one great family, so that "within the four seas, all men are brothers." There is order and even discipline within a family, but the controlling motivation is not fear but a positive desire to cooperate in carrying out shared purposes. So it should be in government.

"The Master said, 'If one tries to guide the people by means of rules, and keep order by means of punishments, the people will merely seek to avoid the penalties without having any sense of moral obligation. But if one leads them with virtue [both by precept and by example], and depends upon *li* to maintain order, the people will then feel their moral obligation and correct themselves.' " Here is the essence of Confucius' political philosophy. Not negative punishment but positive example; not tirades about what the people should not do but education as to what they should do. Not a police state dominated by fear but a cooperative commonwealth in which there is mutual understanding and good will between the rulers and the ruled. On this point he agreed with the most modern democratic theory. "A democratic society," writes A. D. Lindsay, "stands or falls with the mutual understanding which each has of the purposes of others besides himself."

Every political philosophy reflects, to some extent, the political circumstances of its author. Ancient Greece had a good deal of experience with democracies, not always fortunate; for this reason both Plato and Aristotle, while in some respects democratically inclined, had grave reservations about "pure" democracy. In ancient China on the other hand no one, including Confucius, had ever dreamed of the possibility of political democracy as we know it. Since the people had never had power, they could hardly be blamed for the ills of the government. Consequently we find Confucius consistently taking the side of the people and blaming their exploiters, the hereditary aristocrats, for all that was wrong. If their rulers were only good and capable, he declares repeatedly, the people would act as they should without any need for drastic punishments. In similar vein his disciple, Tsêng Shên, tells one who has been appointed to a judicial post that when he discovers evidence that a commoner is guilty of a crime he should not rejoice but feel sorrow and pity, since such things result from the fact that the rulers have "long forsaken the Way."

Plato is classed as a philosopher; Confucius is often called a religious teacher. Yet whereas Plato once observed that "human affairs are hardly worth considering in earnest" (as compared with the service of the gods), Confucius was intensely and almost exclusively concerned with the life of men, here and now. "Fan Ch'ih asked about virtue. The Master said, 'It is to love men.' He asked about knowledge. The Master said, 'It is to know men.'" Since the great majority of men, who composed the common people, were severely oppressed, it was his principal desire to reform the government so as to contribute to their well-being. He reserved his highest praise for rulers who treated the people well.

He was no stranger to the doctrine that all other reforms are of little avail while the people are left in dire poverty. When asked what was the first thing to be done for the masses he replied, "Enrich them." Toward great wealth and those who possessed it he was disdainful and even hostile. He blamed his disciples for amassing fortunes, either for themselves or for others. "A gentleman," he said, "helps those in want, but does not make the rich still richer." We have already seen that when the disciple Jan Ch'iu tightened the screws of taxation to heap up still more treasure for the Chi family Confucius disowned him.

Many political theorists have argued that a rich man should have somewhat more influence in the government than a poor man. Confucius, however, had no such idea. In ancient China, trade was slight; the principal way of becoming rich was by being a ruler and levying taxes. To become very rich, one must tax excessively. Thus Confucius quite naturally considered the very wealthy to be oppressors. He was not a communist; he believed that rulers were entitled to live, not in riotous luxury, but in a manner befitting their station if they did their jobs. If they governed in the interests of the people, no one would begrudge them this. But if not, they were leeches. "The Master said . . . 'If a state is governed according to the Way, poverty and obscurity are things to be ashamed of; if it is not, then it is shameful to have wealth and rank.'"

Once the people's poverty has been relieved, Confucius said, they should then be educated. We have already seen that he advocated at least some education for all the people. He once declared that if any man, no matter how humble, came to him seeking truth he was prepared to spend all the time that was necessary in helping him solve his problem. He boasted that he had never turned away a student, and in fact he seems to have accepted them, for training in the art of government, without regard to qualifications of birth or wealth, if only they were intelligent and industrious.

In thus advocating some education for all, and undertaking to make educated "gentlemen" out of ambitious commoners, Confucius was striking a blow that was ultimately fatal to the hereditary aristocratic order. It is hard for us, who take universal education for granted, to realize how revolutionary this was. Writing of Western Europe, C. Delisle Burns says that "the spread of education hardly began before about 1850. In former centuries it was regarded as useful only for the ruling classes. . . ." It is true that Confucius trained his students to serve in the government, but he accepted for such training poor men of relatively humble origin; this was subversive of the *status quo*.[5] This point was appreciated by an English clergyman, the Reverend J. Twist, who in 1822 wrote a pamphlet on *The Policy of Educating the Poor* in which he warned that "the possessing of those classes with the absurd notion that they are on a footing with their superiors, in respect of their rights of mental improvement, may be in effect as dangerous to the public peace as the projects of certain revolutionary maniacs who teach the people that the convenience of man, and not the will of God, has consigned them to labour and privation."

The revolutionary nature of his educational doctrines seems not to have been appreciated in Confucius' own day, or perhaps they were considered too visionary to have any practical effect. Only after the virus of knowledge had spread considerably do we find its dangers condemned. The author of the Taoist work, *Lao Tzŭ* (which most scholars today believe to have been written considerably later than the time of Confucius),[6] declared that "the reason the people are hard to govern is because they know too much." The Legalist Han Fei Tzŭ asserted that entirely too much time that ought to go into economic production was being wasted, in his day, on study, due to the pernicious example of Confucius and others. To correct this abuse he recommended that literature be abolished.

The fact that no one, apparently, became thus alarmed in Confucius' own day speaks well for his tactics as a reformer. He never, like Mencius, flatly declared that oppressive rulers ought to be put to death, or that there was no inherent difference between a peasant and an emperor. If he had, it is very probable that his whole campaign would have been stopped before it was well started. By being somewhat more tactful, he laid the foundation on which it was possible for Mencius to be blunt with impunity, a century later. This seems to have been a matter of definite policy. He once observed that when one finds himself living under a corrupt government he should be prepared to act boldly when the opportunity presents itself, but in his speech (which cannot of itself right conditions) he should be somewhat cautious.

Yet he was not always cautious, and in any case he seems to have made no effort to conceal his conviction that human beings, as such, are of great and essentially equal worth. He once praised his disciple Tzŭ-lu as one who, "dressed in a tattered hemp-quilted robe, can take his place beside those wearing fine furs, without feeling the slightest embarrassment." Mencius quotes Confucius as having said that if he were not right, he would fear to contend even with the humblest man, "but if, upon examining my heart, I find that I am right, I will go forward against thousands and tens of thousands." Similarly he declared the conscience of a minister to be a higher authority than the command of his ruler. He believed that the important differences between men were moral. While few men were great, almost any man might be. True worth had nothing to do with birth, wealth, or position. It depended upon one's conduct, that is, upon one's self.

Confucius would not have agreed with the statement of the Declaration of Independence, that "all men are created equal." But he would have agreed with the French Declaration of the Rights of Men and of Citizens, of 1789, that men are "equal in respect of their rights." We have seen that he said of one of his disciples that he might properly occupy a throne, even though this disciple was not the son of a ruler, and seems to have been under the cloud of some hereditary blight. But this did not matter, for he was virtuous and capable. We have also noted Confucius' insistence that all men have an equal right to education, limited only by the intelligence and industry of each individual. This was of fundamental importance. For since he believed that governmental office should be apportioned strictly on the basis of virtue and capacity, equality in education meant almost unlimited equality of opportunity to rise in the social and political scale.

Clearly, Confucius was on the side of the people. We never find him speaking disdainfully, like Cicero, of "the ignorant mob." Nevertheless Confucius did consider the people ignorant, as indeed they were, and he never for a moment suggested putting the government into the hands of the masses. He had no more faith in the correctness of the judgment of the multitude than in that of a hereditary aristocrat; he thought they were all in need of education. He once said that "the common people may be caused to follow the proper course of action, but not to understand it." But against this somewhat pessimistic statement we must place another in which he advocated teaching the Way to the man on the street as a means of facilitating government.

In one respect, indeed, Confucius took the common sense of the ordinary man as his standard. We saw in the previous chapter that he had no fixed authority for truth. Neither does science. Yet it would be absurd to say that, for science, all men are equal; this would be to say that anyone could safely be set to supervise a chemical laboratory or a hospital. For science, only the properly educated man is competent, but any normal and intelligent man is capable of such education. The same thing was true for Confucius. He undertook to take any intelligent student, of whatever background, and educate him to the point where he should be capable of making his own moral judgments. But he did not depend, to secure acceptance for his views, on any divine revelation or any claim of special authority for himself. Like the scientist, he believed that he could convince men through an appeal to their reason. This seems to be the sense of a somewhat obscure passage in the *Analects* in which he declares that the common people are the standard by which the justice of his actions may be tested.

Confucius conceived the highest political good to be the *happiness* of the people. This is of the utmost importance and is quite different from aiming merely at their welfare. Most tyrants have probably claimed, and even sincerely believed, that they ruled with omniscient benevolence for the welfare of the people. The totalitarian ruler of the third century B.C., the First Emperor of Ch'in, caused countless thousands to be driven literally to death at forced labor, building great palaces and vast public works, yet he assures us, in a personal statement, that he was "saintliness personified . . . toiling unremittingly at government . . . so that all should benefit by his sacred benevolence." But very often, as the Legalist Han Fei Tzŭ pointed out, the people are too stupid to appreciate the benefits conferred upon them by such rulers.

The claim that a government brings about the welfare of the people may mean anything. But happiness is something else. "The Duke of Shê asked about government. The Master said, 'When there is good government, those who are near are made happy and those who are distant come.' " Another time he said that when the people of other states heard of a really good government they would be so eager to live under it that they would "come carrying their children on their backs." The important point about such statements is that they make the common people, and nobody else, the judges of what is good and what is bad government. Men can be forced to be orderly and to be productive, but they cannot be forced to be happy any more than a horse can be made to drink. They can be made happy only by a government that is good by their own standards.

We must ask a further question. When Confucius spoke of the common people, did he mean *all* men who were not aristocrats? From our point of view, Greek democracy was gravely marred by the existence of a large class of slaves. Both Plato and Aristotle seem to have accepted, however reluctantly, a situation in which some men were merely the "instruments" of others. It is important for our inquiry to consider whether Confucius did so.

There seems to be no mention, in any genuine statement by Confucius, either of slaves or of slavery. This would appear to mean either that he found slavery wholly acceptable, requiring no comment, or that slaves were so few in number in his day that the institution of slavery was relatively unimportant. It seems clear that the latter is the correct explanation. We have evidence that there were slaves before and during Confucius' time, but it is slight and sporadic. C. Martin Wilbur, in his study of *Slavery in China During the Former Han Dynasty*, says that the indications are that before Han times there was only a "weak and under-developed system" of slavery in China. He estimates that in Han times slaves made up no more than one per cent of the population, while previously they had probably been even fewer.

It cannot be assumed, however, that the rest of the population was wholly free. There are many indications that the people in general were in a condition very much like serfdom. We have seen that there was almost no check on the control of powerful rulers over their subjects; and if we may believe the *Tso Chuan* and the *Discourses of the States*, they often supervised many aspects of their lives very closely. It appears that in some cases, at least, even high ministers did not own the houses they occupied at the capital but might be moved about at the ruler's will; the common people were told where they might live and what work they must do and punished if they did not comply. Undoubtedly these later works elaborated on the facts and represented that there had been more plan and precision to the supervision of the people than was in fact the case. Nevertheless it seems fairly clear that when, in late Chou times, the Legalists advocated strict regimentation of the people, it was they (who have been considered innovators) and not the Confucians who were in fact calling for something like a "return to the ways of antiquity." And it was against such compulsory regulation and in favor of greater freedom that Confucius waged his fight.

We have now seen what Confucius wanted. In place of arbitrary rule by hereditary aristocrats, he believed that the most virtuous and capable should rule in the interests of the whole people. Instead of a predatory world in which the powerful lived by exploiting the weak, he wished to see a cooperative society in which each contributed what he could do best, for the sake of all. A beautiful ideal; but how was it to be realized?

In a recently published book Kuo Mo-jo, a brilliant Chinese scholar of decidedly leftist tendencies, has depicted Confucius not merely as a champion of the people but as a fomenter of armed revolution. His evidence for the latter point is decidedly weak, however, and it seems clear that in his enthusiasm to clear Confucius of the ancient and erroneous charge that he was a tool of the "vested interests" of his day, Kuo has gone to the opposite extreme.[7] It is quite true, as we have seen, that Confucius was twice tempted to join the party of men who were revolting against their superiors, but even if he had done so and they had succeeded, this would merely have replaced one set of hereditary aristocrats with another. True revolution, in the sense of a forcible and thorough-going change in the form of government, was hardly possible in his day. Revolts by aristocrats were common. Sometimes the common people turned and struck out blindly against their oppressors, but such riots were never even intended to change the form of government. The people would not have known how to rule; they did not even suppose that they had the right or the ability to rule. It was only after centuries of Confucian education that men of plebeian birth came to sit on thrones. For Confucius to seek to implement his ideals by armed force would have been both impracticable, and repugnant to his nature.

Nor could he, of course, have used the vote. Not only was there a complete absence of the necessary education among the people; even more important, no one in ancient China seems ever to have thought or heard of the technique of voting, although it was well known in ancient Greece. It was clear that Confucius would have to work through the hereditary aristocrats who occupied the thrones. It is equally clear, as we have seen, that he had no liking for the hereditary principle, but he had no choice.

It has often been supposed that Confucius was seeking to restore the power of the nominally reigning Chou king, but there is little evidence for this. In the *Analects* he never so much as mentions the reigning king. The Chou kings had long been puppets, lacking alike in political power and force of character; during Confucius' lifetime a long and sometimes bloody struggle went on between several pretenders to the throne. Confucius indicated his view sufficiently by observing that China "has no ruler." To attempt to restore the incompetent Chou line to power would have done no good to anyone, and Confucius had no such idea. On the contrary he (like Mencius later) thought rather of building up a new central authority to take its place; this is undoubtedly what he meant when he said he hoped to make a "Chou in the east." He believed that if one state were governed really well, the people of the whole country would be so powerfully attracted that its ruler would soon control all of China.

For this undertaking he would have liked to find a truly virtuous and enlightened ruler. Although Confucius never stated the doctrine of the right of revolution so bluntly as Mencius did, he repeatedly made it clear that in his view mere inheritance did not confer the right to rule, and that any ruler who did not properly perform his functions had no proper title to his place. "The Master said, 'If one is able to correct himself, what difficulty will he find in carrying on government? But if a man cannot govern himself, what has he to do with governing others?' " [8] Since most of the rulers of his time were conspicuously lacking in self-control, such remarks were peculiarly trenchant.

It is unnecessary to list the qualities that Confucius believed a ruler ought to possess; they were precisely the qualities of the ideal Confucian. One is reminded of Plato's words: "Until philosophers are kings, or the kings and princes of this world have the spirit and power of philosophy, and political greatness and wisdom meet in one . . . cities will never have rest from their evils,—no, nor the human race, as I believe . . ." But Plato admitted that this was indeed a very difficult state of affairs to bring about, and Confucius, who spent many years in fruitless journeyings seeking a ruler who would study his philosophy, came to realize that the entire fate of the world could not be left to depend upon so slender a hope. Thus we see him, in a number of sayings, relegating the ruler to the place of one who in fact "reigns but does not rule." "The Master said, 'Was it not Shun who may be said to have done nothing and yet ruled well? What did he do? He merely corrected his person and took his proper position as a ruler.'"

This did not mean, however, that no one in the government did anything. Rather, such a ruler left all of the administration to his ministers, but of course he had to select good ministers. Once when Confucius said that a ruler should "promote the upright" and one of the disciples did not understand, Tzǔ-hsia cited, as an instance, the tradition that "Shun, choosing from the multitude, raised up Kao Yao [who became a virtuous and celebrated minister], whereupon the wicked fled." In the *Analects* Confucius repeatedly emphasizes the importance of selecting and promoting officials purely on the basis of their virtue and ability. Thus, although the celebrated Chinese examination system for choosing officials did not take even its earliest form until some centuries after his death, there is no question that Confucius conceived of its objective and that his statements on this subject must have helped it to become established.

The emphasis in administration was placed, therefore, not on the ruler but on his ministers. Describing the political theory of China before the establishment of the Republic, Paul M. A. Linebarger has written, "In the normal routine, the emperor himself was not to govern; but he selected and supervised his ministers, who did . . ." The fact that this view came to be accepted was probably due, in chief measure, to the influence of Confucius.[9] It was strongly combatted by the Legalist Han Fei Tzǔ, who asserted that no wise ruler would confide power to his ministers. The enlightened ruler will not, Han Fei Tzǔ said, use wise ministers, for they would cheat him; nor will he have pure ministers, for they would be duped by others.

It seems very likely that Confucius' personal experience has influenced this basic aspect of Chinese political theory. If he had found a congenial ruler, ready to use his power to put Confucius' ideas into practice, Confucius might not have been so anxious to distribute that power. He had little success, however, in finding sympathetic ears among the rulers, but much more with those who were or might become ministers. Thus we find him exalting the minister even to the point where he says that it may be less important that the ruler be good than that he have good ministers.

He also assigned the minister a higher position of moral responsibility. For the minister ought to have been educated in the Way, a qualification that could not always be demanded of the hereditary ruler. Thus, while a minister ought to be loyal to his ruler, "can there be loyalty," Confucius asked, "which does not lead to the instruction of its object?" When Tzŭ-lu asked how a prince should be served, "The Master said, 'Do not deceive him, but when necessary withstand him to his face.'" Confucius himself practiced this kind of plain speaking when he told Duke Ting of Lu that if a ruler's policies are bad and yet none of those about him oppose them such spinelessness is enough to ruin a state.

Thus, though a minister should be loyal, he must not be supine, and his ultimate loyalty is due, as we have seen, not to any individual but to the Way. This did not, however, mean that Confucius had no respect for authority. On the contrary, he deplored the political anarchy of his day and condemned those who usurped the powers and privileges of their superiors.[10] From this it has sometimes been supposed that he was making a staunch conservative's defense of the *status quo*. But it has been pointed out that even today "the organs of power in a democratic state are not and cannot well be themselves democratically organized. . . . A hierarchical disciplined organization is much the most efficient way to secure technical efficiency." Confucius would have liked thoroughly to reform the government of his day, but after that was done it would be necessary, he recognized, for those taking part in it to give proper obedience to their proper superiors. "The ruler must be a ruler, the subject a subject, the father a father, and the son a son." [11]

The weak point in this political program is obvious. Ultimately, good government still depended upon the rulers, for they held the power and there was no way of compelling them to choose good ministers if they did not wish to do so. Yet the fact is that there was no way by which Confucius could have compelled them. He had to depend, therefore, on influencing young men who were to be ministers and, when possible, those who were to be rulers, through education, and upon the force of social pressure resulting from an educated public opinion. In his own day, when the movement was in its infancy, these had little efficacy; in the course of the centuries they became, as we shall see, irresistible. For the Confucians happened to be the people chiefly interested in books, and they gradually achieved almost a monopoly of literature and of education. They wrote (and revised for propaganda purposes) most of the histories, and ultimately came to educate most of the princes.

So the emphasis comes back to the Confucian individual and the individual Confucian. Barred from the exercise of political power and the execution of practical reforms, Confucius turned to the production of such men, through education, as the only practicable means of promoting his reforms. The Confucian was first a student and later, in many cases, a teacher; if the circumstances were favorable he became an official of the government. Since, as Confucius insisted, the Confucian gentleman was not a specialist, he was fully equipped, like a seed, to take root in any favorable soil and propagate the movement by whatever means were available.

Confucius believed that such a scholar ought to take office only under a good government, or under one which was prepared to follow his guidance, but that "when the state lacks the Way, he rolls up his principles and keeps them in his bosom." On the basis of such statements some, though by no means all, of later Confucians have found it convenient to suppose that Confucius thought one should not risk his person or his tranquility by taking action in any situation of possible danger. This cannot be reconciled, however, with his statement that "to see what is right and not do it is cowardice," nor with other passages in the *Analects*. In fact, as T'ang Yung-t'ung has pointed out, this Confucian principle is one of refusal to compromise with corruption; for it, Confucians have sometimes laid down their lives.

Plato seems to have expressed Confucius' idea perfectly. In *The Republic* he makes Socrates say that the true philosopher, finding himself in an evil environment, "will not join in the wickedness of his fellows, but neither is he able singly to resist all their fierce natures, and therefore seeing that he would be of no use to the State or to his friends, and reflecting that he would have to throw away his life without doing any good either to himself or others, he holds his peace, and goes his own way . . . he is content, if only he can live his own life and be pure from evil or unrighteousness, and depart in peace and good-will, with bright hopes.

"Yes, [Adeimantus] said, and he will have done a great work before he departs.

"A great work—yes; but not the greatest, unless he find a State suitable for him; for in a State which is suitable to him, he will have a larger growth and be the saviour of his country, as well as of himself." [12]

Since attention was thus focused on the individual, it followed that with regard to government the Confucian emphasis fell on the character of the official and not on the machinery of administration. Hsün Tzŭ said, "I have heard of the way in which one may cultivate his character, but I have not heard how to govern a state." The former, if done well, was complete preparation for the latter. This is an exaggeration, of course, but it is an exaggeration of a tendency that receives too little emphasis in the West. We inquire closely of a candidate for a judgeship whether he has a knowledge of the law but are far less insistent that he possess wisdom, humanity, and breadth of mind. This Confucian attitude is a part of the general Chinese habit, which persists to this day, of dealing with matters in a personal rather than an impersonal manner (in terms of what some sociologists would call "primary contacts"), considering the man more important than the office, the individual more important than the organization. The Legalists, on the other hand, placed almost the whole emphasis on the administrative system and the law; if these were well ordered, the government would almost run itself, in their view. Here we have, in sharp relief, what Aristotle called "the vexed question whether the best law or the best man should rule." In fairness it must be noted that Han Fei Tzŭ (probably the ablest of the Legalists) was not so deluded as to suppose that the government could prosper if the ruler himself were devoid of intelligence and energy, but he did believe that the ruler should hold something like a monopoly on personal force and initiative. It is not always recognized, however, that while Confucius had a rather low opinion of law conceived as a set of rules designed to force men to be good, and believed that government should rely on the creative judgment of good men in office, he did not believe that they should rule by arbitrary whim. On the contrary, he would have them prepared for public trust by a very thorough-going education in the principles of morality and government, and selected for their posts on the basis of their proved assimilation of such education. Nor would he ever have freed them from the dominion, via conscience and public opinion, of the Way. Confucianism has been in a sense anti-legal, but it has never been lawless.[13] In writing of the traditional system of government in China, which has been predominantly a Confucian system, Linebarger says, "The scholars were as much subject to established tradition as the humblest Chinese, and everyone knew the tradition."

Aristotle opined that "the rule of law is preferable to that of any individual." Nevertheless, he said, "customary laws have more weight, and relate to more important matters, than written laws, and a man may be a safer ruler than the written law, but not safer than the customary law." This is close to the thinking of Confucius, but it leaves the guidance of society to custom, which is not wholly ideal.

The Greeks, according to Lindsay, did not "before the time of the Stoics, arrive at the notion of an all-pervading supreme law of nature to which positive laws should be subject. . . . The Greeks had little conception of law as a universal principle guiding the deliberations of a judge who is both declaring and developing law." Such a principle was found, however, in the Roman conception of the *jus gentium*, which seems to have been important in the development of democratic ideas in the West, and which Cicero defined as "the law which natural reason has established among all nations." The Stoic conception of natural law based on human equality performed a parallel function. The similarity of these ideas to the Confucian concepts of the Way and of *i*, "righteousness," is so apparent as to need no discussion.

We are now ready to consider the question of whether, and to what extent, the reforms which Confucius advocated may be said to have been "democratic." The question is not absurd; but our treatment of it would be if we did not at once recognize that what Confucius advocated was not, and could not possibly have been, the same thing that we call democratic government at the present day. The latter is a product of the nineteenth and twentieth centuries, based in considerable measure on recently broadened human experience and on such modern innovations as the sciences, physical and social, and industrialization. Yet precisely because of the vast difference in the circumstances of Confucius on the one hand, and of modern advocates of democracy on the other, any correspondence between their ideas is peculiarly interesting.

In asking whether Confucius was democratic we must also ask, what is democracy? Aristotle wrote long ago that "there is certainly more than one form . . . of democracy," and the problem has not become simpler since his day. So many have written, and written well, on this subject that it is difficult even to summarize their views. Charles E. Merriam has stated "the principal assumptions of democracy" as follows:

   1. The essential dignity of man, the importance of protecting and cultivating his personality on a fraternal rather than a differential principle, and the elimination of special privileges based upon unwarranted or exaggerated emphasis on the human differentials.
   2. Confidence in a constant drive toward the perfectibility of mankind.
   3. The assumption that the gains of commonwealths are essentially mass gains and should be diffused as promptly as possible throughout the community without too great delay or too wide a spread in differentials.

4. The desirability of popular decision in the last analysis on basic questions of social direction and policy and of recognized procedures for the expression of such decisions and their validation in policy.

5. Confidence in the possibility of conscious social change accomplished through the process of consent rather than by the methods of violence.[14]

It is clear that four of these points (all but number 4) are in essential, and in some cases remarkable, agreement with the ideas of Confucius. The remaining point, which in effect has to do with voting, may well seem to be crucial, and it is clear that Confucius never conceived of any way in which the mass of the people could control the government. Yet we have already noted that the idea of voting seems to have been unknown in ancient China. And if, when the French constitution of 1791 was propounded in the middle of the French Revolution, "the rejection of universal suffrage could be defended on the ground that the proletariat was illiterate, and that the function of voting demanded a measure of training and experience," it is not remarkable that Confucius did not propose that the government of China be turned over to the peasantry of 500 B.C.

Any such proposal would in any case have been quixotic and futile. A more important question is whether Confucius believed that, under ideal conditions of education and the like, the mass of the people ought to control the government. This is hard to answer. Perhaps the answer is no. But let us set forth (as Confucius seems never to have done) a coordinated statement of his opinions concerning governmental authority, gathering together what has already been said. He appears to have believed that:

> The proper aim of government is the welfare and happiness of the whole people.
>
> This aim can be achieved only when the state is administered by those most capable of government.
>
> Capacity to govern has no necessary connection with birth, wealth, or position; it depends solely on character and knowledge.

Character and knowledge are produced by proper education.

In order that the best talents may become available, education should be widely diffused.

It follows that the government should be administered by those persons, chosen from the whole population, who prove themselves to have profited most by the proper kind of education.

It is evident that this is not the same thing as saying that the people as a whole should control the government. But it does say that every man should have the opportunity to show whether he is capable of taking part in its control and its administration, and that if he proves himself so capable he should be not only permitted but urged to participate. This is in effect an aristocratic system, of government by an aristocracy not of birth or wealth but of virtue and ability. From the democratic point of view Confucius' system has the defect that there was no machinery by which it could compel the employment of the most capable, but that was an inescapable fact of his historic situation. More important, it provided no very effective way in which the whole people could influence the government. To be sure, the principle that government ought to make the people happy gave them a vague power of veto "in principle," but nothing more.

On the other hand, some staunch believers in democracy have been afraid that we might be moving too far in the direction of "popular" government. It is this sort of fear that caused Immanuel Kant to denounce what he called democracy in the same essay in which he declared that "the civil constitution of every state ought to be republican." Alan F. Hattersley says, in his *Short History of Democracy,* "The participation of the people in the executive and judicial branches of government rests on an extreme interpretation of the doctrine of popular sovereignty. Governmental institutions must be judged by their working in practice, and the theory that everyone has an indefeasible right to share, irrespective of fitness, in the government of the community, has borne fruit in incompetent administration and lack of continuity in policy. Popular election of executive and judicial functionaries ignores the need for special qualities which the general public is manifestly incompetent to estimate."

Other authorities emphasize that democracies cannot dispense with the services of the skilled and the capable in office. A. D. Lindsay states that "in a democratic state those who have power and expert knowledge are to serve the community and be controlled by the ordinary people who have neither power nor knowledge. . . . Democracy is not, properly speaking, government *by* the people." Merriam observes, "Far from crushing out talent, democracy may place the highest premium upon it and strike at all artificial limitations." Arthur N. Holcombe asserts that in fact "modern democracy is a kind of aristocracy," in which "many of the offices, including some of the most important, are distributed according to merit regardless of wealth or popularity." "The further extension of the merit system and in general the better organization of national planning mean the attraction of wiser and abler men into the public service and the development of the power of the whole system of government. This is the essence of true aristocracy." If it is true that Confucius advocated aristocratic government, it was in a sense having much similarity to this one.

The forms and the machinery of government have an importance that ought never to be minimized. Nevertheless, human experience has abundantly proved that these are less important than the spirit and the philosophy which underlie them and in which they are carried out. It has also become clear that any philosophy which looks upon truth as a fixed and absolute entity is likely to tend in the direction of political authoritarianism, while the belief that truth (or at the very least the understanding of truth) is constantly in the process of development or unfolding, and that all men may claim a share in its creation or discovery, tends toward political democracy.

There is good reason for this. If truth is fixed and absolute, and certain members of the community are in possession of it, it is right and indeed benevolent for them to compel the less enlightened to conform to it. But if no one can be absolutely certain what the truth is, and the search for it is a tentative and experimental process, there is scope for the participation of every member of the community in a cooperative (*i.e.*, democratic) effort to determine what the ends and the methods of political life shall be.

The affinity between the modern totalitarian state and philosophical absolutism has often been noted. C. Delisle Burns observes that in the educational systems of dictatorships "what is taught is fixed beforehand as the truth revealed to infallible leaders. . . ." Herman Finer writes that dictatorial systems "are convinced, or at any rate claim, that the final pattern of social perfection has already been revealed to man. . . ." But in democracies, he says, "there is inherent a sense that the pattern of perfect policy has not yet been found, that it is still to be searched for in an ever-developing world . . ."

It is evident that in this debate Confucius stood, not on the side of absolutism, but on that of the continuing search for truth. To be sure, he felt confident that he had a program which would get results; some of our modern proponents of democratic reforms are no less self-assured. But he gave his disciples neither a statement of the truth nor an absolute standard, but training in arriving at the truth for themselves. "The Master said, 'Men can enlarge the Way; but the Way cannot [of itself] enlarge the man.' "

This emphasis on the primacy and worth of the individual as such places Confucius firmly in the democratic camp. Few totalitarians would hesitate over the proposition that the bad should be put to death for the sake of the good, but Confucius refused to accept it. He did not flatly condemn all capital punishment, but he preferred to believe that if the government and education were properly ordered there would be no need for it. Totalitarian theory holds that the individual as such has no rights as against the state, but must wholly subordinate himself to it. "The dictatorial State," says Finer, "removes responsibility from the conscience of the individual Party member and tries to chloroform or hypnotize the mind; in the democratic the conscience of the individual is fully responsible, refreshed by the beating waves of dynamic opinion, and troubled." Confucius said, "If a man does not constantly ask himself 'What is the right thing to do?' I don't know what is to be done about him."

Since a democracy is ideally a community of men who regulate themselves, it is natural that the democratically minded should consider "the state's use of force as its inherent defect and not as its glory." Some have believed, with Thomas Paine, that "the more perfect civilization is, the less occasion has it for government, because the more does it regulate its own affairs and govern itself." There is much evidence that this was the view of Confucius; he once observed, "At deciding lawsuits I am no better than anyone else; but what is necessary is to bring about a state of affairs in which there will be no lawsuits."

Clearly, this would be an ideal condition, and just as certainly it could not be brought about unless men were thoroughly imbued with positive ideals. The greatest problem of democracy vis-à-vis totalitarianism is that in the latter many men work with fanatical zeal to forge the chains that bind their society, while in democracies too many are indifferent toward, and even unconscious of, their freedom. Democracy requires for its continuance, and always has required, some understanding and conviction of the rightness of its principles among all the people, and genuine enthusiasm for its ideals on the part of the many who take the initiative in political activity.

It is the great merit of Confucius that he was able to kindle such enthusiasm. He permitted his followers to keep their consciences and even insisted that they must be surrendered to no one, but he demanded everything else for the service of mankind. Neither wealth, nor worldly honor, nor life itself, might be enjoyed if this were incompatible with the Way. This creed had the zeal of a religion; "If a man hear the Way in the morning, he may die in the evening without regret." Mere intellectual acquiescence in the Way was by no means enough. "Those who merely know it," Confucius said, "are not equal to those who love it; and those who love it are not equal to those who delight in it."

It was not, however, a religion, and this was its strength. Faiths that are tied to particular metaphysical theories, ironclad dogmas, or speculations about the nature of man and the universe, must suffer whenever the growth of human knowledge attacks their foundations. But the lack of absolutism in Confucius' thought and the fact that it stayed close to simple human needs and human sympathies permitted its basic principles to survive through the revolution of a whole galaxy of intellectual systems.

It has been observed that in the Middle Ages "the existence and prestige of the church prevented society from being totalitarian, prevented the omnicompetent state, and preserved liberty . . . by maintaining in society an organization which could stand up against the state." C. Delisle Burns has even suggested that today "there may be a place for something of the nature of a 'religious order,' uniting those who are more enthusiastic in their advocacy or their work for the common good . . . an association for spreading ideas and new habits without compulsion." Confucianism has performed such functions in China.

It has been fortunate, however, in that it has neven been organized. Having no head, no creed, and no organs, it could never be destroyed nor completely controlled. There have been sacrifices to Confucius but they have been functions of the state, not of Confucianism.

We have seen how Confucianism started, as a seemingly spontaneous reaction of the disciples to the personal magnetism of Confucius. He expected them to be true to the Way, but their deference to him personally was never a matter of discipline but, as Mencius said, "a glad and sincere submission of the heart." Since even in government he believed in voluntary cooperation rather than in rules, he did not found an organization, but there is no doubt that he consciously initiated a movement.

This movement was designed to provide a counterpoise to the hereditary and predominantly military aristocracy, which held a monopoly on power and privilege. Like the "chivalrous" knights of medieval Europe, many of these aristocrats considered war a game and valued reckless courage and the killing of men as ends in themselves.[15] Confucius was by no means the only man in ancient China who deplored their emphasis on destructive rather than constructive achievement. The *Discourses of the States* records the indignant speech of an official who told

his overlord that all his years of loyal and distinguished service
in the administration of the state had gone unrecognized but
that now that he had killed men in battle, "because for a single
morning I have become sick with madness you say, 'I must
certainly reward you.'"

Confucius was not a pacifist, and he did not break completely
with the customs or the traditions of the aristocracy. He himself shot with the bow and commended the exercise; scholars
seem to have been archers even as late as the Han period. But
he did seek to change the aristocracy completely, so that it
should be based on merit rather than heredity and dedicated to
service rather than being predatory.

While war might be necessary, he regarded it as definitely
an evil. For military valor he had no regard unless it were en-
listed in the service of the right, and in any case he valued physical far below moral courage. He thought little of feats of
strength and the use of force in general, reserving his praise
for those who benefited mankind.

Inevitably such sentiments drew the scorn of the swashbuckling aristocrats. It seems probable that it was they who first,
in derision, called men who depended on learning rather than
valor by the name of *ju*, "weaklings." [16] Confucius used it in
only one passage in the *Analects*, and it seems to have been
taken up only slowly by the Confucian group itself, although
others used it of them.[17] By the third century B.C., however, they
were using it proudly, and its origin had probably been forgotten.

It was to this band of "weaklings," then, that Confucius
confided his hopes. He did much for them in his own day,
kindling in their hearts a flame that has been handed down in
unbroken line even to ours. He could not take for them the
hereditary places of power, but he subtly appropriated for them
the name "gentleman," which henceforth more commonly
meant a man of learning and gentle bearing than a man of
noble birth. He called them "knights" and demanded of them
(with a surprising degree of success) that spirit of self-sacrifice
and devotion to the common good, for the constructive purposes
of peace, that men usually reserve for the strife of war. As
weapons he gave them pens, and as shields books. He gave them

a mission: to go forth boldly and replace the mighty in the seats of power, governing the world in the name and the interests of humanity.

As he died, the hope for success must have seemed to him a forlorn one.

ЛЛЛЛЛЛЛЛЛЛЛЛЛЛЛЛЛ

CONFUCIANISM

CHAPTER XI

THE "WEAKLINGS"

THE term *Ju,* "weaklings," is commonly translated as "Confucians," and we shall follow that convention. The name of Confucius has only rarely been used in China in connection with his school, and while it is clear that *Ju* was not yet a current term for "Confucian" in the Master's own day, it soon became so.

Confucianism is commonly considered to have triumphed in the second century B.C. But it did not do so without many vicissitudes, and like any veteran of many campaigns it acquired numerous scars; at the end of its three centuries of struggle it was not what it had been at the beginning. Similarly, the conception of Confucius had undergone great modification.

No comparable period in China's history has so decisively influenced its intellectual, social, and political life as did the three centuries after the death of Confucius. It was a time of the most intensive change; almost everything seemed to have broken loose from its old moorings. Men rose and fell in the social scale with dizzying rapidity. Communications were greatly improved and men traveled as never before. Money became current, trade developed on a considerable scale, and private ownership of land gradually replaced the feudal type of tenure. War achieved a

173

new scope and new horror. Politically, the tide of decentralization, near its flood in Confucius' day, reversed itself. At an
increasing pace, weak states were conquered and annexed by
their stronger neighbors. Some of the minor aristocratic families,
which had already usurped the actual power of the rulers of
states, succeeded in taking the thrones as well; once seated they
took care to develop strong administrations that should prevent
others from replacing them. In doing so they found it safer to
employ men of relatively humble origins, trained in the art of
government, rather than to give authority to their relatives
and other powerful aristocrats.

We have seen that even Confucius hoped that he might be
able to set up a new authority to replace the Chou kings, now
miserable puppets, in ruling all of China. It was generally
recognized that a new dynasty was sure to come; the only question was, who could establish it? Almost all of the more powerful heads of states cast covetous eyes on the royal throne and
organized their states and drilled their armies for the great contest.

It might be thought that in such a state of affairs no one
would have time for philosophy. The reverse was true. Philosophers were sought after and courted by rulers as they have
seldom been anywhere. Even the First Emperor of Ch'in, the
totalitarian monarch who ordered books burned and tried to
forbid the study of philosophy among all save his officials, is
reported to have said, after reading two essays by Han Fei Tzǔ,
"Ah, if I could but see this man and get to know him, I could
die without regret."

Such interest among the rulers was not based on purely intellectual grounds. Chinese philosophy has usually stayed fairly
close to human concerns and ethical and political considerations. It was believed (and the philosophers did not discourage
this opinion) that if only a ruler could get hold of the *right*
philosophy it would enable him to control the entire Chinese
world. Both of the two most famous early Confucians, Mencius
and Hsün Tzǔ, stated flatly that a ruler who put into operation
Confucian principles and employed Confucians to administer
his government would be certain to rule all of China. Their

opponents denied this, and made comparable claims for their own philosophies.

It is customary to speak of the philosophic "schools" of Confucianism, Moism, Taoism, and Legalism. This is useful in helping us to distinguish different currents of thought, but it would be misleading, as many scholars have recognized, to think that each of these was a closed and organized group. Before Han times this seems to have been true only of the Moists. Men are not papers, which can be sorted into pigeonholes, and while most individuals no doubt thought of themselves as belonging predominantly to one intellectual tradition or another, in fact each was influenced by all of them. Thus we find a great deal of Taoist and Legalist thinking in what are supposed to be purely Confucian works; conversely, Confucianism influenced the other philosophies profoundly.

The confusion of thought currents was not only due to influences on individuals. Still another type of boring from within seems to have been practiced by the method of inserting foreign passages into books. We have seen, and shall see still more, that there are non-Confucian interpolations in the *Analects*. Hu Shih has pointed out that the first three chapters of the book called *Mo Tzŭ* "have nothing of the Moist spirit"; it would seem, indeed, that they may well be Confucian additions to the text. Such foreign matter is common, even in the principal works of each school. This makes a confusing situation, yet, while difficult, it is not hopeless. There were, after all, certain main principles around which each of these philosophies was organized, and while we may never be able to purge the texts completely, it is by no means impossible to detect additions that flatly contradict the main tenets of the work in which they occur. This is necessary if we are to understand even the outline of the development of ideas during these three hundred years, and we must understand it if we are to trace the development of Confucianism and the metamorphosis of the conception of Confucius.

As we have seen, there were considerable differences not to say quarrels between the disciples even while Confucius was alive. As soon as the Master's authority was removed by death these must have become greatly accentuated. Mencius states that there was an attempt to make Yu Jo a successor to Confucius, but it failed. Han Fei Tzŭ says that the Confucians came to be divided into eight schools, and that "each one insisted that it alone carried on the true Confucian tradition." The *Historical Records* relates that "after the death of Confucius his seventy disciples scattered and traveled about among the feudal lords. The greater among them became teachers [of rulers], or ministers; the lesser were friends and teachers of officials, or went into retirement and were no longer seen." Of four disciples of Tzŭ-hsia it says that they "all became the tutors of kings." Tzŭ-hsia himself was tutor to a ruler of Wei. Mencius tells of two early Confucians who were ministers of states; one of them, Confucius' grandson Tzŭ-ssŭ, was a minister in two states, presumably successively.

This grandson of Confucius is quoted as having told his duke that it was the place of rulers to serve scholars but not to presume to be friends with them. The scholars were beginning the process of turning the tables on the hereditary aristocrats, and "putting them in their places." Mencius said that "those who counsel the great should despise them." Hsün Tzŭ declared that the true gentleman "is the equal of Heaven and earth," and that though a great Confucian might be in the direst poverty yet "kings and dukes cannot vie with him in fame."

Mencius seems to have believed that he ought, if he had his deserts, to be king. But since there was no chance of that he developed a sour-grapes philosophy and asserted that among the things in which the true gentleman takes pleasure "being king of the world has no place." Instead he, and other Confucians, put forward the idea that they belonged to a grandly superior species, which might deign from time to time to assist the rulers by taking office but found it even more pleasant to act merely as free-lance consultants, receiving gifts in return for their advice but accepting no galling responsibilities.

All this was undoubtedly delightful for the Confucians, but why, we are constrained to ask, did the rulers tolerate it? Why did arbitrary despots, who could have had them made into mincemeat for a whim, permit them to preach revolution, accept their deadliest insults, and beg them not to go away? One reason we have already noted; the rulers hoped that they could help them in the struggle for the possession of China. Furthermore, times were changing; in northeastern China at least (where most of the Confucian activity took place) the people were becoming increasingly educated and emancipated. Regardless of the theoretically arbitrary powers of the rulers, they could not safely oppress their subjects beyond a certain point, and the Confucians held a working philosophy of government which was at least philanthrophic if not democratic. There was still another reason, which we considered earlier; the Confucians, and apparently they alone, had a regular discipline for training men for government service. By modern civil-service standards it may have been rudimentary, but it was considerably better than nothing.

Whatever the reasons, the rulers vied with each other to obtain their services or advice. In fact, scholars and philosophers of various complexions were courted and pampered. Mencius is said to have "traveled about followed by several tens of vehicles and several hundred men, living off one feudal lord after another." He was lodged in palaces and supported by large gifts of money from the rulers. King Hsüan of Ch'i (by this time a number of the rulers of states called themselves kings), who reigned 332–314 B.C., was especially noted as a patron of philosophy. A Han author says that he had assembled more than a thousand scholars, and that such men as Mencius "received the salaries of high officials and, without having to undertake the responsibilities of office, deliberated upon affairs of state." The *Historical Records* adds that King Hsüan built lofty mansions for these philosophers and treated them with the highest honors so as to attract others. In the following century the Legalist Han Fei Tzŭ declared that the rulers gave wealth and rank so lavishly to useless scholars that no one wished to perform useful work.

Confucius appears to have been a good judge of character and to have demanded a high standard of quality in his disciples. Yet even his followers included some who were lazy, insincere, and mercenary. It seems obvious that in the centuries after his death the average of intellect and character in the Confucian group as a whole must have declined greatly. Before Confucius, almost the only way to attain high station was by being born to it. But now a man of the humblest origin might hope, through acquiring learning and having a clever tongue in his head, to live in a palace, wear the finest furs, have beautiful concubines and enjoy the most exalted social position. He might become a prime minister, and if he could not be ruler, he could at least have the satisfaction (if he were accomplished enough) of despising and insulting the rulers with impunity.

When by cultivating learning and clever talk one may acquire wealth and honors without toil or danger, "then who," asks Han Fei Tzŭ, "will not take them up?" Who indeed? It is no wonder that, as one work tells us, men traveled by chariot and on foot for hundreds of miles to study with famous teachers.

The result was inevitable. Many of the men who came to call themselves Confucians were devoted scholars of whom the Master would have been proud, but many more were primarily interested in a pleasant and lucrative career. To learn this we need not look only at the books of the enemies of the Confucians; even the Confucian works tell us so. Mencius said that in his day men cultivated character only for the purpose of attaining high position and that once they had achieved success they threw away their principles, as no longer necessary. Hsün Tzŭ, himself a Confucian, made a blistering denunciation of those he called "vulgar Confucians." They made a point, he said, of wearing peculiar hats and clothing; their learning was slight and confused; in dress and action they were "in accord with the fashions of the vulgar"; they "talked about the former kings in order to cheat the stupid and get a living"; they lived as the hangers-on of the rulers' favorites and retainers. The *Records on Ceremonial*, which is one of the Confucian Classics, has one passage that states: "Those whom the multitude today calls 'Confucians' are no genuine Confucians." [1]

The enemies of the Confucians condemned them all, even more severely, but such attacks inspired by obvious malice carry less conviction. It is evident, however, that there were a great many Confucians of whom their more admirable brethren could not be proud. Nor is it likely that these "vulgar Confucians" were a minority; when any profession becomes both easy and profitable it attracts riffraff as carrion draws vultures. How, then, did they make a living? Only a small proportion of them could have had the qualities necessary either for successful teachers or politicians. In the book called *Mo Tzŭ* there is a passage that is certainly from a date later than that of Mo Tzŭ himself,[2] but that is none the less interesting. It says of the Confucian:

> "Greedy as regards food and drink but too lazy to work, he suffers from hunger and cold and is in danger of freezing and starvation. . . . In spring and summer he begs for grain. After the harvest he betakes himself to the funerals. His sons and grandsons go along, and all fill themselves with food and drink. He needs only to manage a few funerals. . . . When he hears that there is a death in a rich family he is overjoyed and says, 'Here is a chance to get clothes and food!' "

This is of course a malicious caricature, yet there is undoubtedly some truth in it. We saw that certain of Confucius' personal disciples paid a great deal of attention to the proper performance of ceremonies and disputed over small points of procedure. In the *Records on Ceremonial*, and particularly in its section called *T'an Kung*, there is a great deal of minute detail as to how funeral and mourning ceremonies should be conducted, contained in statements supposed to have been made by Confucius and his disciples. This ascription is doubtful, but these books certainly reflect the interests of Confucians. Since there were no professional priests in ancient China and the Confucians were versed in ritual, it is reasonable to believe that many of the less able and more needy of them did eke out a living by directing funerals for families able to pay them.

All of this was as far from the intention of Confucius as anything that could be imagined. He specifically warned against attention to the letter of ritual and neglect of its spirit, and denounced those who pretended that their hearts were set on the Way yet were concerned with their personal comfort and prosperity. Nevertheless, we cannot absolve the Master from all blame for the way his flock strayed. It would be unfair, perhaps, to reproach him for the manner in which he insisted that all should be received for instruction. He was merely advocating free access to education. But undoubtedly his statements on this subject made it more difficult for later Confucians to enforce suitable "entrance requirements" for the selection of proper students.

More serious was his mistake in instituting a kind of education that was almost certain never to produce another Confucius. Confucius himself had to struggle as a youth, and this is undoubtedly what made him. He grew up in humble circumstances, and he never lost his sympathy with the great mass of the people. Plato pointed out that the greatness of Darius, the Persian, may be attributed to the fact that he "was not the son of a king, and had not received a luxurious education." This salutary observation was made more than once in ancient China; Mencius said, "Men of virtue and wisdom will generally be found to have lived through trials and hardships." [3] Unfortunately, however, Confucius did not appreciate this point. He dismissed his own early struggles as unimportant and advocated a kind of education that, being concerned almost exclusively with the art and philosophy of government and the life of the court, tended to divorce the student from the life of the people about him. It was an unusual young man who, nurtured in such a curriculum and feeling himself destined for great things, could refrain from becoming a snob. Confucius, being a great humanitarian and a great teacher, could prevent this in his own students, but few who came after him could administer his discipline as the Master did.

It would be wrong and utterly libelous to say that all, or anything like all, of the Confucians were narrow, vain, and self-seeking. Many of them were men of remarkable breadth, scholarship, and selflessness. But such men are never the majority in any large group of human beings. And it limits our understanding of what went on inside Confucianism if we do not recognize (as Mencius and Hsün Tzǔ did) that there were the few great Confucians and the many ordinary Confucians. A great many of the ordinary Confucians had neither the wit nor the energy to write books, and when they did they could produce nothing more exalted than the more pedestrian portions of the *Records on Ceremonial* and the Appendices to the *Book of Changes.* We read these latter works once to ten or a hundred times for the *Mencius* and the *Hsün Tzǔ*,[4] which gives us a precisely reversed perspective on Confucian thinking. For while a single member of the rank and file was not as influential as a single genius, collectively their influence was overwhelming. They created an intellectual environment that perforce affected even the mental giants among them, and they gradually bent the principles of Confucius into something more comprehensible, and more practically useful, to men of limited understanding. Little was actually known about the real Confucius, but they supplied this lack abundantly by creating and embroidering traditions. It is perfectly natural that in doing so they pictured Confucius as being like themselves, or like the persons they admired: powerful, courted, fashionable, sometimes sly. We must now briefly trace the development of the tradition; to do so, we shall also have to consider the schools of thought that opposed Confucianism.

⎍⎍⎍⎍⎍⎍⎍⎍⎍⎍⎍⎍⎍⎍⎍⎍⎍

CHAPTER XII

FROM MAN TO MYTH

Mo Tzŭ was born just after Confucius died. He founded the philosophy known as Moism and the tightly organized group known as the Moists. Both were important for a time but had declined greatly by the Han period and have been virtually extinct ever since. Mo Tzŭ, like Confucius, was sincerely alarmed at the widespread suffering caused by poverty, disorder, and war, and he traveled about preaching his remedies for these conditions. In recent years it has rather frequently been held that the Chinese people are greatly at fault for having preferred the doctrines of Confucius to those of Mo Tzŭ. It is no part of our present task to describe at length, or to pass judgment on, the ideas of Mo Tzŭ; it is pertinent, however, to note that his sayings which have come down to us show serious intellectual shortcomings. He was often correct in his criticisms of the Confucians and others, but his argument against fatalism, that "fate does not exist because no one has ever heard or seen fate," is scarcely worthy of a philosopher. His remedy for war, "when feudal lords love one another there will be no more war," is not impressive. And his practice in getting a young man to become his student by promising to get him a position, but later telling him that he had made the promise merely to trick him into studying for his own good, is ethically dubious.

The book called *Mo Tzŭ* contains some material from later hands and some that is not even Moist, but it seems possible to separate out this foreign matter with some assurance.[1] What remains gives us perhaps our only contemporary picture of Chinese thought in the period just after Confucius. Mo Tzŭ is said to have studied as a Confucian, but later broke away and formed his own group. Emphasizing his independence, he criticized the Confucians bitterly, but it is obvious that much of the broad basis of his doctrines was in fact the Confucianism of his day. Thus we can learn about it both from the points he attacked, and from those he seems to have shared with it.

Mo Tzŭ condemned fatalism, which he asserted to be a Confucian doctrine. We have seen that it would hardly be correct to call Confucius a fatalist, but it is probable that this doctrine gained headway in the Confucian group after his death. Mo Tzŭ also denounced the practice of lavish funerals, which he said would cause "the death of a common man to exhaust the wealth of a family, and that of a feudal lord to empty the treasury of the state." On this point it is clear that Confucius would have agreed with Mo Tzŭ, and one of the latter's remarks may indicate that the Confucians were divided on it in his day.[2] If it is true that "vulgar Confucians" made a living by conducting funerals it is understandable, however, that they would have favored lavish expenditure, and when we come to the time of Hsün Tzŭ we find him defending sumptuous funerals.

From the *Mo Tzŭ* we get the impression that the Confucians of that day were very particular about imitating a certain antique style in their clothing, and in other respects too were slavish imitators of the past. In a ruler's court a Confucian would "speak only when asked for his opinion." We cannot expect that Mo Tzŭ, as the leader of a rival school, would have chosen the best Confucians for his description, but there can be little doubt that the group included only too many men who knew or cared little for the true Confucian principles but were eager to do what would best further their political careers.

One chapter in the *Mo Tzŭ* is entitled *Against the Confucians (Fei Ju)*. It condemns the whole group and includes savage attacks on Confucius; it charges, for instance, that at one period he lived on the proceeds of thefts by his disciples. Some of these stories are accompanied, however, by the most glaring historical inaccuracies, and the chapter as a whole differs from the rest of the book. Undoubtedly, as Mei Yi-pao has stated, it was "written at a much later date" ³ and added to the text. In the genuine chapters, Mo Tzŭ mentions Confucius personally very seldom; in almost the only descriptive passage he classes Confucius with the stupid.

Mo Tzŭ believed that he knew better than anyone else how to rectify the ills of the world, and unlike Confucius he was not willing to leave anything to the free choice or judgment of others. To quote him, "My teachings are sufficient. To forsake my teachings and try to think for one's self is like abandoning the crop and picking up a few grains." No one else, he said, could possibly refute his doctrines. Thus in his school he put his students under stern discipline and demanded lifelong obedience; it has been held that the leader of the Moist group (the office was inherited) exercised the power of life and death over its members. Mo Tzŭ believed that the ills of the world, including poverty, disorganization, and war, could be remedied by strictly authoritarian organization. In each group, every member should "identify himself with the leader," and each leader of a group must in turn identify himself with his superior, until the Son of Heaven is reached. "What the superior thinks to be right, all must think to be right; what the superior thinks to be wrong, all must think to be wrong." Those who fail to comply should be punished. It is interesting to compare this with the statement of Adolf Hitler in *Mein Kampf*: "The principle of the establishment of a whole State constitution must be the authority of every leader to those below and his responsibility upwards."

But how is it to be assured that the supreme leader, the Son of Heaven, has right principles and pure motives? He must in turn identify himself with Heaven. But how can it be known whether he has done so? Very easily, says Mo Tzŭ. If he does not, then "Heaven sends down cold and heat without moderation, together with unseasonable snow, frost, rain, and dew. The five grains do not ripen and the six domestic animals do not mature; there are disease, epidemics, and pestilence. Repeated visitations of hurricanes and floods are the punishments of

Heaven on men below for failing to identify themselves with it."
Sometimes Heaven displayed its displeasure really impressively,
according to Mo Tzŭ, so that "it rained blood for three days,
dragons appeared in the temple," and so forth. Mo Tzŭ bol-
stered his case by citing many instances of such occurrences,
which he claimed to be historical. It is at least plausible that he
did not himself make them up, but drew on a body of lore that
was popularly believed.

To us today this kind of talk sounds ridiculous, and it would
have sounded just about as much so to Confucius. Mo Tzŭ
himself denounced the Confucians for denying the existence of
ghosts and spirits, in which he believed devoutly. Nevertheless,
Mo Tzŭ's idea that natural calamities were the punishment of
Heaven, and denoted a wicked government, occurred in almost
the same (though more elaborate) form in what was called
orthodox Confucianism in the Han dynasty. Why? It is doubtful that Mo Tzŭ directly influenced Confucianism. Rather, it is
probable that both Moism and, in the long run, Confucianism
were influenced by a mass of vulgar superstition that had far
more popular appeal than did the rational philosophy of Confucius.

Confucius has commonly been supposed to have placed great
emphasis on the authority of ancient books and to have pointed
to the example of the "sage-kings of antiquity." We saw, nevertheless, that the *Analects* gives little support to this idea. Mo
Tzŭ, however, constantly cited books and the sage-kings to
prove his assertions. He declared, "All words and all actions
which conform with those of the sage-kings of the three dynasties, Yao, Shun, Yü, T'ang, Wên, and Wu, are to be practiced.
All words and all actions which conform with those of the
wicked kings of the three dynasties . . . are to be shunned." It
is hard to imagine that the Confucius of the *Analects* could
have laid down any such authoritarian yardstick for conduct.
On the other hand, there is no reason to believe that in this
respect Mo Tzŭ was much different from the contemporary
Confucians, from whom he had received his early instruction.

Confucius gave principles for thinking but not a fixed standard for truth; he left the individual responsible for finding his
own truth and free to do so. But men in general do not want in-

tellectual freedom, since it carries with it the necessity for intellectual work. It has been pointed out that even today among us "men in any walk of life whatsoever [including most philosophers] require of their philosophies that they shall be closed systems establishing once and for all the ultimate nature and destiny of man and the universe." Confucius, however, offered men's minds "not peace, but a sword." Is it any wonder that few of his disciples understood him well, or that his corpse was no more than cold before Confucians began erecting snug intellectual havens in which they could find the comforting authority of sacred books and infallible sages?

The legends about the early sage-kings now multiplied rapidly. We saw that in the *Analects* Yao, Shun, and Yü appeared as good kings of antiquity. But (except in the last chapter, which is generally recognized as being late and which we shall discuss below) there is no suggestion in the *Analects* that any of them did not become king in the normal manner, save for Yü. Yü is supposed once to have been a farmer, but this has been the case with more than one obscure scion of a royal house. In the *Analects* it was declared that ministers should be selected from among the whole people on the basis of their virtue, and that in antiquity this had been done.[4] The logical next step was to declare that kings, too, should not inherit their positions but should be selected for their virtue and ability. Confucius undoubtedly believed this, but there seems to be no record that he stated it explicitly. In Mo Tzŭ's generation it was so stated. Moreover, it was declared that in the time of the ancient sage-kings it had been normal for the ruler to choose his heir, from among all the people, on this basis. With this doctrine the scholars turned the tables completely on the hereditary aristocrats, telling them in effect that they were nothing more than usurpers of their thrones, which ought to be occupied by able and virtuous scholars.

Our earliest statement of this doctrine is in the *Mo Tzŭ*. For that reason and others it has been held that Mo Tzŭ originated it, but this is unlikely.[5] Mo Tzŭ himself believed it, but he also quotes a Confucian as saying, "Anciently when the sage-kings assigned rank, they established the most sage as Son of Heaven, and those next in merit as ministers and great officers. Now

Confucius was widely versed in poetry and historical documents, discriminating with regard to *li* and music, and possessed an intimate knowledge of all things. If Confucius had lived under a sage-king, he would surely have been made Son of Heaven!" Mencius later said almost the same thing. It seems fairly clear that the idea that the sage-kings of antiquity had not inherited their thrones, but gained them through their virtue, arose shortly after the death of Confucius [6] and was espoused by both the Confucians and the Moists.

Nevertheless some Confucians regarded it with caution. As propaganda to enhance the prestige of the scholars as a group it was fine, but if the aristocrats took it *too* seriously it could make trouble. Even today some very democratic persons favor a constitutional hereditary monarchy because of its stability. It was realized that if the rulers began looking around for worthy individuals to whom to give their thrones, the result was likely to be that the best talkers would be crowned, and chaos might ensue. Precisely this did happen in the state of Yen, in 314 B.C.

As the legends developed, it was alleged that the sage-kings had abdicated in their old age, in favor of worthy ministers. In Yen it was represented to the ruler that he should offer his state to his prime minister (the suggestion came from a relative of the minister, who was given a bribe). The ruler was assured that the minister would refuse, but in fact he accepted. Three years later there were revolts in which "several tens of thousands lost their lives." [7]

Mencius criticized this action of the ruler of Yen in giving away his state,[8] and declared that only Heaven had the right to give a state to any one other than the heir to its throne. When we inquire what is meant by Heaven's giving the throne to a man, it appears that this may be judged by the people's acceptance of him as their ruler. Hsün Tzŭ believed that in ancient times rank had been assigned according to virtue, and that for this reason the throne had sometimes passed out of the emperor's family after his death; but he denied that the sage-kings had abdicated while they were living. Much later Emperor Wên, whose reign Dubs considers to mark the beginning "of the Confucian influence" in the Han dynasty, took these legends much to heart. In 179 B.C. he issued an edict saying that he ought properly to "seek extensively throughout the empire for a capable, sage and virtuous man, to whom to resign the throne." At any rate, he said, he ought not to make his son his heir. His official advisers, however, demurred. They insisted (successfully) that the stability of the empire would best be served by maintaining the hereditary transmission of the throne.

The position of the Confucians on this point was perfectly understandable. The principle that ministers must be selected for their virtue and ability was necessary to good government. The idea that rulers had in the past been, and even *ought* in the present to be, selected on that basis greatly enhanced the prestige of the scholars and was a most useful psychological curb on the impulses of sovereigns who could, if they liked, be arbitrary despots. But if it had in fact been practiced, it would have made the throne the plaything of the most violent intrigue. Furthermore, a ruler who believed that he had gained his throne because of his wisdom and virtue would have been far more arbitrary and far less amenable to reason than a hereditary ruler who had been properly chastened by a Confucian education. It is no wonder, then, that the wisest Confucians wanted to keep the principle of leaving the throne to the virtuous as a beautifully remote aspect of history.

It was not really history, of course. In ancient China, until we reach a time very close to that of Confucius, it is doubtful that a man of plebeian origin could rise even to become a high official, to say nothing of a ruler.[9] There is a great deal of evidence, on the other hand, that important offices were commonly handed down in noble families.[10] But when the scholars argued that the virtuous had been made rulers in antiquity, they needed to be able to point to historical documents to prove this. The demand, as usual, stimulated supply, and it was not long before historical documents proving this point existed in profusion. One of them, called *The Canon of Yao*, was apparently written (in first draft at least) at some time during the first hundred and fifty years after Confucius died.[11] A little essay on the succession of Yao, Shun, and Yü was also inserted into the *Analects*, as the first section of its last chapter; it does not refer to Confucius at all and has long been recognized to be an extraneous addition to the *Analects*.

It is clear that forged documents were written in China at least as early as the beginning of the Chou dynasty. But the flourishing period of this type of manufacture did not begin, it would seem, until around or shortly after the time of Confucius. By Mencius' day, as we have noted, there were so many dubious works that he said, "It would be better to have no historical documents than to believe all of them." Yet the forgers went busily on, writing back into what was supposed to be history the various things that legend said had happened in the past and the various utopian schemes that they would have liked to see practiced in the future. In the *Book of History*, for instance, only about one fourth of the documents were really composed when they are alleged to have been, while the rest are forgeries. For some other books the case is much worse. Thus ancient Chinese history became a glorious and almost hopeless mélange of fact and fiction, which scientific scholarship has only recently begun to sort out with any great success.

The result for the understanding of Confucius was disastrous. Not only were the facts about his life and thought completely distorted; much worse, his whole historical background was so falsified that it was no longer possible to see him in perspective. It was alleged that in antiquity men had achieved thrones not by inheritance but by virtue. Yet Confucius never clearly stated that this ought to be the case. Taken together, these things make it appear that Confucius believed in the hereditary principle. Yet we know that the fact is that he did not, and that it was a daring step for him to insist that the highest ministers should be appointed for their virtue and ability, regardless of birth.

Mencius was born shortly after 400 B.C., about a century after the death of Confucius. He is said to have studied with disciples of Confucius' grandson, Tzŭ-ssŭ. Of all Confucians whose ideas have come down to us reasonably intact, he is the earliest. The long work called *Mencius* was probably put together by his disciples; it seems to be more reliable than most ancient texts. Mencius, like Confucius, traveled about seeking office, and seems sometimes to have attained it.

Like Confucius he believed that "the people are the most

important element in a state," that their welfare must be the first object of government, and that (in almost these very words) "governments derive their just powers from the consent of the governed." He even advocated that the ruler should se- cure the concurrence of the people before carrying out the death penalty. Government, he declared, should be put into the hands of virtuous and capable Confucian scholars and not in- terfered with by the rulers, who had never studied how to gov- ern. He improved on Confucius in advocating specific economic measures; his words on conservation of natural resources sound very modern. Yet he was wise enough to insist (like both Con- fucius and Kant) that the motive of profit alone cannot be the foundation for the policy of a state.

Mencius agreed with Confucius that an incapable ruler had no legitimate title to the throne. He went further and declared that when a sovereign ceased to bring about the welfare of the people it became a solemn duty to rebel and replace him. His ministers, however, ought to prevent this from happening by correcting his faults. As we have already seen, Mencius claimed for the scholar the place of highest worth and honor. He com- plained about the gifts presented by the rulers to scholars, not that they were not enough but that they were presented in such manner that the scholars had to give thanks for them. Even an emperor, he said, should not presume to summon an eminent scholar to himself, but should go to see him, as had been the practice of "the able and virtuous rulers of antiquity." And a teacher stands in relation to a former pupil, even if the latter is a ruler, in the relation of a father or an elder brother rather than that of a subject. Since most scholars and therefore most tutors of princes were Confucians, this principle was destined to play an important role in gaining power for Confucianism.

Mencius not only asserted such claims for the Confucian scholar, but he seems to have done so with some success since he enjoyed favor at several courts. Reading his persuasive argu- ments we might suppose that the reign of true Confucianism was just around the corner. But Mencius, who was undoubtedly one of the best of the better Confucians of his day, had certain weaknesses that were typical of many in the group.

The fact is that Mencius was a snob. He lived and traveled

in style, but he was deeply envious of the princes who had yet greater luxury. As we have seen, he believed that if justice were done Mencius would be emperor. Since this was impossible, he pretended to despise position and luxury and to care for nothing but virtue, but like a certain lady he protests too much. By a number of statements he betrayed his sympathy with the hereditary nobility. He said, "The practice of government is not difficult; one needs merely not to offend the great families." By gaining favor with these important noble houses one could, Mencius said, "spread his virtuous teachings over the whole world." Although he often claimed to consider that virtue gave the truest title to office, he also said, "The ruler of a state should promote the worthy only if it is unavoidable. For he will thereby cause the low to go above the honorable, and those not related to the ruling house to rank above his relatives. Can he do so otherwise than with caution?"

This is quite inconsistent with some of Mencius' other statements and of course quite at variance with the ideas of Confucius. Yet this kind of inconsistency runs through a great deal of the relatively early Confucian literature, because the Confucians were human beings. On the one hand they were aligned, as a group, with Confucius in his struggle against the hereditary aristocracy. But as individuals, some of them were scions of aristocratic families and all of them were dependent upon the favor of particular aristocrats for office, for eminence, and perhaps even for their daily bread. It is not surprising that their loyalties and their principles sometimes became confused.

Despite this confusion, Mencius was a strict believer in human equality. It might be argued that this was to prove that he was as good as the rulers, but at least it must be admitted that he did not claim to be any better, innately, than anyone else. In fact, Mencius believed that all men are by nature good, and that the great sages of antiquity were simply men who fully developed their innate propensities. Mencius said a great deal on this point and on psychology which psychologists and psychiatrists find interesting even today. His thinking on this subject was original and penetrating; nevertheless it had consequences that were not wholly fortunate.

The doctrine that men are naturally good might spur men to

work harder since it opens the possibility for all to reach the top. On the other hand, it might also curb initiative since after all one has virtue without having to work for it. Mencius certainly said that men should cultivate their characters, but we do not find in him the same stern insistence on the responsibility of each individual for his own destiny that there is in the *Analects*. This is perhaps natural. When a submerged group first starts to combat hereditary privilege, the emphasis is on the fact that some individuals born humble are just as worthy as the aristocrats. But as the ideological battle begins to be won the emphasis shifts to equality, and the individual is submerged. Thus the French philosophers who preceded the French Revolution were individualists, but the slogan of the revolution spoke of equality.

In Mencius there was a relaxation from the struggle that characterized Confucius' thought, not only in the moral but in the intellectual realm as well. Human nature, Mencius believed, was not only good but a sort of microcosm, so that "all things are complete within one's self." From this he deduced that one could gain a knowledge of the universe by the relatively simple method of looking within his own heart. Lorraine Creel has pointed out that Mencius could hold this view because he felt that moral principles were the only aspect of the universe that was of any interest, and that these beliefs caused him to give far less emphasis to the need for study than Confucius did.[12]

Philosophy was young in China, but already men were becoming weary of Confucius' insistence that it is not only the right but the duty of every individual to find the truth for himself, and constantly to correct his understanding in the light of new experience. They wanted an easier way, and of course they found it. Compare the methods for judging character proposed by Confucius and by Mencius. Confucius said:

> "Look closely into a man's aims, observe the means by which he pursues them, and discover what brings him content. How can a man hide his character?"

But Mencius had a simpler way, to wit:

> "Mencius said, 'Of all the parts of a man, there is none more excellent than the pupil of the eye. It cannot conceal

wickedness. If within the breast all is correct, the pupil is bright; if not, it is dull. Listen to a man's words and look at the pupil of his eye; how can a man hide his character?' "

Mencius' recipe has almost the smooth efficiency of a magical formula. We shall see this characteristic appearing in Chinese thought again.

The quest for easier ways meant less study, in so far as study means the search for a personal understanding of truth. But, although this may seem paradoxical, it did not mean less but more emphasis on antiquity and on books that were regarded as scriptures. For if one is not going to find the truth for himself, he must then have convenient books and traditions which supply it ready to use. Thus we find Mencius saying, quite like Mo Tzŭ but quite unlike Confucius, that "there has never yet been one who followed the ways of the former [sage] kings and yet fell into error." Those who wish to be perfect rulers and ministers "need only to imitate Yao and Shun—nothing more." The government of Yao and Shun was not only perfect, but suited to all times and places, so that it is equally wrong, Mencius said, to tax more or to tax less than they did. As for the literature, while Mencius does not seem to have placed such emphasis on its study as Confucius did, he quoted from it a good deal more.

Since in many ways the thought of Mencius was so different from that of Confucius, we might expect that in the *Mencius* we would find Confucius represented as being very different from the Confucius of the *Analects*. On the whole however this is not the case. In fact, the Confucius we see in the *Mencius* is more like the Confucius of the first fifteen chapters of the *Analects* than is the conception presented in much of the last five chapters of the *Analects*, which as we know were compiled later.[13] This speaks well for the accuracy both of the *Analects* and of the *Mencius*. Nevertheless, it would be too much to expect that the traditions concerning Confucius had not altered at all. Mencius believed that Confucius was the greatest man who had ever lived and felt it necessary to explain how it happened that he had not become emperor. It would have been difficult for Mencius to realize the truth, that Confucius had

had no governmental position at all a good deal of the time and that he never achieved a place of real authority. Thus, although he rejected some stories about Confucius as being mere fictions, he seems to have believed that Confucius was in office most of the time, even on his travels, and he stated that Confucius had been minister of crime in Lu. This passage in the *Mencius* seems to be the earliest statement that Confucius held so high an office.[14]

Even though Mencius did not himself misrepresent the thought of Confucius to any considerable degree, the book of *Mencius* has contributed greatly to such misrepresentation. For the *Mencius* is the earliest long, clear, connected discourse on Confucian philosophy that we have, and is much easier to understand than the *Analects*. It is only natural, then, that where the *Analects* is obscure or silent students have (sometimes unconsciously) used the *Mencius* to repair the omission. The fact that Mencius on occasion defended the hereditary aristocracy, and showed some interest in the institutions of feudalism, has lent support to the idea that Confucius was a champion of feudalism. Since Mencius said that men need only to imitate the ancient sage-kings, it has been assumed that Confucius gave the same advice.

When Mencius said that "all things are complete within one's self," he was talking in a way which tends toward mysticism, or at least is very far from the usual common sense of Confucius. He was still farther when he said, "The multitudes follow the Way throughout their lives without understanding it," and when he described life under a sage-king as follows: "His people have an air of deep contentment. Although he slay them they do not resent it; when he does what is to their advantage they do not feel benefited. They daily make progress toward the good, without knowing why. Wherever the true gentleman passes, things are transformed; wherever he abides, his influence is like that of a spirit; it flows upward and downward, together with that of Heaven and Earth." On the other hand, this is extraordinarily similar to passages in some of the Taoist books.[15] If these portions of the *Mencius* are genuine, they would seem to indicate that Mencius had been influenced by Taoist ideas.[16] In any case, it is well recognized that Taoist thinking soon came to influence the whole stream of Confucian thought profoundly.

Taoism is a subject to which justice could be done only in volumes, but here it must be dealt with in a thumbnail sketch. The most important Taoist works are, as is well known, the *Lao Tzŭ* and the *Chuang Tzŭ*. The traditional view has been that the *Lao Tzŭ* (also called the *Tao Tê Ching*) was written by a slightly older contemporary of Confucius, named Lao Tzŭ. More recently evidence has been brought forward to show that Lao Tzŭ is perhaps a legendary character and that the book called *Lao Tzŭ* was written no earlier than about the time of Mencius, if that early. This latter view seems clearly to be correct, and today is probably accepted by most scholars although the subject is still debated.[17] Chuang Tzŭ is believed to have lived at about the same time as Mencius. However, it is improbable that either the book called *Lao Tzŭ* or the *Chuang Tzŭ* is by one man; some scholars believe that they were changed and added to even as late as the Han period. They do not set forth identical philosophies, and indeed there are inconsistencies within the works themselves; nevertheless, they do represent a distinct Taoist type of thought.

Taoism was essentially a reaction against the prevalent modes of thinking. The rulers and their lackeys were intent upon enslaving and exploiting as much of mankind as they could. The Confucians and the Moists, in their different ways, proclaimed men's duty to enlist in the struggle for peace, justice, and humanity toward men. The Taoist said, "A pox on both your houses!" and declared his right as an individual to live an independent life of his own. Men talk about one's duties, but who knows what they are? Men eat steaks, owls eat mice; which is right? And if all things are relative, what happens to the validity of the benevolence and righteousness about which the Confucians talk? "Formerly Chuang Chou [*i.e.*, Chuang Tzŭ] dreamed that he was a butterfly flying about enjoying itself. He did not know that he was Chou. Suddenly he awakened and was himself again. But now he does not know whether he was formerly Chou dreaming he was a butterfly, or is now a butterfly dreaming he is Chou."

This is basically a mystical philosophy. The *Tao*, which for

Confucius was a way of conduct, is for the Taoist the basic principle and stuff of the universe. It was originally formless, desireless, without striving, supremely content and therefore happy. It existed before Heaven and Earth. In the course of the generation of things and institutions, the farther man gets away from this primal state the less good and the less happy he is. Therefore all artificiality is bad. Virtues came into vogue only after virtue had ceased to exist. Study is futile and even dangerous since we may overstrain ourselves. Anyway, "the wise are not learned, and the learned are not wise." "When we renounce learning we have no more troubles." Government, as an artificial institution, is wrong. "Small robbers are put in prison, but great ones become feudal lords." The *Lao Tzŭ* inveighs, in a manner quite like that of the Confucians, against oppressive punishments, excessive taxes, and war. The Taoist sage values contentment, and refuses high office or even the throne itself if it is offered to him.

This aspect of Taoism ends in almost pure individualism. "The true object of the *Tao* is the regulation of one's own person." When a Taoist is asked in the *Chuang Tzŭ* how to govern the world he replies, "Let your mind find its enjoyment in pure simplicity; blend yourself into the ether in idle indifference; accord with the natural order of things; and admit no selfish consideration. Do this and the world will be well governed."

Thus far Taoism is challenging, brilliant, and consistent. This basic core of Taoist philosophy has touched the mind of every Chinese, of whatever school of thought or religion. It is responsible for much of their good-humored scepticism, their tolerance, and their ability to enjoy life regardless of circumstances. Without it, painting and poetry in China would be very different things. It is one of the prime ingredients of Chinese culture.

There is another aspect of Taoism, however, which had less happy consequences, since it led to the endorsement of totalitarianism. It should perhaps be considered an abandonment of "pure" Taoism, but it is found in some parts of even the earliest texts. Since the Taoist sage recognizes his identity with the totality of the universe, insult, injury, even death cannot harm him. Thus he is impregnable and (note the transition) therefore irresistible. Since he cannot be either raised or humbled, he is the highest of all creatures. Being at one with the *Tao* he has its attributes and wields the mighty power of Nature itself. Like Heaven and Earth, he is not benevolent but treats the mass of little men as his playthings, indifferent whether he seem kind or cruel. In fact, the Taoist sage plays God.

Since men ought to return to a state of primitive simplicity it was difficult, at least for some Taoists, to resist the feeling that they should compel them to do so. Thus we find rather surprising statements concerning the manner in which the Taoist may "get control of the world," and how he should rule, restraining the people and making them desireless. "The sage rules," the *Lao Tzŭ* tells us, "by emptying the people's minds and filling their bellies, weakening their wills and strengthening their bones, constantly keeping them in a state without knowledge and without desire." In the *Chuang Tzŭ* we read, "What is harsh, and yet must necessarily be set forth, is the law." Such ideas clearly conflict with the philosophic kernel of Taoist thought, and they may represent perversions of it, but they have been extremely influential.

The *Lao Tzŭ* never refers to Confucius or the Confucians by name, though it clearly attacks their philosophy. The *Chuang Tzŭ* recognizes Confucianism as its chief foe, and discusses Confucius in no less than twenty-one of its thirty-three chapters. In some passages the *Chuang Tzŭ* attacks Confucius directly, accusing him of misdemeanors and ridiculing and reviling him. Usually however it is much more subtle and claims that Confucius came to see the error of his ways and was converted to Taoism. Thus Confucius is repeatedly quoted as talking in a thoroughly Taoist manner and making fun of those who practice Confucianism.

While relatively few scholars believe these stories today, many have believed in the past that Confucius was indeed converted to Taoism, by Lao Tzŭ, late in his life. But these tales have many flaws. It cannot be held that the *Analects* all comes from a period before Confucius' conversion to Taoism is supposed to have taken place, for there is proof to the contrary; [18] nevertheless, the *Analects* gives no hint of such a change. Also, the *Chuang Tzŭ* puts into Confucius' mouth language that was unknown in his day.[19] Finally, the *Chuang Tzŭ* is not consistent with itself on the date of Confucius' conversion. He is said to have been instructed in Taoism, by Lao Tzŭ, as early as his fifty-first year and to have been converted when he was sixty. Yet another passage quotes him, at sixty-nine, as saying that he has never heard the Taoist doctrine; he is converted again. Nevertheless, in another part of the same work Confucius is berated as having been, at seventy-one, an unregenerate Confucian, with no suggestion that he had ever been a Taoist.[20]

No modern man can read these Taoist books, with their dazzling paradoxes and trenchant criticisms, without being profoundly impressed. It is no wonder that they struck the thought world of ancient China with the impact of a thunderbolt. A very large proportion of those who called themselves Confucians were deeply influenced. After all, had not the Master himself been a disciple of Lao Tzŭ, according to *Chuang Tzŭ?* Thus we find that in the latter part of the *Analects,* which was put together relatively late, there is a good deal of Taoist influence even on what Confucius himself is supposed to have said.[21]

This was merely one aspect of a wholesale infiltration of Confucianism by a type of thinking that, if not all Taoist, tended to be associated with Taoism. We have seen that the common run of Confucians found Confucius' formula for arriving at truth—study and hard straight thinking—much too arduous. The *Lao Tzŭ* offered a much easier way. If one achieved the enlightenment of a Taoist sage he could "without going out the door know the whole world, without looking out the window see the way of Heaven. . . . Therefore the sage does not travel yet knows, does not see things yet is able to call them by their right names, does not work and yet achieves." This was most attractive.

Other short cuts to knowledge were being developed. The theory that all things consist of *yin* and *yang,* the negative and positive principles, and that complex natural phenomena could be explained very easily on this basis, grew up around this time.[22] Men also began to be fascinated with numbers, regarding them as a simple key to the mystery of the universe.[23] These principles were applied to the study of the ancient fortuneteller's manual called the *Book of Changes.* Its original text dates from a time earlier than that of Confucius, but there were now added to it ten appendices, called its *Ten Wings*. They date from various periods; all of them seem to be later than the time of Confucius, and some parts of them may be from a time no earlier than the Han dynasty.

In order to give these appendices authority, they were said to have been composed by Confucius. There are really only seven of them, rather than ten, but each of the first three is divided into two parts. They are obviously by different authors, so that they ought to be dealt with individually, but this would prolong our discussion unduly. In general, they comment on and amplify the text; they are more intelligible and more philosophical than the text itself. Both the third and the fourth appendices have, very frequently, the words "The Master said," evidently referring to Confucius; [24] this fact in itself indicates that he was not their author.

That he can scarcely have been is shown by the frequent occurrence in these appendices of terms that are not found in any Chinese literature as early as Confucius, not found in the *Analects*, and not even found in so late a work as the *Mencius*. This is the case with the dualistic concept of *yin* and *yang*, which occurs in all of the appendices except the last two.[25] Similarly the concept of Ti 地, Earth, as the counterpart of Heaven in the metaphysical Heaven-Earth dualism, is unknown to the pre-Confucian literature and does not occur in the *Analects* yet is found as a definitely metaphysical term in all of the appendices but the last two.[26] The absence of these late terms from the last two appendices is doubtless significant, but it has little importance for our present inquiry. These two treatises are extremely brief and utterly superficial; there is no reason to suppose that Confucius would have bothered even to read, much less to write, such trifles.

The bulk of the other appendices is also trivial. Much is absurd, and most of what is not absurd is utterly trite and commonplace. The work is reminiscent of those handbooks of palmistry, phrenology, and occult science that are published at the present day, whose authors, as rich in vocabulary as they are poor in ideas, attempt by employing impressive terms to conceal the fact that they have nothing of the slightest interest to say.

The most convincing evidence that Confucius did not write

these appendices is the fact that they are pervaded by a philosophy that is not only absent from, but even opposed to, that of the *Analects*. The *Analects* says that Confucius did not speak of "strange phenomena" or of spirits. Yet the fourth appendix tells us that "the Master said . . . 'Clouds follow the dragon, and winds follow the tiger,' " and the appendices in general are full of mysterious and metaphysical language. Confucius believed that knowledge is a thing hard won through experience and thinking, but the *Book of Changes* offered a far easier way. One needed only to study this book, with its mystic science of numbers ("the number corresponding to all things is 11,520") and its hexagrams; one who has done so sufficiently "knows everything."

If Confucius had believed that there was so simple and sovereign a way to resolve all doubts, there should be some mention of that fact in the *Analects*. Yet, except for *Analects* 7.16, which has undoubtedly been interpolated,[27] there is none. Furthermore, none of the early sources ever says that Confucius made any use of divination. This is a striking fact, for it was a very common practice. Long before his day, in the Shang period, the guidance of divination was sought constantly, and we know that it was practiced in early Chou times. The *Tso Chuan* and the *Spring and Autumn Annals* make it evident that in Confucius' own lifetime, and in his own state, divination was used regularly, both by individuals and by the government. Likewise the *Book of Changes* tells us that the gentleman always divines before he acts. Yet Confucius, in so far as we know, never had recourse to divination. Nor, apparently, did Mencius.

The fact is that the whole philosophy of divination and the view of the world that is found in most of the appendices to the *Book of Changes* is utterly foreign to the thinking of Confucius and even of the earliest Confucianism. A number of scholars, Chinese, Japanese, and Western, are agreed on this conclusion.[28] In the one passage in the *Analects* in which Confucius refers to divination, he criticizes it.[29] Furthermore, as Fu Ssŭ-nien has noted, "Mencius says not a word about the *Book of Changes*, and while Hsün Tzŭ mentions it in passing . . . he condemns the practice of divination." When Hsün Tzŭ listed

the books that a Confucian should study he made no mention
of the *Book of Changes*.

It would be unreasonable, however, to expect that Confucian
doctrine should have been created exclusively by Confucius and
the great Confucians. Gibbon has well remarked, "A state of
scepticism and suspense may amuse a few inquisitive minds.
But the practice of superstition is so congenial to the multitude
that, if they are forcibly awakened, they still regret the loss of
their pleasing vision." And they take steps to recover it, in
ancient China as in ancient Rome. The great mass of Confucians wanted Taoism, they wanted divination, and they wanted
the blessing of Confucius on these things. In the appendices to
the *Book of Changes* they got all three.

These appendices mix Taoist and Confucian ideas inextricably.[30] Some of them repeatedly quote Confucius, referring to
him with the utmost respect as "the Master." Thus the Master
is made to call the *Book of Changes* perfect and to recommend
it to all. He is also quoted as endorsing its easy road to truth,
and asking, "What need is there of thinking, what need is there
of any anxiety?" These same words appear verbatim in the
Taoist work, *Chuang Tzŭ*; it seems perfectly clear that they
were lifted from that source and put into the mouth of Confucius. Here we have come a long way from the Confucius of the
Analects, who said, "He who has no anxiety about what is
distant will find sorrow close at hand." The *Chuang Tzŭ* fur-
thered this fraud by quoting Confucius as saying that he had
studied the sciences of numerology and *yin* and *yang*. It also
made him say that he had studied the *Book of Changes*. By Han
times Confucius was declared to be the author of all ten appendices; while this view has been challenged from time to time,
some scholars continue to believe even to the present day that
he wrote some or all of them.

Yet one thing was lacking. The *Analects* made no mention
of the *Book of Changes*. That, too, was taken care of. Some
scholars believe that a single character in *Analects* 7.16 was
merely altered to make it appear to refer to the *Book of Changes*;
others think that this whole passage was added to the text.[31]
Analects 7.34 was also altered so as to make it refer to divination, but this changed version of the passage occurs only in a

Taoist work; it did not find a place in the *Analects* as it has
been transmitted.[32] Still another passage was probably added to
the *Analects* under this same influence. In section 9.8 Confucius is quoted as saying, "The phoenix does not come, the river
puts forth no chart; I am finished!" The phoenix is a bird of
good omen, the river chart a fortunetelling device. Neither is
mentioned elsewhere by Confucius, and as Ku Chieh-kang has
pointed out this passage contains the only references to the
supernatural ascribed to Confucius in the *Analects*. Ku rightly
considers it "open to grave suspicion." [33]

The new currents in Chinese thought produced great changes
in the conception of Confucius. These may be traced in a number of books.

The *Tso Chuan* has already been referred to many times.
This is perhaps our most important single source on Chou
dynasty China; it has been a gold mine of both information and
misinformation. The studies of a number of scholars have resulted in dating its composition, on the basis of many different
criteria, as having taken place somewhere in the neighborhood
of 300 B.C.[34] The text as it stands is supposed to be a commentary on the *Spring and Autumn Annals*, but as many scholars
have noted the *Tso Chuan* at many points has nothing to do
with that work. It seems rather to be a composite book, containing material from a number of older documents. Nevertheless, it
does not appear to be merely a collection of miscellaneous
pieces, thrown together without editing. On the contrary, Chang
Hsin-hai seems to be quite correct when he says that "the *Tso
Chuan* is inspired by a dominant motive . . . facts were . . .
selected in order to illuminate the historian's personal conviction. . . ." On the whole the point of view presented is a Confucian one; while scattered passages to the contrary may be cited,
this is not remarkable in so huge a work.

It seems clear on the one hand that the author or authors of
the *Tso Chuan* had authentic historical documents to work with,
and on the other that they did not hesitate to embellish them
in order to prove their points. It is difficult to account, in any
other manner, for the consistent way in which characters in the
Tso Chuan predict the future, time after time, often with un-

erring accuracy.[35] Maspero has pointed out that it includes a prediction, under the date of 629 B.C., that there would take place after 300 years an event which in fact happened in 320; it must clearly have been added to the materials by those who made up the *Tso Chuan*, around 300. Furthermore, this text constantly uses the language of that period. It abounds in references to such phenomena as weird omens, dragons, malignant ghosts, a corpse that revives after six days, a speaking stone, and so forth. It refers frequently to divination by the *Book of Changes* (with uncanny results) and includes a number of references to concepts such as *yin* and *yang*, and the *wu hsing* (usually translated "five elements"), which were in fact unknown at the time of which the *Tso Chuan* speaks, 722–464 B.C.[36] This fact has misled even some modern critical scholars and caused them to believe that these concepts existed early because they are mentioned in conversations, in the *Tso Chuan*, that are alleged to have taken place at an early date.

Nevertheless it is abundantly evident, as was mentioned earlier, that many of the conversations in the *Tso Chuan* are in large measure works of fiction. Purporting to date from a time from which our other records have the spare and terse character of the *Analects*, it records in lengthy detail the language even of secret conspiratorial conferences, and lays bare the motives of men's hearts. It is excellent creative writing; but as history it is comparable rather to Shakespeare's *Julius Caesar* than to Caesar's *Gallic Wars*. Yet it is not always as consistent as Shakespeare, for its primary motive seems to have been neither art nor history but propaganda. Thus each lengthy speech is an opportunity to slip in some Confucian aphorisms. The result is sometimes incongruous. A high officer of Lu is recorded as having made a long and high-sounding address on the unpardonable evil of regicide. This is not necessarily incompatible with the fact that he elsewhere publicly admits that he himself has been guilty of that very crime; but when we note that this long harangue, attributed to 609 B.C., refers constantly to Yao, Shun, and many more characters of late legend, we must regard it with grave suspicion.

King Chuang of the "barbarian" state of Ch'u, who ruled 613–591 B.C., was pleasure loving, tyrannical, and warlike.

When a minister of another state killed its utterly debauched ruler, Chuang attacked that state, appropriated its territory, and had the minister pulled to pieces by chariots.[37] He wanted to take the minister's mother, a famous beauty, to his harem, but when persuaded that this would be impolitic gave her to a subordinate. He continued a career of aggressive war until his latest years. Yet the *Tso Chuan* records speeches that this warrior is supposed to have made in the very middle of his career in which, in quite Confucian terms, he descants upon the necessity of humility and good faith, condemns war, and damns himself as a cruel aggressor.

It seems clear that the author or authors of the *Tso Chuan* saw nothing reprehensible, but quite the reverse, in adding little Confucian homilies to their text wherever they could fit them in. On the other hand they seem to have been conscientious historians to the extent that they did not change the facts as they found them; at least, they did not change them enough to make the speeches they wrote for their characters wholly plausible. There is nothing unusual in this insertion of imagined speeches. Macaulay wrote that "Machiavelli and Guicciardini, in imitation of Livy and Thucydides, composed speeches for their historical personages," and that he feared that the practice still (in 1828) was followed by some European writers.

We will not expect, of course, that the Confucianism of the *Tso Chuan* will be identical with that of Confucius, or that the Confucius it portrays will be wholly historical. It is perfectly natural that we find Confucius, in this text, foretelling the future and showing supernatural knowledge, and studying with a man versed in the lore of dragons and other occult matters. Nor is it surprising that Confucius' genealogy is so traced as to make him a descendant of the Shang kings and rightful heir to the throne of the state of Sung.[38] It is not even very remarkable that the *Tso Chuan* quotes Confucius as reproving those who have the temerity to criticize the wrong-doing of the powerful; [39] by this time there were, among those who called themselves Confucians, many "sensible" men, who well knew that discretion is the better part of valor.

What is surprising is the fact that in this historical work, covering the period of Confucius' lifetime and written under intensely Confucian auspices, there is very little indeed about the life of Confucius. There is no biography nor even the material for one; all it records is a very few scattered incidents, of which some are quite evidently not based on fact. The one instance it cites in which Confucius is supposed to have played an important political role is a long and involved anecdote that is so absurd that a committee of Chinese scholars, which edited the *Tso Chuan* under imperial auspices in the eighteenth century, omitted it, quoting the opinions of many previous critics, as a falsification by "vulgar Confucians."

The two other early commentaries to the *Spring and Autumn Annals*, called the *Kung-Yang Chuan* and the *Ku-Liang Chuan*, tell almost nothing about Confucius' life, although both are Confucian works. Even stranger is the case of the *Discourses of the States* (*Kuo Yü*). This work, which Karlgren's researches indicate may have been written around the same time as the *Tso Chuan*,[40] includes two chapters on the history of the state of Lu. Here we should certainly expect to find the story of Confucius' life. But it has nothing of the sort. It merely relates a number of incidents in which Confucius is consulted as a wise man, commonly on supernatural matters; he gives answers that frequently refer to spirits and omens. But nowhere is it suggested that Confucius held any office. Clearly, when Confucius had been dead for around two centuries the facts about his life were very little known, and the rich development of legend that later came to fill the gaps had only begun.

This situation could not last. Very soon imagination supplied whatever history left blank. A rich harvest of its productions was gathered into the work called the *Discourses of the Confucian School* (*K'ung Tzǔ Chia Yü*). Scholars debate its date; Waley believes that it "represents the Confucian legend as it developed during the 3rd century B.C.," while others are equally assured that it is a forgery of the third century A.D.[41] It seems to be beyond question that the work we now have is not identical with the ancient book of that name, but it has been suggested that the ancient book was merely somewhat changed and added to. In any case, we cannot hope to find in this book information about Confucius that is certainly true. Even if some of its incidents are genuine (and some may be) they are intermixed with a welter of complete absurdities which discredits the whole. Confucius repeatedly reads omens and foretells the future; in fact, this work quotes one of the disciples as saying that "there is nothing that the Master does not know."

This book, and others that similarly report late and fanciful stories about him, have unfortunately had more influence upon the generally accepted picture of Confucius than has the *Analects*. We have seen that Hsün Tzŭ complained that in his day too many of the Confucians were mere lackeys and hangers-on of the aristocrats; the *Discourses of the Confucian School* duly reflects their snobbishness, putting into Confucius' mouth approval of strong class distinctions. It also depicts him as having engineered an extensive program of intrigue, plunging a large part of eastern China into sanguinary war, in order to avert a single attack on the state of Lu; historical anachronism, if nothing else, proves this false. It makes Confucius approve of "cheating barbarians" and recommend capital punishment for a number of crimes including "inventing strange clothing"; in both respects it directly contradicts the *Analects*. There is much more of this sort, but it would be tedious to catalogue it.

To what extent the falsehoods of the *Discourses* concerning Confucius may be malicious is uncertain. There is no doubt, however, that the work was written under strong Taoist influence. It relates that Confucius collected books on divination and divined using the *Book of Changes*. At least once it puts a paraphrase from the *Lao Tzŭ* into the mouth of Confucius.[42] It relates, as do some other late works, that Confucius sought out Lao Tzŭ in order to study with him. It makes Confucius call Lao Tzŭ "my teacher" before he has ever seen him, and dates Confucius' great popularity as having started only after he was enlightened by the Taoist sage. After carefully checking this story of an interview between Confucius and Lao Tzŭ, one can only agree with Chavannes that it is "an invention of the Taoists who . . . give the freest play to imagination and make no pretense of accuracy . . ."

There are a number of other books containing anecdotes about Confucius which (although some of them pretend to be very old) critical scholarship now dates as having been composed in the third century B.C. or later. It is impossible for us to survey all of these stories; what has been said of the *Discourses of the Confucian School* will apply, broadly speaking, to most of the anecdotes about Confucius in these works. In any case, they cannot be used with any assurance by one who seeks to know Confucius as he really was.

The last of the great Confucians of the early period was Hsün Tzŭ. The dates of his birth and death are uncertain, but it seems clear that he was alive during all of the first half of the third century B.C. Hsün Tzŭ was born in the northern state of Chao. He traveled to Ch'i, where he had an official post. Later he went to the great southern state of Ch'u and held office there. In addition, he visited the state of Ch'in. Therefore it seems probable that Hsün Tzŭ's experience was more wide and varied than that of either Confucius or Mencius. This fact was reflected in his thinking.

Hsün Tzŭ had one of the world's great minds. Much of his thinking was of the sort that, being admirable, we like in our temporal provincialism to call modern. There is more of incisive analysis and profound wisdom in his single chapter on *The Correct Use of Terminology* than in the collected works of some philosophers. Much of his thinking was a logical development of the high intellectual tradition of Confucianism to a new plane of clarity. Although (for reasons we shall soon consider) he did not enjoy great favor among later Confucians, much that is best in later Confucianism was given its definitive stamp by Hsün Tzŭ. He greatly developed the theory of the role of *li* in education, which Confucius had merely suggested; in fact a large portion of the highly influential classic, the *Records on Cere- monial*, was copied verbatim from the book called *Hsün Tzŭ*. He was forthright in his condemnation of the flourishing superstitions of his day. He interpreted Heaven as being the order of nature, and declared that rather than fearing omens and ghosts men should fear bad government and disorder. To those who asked why prayers for rain were followed by rain, he answered that it would have rained whether the prayers were made or not.

In some respects Hsün Tzŭ's thinking marks the high point of early Confucianism. But the Chinese have a proverb that says that the moment of greatest success is also the moment in which decline begins. There is no question that in some respects Hsün Tzŭ turned Confucianism in directions which Confucius would have deplored. The fundamental reason would seem to be that Hsün Tzŭ had little faith in humanity. The essence of Confucius' thought was the belief in the possibility of a cooperative world in which men should work together in mutual understanding and confidence, not merely herded like sheep but having some part in choosing their own ends. Hsün Tzŭ believed, however, that they must be firmly directed into the way in which they should go.

Mencius, in his almost sentimental insistence upon the goodness of human nature, went beyond anything that Confucius had said. It may be because Hsün Tzŭ had wider experience of different cultural environments that he insisted that men's natures could not be depended upon to make them good. He had seen that in differing environments the same kind of men came to be very different; for this reason he emphasized the predominant role of nurture.[43] He went further and declared that "the nature of man is evil; his goodness is only acquired training." We have seen that Mo Tzŭ preached authoritarianism. Hsün Tzŭ's idea that unless properly taught men would invariably be "selfish, vicious, and unrighteous" moved him in the same direction.

If men of themselves are evil, something must be added to them from outside to make them good. "Therefore," Hsün Tzŭ tells us, "the former [sage] kings invented for them *li* and righteousness." For Hsün Tzŭ wisdom and morality were a fixed body of truth, which one might learn, but to which one could contribute nothing. Indeed, he could not even learn without having a qualified teacher, and with such a teacher he must never dare to differ. "Not to consider right the rules laid down by one's teacher, but to prefer one's own ways, is as if a blind man were to try to distinguish colors, or a deaf man to distinguish sounds; there is no way to avoid confusion and error."

The only way to escape from one's natural depravity was to study, and Hsün Tzŭ strongly emphasized the importance of study. But for Hsün Tzŭ study did not constitute, as for Confucius, a process of "hearing and seeing much," and interpreting it for one's self in the light of one's own experience and understanding.[44] Rather, he believed that it must be confined to the intensive study of a precisely delimited body of subject matter. In this he may have been influenced by Taoism. Unlike many Confucians, Hsün Tzŭ was not bemused by Taoism. His forthright rejection of superstition and mysticism opposed its grosser aspects, and he criticized both Lao Tzŭ and Chuang Tzŭ by name.[45] Nevertheless, Taoist ideas were so generally current in his day that he could hardly avoid being affected by them.

Confucius, as we saw, was an exceedingly hard taskmaster to his students, demanding the unceasing search for truth. The Taoists ridiculed this, declaring that such exertion was both useless and dangerous. Such a position has great appeal to men's natural desire for moderation, not to say laziness. The *Chuang Tzŭ* says, "Our life has a limit, but knowledge has no limit. To use the limited to seek the unlimited is indeed dangerous." In different words, Hsün Tzŭ made exactly the same point. Thus he denounced all kinds of study and investigation except that which pertained to what he regarded as the true tradition, and he specifically prescribed the study of a set list of Classics. Study, he said, "begins with reciting the Classics and ends with learning *li*." As Dubs has well said, "Hsüntzŭ developed Confucianism into an authoritarian system, in which all truth was to be derived from the sayings of the Sages."

This authoritarianism did not stop with the intellectual sphere. Since he believed that the sage-kings of the past had invented *li* and righteousness to control the people, it was perfectly logical for Hsün Tzŭ to deplore heretical ideas and to declare that the wise king of the present ought to "deal with the people with authority, guide them in the Way . . . and restrain them by punishments." Fung Yu-lan has suggested with reason that such thinking by Hsün Tzŭ may be blamed, in part, for the slightly later development of thought control under Legalist totalitarianism.

Whereas Mencius had said that all men alike were by nature good, Hsün Tzŭ said that all were by nature evil; in both cases, all men were put on the same level. Hsün Tzŭ seems to have gone further than Mencius in asserting that men should be given positions on the ground of ability rather than of heredity. Yet whatever their basis, Hsün Tzŭ believed strongly in class distinctions, which he declared to be necessary to good order. And whereas Confucius had wanted to "enrich the people," Hsün Tzŭ asserted that the people had been divided into "poor and rich, noble and plebeian" by the sage-kings, for their own good. Those of noble status should be "regulated by *li* and music," while the common people should be controlled by the rigors of the law. Here again Hsün Tzŭ was breaking with Confucius and foreshadowing the special privilege of the new Confucian aristocracy of talent that was to come later.

In the book called *Hsün Tzŭ* what is said of Confucius does not, for the most part, vary greatly from the kind of thing we find in the *Analects*. The stories have grown, naturally. It is not only said that Confucius was minister of crime in Lu, but also that this produced a remarkable change in the manners of the people. Yet there is little of the marvelous or unbelievable element. This is not true of the last six chapters, which include a number of strange anecdotes, and promote Confucius to the position of "acting prime minister" of Lu. There seems to be little doubt, however, that these chapters are later additions to the book.[46]

ⁿⁿⁿⁿⁿⁿⁿⁿⁿⁿⁿⁿⁿⁿⁿⁿⁿ

CHAPTER XIII

DISASTER

WE have seen that the process of political decentralization reached a culmination around the time of Confucius. Disorder became so great that the necessity for a remedy was widely recognized, and many different men undertook to reunite China by different means. Confucius hoped for a voluntary association of enlightened men. His ideal had considerable resemblance to that of modern democracy, but since education was not general and he devised no machinery for putting democracy into effect, this hope was not capable of realization. Mo Tzŭ's solution was even less so.

There were others, however, who had plans that seemed much more practical. They are known as the Legalists, because they emphasized the role of law in government. In fact, however, they might even more descriptively be called totalitarians, for they advocated the strongest kind of centralized administration and wished to make the individual wholly subservient to the state.

The thinkers who are called Legalists did not actually form a school; on the contrary they criticized and, in one celebrated case, even destroyed each other. Furthermore, some of the books that have been called Legalist are dubious as to date and authorship, and miscellaneous as to content, so that various types of opinion (even including Confucian) are included in different portions of the works. Obviously, by making various selections of materials from such books, one might obtain a number of different versions of Legalism. Here we shall concern ourselves primarily with that type of Legalism which came to be embodied in the practices of the Ch'in empire in the third century B.C. For its ideological background we shall take as our chief source the genuine portions, in so far as they can be ascertained, of the book called by the name of the Legalist philosopher Han Fei Tzŭ.[1] This is reasonable since both the founder of that empire and his principal Legalist adviser seem to have been strongly influenced by the ideas of Han Fei Tzŭ.

A number of motifs and motives underlay Legalism. Those who professed it claimed to be anxious to bring about an orderly and disciplined world for the good of the people; in some cases they were undoubtedly quite sincere. Rulers were attracted by the fact that it offered them absolute despotic control. There was a considerable Taoist element in Legalism. Han Fei Tzŭ, probably the greatest thinker among the Legalists, quoted Lao Tzŭ, and the *Historical Records* stated that his ideas were based upon Taoism. Both Taoism and Legalism were archenemies of Confucianism. We have already seen that while Taoism ought logically to have espoused anarchism, it in fact licensed the ruler, if only he were a Taoist sage, to play God as an unbridled despot. It seems to be a tendency of totalitarianism, which can be seen in other places than ancient China, to couch its claims in wild and mystical rhetoric. In Taoism the Legalists found such language waiting for them. The later Chinese conception of the emperor as a mysterious sage of awe-inspiring power, occupying a "dragon throne," did not come originally from Confucianism, but from Taoism by way of Legalism.

Furthermore, the wedding of Taoism and Legalism was in line with the tendency of the times to seek easier ways to do things. In many respects Legalism was extremely hard-headed and realistic, but the Legalists were by no means averse to presenting their formulae as having metaphysical authority and an almost magical efficacy. The most Legalistic ruler in Chinese history, the First Emperor of the Ch'in dynasty, was steeped in

Taoist superstition and magical practices. Such a man could not fail to be attracted by the Legalists' claim that, if he would only use their methods, he might "repose on a couch and listen to the sound of stringed and bamboo instruments, yet the empire would be well governed." [2]

The Confucians of the third century B.C. were generally believed, even by themselves, to be the party that desired to revive the ways of antiquity. The Legalists, in contrast, proclaimed themselves as bold innovators, with new measures for new times. This claim was partially justified; many of their measures were new. Some of their economic policies, such for instance as that permitting the buying and selling of land, tended to give the plebeian individual greater liberty of action. Nevertheless, as regards liberty in general, the position of the Legalists was distinctly reactionary. It was the Confucians who were the champions of the new freedom of the individual, which had been unknown when feudalism was at its height. The Legalists, on the other hand, considered this freedom subversive. Han Fei Tzŭ stated the case against the scholars (and he spoke especially of the Confucians) very clearly: "Cultivating benevolence and righteousness they are trusted, and given governmental posts; cultivating literary learning they become famous teachers, renowned and exalted; these are the accomplishments of a common fellow. Thus it comes about that without any real merit they receive posts, and though without noble rank they are exalted; when the government follows such practices the state must fall into disorder, and the ruler be endangered."

The Legalists wished to abolish feudalism, which had made strong central government impossible. Nevertheless the kind of totalitarian power they sought for the ruler was in fact most closely akin to that which the feudal lord had exercised over his helpless and ignorant serfs. Thus they, like the Taoists, wished to "weaken the people" and keep them in a state of simple ignorance. From this point of view the *Lao Tzŭ* diagnosed the case perfectly when it said, "The reason the people are hard to govern is because they know too much."

But this poison of enlightenment, which both Taoists and Legalists quite correctly blamed on the Confucians, had corrupted the more civilized parts of China too thoroughly; the calendar could not be turned back permanently although the Legalists tried very hard. A glance at history would seem to indicate that totalitarianism has seldom really flourished except among peoples long habituated to be submissive to discipline and despotic rule. It is no accident, therefore, that Legalism did not take its rise in the most cultured parts of China, which had seen the development of the new freedom. Of the three most famous Legalists Han Fei Tzŭ was born, and Shang Yang is said to have acquired many of his ideas, in states that, while Chinese, lay to the west of Confucius' principal sphere of action. The third, Li Ssŭ, was born in the still partly barbarian state of Ch'u. But it was only in the far western state of Ch'in that their doctrines were fully appreciated and practiced.

There is manifold evidence that Ch'in was culturally, as J. J. L. Duyvendak has said, "a backward country, more than half 'barbarian' in origin." Constant fighting with neighboring barbarian tribes had kept its people warlike and given them little leisure for culture. This appears to have kept them, as individuals, well disciplined and submissive to authority. When the Confucian philosopher Hsün Tzŭ visited Ch'in he noted with great admiration that everyone went strictly about his business as it was laid down by the state, having "no private concerns." His words sound as if he were describing an ant hill. He seems to have liked very much the fact that the people "were deeply afraid of the officials, and obedient" (a circumstance on which Confucius would certainly have commented differently). Indeed, the only fault Hsün Tzŭ could find with the situation was that there were not many Confucians in Ch'in. He was like some modern men who like both the freedom of democracy and the so-called efficiency of totalitarianism, and see no reason why it is not possible to have both.

Ch'in is supposed to have been set upon the path of glory by Shang Yang, a scion of the ruling house of the state of Wei (衛). He was unappreciated in the east but was given honor and power when he went to Ch'in, about the middle of the fourth century B.C. As a high minister he is said to have reformed the government, repressing the nobility and instituting a strong central administration. He introduced economic reforms, broke up the unity of the patriarchal family, and set the people against each other by offering rewards to informers. In various ways, according to the tradition, he strengthened Ch'in for the coming battle for China, and as a general extended its territories both by strategy and by treachery.[3]

For more than a century the contest continued, as Ch'in gradually enlarged its territories and the other states struggled against extinction. Sometimes they combined, but never permanently nor effectively. The military prowess, and perhaps better methods, of Ch'in's armies were important. But that state did not rely on battles alone. Secret agents were also sent into the various states, to win allies and sow dissension by means of bribery and, when necessary, assassination.

An important role was played by two students of Hsün Tzǔ. That Confucian scholar denounced Ch'in's career of conquest and opposed many aspects of Legalism. But he had given up (no doubt unconsciously) the ideal of a cooperative society advocated by Confucius, in favor of authoritarian control, and his idea that human nature is evil suggests Legalism as one of its possible corollaries. Thus it is not wholly surprising that his brilliant pupil, Han Fei Tzǔ, became the greatest Legalist philosopher.

Han Fei Tzǔ was a prince of Han, a neighboring state and principal enemy of Ch'in. He is said to have turned to writing because of an impediment in his speech. The book called *Han Fei Tzǔ* that has come to us certainly includes additions and interpolations, but it seems possible to distinguish certain sections which are clearly his. They set forth, with ruthless clarity and astringent logic, a system of utter totalitarian despotism. Han Fei Tzǔ recognizes the supremacy of nothing but force, and aims at making the ruler rich and powerful. The people are to be used completely as instruments of the ruler's designs, living or dying as suits his purpose. For a ruler to be benevolent, or oppressive, is equally bad and equally irrelevant. The poor should not be helped for this only pauperizes them, and the good will of the people is worthless. The ruler must firmly hold all power himself. He must choose his ministers for their ability and reward them with wealth and rank, but not with power and influence. They need not be virtuous; such men are few. They ought not to be wise; such men would deceive the ruler. They should not be pure; such men would be deceived by the people. The ruler need only keep them and all of his subjects in such a state of fear that they will dare to do no wrong. Above all, he must compel every individual to live only for the state. Every personal thought and feeling must be suppressed. "All speech and action which is not in accord with the laws and decrees is to be prohibited."

After Han Fei Tzŭ, the policies of Machiavelli's *Prince* seem timid and vacillating. Upon reading two of Han Fei Tzŭ's essays the ruler of Ch'in is reported to have been delighted and declared that he wished to see him. A little later Han Fei Tzŭ was sent as ambassador to Ch'in, where he did see the ruler, but another Legalist had preceded him to that state.

This was Li Ssŭ, previously his fellow student under Hsün Tzŭ. Li was much less brilliant than Han Fei Tzŭ and seems to have known it, but he had the advantage in that he had been in Ch'in for some time and had the ruler's confidence. He contrived to have Han Fei Tzŭ put to death.[4] Thereafter Li Ssŭ steered Ch'in to victory, guided chiefly, it would seem, by the ideas of his murdered colleague.

Ch'in's rise was bloody. It is recorded that on one occasion 400,000 soldiers who had surrendered to Ch'in were massacred; the figure is undoubtedly exaggerated, but suggestive. By 221 B.C. Ch'in had swallowed up all of China. The Legalist, totalitarian state had become supreme.

Efficiency was the order of the day. "Laws and regulations were made uniform, weights and measures standardized, cart wheels spaced the same distance apart,[5] and the forms of written characters made uniform." In the same spirit of simplification the Ch'in ruler took the title of "First Emperor," and directed that (since there would never again be a change of dynasty) his successors on the throne should simply be numbered "up to a thousand and ten thousand without end." If this suggests megalomania the impression is correct. We have already noted that the First Emperor was very superstitious. In 219 he became angry with a mountain and sent 3,000 convicts to cut down every tree on it. At this we may smile, but when human beings were the objects of his wrath or his whim the results were less humorous. Savage punishments were imposed, on Legalist principle, for small infractions of the law. Great numbers of persons were transported to distant regions, like pawns. He built many palaces and vast public works with convicts and forced labor. In the area near the capital alone he is said to have had 270 palaces, all filled with fine things and beautiful women. On his tomb 700,000 men are said to have labored; the building of the Great Wall cost a great many lives. Extremely heavy taxation was necessary to support these projects.

A century earlier Aristotle, in Greece, had listed "the ancient prescriptions for the preservation of a tyranny"; they read as if he had been describing the policies of the Legalists and the First Emperor. Heavy taxation and great public works "to occupy the people and keep them poor" are included. The tyrant also, Aristotle says, forbids education and "must prohibit literary assemblies or other meetings for discussion." Quite in accord with this, Han Fei Tzŭ had denounced learning, declaring that time spent in study was time taken from useful work, and thus interfered with the people's duty to strengthen the state and enrich the ruler. "Therefore in the state of an enlightened ruler there is no literature."

The scholars, among whom the Confucians were a prominent element, proved hard to assimilate into the First Emperor's totalitarian state. They even had the temerity to criticize the First Emperor, a practice which he found "utterly unspeakable." The principal criticism of the scholars is said to have been directed against the fact that the First Emperor did not give fiefs to his relatives and did not follow the ways of antiquity. If this is true, it indicates that the Confucians of the time were a poor lot. Still, they gave enough trouble so that it was considered necessary to prevent them from agitating the populace. Approval was given to a proposal by Li Ssŭ that, in order to prevent the spread of "doubt and disorder among the people," all books in the hands of the people, except works on medicine, divination, and agriculture, were to be burned. Those who failed to give up their books were to be branded and sent to forced labor. All persons who henceforth dared to discuss the *Book of Poetry* or the *Book of History*, or to "use the past to discredit the present" were to suffer death.

Just how many persons lost their lives is uncertain. In the

next year, 212 B.C., the First Emperor had 460 "scholars" buried alive, but it appears that he was merely venting his pique because he had been told that someone was criticizing him.[6] Furthermore, many of these "scholars" were in fact magicians. Nevertheless, it is clear that some Confucians were suffering.

The amount of literature that is lost to us as a result of "the burning of the books" has perhaps been exaggerated, and the persecution of Confucianism under Ch'in probably strengthened it as a movement, rather than the reverse. The real harm done to Confucianism by Legalism was not its suppression, but its perversion. It has often been remarked that the authoritarian Confucian orthodoxy of Han times had in fact more than a little of Legalism in its character. We have already seen that Hsün Tzŭ, in his authoritarianism and his approval of punishment as a means of social control, leaned toward Legalism. In fact, Legalism seems to have steadily infiltrated Confucianism over a long period.

This process was not one-sided. There are passages in the *Han Fei Tzŭ* that controvert Legalist philosophy, which were probably added to the text by Confucians.[7] But the Legalists played this game too, and skillfully. Confucius is frequently criticized in the *Han Fei Tzŭ*, but in parts of the book that may be by later Legalists Confucius and one of his disciples are made to talk as Legalists. Though the falsity of at least one of these stories is wholly obvious,[8] they were doubtless believed even by many Confucians. In one story, told to make a Legalist point, Confucius was represented as having been prime minister of the state of Wei; this was no doubt intended to make it more difficult for Confucians to reject the tale.

The real triumph of the Legalists, however, was the injection of their ideas into the very heart of Confucian literature. It is not always easy to be sure whether this is a matter of interpolation by Legalists or the result of Legalistic tendencies among Confucians. This question hangs, for instance, over sections of the *Book of History* that were composed late and that include some quite Legalistic material.[9] Sheer falsification, however, seems to be the only explanation of the Legalistic statements and actions (including the summary execution of a rival) that are fathered upon Confucius in one of the final chapters of the

Hsün Tzŭ, undoubtedly by a Legalist who tampered with the text. The Legalist technique is familiar; Confucius is here honored with the title of "Acting Prime Minister" of Lu.

This fraud has long been recognized by scholars, but some Legalist intrusions were less obvious. The *Records on Ceremonial* (which we shall discuss at more length later) includes a document called *The Doctrine of the Mean.* Although many scholars have recognized that this work is at least in part a late compilation, it has enjoyed the greatest influence, especially since the Sung dynasty; at that time it was made one of the Four Books, which have been the particularly sacred scriptures of recent Confucian orthodoxy. When *The Doctrine of the Mean* speaks of "the Master," it means Confucius. It includes the following passage:

> The Master said, "If one who is ignorant is fond of using his own judgment, if one without rank desires to control himself, if one who lives today goes back to the ways of antiquity—disaster will certainly fall on all such persons. Only the Son of Heaven may pass judgment upon *li,* set up standards of measure, and establish the forms of characters. Today in the empire all carts have their wheels the same distance apart, books are written in uniform characters, and for conduct there are uniform regulations." [10]

This is transparently Ch'in dynasty Legalism, put into the mouth of Confucius in one of the most sacred Confucian scriptures. Its last statement uses the very words in which the standardizations by the First Emperor were described, and could scarcely have been written before the unification of China in 221 B.C. The statement that "only the Son of Heaven may pass judgment upon *li*" would never have been made by Confucius. In fact, he did not speak at all of the emperors living in his own day, but he knew well enough that all of the hereditary aristocrats were sadly in need of guidance in all intellectual matters. It is only in a totalitarian state that the possession of political power makes the ruler the arbiter of all things. Likewise the condemnation of "one without rank who desires to control himself" is pure Legalism. Confucius said that he himself as a young man was "without rank" (the word is the same) yet he refused to submit his will, or that of his disciples, to any ruler. As for Confucius' alleged disapproval of one who "goes back to the ways of antiquity," this is exactly what Han Fei Tzŭ and Li Ssŭ repeatedly accused the Confucians of doing.

The same words are attributed to Confucius in the *Discourses of the Confucian School*, with differences that are negligible in all respects but one; there he is quoted as praising those who "living today, set their minds on the ways of antiquity." By this time matters were so confused that few could tell what Confucius had or had not said. Legalist influence even went so far as to be reflected in statements attributed to Confucius in the *Analects* itself.

Analects 16.2 reads, "Confucius said, 'When the Way prevails in the empire, then *li*, music, and punitive expeditions are originated by the Son of Heaven; when it lacks the Way these things are originated by the feudal lords. When this happens, it is rarely that they do not lose their states within ten generations. If they are originated by great officers [*tai fu*] of the feudal lords, it is rarely that they do not lose their power within five generations. When retainers of ministers seize power within a state, they usually fall within three generations. When the Way prevails in the empire, government is not in the hands of great officers. When the Way prevails in the empire, the common people do not discuss public affairs.' "

Although the emphasis upon the feudal hierarchy in this passage is not characteristic of Legalism, the influence of Legalist ideas is nevertheless evident. Here again we have the totalitarian ruler whose political power makes him the arbiter of music and of all things. All power and intellectual initiative are centered in him and descend by a graded hierarchy to his subordinates. The function of the learned and virtuous minister, so important for Confucius, is not discernible here. Whereas elsewhere in the *Analects* Confucius advocates teaching the people the Way, here they are not even to talk about matters of state.

The language of this passage betrays it in a number of ways; it was undoubtedly a late addition to the text.[11] Nevertheless it has played a crucial role in fixing the conception of Confucius' ideas current even among critical scholars; *Analects* 16.2 is chiefly responsible for the idea that Confucius was trying to revive the power of the Chou emperor, that he favored imperial authoritarianism, and that he was a champion of feudalism.[12]

Another passage in the *Analects* that seems clearly to be a late addition is 13.3, in which Confucius is made to state the doctrine of "the rectification of names" and to lay great emphasis upon the use of punishments in government. This passage was either written by Legalists or under definite Legalist influence.[13] This is probably also true of *Analects* 16.9, in which Confucius is made to say, "Those who are born with knowledge are the highest class; those who acquire knowledge by study are next." Here we have the idea that sages (including Confucius) were born with magically all-embracing knowledge. This is very different from Confucius' own emphasis upon the acquisition of knowledge by experience, reflection, and unremitting study. The Legalists, however, were contemptuous of study and wished to discredit those whose only title to consideration was that they were learned. Thus Han Fei Tzŭ wrote, "Whether one is wise depends upon his innate character . . . wisdom is not something which can be acquired by studying with other men." This very closely resembles the point of *Analects* 16.9, which was probably written under Legalist influence. Nevertheless, *Analects* 16.9 succeeded in firmly establishing within Confucianism the idea of the sage who is omniscient from birth, a conception which cut the very foundation from under Confucius' own theory of knowledge.[14]

It is impossible to date the infiltration of Legalist doctrine into Confucianism with entire precision; it appears to have continued well into the Han period. But one thing is clear: by the time the Legalists had completed their work of sabotage, the true nature of the thinking of Confucius had been thoroughly obscured.

CHAPTER XIV

"TRIUMPH"

It has commonly been held that when, during the second century B.C., one of the Han emperors gave official recognition to Confucianism, he did so because it was a doctrine that would bolster his authority. Since the reasons for historical events are seldom simple, there is probably some truth to this. But even more true is a proposition which may seem to be its opposite: that Confucianism owed its ultimate success to the fact that it was favored by the common people, who over a period of many years almost forced it upon their rulers.

Seldom have two political principles been so clearly opposed, and so plainly tested, as in China during the latter half of the third century B.C. On the one side there was that of Confucius, who believed that government must be judged by its ability to give satisfaction (not merely welfare) to the people, and that the state is a cooperative venture; for this reason education must be general, and government must be entrusted to those who, chosen from among the whole people, prove the most competent and virtuous. Opposed to this was the doctrine of the Legalists. They believed that everything should be directed and dictated by the ruler. The people should not understand but obey; they should not be educated but made to fear the law.

Han Fei Tzŭ put it succinctly: "Those who know nothing about government say, 'The ruler must gain the good will of the people.' . . . In effect, this would amount to taking orders from the people! But the people's 'wisdom' is useless; they are like babies."

The question was clearly put: Is, or is not, the good will of the people necessary for successful government? The First Emperor espoused the totalitarian position, that it was not. It should not be supposed, however, that he was a thorough-going philosophical Legalist; it is doubtful that he ever thoroughly understood Legalism. He was moved by more personal motives.

The First Emperor succeeded, at the early age of thirteen, to the throne of the expanding state of Ch'in; his position cannot have been an easy one for a boy. His father was dead. His mother is said to have once been a courtesan; whether this is true or not, she had lived with another man before marrying his father and was celebrated more for her beauty than for her virtue. The First Emperor (undoubtedly at his mother's insistence) richly enfeoffed her current lover and gave him considerable power. When the First Emperor was twenty his younger brother, in command of an army, raised a revolt that was put down with considerable bloodshed. The next year his mother's lover plotted rebellion and led troops which attacked the Emperor's guards in his very capital, but were in the end defeated. Rightly or not, the First Emperor seems to have believed that his mother was a party to this intrigue. It is no wonder he became convinced that he could trust no one. These experiences, coupled no doubt with a natural liking for despotic control, inevitably made him hospitable to the ideas of the Legalists, who declared that the ruler should be suspicious of everyone and keep all power in his own hands.

As a result, the Ch'in empire was controlled by, and was able fully to avail itself of the services of, only one mind. Those who dared to disagree with the First Emperor or to tell him anything that he might find unpleasant were likely to die; for this reason he rarely heard such things. But he tried very hard to make his single mind adequate to govern a great empire. On the stone tablets singing his praises, which he set up in various parts of China, he has told us how he eliminated the violent and cruel ("by boiling them alive"), how his benevolence extended to all ("even oxen and horses"), and how hard he worked for the sake of the empire. He did, in fact, make all important decisions himself, while allowing his officers to exercise very little initiative. He is said to have carried his insistence on personally supervising every detail of the government to the point of examining more than one hundred pounds of state documents every day and refusing to go to bed until they were finished. It is probable that when he died, at the age of fifty, he had literally worked himself to death for the sake of an ungrateful people. Yet all these efforts proved, in the end, unavailing; for no one mind, however brilliant and industrious, is enough to direct a nation.

Superficially it might appear, however, that the First Emperor was quite successful. There seems to have been no real rebellion from the time he completed the conquest of all China, in 221 B.C., until after his death in 210. The dissolution of the empire that followed was under the reign of a weak boy dominated by a eunuch. Nevertheless, even if the First Emperor had lived, rebellion might well have broken out anyway. At first, when peace came after many years of war, there was wide rejoicing; in such circumstances any peace seems better than any war. At that time the Emperor confiscated all arms and transported to the neighborhood of his capital all the people he thought might be capable of rebellion. Yet even these measures and the most savage repression did not secure complete tranquillity. Considerable numbers of men fled to the mountains and became outlaws. Those who stayed and kept silent for fear of the executioner grew daily more bitter, and contrasted their ruler with the "true king" of Confucian legend.

Yet just as the First Emperor was not really a thorough-going Legalist, neither was he wholly anti-Confucian. He killed some Confucians, just as he killed all those whom he suspected of criticizing him. But before he set up one of his self-adulatory stone tablets he "deliberated with the Confucian scholars of Lu" about the inscription. In his various inscriptions we find an indiscriminate mixture of both Legalist and Confucian ideas and phrases; they use expressions from the *Book of Poetry* and the *Book of History*, and one of them even alludes to the

Analects.[1] The Emperor called to his service scholars of all sorts, and even after the Confucian books had been proscribed he continued, to the end of his life, to have Confucian scholars at his court. It was not against learning as such but against learning among the people, where it might make trouble, that his ire was directed.

However, the Confucians were an increasing annoyance to him. Some of them, at least, criticized him for not giving fiefs to his relatives. Here Confucius might well have sided with the First Emperor, for it was perfectly true that continuing feudalism was likely to lead to disorder; but the Confucians of this day were far more traditionally minded than their Master. What the Emperor probably minded much more was the fact that some Confucians were courageous enough to criticize his whole policy, "fomenting doubt and disorder among the common people"; this led to the proscription of their books and the prohibition of their teaching. That their influence was not to be despised may be deduced from the fact that the First Emperor's eldest son is said to have warned his father that persecution of the followers of Confucius might "cause the empire to be unsettled."[2]

As punishment, this son was virtually exiled to the north. A little later, when the First Emperor died, a eunuch and the Legalist Li Ssŭ conspired to forge a letter which caused this son to commit suicide; they then set up a weakling younger brother as Second Generation Emperor.

The standard of rebellion was first raised by a peasant, Ch'ên Shê. Like many another before him, Ch'ên had been drafted for labor service and had been prevented by heavy rains from reporting on time. He and those with him were therefore subject, according to Ch'in law, to the death penalty. He persuaded his companions, since they could only die once, to sell their lives as dearly as possible. Only a spark was needed to start the rebellion. It was very popular throughout the east; men flocked to join Ch'ên Shê, and he was soon able to take the title of "King of Ch'u."

Although only a peasant, Ch'ên was ambitious and clever. He knew that it would not be easy for him to win acceptance as a leader; therefore he did everything he could to play upon the superstition and the sympathies of his followers. On the one hand he tried to make them believe he was favored by the spirits. On the other he declared that he was espousing the cause of the First Emperor's murdered eldest son. This son was liked because he had criticized his father; it will be remembered, too, that he is supposed to have defended the Confucians. It was probably because the Confucians were popular that Ch'ên had the direct heir of Confucius, in the eighth generation, with him as an adviser. Both the Confucians and the Moists of the northeast are said to have flocked to Ch'ên's standard as soon as it was raised.

Considering its later importance, our lack of knowledge of the early history of Confucianism is astonishing. The *Historical Records* says that from the time of Confucius to the Ch'in period Confucianism was little esteemed anywhere except in the northeast, in the states of Ch'i and Lu. Nevertheless, Confucian ideas were gradually spreading, and not only among the rich and powerful. We know, for instance, of one son of a very humble man (probably a farmer) in what is now northern Kiangsu, who during the Ch'in period studied the *Book of Poetry* with a disciple of Hsün Tzǔ. The banning of Confucian books and the repression of Confucian scholars by the First Emperor probably added greatly to their popularity; it was hard to avoid the conclusion that whoever was an enemy of the Emperor was a friend of the people. It is probably for this reason that Ch'ên welcomed the many Confucian scholars who joined his rebellion, and made the descendant of Confucius an official "scholar of wide learning" in his administration. When, a short time later, the armies of Ch'in proved too much for the peasant king and he was killed, this descendant of Confucius died with him.

The revolution went on, however. By this time the totalitarian government of Ch'in was falling into disorder, while the protagonist of relatively democratic rule was dead. Yet the struggle between the two principles did not cease. Two new champions rose to espouse them, each, this time, within the ranks of the revolutionists.

After the death of Ch'ên the actual leadership of the revolution gravitated to Hsiang Yü, who did not, however, assume the titular rule. Hsiang's ancestors had been generals of the state of Ch'u for generations and held a fief there. He was such an excellent general that, it is said, he never lost a battle which he personally commanded. He was extremely domineering; "when he entered the camp there were none who did not advance on their knees, and none dared lift their heads to look at him." In battle, we are told, his mere glance was enough to paralyze the arm of the stoutest enemy and even to cause horses to flee in terror. He seems to have delighted in murder; in fact, he was one of the great murderers of history. Sometimes he assassinated openly, sometimes by stealth; sometimes he massacred surrendered soldiers (200,000 on one occasion, it is claimed), and sometimes had the population of whole regions slaughtered for no apparent reason. Those who had shown themselves exceptionally brave and loyal, but not to him, he killed by boiling or burning. He was once dissuaded from massacring the people of a surrendered town by a thirteen-year-old, who pointed out that this would only stiffen other towns in their resistance; it would seem that he might have arrived at this conclusion by himself. Few noble or unselfish actions by Hsiang Yü are recorded.

Shortly before his death he declared, "It is Heaven that destroys me; I have committed no military error!" He could never understand why, although he was invincible in battle, those who had supported him gradually fell away. But others understood. In the next century a historian wrote, "Under the pretext of acting as supreme ruler, he wished to conquer the world and control it by sheer force."

The champion of relatively democratic rule was one whom few would have cast in that role. It will be most convenient to call him by the name by which he is known to history, Han Kao Tsu. He was a farm boy, both idle and arrogant, the sort of boy "likely to end on a gallows or a throne." Having talent for leadership, he became a petty officer in charge of several villages. Unintentionally committing a "crime" that was punishable, according to Ch'in law, by death, he fled to the wilds and became a bandit chief. When the revolution came he joined it and became a general. After Ch'in had been conquered, Hsiang Yü and Han Kao Tsu fought between themselves for four more years to decide who should have the empire.

Initially Hsiang had the advantage of possessing greater authority, controlling far more troops, and being a much better general than Kao Tsu. But the latter was more intelligent, he was willing and even anxious to take good advice from others, and he knew how to cultivate good will among his associates and among the common people. In many ways he made the people feel that he was their friend. Whereas Hsiang pillaged and massacred as he went, Kao Tsu tried to discipline his soldiers and make them treat the people well. As he went about the country he made a practice of meeting with the elders of the people, explaining his aims to them and establishing a broad basis of support. He provided coffins for his soldiers and returned their bodies to their homes. After he became emperor he freed "those who had sold themselves into slavery because of famine or hunger," [3] and from time to time proclaimed various amnesties and remissions of taxes. He permitted the people to use the many parks and preserves that the Ch'in rulers had enclosed for themselves. All of this stood in the sharpest contrast to the practices of Ch'in and of Hsiang Yü.

Kao Tsu could pose as "the friend of the common man" the more convincingly because he *was* a common man, and never forgot it. His deliberately rude manners offended the cultured but undoubtedly delighted the vast majority of his subjects. And when, because one of his officials built for him a grand and luxurious palace, he protested saying, "The world has been filled with the cries of the toiled and suffering for many years . . . why do you build these palaces and halls beyond all measure?" [4] his words seem to carry a ring of sincerity.

Kao Tsu was by no means an entirely admirable and benevolent character. He was a shrewd politician who could be ruthless in eliminating those whom he thought to endanger his power. But he was intelligent enough to know that he could not afford to *seem* to be arbitrary and despotic if he wished to hold his authority. Where his predecessors had made a point of inspiring terror, he tried to make friends; where they had met treason with summary punishment, he often tried to avert or palliate it with clemency.

The keynote was struck when Kao Tsu first conquered the region that included the Ch'in capital. He might have been expected to put the population to the sword (later on Hsiang

Yü did). But instead Kao Tsu called together leading men from the various districts, told them to have no fear, and declared that he was repealing the Ch'in laws. He said, "Fathers and Elders, you have suffered long enough from the Ch'in laws . . . I am merely going to agree with you, Fathers and Elders, on a new code of laws in three articles." The important word here is "agree." To the newly conquered people of Ch'in, if ever, he might have been expected to lay down the law; instead he "agreed" with them. The fact that they had no real voice in the matter is unimportant; the attitude displayed set a very important precedent. Later, no doubt as a propaganda move in his struggle with Hsiang, Kao Tsu had his officials select, in each district, a man whose years and character commanded the respect of the people, who was to represent the people and advise with the administrative officials. Thus the people were given some voice in the government.

Kao Tsu publicly gave the credit for his achievements to his advisers, ministers, and generals; for himself he claimed only the ability to judge and make use of the talents of others. Even after his power as emperor was firmly established he maintained the pretense, at least, of acting not on his own impulse but on the advice of others. It was probably not difficult to get the kind of advice he wanted, but the influence of this practice on the theory of government was fundamental. It resulted in the principle, which became basic in Chinese governments henceforward, that "in the normal routine, the emperor himself was not to govern; but he selected and supervised his ministers, who did . . ." Under the immediate successors of Kao Tsu this principle limited the theoretically absolute power of the throne in actual practice. It is, of course, quite Confucian.

Dubs has pointed out that "the accession of Kao Tsu marks the victory of the Confucian conception that the imperial authority is limited, should be exercised for the benefit of the people, and should be founded upon justice, over the legalistic conception of arbitrary and absolute sovereignty." He has shown how Kao Tsu, beginning as a rude peasant who was contemptuous of Confucians, was subjected to a long course of Confucian influences, which gradually made themselves felt. Kao Tsu probably never got over some of the uneducated man's suspicion of bookworms.[5] Yet his younger brother, a Confucian who had studied with a disciple of Hsün Tzŭ, was one of his closest advisers, and some of his best counselors were more or less thoroughly Confucian. They went to considerable pains to Confucianize their ruler; one even wrote a book for the purpose, with which Kao Tsu was greatly pleased. Since he had no use for mere pedants he kept none about him, but most of the Confucian advice he got was well seasoned with common sense and it worked; undoubtedly it was the latter fact that attracted him.

During his long struggle with Hsiang Yü, Kao Tsu was advised, in language strongly reminiscent of the *Analects* and *Mencius*, to declare a crusade against his adversary. He did so, in a proclamation which asserted that Hsiang Yü "lacked the Way"; by this means he was able to gather numerous adherents to his cause. Other pronouncements issued under Kao Tsu have a definitely Confucian flavor. This is particularly true of the words in which his subordinates petitioned him to become emperor; after declining the honor in properly self-deprecatory language, he accepted "for the good of the people."

We may be quite sure that Kao Tsu would not have made so much concession to Confucianism if he had not believed that to do so would be a popular, and therefore a politically sagacious, move. That he did think this became particularly clear when the question of his heir arose. It is not surprising that he came to have little love for his wife (she later showed herself extremely cruel and vindictive); also, he feared that her son was a weakling, which proved true. He wished to change the succession but was dissuaded largely, it would appear, because certain Confucians whom Kao Tsu could not himself attract became adherents of the heir. "Thus," Dubs says, "Kao Tsu finally bowed to the influence of Confucianism."

This did not mean, however, that other philosophies were abandoned. Taoism, by this time less of a philosophy than a complex of gross superstitions, continued important and was dominant at the court at some periods in early Han times. Various religions as well as philosophies were tolerated. Legalism, although it seems never to have been a very widely espoused "school," continued to underlie much of the actual practice of government. The harsh and numerous Ch'in laws seem to have continued in effect, for the most part, despite the fact that Kao Tsu had announced that they were abolished. The law against the possession of proscribed books, for instance, was not rescinded until after his death.

Indeed, it was inevitable that Legalistic practices should continue in the government. For the Confucians had no experience in and no methods for governing a great centralized empire. Personnel and practices had to be taken over from the Ch'in administration; in consequence, much of the working philosophy of the administrative officials continued to be Legalist. This does not mean that individuals were always clearly either Confucian or Legalist. We have seen that Confucian philosophy had already begun to be heavily influenced by its adversary.

The influence of Confucianism increased steadily, nevertheless, for several reasons. One was the fact that the Confucians were the conservators of court ritual, for which even the uncouth peasant, Kao Tsu, found it necessary to call upon them. More important was their position as almost the sole custodians of the literature and ancient culture; for this reason they were usually the tutors of young emperors, which assured that their influence was likely to grow with each generation. But most important of all was the fact that they stood for relatively mild and even relatively democratic government, as opposed to harsh and autocratic rule. The common people did not, of course, know books like the *Analects* and *Han Fei Tzŭ*, but they understood well the difference between mild government and decapitation, between light taxation and the virtual confiscation of their livelihood. Furthermore, there were many Confucian scholars to tell them that the former were the methods of the ancient sages and Confucius, while the latter had been the ways of the Legalists and of Ch'in. Many of the Confucians were poor and humble; [6] for this very reason they had the ears of the people.

The importance of the popular good will that the Han house had established appeared at the time when the family of Kao Tsu's wife tried to take over the throne. After Kao Tsu's death his widow gradually consolidated the power of her family, and at length fraudulently made one of them, a mere babe, emperor. The ministers, however, did not ratify this action; the question

was, then, whether the imperial authority was unlimited or
could be exercised only with the consent of the ministers.
When the Empress Dowager died, in 180 B.C., conflict broke
out at once between her family and the Han. The issue turned
on the allegiance of the common soldiers of one of the armies;
asked to choose between the two houses, they declared for the
house of Han. The ministers then wiped out the rebellious family and invited the eldest living son of Kao Tsu to go to the
capital to become emperor. He feared a plot, but one of his
officers told him he need have no fear, for the following reasons among others: "When the Han dynasty arose, it did away
with the harshness and vexatiousness of Ch'in, reduced the
number of its laws and ordinances, and showed its virtue and
beneficence. All are content, and it would be hard to shake
their allegiance." He called attention to the fact that the common soldiers had declared for Han, and said, "Even if the great
ministers wished to make a change [from the Han house] the
common people would not permit themselves to be used by
them. . . . Your worth, your sageness, your benevolence, and
your filial piety [all of these are Confucian virtues] are known
everywhere; thus the great ministers are according with the
wishes of the whole world in desiring to welcome you and make
you emperor." He was enthroned, as the Emperor Wên.

It seems possible that of all the emperors China has had,
Wên is that one whom Confucius would have found most congenial. That is not to say that he was a doctrinaire Confucian;
he was not (neither was Confucius). But the spirit of his reign
seems to have been truly that of Confucius. As Dubs has written, "Emperor Wên accepted whole-heartedly the Confucian
doctrine that the ruler exists for the welfare of his subjects and
put that doctrine into practise. He reduced the taxes and light-
ened the burdens of the people, economizing in his personal
expenses and avoiding any grand displays. . . . He asked the
people for criticism of his rule (in his case this request was
sincerely meant) and he sought for capable commoners to assist
in the administration. He . . . was much worried by famine and
scarcity, even going so far as to abolish the land tax on cultivated
fields (soon revived by his successor)." He took practical measures for famine relief at government expense and provided

pensions for the aged; the means he employed for these purposes were in part modeled after recommendations of the book of *Mencius*, and his edicts quoted from that text although they did not name it.[7] He issued an edict freeing government slaves.[8] He repealed the laws punishing criticism of the government and the emperor, asserting that such laws made it impossible for the ruler to "hear about his mistakes and errors." He abolished punishment by mutilation and so regulated the administration of justice that capital punishment became rare. He seems seriously to have considered leaving his throne to the most worthy person he could find rather than to his son. In his will he decreed that mourning for him should be reduced to an absolute minimum; he did not wish to bother the people and felt that it should be cause for rejoicing rather than sorrow that he had been able to end his years without falling into serious error.

Such an emperor seems too good to be true, but there is ample evidence that the picture is genuine. He undoubtedly made life more tolerable for the people than it had been (or was in the future to be) for some time. China became prosperous and populous. Yet if Wên had the virtues, he also had the shortcomings of Confucianism. Although Confucius was no pacifist, he seems to have had more faith in the power of virtue than may have been warranted; in the Confucians that faith became huge. Being both pacific and economical, Emperor Wên allowed China's defenses to decay, and the Huns to the northwest took advantage of that fact to make serious raids deep into China.

Wên was superstitious, a fact which did not mark him off from most of the Confucians of his day. At his court he had scholars for other philosophies as well as for Confucianism, and he appointed a Legalist as tutor to his heir. The reign of this heir was not especially noteworthy, except for the fact that at the instigation of his Legalist tutor feudalism, in the modified form in which it had existed under the Han, was almost abolished as an important factor, with great accrual of strength to the imperial government. The next emperor, however, was under strong Confucian influence at the beginning of his reign; this was the Emperor Wu.

Emperor Wu of the Han dynasty is one of the most impor-

tant of all Chinese rulers. His reign is of outstanding importance
in the history of Confucianism. His action in giving state recognition to Confucianism has been compared with Constantine's
espousal of Christianity. Wu [9] was well trained in literature,
and his edicts have a distinctly Confucian flavor. They speak
repeatedly of his concern for the common people, stress the
importance of *li*, music, and study, and quote from the *Book of
Changes* and the *Analects*. His reign was celebrated for the re-
discovery of ancient literature, especially the Confucian Classics.

In his first year on the throne he approved a memorial proposing that, among certain scholars who had been recommended
for office, those who had studied Legalist doctrines should be
dismissed. He established the positions of official "scholars of
wide learning" for each of the Confucian Five Classics, and
provided livings for each of fifty disciples of these scholars, who
were the official exponents of learning at the court. This laid
the foundation of the Imperial University, from which as time
went on most of the minor officials of the government were
drawn; this fact assured that the government would increasingly
be permeated by Confucianism. By repeated examinations Wu
drew learned men into the government; he gave offices to two
descendants of Confucius. He appointed to the highest office
in his government a former swineherd who had achieved reputation for his knowledge of the *Spring and Autumn Annals*. It is
not surprising, therefore, that many scholars have fixed upon
the reign of Emperor Wu as the period of the triumph of Confucianism.

His reign was also one of more centralized, despotic, and
authoritarian government than had prevailed in China since
Ch'in times. Wu rejected the previous practice of loose rule, in
which the emperors had leaned largely on the advice of their
ministers; instead, he held the reins of government tightly in
his own hands. Since this development came at precisely the
same time at which Confucianism came to be officially patron-
ized, it is not surprising that a great many students, including
some of the most critical, have held and still hold that the
theory that the emperor should rule autocratically was a Confucian doctrine. Indeed, a high official of Emperor Wu's court
(not himself a Confucian) stated that according to the Con-

fucians "the ruler sets the tune, the ministers chime in; the ruler precedes, the ministers follow."

Ever since the time of the Han Emperor Wu, this has often been true of many Confucians. The same attitude has been read back into earlier Confucianism, and even into the ideas of Confucius himself. Since the reign of Wu has thus played a dominant role in the interpretation of Confucianism, and even of Confucius himself, it is necessary that we examine with considerable care what actually took place in his time.

Wu succeeded to the throne at the age of fifteen. His principal ministers at that time were Confucian, and it was under their influence that he dismissed certain Legalist and other scholars who had been recommended for office. These ministers invited to the court a certain venerable Confucian, and Wu asked him for advice on how to govern. But the old scholar was sour; he had been severely punished (possibly castrated) by a relative of the Emperor, and he replied curtly that government was a matter of deeds, not words. The boy ruler, who up to that time had been enthusiastic in his literary studies, was offended, but he treated his ancient guest politely. A little later the Confucian group was ousted from power by the Grand Empress Dowager, who was a Taoist. Although Confucians came back to high office later, especially after her death, Wu's personal ardor for Confucianism had cooled.

There were fundamental reasons, going far beyond court intrigue, for this change. Confucianism had always stood for the theory that the ruler's business was to bring about the welfare and happiness of the people, and that if he did not do this he had no just title to the throne. Such a doctrine was useful to revolutionaries, and the founder of the Han dynasty had found it so. For the same reason it was dangerous to an established sovereign, especially if he wished to rule despotically. At the court of Wu's father a Taoist had argued that the ancient sage-kings, founders of dynasties, who were praised by the Confucians, had in fact been only insubordinate regicides. A Confucian asked what, in this case, was the status of the founder of the Han dynasty? The Emperor stopped the debate, strongly hinting that scholars who avoided this topic would live longer. "From this time," a contemporary historian wrote, "no scholar dared" to discuss this subject. It seems significant that although this same forthright Confucian was recommended to Emperor Wu, he found no favor at Wu's court.

All of the great Confucian teachers—Confucius, Mencius, and Hsün Tzŭ—had explicitly stated that rulers should entrust the administration of government to virtuous and capable ministers, and that ministers owed their primary allegiance to principle, to the Way, not to the ruler. They all declared that proper ministers should oppose the ruler if he acted wrongly.[10] To a man of the arbitrary and tyrannical temper that Emperor Wu increasingly displayed, this was naturally repugnant.

Nevertheless the Confucians might have been forgiven some of these things if they had been capable of practical administration. Most of them were not. They had begun to fall into that preoccupation with purely literary studies against which Confucius had explicitly warned, and were so deeply tinged with Taoist metaphysics that many of them seem to have conceived the art of government as a vast system of magical practices. Their enemies, and sometimes even their friends, characterized them as narrow pedants without either the practical training or the grasp of practical affairs needed for the running of a great empire. The Confucians minimized the very real dangers of the barbarians who pressed upon the borders, and condemned the vigorous military measures of Emperor Wu as sheer imperialism which impoverished China needlessly. They insisted that if China's emperor would only extend his virtue and favors to cover them, the barbarians would submit of their own accord.

The Confucians were an annoyance to Wu, as they had been to the Ch'in First Emperor. But Wu was quite familiar with the experience of his totalitarian predecessor, who had repressed and executed Confucians only to have them join in destroying his dynasty. Wu's tactics were infinitely more subtle and effective.

These tactics appear clearly in connection with his treatment of the Confucian scholar Tung Chung-shu, who was renowned as a student of the *Spring and Autumn Annals*. Under previous emperors a system had been developing whereby scholars were recommended to the court from over the empire, and sometimes given examinations. Early in Wu's reign Tung Chung-shu was one of some hundred scholars who were recommended to and examined by the emperor; the examination and Tung's reply are preserved to us.

The Emperor begins by saying that he has most diligently set his mind to the problems of good government, but that when he looks over the course of history he wonders whether after all the earnest and meticulous "endeavor to pattern after high antiquity is useless." On such problems he hopes the assembled scholars will give him their counsel, without concealing anything.

In his reply Tung Chung-shu informs the Emperor that he has discovered a method of governing by reference to the *Spring and Autumn Annals*. It is only necessary, he explains, to observe the phenomena of nature and then seek analogies in this work; if the government is bad Heaven warns the ruler by sending natural calamities such as flood, famine, or eclipses. This book also, he contends, contains profound teachings on the philosophy of government; as an example he quotes this passage: "In the spring, the first month according to the royal calendar." By means of a pun, Tung reads deep significance into these words.[11]

Tung also vigorously criticizes the government, declaring that the poison of Ch'in Legalism has persisted under Han. "The present practice of doing away with officials who use the virtuous teachings of the former kings, and placing the government of the people entirely in the hands of those who use penal law—is this not to depend entirely upon punishments? Confucius said, 'To put men to death without having first instructed them is called cruelty.' " [12] Tung softens his criticism by praising the Emperor's virtue, but declares it is ineffective without proper education. He asks that a state university be established for this purpose, and that the government be basically reformed.

Wu was not much pleased by the replies he got on this examination, and wrote a criticism. In fact, he said, the early rulers whom the scholars admired used a variety of methods of government. Some were energetic, some lax; some used stern punishments, while under others the prisons were empty; Wu said he found this confusing. The papers of the scholars did not, he said, give him much help; they were learned, but their proposals "examined in the light of present conditions would be difficult to carry out." He asked them to try again.

To this Tung replied in similar vein, declaring that the differences between the sage-kings were more apparent than real. In order to benefit the people, he again insisted, a university should be established to support scholars. He also suggested the establishment of a merit system for the promotion of good officials. Again the Emperor was not satisfied with the replies, saying that the scholars showed great knowledge of antiquity but asking, "Why are you so confused with regard to the affairs of the present?" He again asked them to write for him. Tung Chung-shu thereupon repeated his insistence that there was no essential difference between the past and the present. He also made another attack upon the methods of the government, denouncing oppressive administration of the laws and declaring that the Emperor's favored officials were becoming rich by engaging in trade, and grinding down the people. Finally, he asked that all but the Confucian teachings be suppressed.

For such criticism the Ch'in First Emperor would have buried Tung Chung-shu alive. But Wu knew better than to make a martyr of such a prominent Confucian. Instead, he gave him a high office. But, we must ask, what office?

Wu had an elder brother who ruled a vassal kingdom in the southeast. A militant, arrogant swashbuckler who collected bravos about him, he was something of a thorn in the side of the Emperor. Wu sent Tung Chung-shu to be his minister. The Emperor must have thought it a rare joke to send this preaching pedant to his swaggering brother. In addition, since such kings often killed ministers who displeased them, Wu probably hoped he would never see Tung again. If so he was mistaken, for Tung tamed the lion and held his post with great success. Later on Wu appointed Tung, at the instigation of one of his enemies, to the court of another and even fiercer brother; this time the scholar saved himself by resigning, after a short time, "for reasons of health." Thereafter Tung lived at home as a retired scholar. From time to time Wu sent messengers to ask his opinions on matters of state; that the Emperor often acted on his advice may be doubted, however.

In this manner Wu was able, without ever being seriously

bothered by Tung Chung-shu's recalcitrance, not only to avoid making a martyr of him but even to enjoy the reputation of being a patron of this famous scholar. In fact, the Emperor once magnanimously "saved his life," by pardoning him after he had been sentenced to death for writing a "stupid" book.

Another of Wu's examinations is preserved; from this we may see the kind of Confucian he liked. This is the examination of Kung-Sun Hung. As a young man he had been a jailer. For some fault he lost his place and had to herd swine. In his forties he studied the *Spring and Autumn Annals,* and was more than sixty when he was recommended and given an official post. He had the temerity to disagree with Wu and was dismissed, but he was again recommended and in 130 B.C. was given an examination.

In setting this examination Wu, although he uses Confucian language, seems to have been deliberately making an opening for the expression of non-Confucian ideas by the scholars. There were disasters, he says, even under the rule of the ancient sages; why? And how can the Confucian virtues of benevolence, righteousness, *li,* and wisdom be put into actual practice?

Kung-Sun Hung began his reply in an orthodox Confucian manner, stressing the importance of sincerity. He then listed "eight fundamentals of government"; his last two, punishments and rewards, are Legalist points. From here on his essay reads much like a Legalist treatise. He described all four of the Confucian virtues in terms that were far more Legalist than Confucian, and much of the terminology he used came straight out of the book of *Han Fei Tzŭ.* In order to rule properly the sovereign must set forth the laws, and use "methods" (*shu,* a Legalist term). He must "monopolize the handles which control life and death" (a paraphrase of a passage in Chapter 48 of *Han Fei Tzŭ*), and maintain firm personal control of the government.

The officials who graded the replies were undoubtedly scandalized by this piece of thinly disguised Legalism. Among more than a hundred papers they graded it last, before sending them on to the Emperor. Wu, however, was delighted, and moved Kung-Sun's paper to first place. This is not surprising. Wu was actually using Legalist methods more and more, and as early as his examination of Tung Chung-shu he seems to have shown a knowledge of the book of *Han Fei Tzŭ*.[13] A few years later, in an edict, Wu quoted from a memorial of the Legalist Li Ssŭ and from the *Han Fei Tzŭ*, without, however, mentioning his source in either case. To avow himself as a Legalist would not have been good politics, and Wu was too astute for that. But there seems to be little doubt that he was privately inclined more and more in that direction. If he kept his own counsel, he was merely following the injunction of the *Han Fei Tzŭ*: "The ruler must not reveal his thoughts. . . . Hear but do not be heard, know but do not be known." [14]

The Emperor Wu liked the ex-jailer because Kung-Sun Hung was in fact a good deal of a Legalist; [15] but he found him valuable because he was in name a Confucian. Ssŭ-Ma Ch'ien, the historian who was himself an official at Wu's court, put it plainly; he said that the Emperor was greatly pleased with the fact that Kung-Sun "could use Confucian doctrines to adorn the administration of the laws and of official business." [16] Esson M. Gale, writing of the early Han emperors and especially of Wu, points out that while "in the actual administrative measures of the state, they reverted to the execrated policies of the *legalist* statesmen of Ch'in," for purposes of prestige "they erected a façade of conformance to 'Confucianism.' "

For such a false front, a purely nominal Confucian like Kung-Sun Hung was perfect material. On one point, opposition to Wu's vast program of imperialist expansion, he did take a stand and got a concession from Wu on one occasion. For the most part, however, Wu merely ignored his opinions when they did not agree with his own. Kung-Sun took care seldom to show such disagreement, and never to contend with the emperor openly—thus exactly reversing the injunction of Confucius in *Analects* 14.23.

Ssŭ-Ma Ch'ien, who had probably known him, called Kung-Sun Hung "a suspicious man, outwardly magnanimous but inwardly scheming," who pretended to be friendly with those who disagreed with him but got his revenge in the end. Forthright Confucians like Tung Chung-shu called him a flatterer. It is recorded that one scholar's greatest popularity dated from his public denunciation of Kung-Sun Hung as a toady. His conduct, however, was meticulously correct. He was ostentatious in his filial piety and lived in an extremely frugal manner, winning praise because he gave most of his salary away to assist other scholars and friends.

The Emperor advanced Kung-Sun rapidly. Within a few years he was given the highest office in the government and enfeoffed as a marquis. Such preferment of one of their number, which seems to have been unprecedented, made a deep impression on all the scholars. Kung-Sun then succeeded, where Tung Chung-shu had failed, in getting the emperor to establish a university, which meant livings for fifty more Confucians. Clearly, it was to the advantage of a "wise" Confucian to be cooperative toward the imperial government.

Although Kung-Sun Hung continued (while heads fell all about him) to be chief minister until his natural death, there is no indication that he took any effective part in the government. On the contrary, it is clear that he was a convenient "Confucian" figurehead for the despotic personal rule of Emperor Wu.[17] Nevertheless, Wu had men who assisted in the formation and execution of his plans, but they do not always seem to have been the men who held the highest offices. The advisers to whom Wu really listened were men versed in finance, in criminal law, and in military affairs, *i.e.*, in the realm of the emperor's practical interests. At least one of them, Sang Hung-yang, appears to have been an openly avowed Legalist, who admired the First Emperor of Ch'in and was contemptuous not only of Confucians but even of Confucius himself.[18]

Aided by such officials, Wu pursued a regime of imperialistic conquest, totalitarian regimentation of the economy, and Legalistic repression of the people. His military measures, justified at first by the barbarian threat, expanded into vainglorious exploits. These exhausted the treasury; to raise more money government monopolies were established on such vital commodities as salt and iron, and the coinage was debased. To maintain "discipline," laws and punishments were multiplied; these also aided the treasury by providing large fines and large numbers of new slaves for the government. Officials lost their lives so regularly that few wanted official posts; a system was then established whereby a man appointed to a position could avoid the dubious honor only by paying the government to excuse him.

These measures, which brought power and glory to the state, meant misery and oppression for the people, but any criticism or "obstruction" of the government's policies met with the severest punishment. Toward the end of Wu's long reign discontent flared into disorder; it occurred, interestingly enough, in regions near the home of Confucius, in the most Confucian part of China. When it was repressed, many thousands of persons were executed.

Nevertheless it is doubtful that Wu could have maintained his power if he had depended on force alone and been as careless of public opinion as was the First Emperor of Ch'in. He was not. He made a great pretense of benevolence and alleged the most altruistic motives for actions that were intended to enhance his own power. What was probably his shrewdest move to nullify popular resentment was his action in supporting large numbers of Confucians, both as officials and as state-subsidized scholars. The Ch'in First Emperor buried Confucians alive; Wu tried to stop their mouths with treacle.

The effects on Confucianism were considerable. From this time on the number of those who studied the Confucian Classics increased rapidly, "no doubt," a Han historian commented dryly, "because this was now a way to gain position and wealth." Recruits made to any cause on this basis are seldom the most desirable; thus it was all the easier for the authorities to turn many of them gently toward "safe" studies and opinions, and away from the "dangerous" criticism of social and political conditions which had characterized Confucianism up to that time. Emperor Wu's action in moving Kung-Sun Hung's paper to first place is a vivid example of the way in which the government could show how well it paid to have the right opinions. The concentration on the study of ancient books, already well under way within Confucianism, was a relatively harmless pursuit which the government encouraged by stressing literature in the examinations. It was from the time of the Emperor Wu, Chavannes wrote, "that there began to be manifested the tendency of the Chinese mind to seek in the classical books for the principle of all wisdom."

The exclusion from official preferment of scholars who studied works other than the Confucian classics did not have the

effect of maintaining the purity of Confucianism; quite the reverse. Its effect was to cause a great many students, whose real
interests lay elsewhere, to become professional Confucians, and
interpret Confucianism in the light of their basic Taoist, Legalist, or other philosophy. Nor is this all. In fact, as Hu Shih has
pointed out, the kind of Confucianism developed under Wu
was made "a great synthetic religion into which were fused all
the elements of popular superstition and state worship . . .
thinly covered up under the disguise of Confucian and Pre-
Confucian Classics in order to make them appear respectable
and authoritative." But "this Confucianism was not at all what
Confucius taught or Mencius philosophized about . . ."

This statement is so true as to be unquestionable. It is also
true, however, that the conception of Confucius current in Han
times has deeply influenced the conception of Confucius himself
that is current even into our own day. Indeed, the period of the
Emperor Wu has interposed an all but opaque veil between us
and any real understanding of Confucius. We need not concern
ourselves here with the rich growth of legends involving the
supernatural, such as those which alleged that dragons and spirits hovered in the heavens at his birth; these discredit themselves. But other stories about Confucius found in Han works,
which are in fact scarcely more credible, still find acceptance.
Here we can consider, as examples, only two books, the *Historical Records* and the *Records on Ceremonial (Li Chi)*.

The latter work, one of the most voluminous of the Classics,
is a collection of treatises dealing in the main with ceremonial
usages, *li*. Compiled by a Han dynasty Confucian, it undoubtedly contains some documents which are somewhat earlier.
Attempts have been made to ascribe to some of them a date
nearly as early as that of Confucius; for this reason some sections
of the *Records on Ceremonial* have commonly been considered
basic sources for the understanding of Confucius. On examination, however, it appears that even the best of these materials
have undergone, at the least, so much later editing and interpolation as to cast grave doubt on them. We have already seen
that the section called the *Doctrine of the Mean* contains late
Legalistic ideas, and there are other reasons which impel us to
agree with those scholars who have considered this work to be

in large part, at least, a late production. This work has been made, since Sung times, one of the revered Four Books of Confucianism, along with the *Analects, Mencius,* and another section from the *Records on Ceremonial* called the *Great Learning.* There seems to be no reason to believe that this latter work, either, was composed very early.[19]

Nor do other sections of the *Records on Ceremonial,* which report on Confucius, inspire much confidence. Some of them are probably based on genuine traditions; these have, however, passed through so many hands as to be doubtful in their present form. Others are quite obviously pure fabrications.[20] The long section called *T'an Kung,* which is often used as a source on Confucius, no doubt contains some more or less authentic material, but it is hard to trust a treatise which includes so much that cannot be credited. The conduct of Confucius in his last days, as depicted here, is that of a querulous, egotistical, superstitious old man, and stands in the strongest contrast to comparable passages in the *Analects.*[21] In this document he is made to act according to the aristocratic code of a Han dynasty Confucian gentleman; here too, as Chinese critics have noted, his conduct conflicts with what is found in the *Analects.*[22]

The Confucius found in many sections of the *Records on Ceremonial* is not the human being who lived in Lu; rather, he is the sage who had been elaborated in centuries of tradition, now made the hero of Confucian anecdotes. And he acted, of course, as a conventional Han Confucian should act. Confucius had previously been converted to Taoism and to Legalism; now he was converted to Han dynasty Confucianism!

Among the works that have caused this Han conception of Confucius to be accepted as the truth about the man as he actually was, none has been more influential than the biography of Confucius which makes up Chapter 47 of the *Historical Records.* Most Chinese and Western students are agreed that, despite certain defects, this biography is the basis of our current understanding of the life of Confucius. This influence is natural. This biography was the first attempt, and remains almost the only major one, to put the incidents of Confucius' life in chronological order. The *Historical Records* was written by Ssŭ-Ma T'an and his son Ssŭ-Ma Ch'ien, both of whom were officials at the court of Emperor Wu; it was the first great history of China, and it is with reason that it "has held a place in the curriculum of Chinese education second only to the classics." A number of its biographies are excellent pieces of literature, in which motivations are established, character is delineated, incidents are related with gusto, and men and women come alive.

The biography of Confucius is, by contrast, a slipshod performance. There is little motivation and almost no development of a consistent character for Confucius. It consists, in fact, of a series of incidents gathered from Confucian, Taoist, and Legalist sources, thrown together in what is alleged to be a chronological order with very little criticism or harmonization. The result is that Confucius moves through the story like a puppet. Anachronisms are not exceptional but almost the rule. Confucius is represented as talking with men who had in fact been long dead (in one case a hundred years), while two men, who are alleged to have been his first disciples, are said to have been advised to study with him at a time when in fact they had not yet been born. The author seems unable to remember where he is in his story; he says Confucius left one state, yet continues to relate his actions there, and later suddenly tells of his actions in another state without having transported him there. The chronology often differs from that given in other chapters of the *Historical Records*, as many scholars have noted.

The biography abounds in absurdities. A minister of war, wishing to kill Confucius, uses the novel method of having a tree under which the sage is teaching cut down. But while this is being done Confucius simply strolls away, and the plot is thus foiled. In spite of all of these things, it might be a more or less acceptable biography if it presented a consistent, credible picture of the man, and one reasonably congruent with earlier works like the *Analects* and *Mencius*. It does not. Its Confucius is a sage of clairvoyant powers, who discourses at great length about the supernatural; this is in direct conflict, of course, with the *Analects*.[23]

It is true enough that most of the stories in the biography were culled from other works. But it is hard to avoid the feeling that it was put together in a manner that was intended subtly and almost imperceptibly to undermine the character of Confucius as an admirable person. He is depicted as having been, not to mince matters, a liar. Twice he is quoted as asserting he knew nothing about warfare, but between these two passages his disciple Jan Ch'iu is quoted as saying that he had been taught strategy by Confucius. On another occasion he is represented as having very flagrantly broken his oath almost as soon as it was given; when Tzŭ-kung, scandalized, protested, Confucius is declared to have replied, "It was an oath given under duress; the spirits will pay no attention to it." [24] This incident has been shown to be unhistorical.

Many things in this biography show an attitude of concealed but definite hostility toward Confucius. This is very clear in the selection of passages quoted from the *Analects*. These run into the scores, and include such gems as *Analects* 10.9: "If his mat was not straight, he would not sit on it." We look in vain, however, for the warm, sincere, human passages that have made Confucius beloved for twenty-five hundred years. Scarcely one of them is included.

Why is this biography so bad? Ch'ien Mu has sought to explain its deficiencies as being due to changes and interpolations made in the text by later hands. No doubt the text has been tampered with,[25] but that seems inadequate to explain the fact that there are not even the remnants of a good biography. Ts'ui Shu put the case strongly when he said that this biography was "seventy or eighty per cent slander," but certainly a large proportion of it is derogatory to Confucius. Why?

Both of the authors of the *Historical Records* were officials at the court of Emperor Wu. The father, Ssŭ-Ma T'an, was a Taoist whose sharp criticisms of Confucianism are preserved in an essay embodied in the *Historical Records*. Scholars are divided as to whether his son, Ssŭ-Ma Ch'ien, was or was not a Taoist; the evidence would seem to indicate that he at least had leanings in that direction.[26] The difficulty is that there seems to be no way to determine which parts of the book were by the father and which by the son, so that critics may select their evidence as suits their theories.

Although it seems impossible to tell whether the father or the son had the principal part in writing the biography of Confucius,[27] it is evident that it draws heavily on Taoist works and embodies many Taoist ideas. It represents Confucius as having sought out the Taoist sage, Lao Tzŭ, and been lectured by him; this incident is not historic, but was probably first invented by the author of a part of the Taoist work *Chuang Tzŭ*, for the purpose of enhancing the prestige of the Taoists as against that of the Confucians.[28]

It seems likely, however, that something more than a tendency toward Taoism may have lain back of the writing of this biography. Both of the authors of the *Historical Records* were officials at the court of Emperor Wu, and it is perfectly clear that, while they admired the type of Confucian scholar who stood resolutely by his principles, they despised what their book called the "flattering Confucians" who assiduously courted their tyrannical master. We have seen that the *Historical Records* condemned Kung-Sun Hung, the "Confucian" lackey who rose to supreme power, in the plaincst language. It points out that after he was made chief minister the oppression of the people became constantly more severe, and the laws were applied with increasing rigor. "Just at this time the emperor summoned to the court and paid honor to men of worth, virtue, and learning; some of them attained to the rank of dukes, ministers, and great officers. Kung-Sun Hung, although a counselor of state, used a cotton coverlet and ate only a single dish at each meal, as an example to the empire. Nevertheless," the historian comments sardonically, "this did not bring about a reform of morals; and men became ever more intent on the race for prestige and profit."

It has been alleged that the *Historical Records* was written chiefly to censure the administration of Emperor Wu. But that was a dangerous game, as Ssŭ-Ma Ch'ien learned when he was condemned to castration for daring to criticize one of the Emperor's actions. When vindictive "Confucians" like Kung-Sun Hung were in power, it would have been impossible not to write about Confucius in a universal history of China, and most unwise to criticize him openly. It seems probable that the authors chose the course of seeming to praise the sage, while in fact they subtly and effectively damned him. They depicted him, in fact, as a mealy-mouthed, hypocritical "Confucian" of the sort that thronged Wu's court; no doubt they shrewdly guessed that these gentry would find nothing in the picture to criticize.

Chavannes asserted that Ssŭ-Ma Ch'ien must have had a high opinion of Confucius because he placed his biography, where it did not properly belong, in "a high place of honor" among the chapters on the hereditary nobility. But Chavannes himself has pointed out that the *Historical Records* is a satirical book, and this was probably the cream of the jest.

The hypothesis that the biography was written as a piece of carefully veiled satire is supported by Chavannes' own difficulty in translating the opening sentence of Ssŭ-Ma Ch'ien's appraisal of Confucius. In 1895 he published a version which interpreted it as enthusiastic eulogy; ten years later he revised his translation of this same sentence to one that damns with faint praise.

Such is the nature of the biography which, despite the dissent of a few, has been received for two thousand years as the definitive portrayal of Confucius.

The things that happened to Confucianism under the Han Emperor Wu had lasting effects. Thenceforward, with some vicissitudes, Confucianism continued to be subsidized by the government, at times very lavishly. Inevitably a large proportion of those who called themselves Confucian became more or less responsive to the wishes of those who dominated the government, and Confucianism came sometimes to be used as a tool for the control and even for the oppression of the people. The subsidizing of scholarship by the government had, in many periods, the unfortunate effect of tending to standarize thought.

The conception of Confucius that was officially sanctioned, and generally received, was one very far from the truth. This, however, was difficult to regulate. For every scholar studied the *Analects*, and in every age some of them saw, through all of the veil of hair-splitting commentary and official interpretation, the things that the lonely scholar of Lu had been trying to say. When the Manchus conquered China in the seventeenth century and imposed a regime of considerable harshness, they took over and cultivated official Confucianism as a technique of control. Some of the most able scholars of the period, however, not only held aloof from taking office under the Manchus but vigorously attacked the whole elaborate structure of Confucian doctrine that had been developed over nearly two thousand years. They condemned absorption in the mere study of books, insisting that scholars must concern themselves, as Confucius had done, with the practical affairs of the world. With remarkable vigor and scholarly acumen they went back to the basic texts of the *Analects* and *Mencius,* and even rejected many of the early Taoist corruptions of the truth about Confucius. They saw that he had been no doctrinaire, formulating dogmas to bolster imperial despotism, but an earnest, practical, and experimental seeker for truth. Naturally, the pioneering efforts of these seventeenth-century scholars had their imperfections, but they laid the foundation for the great critical movement in Chinese scholarship which continues to the present day.

Nor were the efforts of rulers like the Han Emperor Wu, to control Confucianism by subsidizing it, by any means wholly successful. The government tried to swallow Confucianism, but the question is, who swallowed whom? The filling of government posts by means of examinations on the Confucian Classics did allow the court to influence the interpretation of the Classics, but it also ensured that most of the officials and most of the emperors would be heavily influenced by those works. And some of them are, from the point of view of a government with despotic tendencies, decidedly dangerous books.

Neither Wu nor later emperors were ever able to divorce Confucianism from its early function as the champion of the rights of the people against despotism, a force favoring social and political amelioration if not revolution. Confucians of integrity did not sell their consciences to Wu in exchange for favors to their group. We have seen that he was opposed during his lifetime; there is reason to believe that after his death, despite the fact that history has assigned the triumph of Confucianism to his reign, a majority of Confucians held the Emperor Wu in low esteem.[29] Fifteen years after his death his great-grandson, Emperor Hsüan, announced a plan to honor Wu's memory in celebration of his meritorious achievements, including his patronage of Confucianism. The famous Hsia-Hou Shêng, author of a work on the *Analects,* who was then a high official of the court, denounced this plan; despite the fact that punishment was certain, he declared that Wu should not be honored, since he had been a waster and an oppressor, "conferring no benefits upon the people." At around this same time another Confucian, contrasting Wu's methods with the principles of Confucius, is quoted as saying, "When Confucius said, 'If anyone were to employ me, might I not make a new Chou in the east?' he was intimating that he aspired, like Ch'êng T'ang, Wên, and Wu [all revolutionaries who worked to overthrow dynasties], to uproot brutality and do away with the wicked for the sake of the people."

If the emperors could exercise a measure of control over Confucianism, it is also true that the Confucian scholars had means of control over the emperors that were often equally effective, if more subtle. One of the oldest is that elaborated by Tung Chung-shu, whereby the *Spring and Autumn Annals* was searched for analogies to current events. It was taken as a text from which to point out the shortcomings of the emperor's favorites or of the ruler himself, and the certainty of catastrophe if necessary reforms were neglected. Natural calamities were also interpreted, by analogy with the *Spring and Autumn Annals*, as warnings sent by Heaven to show its displeasure with unrighteous government.

The K'ang Hsi emperor, second of the Manchu line, expressed his impatience with such "superstitious and ignorant" ideas. It is equally impossible not to admire his rational temper, and not to suspect that it may have been prompted in part by irritation with Confucian criticism of his rule. In 1699 he appointed a board of well-known scholars to make a new edition of the commentaries on the *Spring and Autumn Annals*, from which they should "eliminate everything not in harmony with the *classic*" (*i.e.*, the *Annals*). When the work was completed the Emperor expressed his satisfaction. After all, he pointed out, even while Confucius' disciples were alive there were varying traditions as to what he had said, and how could Confucians living thousands of years later be sure? In this book, the Emperor said, his editors had merely "selected what was in accord with right." Turning to the book itself, we see that the editors condemned as "not right" passages which asserted that an unworthy or tyrannical ruler had no claim to loyalty, and might properly be removed.

While the influence of Confucianism on the government has been greater at some periods than at others, it has been pervasive, and in general it has tended toward what we call democracy. Perhaps in no other great nation has it so continuously been the accepted theory, for the past two thousand years, that the government exists for the purpose of bringing about the welfare *and satisfaction* of the people, and that if it fails to do so it may properly be criticized and even overthrown. This has given great power to public opinion.

The insistence of Confucius that the administration should be placed in the hands of the most capable men in the land, selected solely on the basis of their virtue and education, resulted in the examination system, which was gradually elaborated from Han times onward. Its specific organization differed from period to period. During the Manchu dynasty it consisted of three kinds of examinations, local, provincial, and national, held every two or three years. The candidates competed, at each level, for three successively higher degrees. The competition was intense; in each examination, only a small proportion of the candidates could hope to pass. Naturally there was corruption, but elaborate precautions were taken to prevent it, and during the better periods under Chinese rulers they seem to have been remarkably successful.

Even the lowest degree gave its possessor, though he might be the son of the poorest peasant, great social distinction. In some cases those who held it were given government stipends, or minor posts in the local administration, which meant that in effect they received state assistance in continuing their education. Possession of the highest degree did not always assure that its holder would be appointed to office, but under Chinese dynasties a large proportion of the most responsible posts were normally filled by men who had excelled in the examinations. Although office might be attained in other ways, it appears that, in many periods at least, the man who had passed the examinations had the best prospect of reaching the top of the official hierarchy.

An important exception must be noted, however, in the case of dynasties established by foreign invaders; they naturally gave many of the highest offices to their own people, without subjecting them to the competition of the examinations. Nevertheless, after all of the necessary qualifications have been made, it remains true that in large measure China has been ruled by a bureaucracy imbued by education with Confucian ideals, and recruited through the examinations from the people in general. This does not mean, of course, that all of the highest posts were filled by the sons of farmers. Entirely aside from favoritism, which did operate, the son of a member of the bureaucracy had natural advantages; his family could afford to give him a good education, and he grew up in a learned and professional atmosphere. It is not remarkable that a great many of the principal ministers were the sons or grandsons of officials, but it is surprising that some of them were able to rise from the ranks of the people without such advantages. Although our information is incomplete, it appears that at least in some periods the lower ranks of the bureaucracy, in particular, were infused through the examinations with fresh blood from the masses in considerable volume.

The content of the examinations was designed chiefly, though by no means exclusively, to test the candidates' knowledge of the Confucian Classics. Confucius had never laid eyes on a number of these books and would certainly have taken sharp issue with a good deal of their content. He would have deplored the emphasis that the examinations laid on mere knowledge of books as such (see, for instance, *Analects* 13.5). A great many of the more vigorous minds among Confucian scholars deplored it, too, but never with great or lasting effect.

Despite its shortcomings, the examination system gave China a unique kind of government which had many advantages. It brought many of the ablest men in the country into government service. In so far as it was effective, it assured that officials were men of culture, not mere wasters who had inherited their positions. Because its very basis was the philosophy and the ethics of Confucianism, it inculcated a body of shared ideals which produced a very unusual *esprit de corps*. Although it fell short of what we today consider political democracy, it gave to the common people a kind of representation in the government, since in each generation some of their number normally won official posts. It did not make a classless society since education automatically raised the status of its possessors, but it did bring about a degree of social democracy that has probably never been equaled in so great a country over such a long period. Where every peasant's son may in theory hope to become the most powerful minister in the government, and one of their number does occasionally reach such a position, a certain limit is set to social stratification.

It will be recalled that Confucius insisted that a minister should consider loyalty to principle above loyalty to his ruler, and must criticize fearlessly. This doctrine received institutional expression in the post of the official censors. It was their duty to examine the conduct of everyone in the government, including the emperor, and to criticize any dereliction without fear or favor. Naturally, the manner in which these duties were discharged varied with the integrity and the courage of the censors; at some times, indeed, they seem even to have been used as the tools of despotic emperors. Nevertheless, there is no question that some of the censors filled their office with the highest idealism. To be sure, the emperor could always condemn a troublesome censor to exile or even to death, but only at the risk of creating a troublesome martyr.

Altogether, these things made for a degree of democracy that is surprising in a theoretically absolute monarchy. Yet the fact remains that it fell far short of fully democratic government. Confucius had made a remarkable beginning toward democratic government, but too little had been added to the principles which he formulated. And principles are not enough. For effective democracy the people in general must have an effective voice in choosing their rulers. This requires that specific techniques for this purpose be created. In China these were never developed; this achievement took place on the other side of the world. Nevertheless Confucianism played an interesting and significant role in connection with it. To consider this we must transfer our attention to Europe.

LLLLLLLLLLLLLLLLLLLL

CHAPTER XV

CONFUCIANISM AND
WESTERN DEMOCRACY

In the Western world democratic institutions made their most rapid and dramatic gains in connection with the American and French Revolutions. It is no doubt true that these revolutions were not "caused" by the philosophic movement known as the Enlightenment; but it is true that this new pattern of thought determined, in very considerable measure, the direction in which men moved once the revolutions had given them freedom of action.

The philosophy of the Enlightenment has some very remarkable similarities to Confucianism. Since it developed during the seventeenth and eighteenth centuries, and this was precisely the period at which Confucianism came to be effectively known in Europe, it has inevitably been asked whether Chinese philosophy did not suggest some of these European ideas. To give a judicious answer is not easy. If one is especially interested in China, he tends to note all influences from that source and pay less attention to any others. In an impressively documented volume on *The Influence of Chinese Thought on European Culture* published in 1940, a Chinese scholar went so far as to declare that "Chinese philosophy was without doubt the basic

254

cause of the French Revolution." Others, contemptuous of both China and the revolution, have sought to discredit the latter by associating it with the former. Less than forty years after the revolution Macaulay, belaboring the "French academicians" of the eighteenth century, asserted that in their circle stories about China "which ought not to have imposed on an old nurse, were gravely laid down as foundations of political theories by eminent philosophers." Another enemy of the revolution, the brilliant French critic and social philosopher Ferdinand Brunetière (1849–1906), blamed much that he did not like in French democracy on the Chinese. Of the French system of education, Brunetière wrote: "There is nothing more Chinese! The Revolution organized the system, but its principles were laid down by 'philosophy,' and by those philosophers who admired and panegyrized China. Everything to competitive examinations and nothing to favor, but above all nothing to heredity! their envious spirit has been seduced by that conception of the mandarinate."

On the other hand, some students of the French Revolution seem almost completely to ignore the fact that Chinese ideas played any role at all in its background. Georges Lefebvre, who has been called "the most distinguished living authority on the period of the Revolution," found it possible to publish, in 1939, an entire volume on the background of the revolution which made no mention of China whatever. Quite naturally, he paid primary attention to social, economic, and political conditions within France itself. At the same time, however, he warned against "forgetting that there is no true revolutionary spirit without the idealism which alone inspires sacrifice," and attributed to the philosophy of the eighteenth century a large share in the forging of that idealism. He wrote:

> From the sixteenth to the eighteenth centuries philosophers proposed that man . . . throw off the fetters that held down his rise on earth; they urged him to become the master of nature and make his kind the true ruler of creation. Different though such doctrine seemed from that of the Church, the two were at one in recognizing the eminent dignity of the human person and commanding respect for it, in attrib-

uting to man certain natural and imprescriptible rights and
in assigning to the authority of the state no other purpose
than to protect these rights and to help the individual make
himself worthy of them.

However correct this may be, it is also true (1) that in certain
very important respects the thinking of the Enlightenment
moved to positions much more similar to those of Confucianism
than to those of the contemporary Church, and (2) that this
fact was recognized and widely proclaimed by leading figures of
the Enlightenment.

At the time this was not only well known but even notorious.
When Christian Wolff, in an oration, said of the Chinese that
"in the Art of Governing, this Nation has ever surpassed all
others without exception," he is reported to have been ordered
to leave the University of Halle within twenty-four hours "under
pain of immediate death." The result was to cause his speech to
be read with enthusiasm as far away as England. Much the
same thing had been said before and would be said again by
many. Leibniz wrote of the Chinese: "Even if we are equal to
them in the productive arts, and if we surpass them in the
theoretical sciences, it is certainly true (I am almost ashamed
to admit) that they surpass us in practical philosophy, by which
I mean the rules of ethics and politics which have been devised
for the conduct and benefit of human life." Voltaire asserted that
"the constitution of their empire is in truth the best that there
is in the world . . . the only one in which a governor of a province is punished if, when he quits his post, he is not acclaimed
by the people . . . four thousand years ago, when we did not
know how to read, they knew everything essentially useful of
which we boast today." In England Eustace Budgell wrote in
1731 that

> the great point in which all Authors, who have wrote of the
> *Chinese,* do generally agree that they excel all other People
> in, is the *Art of Government.* Even the French . . . are
> obliged to own ingenuously that the Chinese do excel all
> other nations in the *Art of Government,* and can never suffi-
> ciently admire those political maxims collected, methodized
> and commented upon by the great *Confucius.*

When François Quesnay first set forth the political principles of his very influential Physiocratic doctrine, he did so in an exposition of the government of China, as he understood it. In the introduction to his final section, concerned with "the natural principles in accord with which prosperous governments are constituted," he stated that it was merely "a systematic account of the Chinese *doctrine,* which deserves to be taken as a model for all states."

If these things are sometimes forgotten, a part of the reason lies in the peculiar circumstances which surrounded the introduction of Confucianism to Europe, and its rise to and fall from popularity. Although travelers had told tales about China for centuries, most of them had learned very little about Chinese culture, and therefore could report little. It was different, however, with the Jesuit missionaries who, after the greatest difficulties and with superb ingenuity, gained access to China just before 1600 A.D. A learned order, the Jesuits used their learning to gain and hold a position in Chinese intellectual circles, and even in the imperial court itself. They served the emperors as astronomers (one of their number held the important office of vice-president of the Board of Astronomy), physicians, diplomats, and even casters of cannon. A few of them came to be intimate friends of emperors. They not only spoke Chinese but read and wrote it, and they came to have an intimate knowledge of China that many later scholars have cause to envy. They kept up a voluminous correspondence with members of their own order and with some of the most famous men of the day in Europe. Some of these letters were published as books and others became the basis on which books were written.

These letters, and the new information about China, became a sensation in Europe. Virgile Pinot has concluded, after a careful study, that in eighteenth-century France China "seems to have been more in favor than England itself," despite the fact that this was also the century in France of "Anglomania." By 1769 it could be written that "China is better known than some provinces of Europe itself"; indeed, it seems probable that literate Occidentals knew more about China in the eighteenth century than they do in the twentieth. Yet since most of this information came through the Jesuits it naturally bore the stamp of their interests, and many have insisted, from that day to this, that they deliberately falsified their accounts from ulterior motives. These accusations grew, to a large extent, out of the celebrated Rites Controversy. The Jesuits held that the ceremonies performed by Chinese in honor of their ancestors and Confucius were not worship, and might be tolerated; other Catholic orders opposed this stand. Ultimately the Jesuits found themselves in disfavor both with the Pope on the one hand and with the Chinese Emperor on the other.

Certainly it is true that the Jesuits sent glowing pictures of China to Europe. Even Voltaire, who defended the Jesuits on this score, admitted that they painted a too flattering picture of the Chinese emperors. It was also charged that, in describing Chinese philosophy and specifically Confucianism, the Jesuits did not give a true picture of these things as they were generally understood in China at that time.

It is perfectly true that the Confucianism which the Jesuits reported with such enthusiasm in their letters to Europe was not the Confucian orthodoxy that was commonly current in China in the seventeenth and eighteenth centuries. That orthodoxy, commonly called Neo-Confucianism, was a complex doctrine. It embodied many of the ideas of Confucius, but these were woven into an elaborate system of metaphysical philosophy that derived many of its elements from Buddhism. Confucius would not have understood it, and it would not have been received sympathetically in Europe by men like, for instance, Voltaire. Nor did it appeal to the Jesuit missionaries, who were men of keen and critical minds. Furthermore, they had their own system of metaphysics, and felt no need of another.

The more they studied the Confucian texts, however, the more they became convinced that this contemporary philosophy was not the same thing as the original Confucianism at all. Matteo Ricci, the great pioneer of the mission, made the observation that its metaphysics "seems to me to have been borrowed from the sect of idols [Buddhism] five hundred years ago." As he delved further into the early texts, he said of this Neo-Confucianism, "This is not Confucius!"

His view sprang from sincere intellectual conviction. It also coincided with the need of the missionaries for a means of winning over Chinese intellectuals to Christianity. As they frequently did in other countries, the Jesuits in China exerted their best efforts toward converting members of the ruling group. These men were predominantly Confucian. Thus, a present-day Jesuit affirms, "It was necessary that they begin by breaking the intimate bond . . . which united Chu-hsiism [Neo-Confucianism] with the moral philosophy of Confucius." They set about this task with great vigor and achieved considerable success; Hu Shih attests that they "won over a number of the most brilliant and serious-minded scholars of the age." One of these converts, taxed with having deserted Confucianism, declared that he had not done so at all, but had rather found in Catholicism a doctrine much closer to the teachings of Confucius than the "distortions" of "later Confucians." Father Intorcetta went so far as to affirm that if Confucius had lived in the seventeenth century "he would have been the first to become a Christian."

The Jesuit attacks on Neo-Confucianism probably bore fruit in China beyond what was contemplated. It has been said that Ricci was the first to deny that Neo-Confucianism represented the genuine thought of the ancients. At any rate, it would seem that when he and other Jesuits began to propagate this opinion, it was not held widely (if at all) among Chinese scholars. The Jesuit contention became generally known, and was widely debated in Chinese intellectual circles. Subsequently, the proposition that Neo-Confucianism was not original Confucianism, but a distortion deriving much of its content from Buddhism, became a basic tenet of the important "school of Han learning";[1] this school arose within a few decades after the death of Ricci. It also appears that it was considerably though indirectly indebted to the Jesuits for scientific method, both in general and in such specific fields as astronomy and linguistics. This "Han learning," as Hu Shih has pointed out, "produced the age of scientific research in the humanistic and historical studies during the last three hundred years." It was also an important factor in the intellectual background of Sun Yat-sen and other leaders of the Chinese Revolution. Thus, although the Jesuit missionaries of the seventeenth and eighteenth centuries did not succeed in converting all of China to Christianity, as they had hoped, they exerted an influence upon her culture that is altogether remarkable in view of their small numbers and the difficulties under which they worked.

In Europe, the effects of their activities as intermediaries between civilizations were likewise noteworthy. The Jesuits sent back detailed and often enthusiastic accounts of China, of Chinese thought, and especially of Confucius. They have often been accused of deliberately painting a picture that was too glowing. Perhaps some of them did. But it seems far more probable that this impression is derived from the fact that they talked most about what interested them most. They did, statements to the contrary notwithstanding, report the religious and magical practices of the day, sometimes at length.[2] That being done, they went on to speak of those things that aroused their enthusiasm, and especially of early Confucianism as it appeared in such works as the *Analects* and *Mencius*. Of the Classics Ricci wrote, "When we have carefully examined all these books, we have found very little which is contrary to the light of reason, and much that is in conformity with it; these books are not inferior to those of any of our philosophers."

Some of the statements which the Jesuits intended to be derogatory did not appear so when they were received in European intellectual circles. When Ricci deplored the fact that the philosophy of Confucius lacked the supernatural element, it was not his intention that this should kindle greater interest in the sage, but that was the effect of such observations in Europe.

Thus it was their conception of an earlier and "purer" Confucianism which, for the most part, the Jesuits reported to Europe. We are not to suppose, of course, that they succeeded wholly in reconstructing the philosophy of Confucius; without a great deal of critical scholarship that was to come later, that would have been impossible. And certainly, many absurdities about Confucius became current in eighteenth-century Europe. Nevertheless, in the circumstances the Jesuits did remarkably well.

This is why Adolf Reichwein wrote, "The Enlightenment knew only the China of Confucius." Striving to break the bonds of a metaphysical ethics and a feudal society, the philosophers of the Enlightenment "discovered, to their astonishment, that more than two thousand years ago in China . . . Confucius had thought the same thoughts in the same manner, and fought the same battles. They read in his book the words: 'If a man make himself understood by his words, the end is attained.' He, too, then had advocated clearness in verbal expression and, therefore, also clearness of logical thought generally. Thus Confucius became the patron saint of eighteenth-century Enlightenment." To see how true this is we need only to turn to Voltaire's *Philosophical Dictionary* where, in a eulogy of Confucius, the French philosopher wrote, "I have read his books with attention; I have made extracts from them; I have never found in them anything but the purest morality, without the slightest tinge of charlatanism." Elsewhere Voltaire wrote: "The happiest period, and the one most worthy of respect which there has ever been on this earth, was the one which followed his [Confucius'] laws."

The position of saint is a most difficult one, however, to maintain. And undoubtedly some of the Jesuits and other enthusiasts overdid things by exaggerating the degree to which the contemporary Chinese and the Chinese government were guided by "pure" Confucianism. For a variety of reasons there was scepticism in Europe from the beginning, and when Chinese culture was used to attack traditional European institutions, counterattack was inevitable. When Leibniz suggested that Chinese missionaries should be sent to Europe to teach "natural theology," and Voltaire declared that in morality Europeans "ought to become the disciples" of the Chinese, it was natural that others should inquire whether the Chinese were in fact so moral after all.

They had little trouble finding testimony that they were not. Enemies of the Jesuits, and traders and other travelers less fortunate in their experiences with the Chinese, bore willing witness against them. On the basis of such testimony Fénelon, writing around 1700, called the Chinese "the most vain, superstitious, selfish, and lying people in the world." And Montesquieu, in his *Spirit of Laws* which appeared in 1748, asserted that "our merchants are far from giving us any such accounts of the virtue [of the Chinese] so much talked of by the missionaries."

If the missionaries were not reliable about the Chinese, why should one believe them about Confucius? As more and more information was received in Europe about the belief in divina-

tion and magic on the part of the masses and even of some
scholars in China, it began to be suspected that the lofty philosophy of Confucius had been nothing more than an invention
of the "wily Jesuits." At best, all the accretions and corruptions
of later Confucianism were now attributed to Confucius himself. Thus Diderot, in the article on Chinese philosophy which
he wrote for the great *Encyclopedia,* sets forth a confusing
array of these things and then, toward the end, gives a summary of material in the *Analects;* from the latter, he says,
"one may see that the ethics of Confucius is much superior to
his metaphysics and his physics." The truth is, of course, that
the bits from the *Analects* are the only part of his article that
has any real connection with Confucius; the "metaphysics and
physics" are the work of later times. But only the Jesuits knew
enough to draw this distinction; and Diderot made it plain at
the beginning of his article that he was no longer willing to trust
them.

However, Voltaire was still writing and China was still in
vogue. The crushing blow to its prestige came from the dis-
crediting of its governmental system. Here its partisans had
undoubtedly gone too far in their praise. The Jesuits naturally
had an optimistic view of a government which had signally
favored them; and indeed as compared with the governments `
of Europe at the time there was no doubt some justification
for their description of its organization as "perfect and exact."
But the seventeenth and eighteenth centuries were not the best
in which to observe its virtues. They began with the corrupt
and oppressive rule of late Ming times, continued with the
Manchu conquest, and saw the Manchus establish their reign
with peculiarly harsh repression. The Ch'ien Lung emperor,
during whose reign Voltaire lauded the Chinese as an example
of tolerance, was one of the greatest destroyers of literature (in
the name of the suppression of "dangerous thought") in all
history.

Gradually these facts became known. In vain did Voltaire
protest, against the assertions of critics like Montesquieu, that
China was in fact not a "despotism" but only appeared to be
so.[3] Other champions of that country boldly declared that it
was a despotism, but the most benevolent and constitutional

of despotisms and therefore the best of governments. Leibniz, much earlier, had been attracted by his conception of the Chinese emperor as an enlightened despot. When Quesnay published his treatise on the political principles of Physiocracy he called it *Despotism in China*. It will be recalled that Quesnay was the physician of Mme. de Pompadour and later of Louis XV, which doubtless caused him to feel tolerant toward "benevolent despotism." But others were not so, and as revolutionary sentiment grew China fell rapidly from general favor.

Let us recapitulate. Chinese philosophy was introduced to Europe by the Jesuits. They reported chiefly on what they considered best, the ideas of Confucius personally and the earliest Confucianism. Being rationalist in temper and tending in a democratic direction, this philosophy was hailed as a revolutionary gospel from another world. A little later, however, Europeans learned more about the later forms of Confucianism, which as we saw earlier were in part a perversion of that philosophy designed to make it serve the purposes of monarchic authority. Simultaneously it was emphasized that in fact the government of China, which had been so highly praised, had at least many of the characteristics of a despotism; indeed, some of its very champions hailed it as such. It was concluded that the virtues of Confucius and of Chinese government had alike been inventions of the Jesuits, perpetrated for purposes of propaganda. At this same time the Jesuit order became so thoroughly discredited that in 1773, after it had been expelled from one country after another, it was dissolved by the Pope. Disillusionment became complete; the "Chinese dream" was over. Never again in the West, since the end of the eighteenth century, has interest in China and esteem for that country risen so high.

This curious chain of events has caused many of those who trace the background of the French and American Revolutions completely to disregard the fact that Chinese ideas contributed to the growth of democratic philosophy. Alan F. Hattersley, in his *Short History of Democracy*, does recognize that new ideas derived from "Asiatic states of ancient civilization" played a role in the development of the ideals of "equality, charity and fraternity." In general, however, even those who are well aware that China influenced the West during the eighteenth century do not emphasize this point. Since China is identified as a despotism, and Confucius with China, it is often supposed that his ideas could hardly have contributed to the growth of democracy.

Gustave Lanson, who has been called "the creator in France of the science of literary history," made an elaborate analysis of the intellectual background of the French Revolution. While not denying that outside influences had made some contribution, he concluded that the revolutionary philosophy had been basically an indigenous development, the result of thought processes long under way in France, stimulated by current conditions in that country. Lanson named three French books, published around 1700, with which he said "there began the movement from which would proceed the political philosophy of the eighteenth century and the doctrines of the revolutionaries." One of these was Fénelon's *Télémaque*.

This inclusion of Fénelon among the precursors of the revolution is very convenient for our investigation. For it happens that in his *Dialogues of the Dead* (which Lanson also cited as representing similar views) Fénelon vigorously attacked the philosophy of Confucius. From this work we may learn, then, what a hostilely inclined French intellectual believed the philosophy of Confucius to be, at the beginning of the eighteenth century. We can also compare the opinions of Fénelon with those of Confucius as Fénelon understood them, and see which appears to be closer to the philosophy of the revolution. Among the dialogues in this volume, which was published in 1700,[4] Fénelon included an imaginary debate between Socrates and Confucius. Fénelon leaves the reader in no doubt as to his sympathies. He damns the Chinese roundly; clearly, Fénelon is talking through Socrates.

Socrates begins by denying the resemblance that is commonly alleged between himself and Confucius. "I have never," Socrates declares, "thought of making the people into philosophers . . . I have abandoned the vulgar and corrupt to their errors, limiting myself to the instruction of a small number of disciples of cultivated spirit."

Confucius replies courteously and says, "As for me, I have

---

avoided subtlety in reasoning, limiting myself to sensible maxims for the practice of virtue among men." "I have believed," Socrates answers, "that one cannot establish true maxims without going back to first principles from which they can be proved . . ."

"But have you," asks Confucius, "been able by means of those first principles to prevent divisions and disputes among your disciples?" No, Socrates tells him, and that fact has caused him to lose his hopes for the human race. For the most part nothing can be done with them. "Example and argument, instilled with the greatest art, have some effect only on a very small number of men who are better born than others. A general reform of a state thus appears to me to be impossible; that is the extent to which I am disillusioned with the human race."

"For myself," Confucius replies, "I have written and I have sent out my disciples, in the attempt to cause moral principles to prevail in every province of our empire." To this Socrates answers Confucius that, being "of a royal house and having great authority in your nation, you were able to do many things not permitted to me, the son of an artisan." In a long speech Socrates then develops his point that in general peoples who have accomplished much have owed this to good leadership. "But to be philosophical, to follow the beautiful and the good from persuasion alone, and from the true and free love of the beautiful and the good—this is what can never be diffused among a whole people; it is reserved to certain chosen souls whom heaven has seen fit to separate from the rest. The people in general are capable only of exercising certain virtues, in matters of custom and opinion, on the authority of those who have gained their confidence." In the remainder of the dialogue Socrates argues, in great detail, that the Chinese are by no means so ancient or admirable a people as they have been represented.

If, as Lanson held, Fénelon (*i.e.*, "Socrates") was a precursor of the revolution, it is clear that he was still a long distance from "liberty, equality, fraternity." Just as clearly, he believed that the philosophy of Confucius was much closer to these sentiments—in fact, altogether too close for his taste.

Lanson developed his thesis, that the philosophy of eighteenth-century France and the political principles underlying the revolution were basically indigenous developments, in two essays. In the first, while acknowledging that external influences (including those from China) played some part, he argued that "the movement which resulted in French rationalism in the eighteenth century . . . was the result of an inner travail which, beginning with the Renaissance, had been transforming the spirit of French society, and which suddenly became more noticeable and more rapid in the closing years of the seventeenth century."

Thus, he says, a transformation came about in the years from 1680 to 1715 which had as its salient points these ideas: (1) The demand for clear and coherent thinking, together with attention to facts and experience, with no concession either to prejudice or to authority; one must seek the truth for one's self. (2) The sovereignty of conscience, independent of dogma; thus good men everywhere, regardless of race or religion, have essentially the same moral principles, and the individual may judge what is good or bad for himself; in general the good is "the golden mean." (3) The good and the pleasant became identified; one should not seek to eliminate but merely to guide one's desires. The emphasis was on enjoying this world; other-worldly sanctions disappeared. (4) The good was found not, as later by Rousseau, in primitivity but only as a product of culture and civilization. (5) The philosophy of pleasure was enlarged to one of reciprocity, whereby one felt the need to make others happy in order to be happy himself. (6) The virtue of "charity" was replaced by that of "humanity."

Lanson acknowledges that the new knowledge of China played some part in the development of the second of these ideas. For all of them, however, he seeks to find indigenous and logical explanations. In some cases these are not wholly convincing. The transition from egoism to altruism, for instance, does not in fact seem to be anything like so simple and almost inevitable a thing as it is here pictured.

Two facts are distinctly worthy of remark. In the first place, as the reader will have noted, in every one of these six respects French thought of the eighteenth century came to positions extraordinarily similar to those of Confucius in the *Analects* and of very early Confucianism. In the second place, the period of 1680 to 1715, in which Lanson dates this transformation, is precisely that in which this early Confucianism was effectively introduced to the French public. The first translation of any of the early Confucian works seems to have been published in 1662, and others followed in the succeeding decades.[5] In 1685 a special party of learned French Jesuits bearing letters from Louis XIV was sent to China, from whence they and others who followed them kept up a voluminous correspondence with a number of the most eminent men in Europe; these letters formed the basis of a number of books published in the succeeding decades that made China, and Confucius, known as never before.

In his second essay Lanson stated that "between the dates of 1692 and 1723 there awoke, in the upper class of French society, a social conscience and a spirit of reform. There had been nothing of the sort before." And he sought to show, without "pretending to underestimate foreign [*i.e.*, British and American] influences," that these things were to a large extent caused by current conditions in France. Though there is merit in his argument, the causes that he cites are sometimes inadequate to account for the effects. No doubt it is true that the spread of "a spirit of reform, of active zeal for the public welfare" was stimulated by the oppressive nature of the late years of the reign of Louis XIV. But that is somewhat beside the point. Our question is, why this particular sort of spirit at this particular time? Obviously it is not always called forth by the simple fact of oppression, in France or anywhere else.

Still less does it seem possible to agree with this statement: "The principle of equality was evolved, but from where? From the consideration of the unequal and oppressive assessment of poll-taxes." Undoubtedly this was a factor. But the very fact that there was protest against unequal treatment implies that men felt themselves entitled to equal treatment, that is, felt themselves to be in some sense equal. It seems probable that the reasons for which they did so were far more complex than Lanson suggests. Among the forces tending in this direction were influences from the Reformation, from England, and from China. It was the idea of basic human equality which Occidentals had been most startled to find prevalent, as they believed, in China. They had been reporting this amazing fact

to Europe for a century prior to 1692, the date which Lanson
sets for the beginning of the awakening of a social conscience
in France.

It is beyond the scope of this book to list the great number of
scholars, philosophers, and statesmen in Germany, England,
and France who were influenced by Chinese ideas during the
seventeenth and eighteenth centuries. This has been done by
others.[6] Nor can we consider in detail each of the resemblances
which exist between cardinal principles of eighteenth-century
philosophy and the philosophy of the French Revolution, on the
one hand, and early Confucianism on the other. Such compari-
sons might easily fill a volume. The concept of natural law,
so important in Europe, is very like the Confucian conception
of the Way, as both Leibniz and Wolff recognized; it has been
suggested that it was on this basis that Turgot, who was a minister of Louis XVI and whom we know to have been deeply
interested in China, suggested to his royal master certain modi-
fications in the operation of the French monarchy. Also common to eighteenth-century France and to China were the ideas
that the proper end of government is the happiness of the people,[7] and that government should be a cooperative rather than
a competitive enterprise; even Montesquieu praised the government of China on this latter score, commenting, "This empire
is formed on the plan of a government of a family."

Since it is impossible even to summarize the evidence on all
these points, let us consider only two principles that were fundamental to the French Revolution: first, the right of revolution
itself; second, human equality.

The revolutionary National Convention declared, "When
government violates the rights of the people, insurrection is
for the people, and for every portion of the people, the most
sacred of rights and the most indispensable of duties." Although
this was completely at variance with the political theory of
medieval Europe it was not, of course, by any means the first
European challenge to the older conceptions. This challenge
must have been significantly reinforced by the discovery of
Chinese political theory. For in China, which was widely proclaimed to be the best governed and most orderly of nations,

the principle that in the face of oppression revolution is precisely "the most sacred of rights and the most indispensable of duties" had long been accepted as an axiom. It is implicit in the *Analects* and explicit in the *Mencius*.[8] The fact that in China the danger of revolution was an everpresent deterrent to tyranny was early reported by the missionaries and was mentioned long before the revolution by a number of writers, as various as Quesnay at the court of Louis XV and Oliver Goldsmith in England. Montesquieu wrote that "the emperor of China . . . knows that if his empire be not just, he will be stript both of empire and life."

The case of the principle of equality is also of interest. In 1789 the Assembly adopted a Declaration of the Rights of Man and the Citizen; Article I states: "Men are born, and always continue, free and equal in respect of their rights. Civil distinctions, therefore, can be founded only in public utility." The resemblance of these words to the preamble of the American Declaration of Independence has often been remarked. It is also worthy of note that a similar statement had been published in Paris at the early date of 1696, by the Jesuit Le Comte. He wrote that in China "nobility is never hereditary, neither is there any distinction between the qualities of people; saving what the offices which they execute makes."

Harold J. Laski has written that "the French Revolution may be said to have contributed to democratic theory the insistence that the career must be opened to the talents, which was, whatever its limitations, a denial that birth or race or creed can bar the road to equality." There is some doubt, however, about the originality of this contribution, since long before the revolution wide publicity had been given to the idea that in China offices were filled strictly on the basis of worth. Virgile Pinot has pointed out that "the admirers of China believed that they found there, and there only, a country where merit permitted one to attain to the highest dignities of the state, a country where each person was classed in the social hierarchy according to his merit, while neither the favor of the prince nor the advantages of birth could permit him to insinuate himself fraudulently into a place to which he was called neither by his virtues nor by his learning. The thing must have been rare or even non-existent in Europe, for all the missionaries, of whatever nationality they might be, celebrated in dithyrambic terms this marvelous Chinese hierarchy which was founded on nothing but merit."

Such reports by the missionaries were made as early as 1602 and continued in unbroken sequence. In a widely read work published in 1735 Du Halde asserted that in China "a student, though the son of a peasant, has as much hope of arriving at the dignity of Viceroy, and even of Minister of State, as the children of the greatest persons of quality."

These observations stirred wide interest. They were discussed in many books, including Robert Burton's *Anatomy of Melancholy*, published in 1621. Another Englishman, Eustace Budgell (who had been a contributor to the *Tatler* and the *Spectator*), proposed in 1731 that the Chinese practice be adopted in Britain. He wrote that he considered it a maxim *"That every Post of Honour or Profit in the Commonwealth, ought to be made the reward of real Merit*. If any Modern Politician should take it into his Head that this Maxim, however Excellent in it self, cannot possibly be observed in so large and populous a Kingdom as *Great Britain*; I beg leave to inform such a Politician, that at this very Time, this glorious Maxim is most strictly follow'd and observ'd in the *Largest*, the most *Populous*, and the best *Govern'd* Empire in all the World: I mean in *China*. . . . No man in China can be made a *Mandarine*, that is, a *Gentleman*, or is capable of any *Post* in the *Government*, who is not really a man of *Parts* and *Learning*." In 1762 Oliver Goldsmith used this same argument as the basis of a bitter attack upon the hereditary aristocracy of Great Britain.

In France it was remarked by a number of writers, including Voltaire, Etienne de Silhouette who became Controller-General of France in 1759, Turgot who held the same position from 1774 to 1776, the royal ambassador Pierre Poivre, and Quesnay who founded the Physiocratic doctrines. In short, at the time when the French Revolution "contributed to democratic theory" the principle that men should be chosen for office purely on the basis of their individual character and attainments, it had been common knowledge for a very long time that this was the theory, at least, of government in China.

Are we to conclude, then, that the new knowledge of China was "the cause" of the French Revolution? Certainly not. The revolution was brought on by many factors, political, economic, social, and intellectual, an exhaustive inquiry into which would be out of place here. Our concern is not so much with the revolution as such, as with the spiritual revolution that gradually re-oriented the thinking of the entire Western world, in the seventeenth and eighteenth centuries, in the direction of democracy. It goes without saying that the new knowledge of Confucianism was only one of many factors which lay back of this spiritual revolution.

It was a factor, however, of which the importance has not been adequately recognized, nor sufficiently investigated. In Europe, and in France in particular, the whole pattern of thought became transformed during the seventeenth and eighteenth centuries, and after the transformation it was in many respects similar to the thinking of Confucius. Neither the transformation nor the resemblances were superficial. It is perfectly clear that in part these resemblances are due to sheer coincidence, but it seems improbable that they are wholly so. To determine to what degree they are the result of influence by one culture upon the other will require careful research, of a sort which has not yet been carried out upon a sufficient scale. When it is, a new and significant chapter may be added to the biography of democracy.

Some indication of the kind of results which may come from such research is provided by an exceedingly interesting essay published in 1948 by Arthur O. Lovejoy, entitled "The Chinese Origin of a Romanticism." It is a meticulously documented study of Chinese influence during the eighteenth century in a single field, aesthetics, in a single Western country, England. Lovejoy concludes that "a new canon of aesthetic excellence" was introduced from China, and says: "A turning-point in the history of modern taste was reached when the ideals of regularity, simplicity, uniformity, and easy logical intelligibility, were first openly impugned, when the assumption that true beauty is 'geometrical' ceased to be one to which 'all consented, as to a Law of Nature.' And in England, at all events, the rejection of this assumption seems, throughout most of the eighteenth century, to have been commonly recognized as initially due to the influence and the example of Chinese art."

This function of Chinese ideas, the presenting of an alternative to the entrenched axioms of European thought, to which it had previously been alleged that all civilized men assented, had repercussions in other fields than art. It had a bearing on such basic questions as that of the value of human happiness. Gilbert Chinard has pointed out that "the whole Christian civilization had been built on the idea that happiness is neither desirable nor obtainable in this vale of tears and affliction." Those who had protested against this were many, but in general they were lone voices, or small groups.

Then the discovery of the East opened to European eyes, as Voltaire graphically put it, "a new moral and physical universe." In China they found a nation which claimed to be the most ancient in the world, and which indisputably possessed that least questionable of all credentials, prosperity,[9] which in calm self-sufficiency regulated itself by principles which were in many respects the very opposite of those prevailing in Europe. Here happiness was not frowned upon, but was rather considered the highest end, not only of the individual but even of the state. Human equality was not denied; rather, those who reported on China asserted, it was the very basis of social and political theory.

Inevitably this "new universe" was appealed to by European nonconformists in support of heterodox notions. No longer could it be said that any practice which conflicted with European tradition "would not work" or "was not done." Voltaire asserted with glee that "the same men who maintain, against the position of Bayle,[10] that a society of atheists is impossible, assert at the same time that the oldest government in the world [the Chinese] is a society of atheists." When defenders of the status quo declared that it would be subversive of good government and order to give political power, on the basis of merit alone, to men of no hereditary status, Budgell could now reply that "this glorious Maxim is most strictly follow'd and observ'd in the *Largest*, the most *Populous*, and the *best Govern'd* Empire in all the World: I mean in *China*."

If European standards were not to be subverted this threat had to be met by the defenders of tradition. They did meet it, as we have seen, and they succeeded in thoroughly undermining the reputation of Chinese and Confucian thought in Europe. The result has been that from the time of the French Revolution on it has been all but forgotten that China made a contribution, of some significance, to the development of democratic ideas in the West.

At the very beginning of the European interest in China Leibniz expressed the hope that there might be an "interchange of civilizations between China and Europe." That was, of course, impossible. Yet perhaps there has occurred, to a greater degree than we realize, a partial yet by no means insignificant transfusion of values.

If Europeans are unaware of the degree to which China influenced their democratic heritage, it is probable that most Americans are only a little more aware of the influence of the philosophy of the eighteenth-century Enlightenment, and especially of French philosophy, upon the development of democratic ideas and institutions in the United States. It is the easier to forget this because of the fact that the American Revolution preceded the one in France and helped to bring it about.

Nevertheless, the ideas of the French Enlightenment played a definite role in the preparation for the American Revolution, and perhaps a still larger one in the development of democratic ideas in America after the revolution. Thomas Jefferson, the author of the Declaration of Independence, has been called the "symbol of the Enlightenment in America." Such influence as the philosophy of Confucius may have had upon the development of democratic thought in America came chiefly and perhaps exclusively through this French influence. Americans who were prominent in their own revolution seem to have shown very little interest in China; this may be explained partly by the fact that, by the period of closest American intellectual contacts with France, China had been largely discredited in Europe.

At least one clear line of connection, however, runs through the Physiocratic doctrines of Quesnay. It has sometimes been questioned that this body of theory, which importantly influenced both Adam Smith and Karl Marx, was in fact derived in significant measure from China. The fact that Quesnay said he got it from China is not of course conclusive, but no one at all familiar with the Chinese literature on political and economic theory can read Quesnay without being struck by the high degree of correlation. Furthermore, a great deal of what Quesnay has to say is quite evidently derived from statements on China by such writers as the Jesuits and Voltaire.[11] Lewis A. Maverick states that the first seven chapters of Quesnay's *Despotism in China*, which first set forth the political aspects of Physiocracy, "were lifted bodily" from a work descriptive of China written by Jacques Philibert Rousselot de Surgy.

Physiocracy emphasized especially the importance of agriculture, and urged that the state should promote it. At the same time the Physiocrats considered trade and industry unproductive. They advocated free trade, with taxes only on agriculture. Quesnay believed that the government should be headed by a monarch of "despotic" power; but his rule should not be "arbitrary and tyrannical," but like that of the emperor of China.

Thus far there is little in Quesnay's theory which could not find a basis somewhere in Chinese literature. There is no doubt, however, that Quesnay and the other members of his school adapted the idea of the despotic power of the Chinese emperor (which as we have seen was a perversion of the ideas of Confucius) to their European theory of "enlightened despotism." Furthermore they emphasized the importance of private property and the role of "rich proprietors . . . established by providence for the purpose of exercising the most honorable public offices," in a manner absent from or even at variance with Confucian theory.

Benjamin Franklin arrived in France in 1767, the year of the publication of Quesnay's *Despotism in China*. In fact, he subscribed for and contributed to the magazine in which it was first published. In Quesnay's home "Franklin found what interested him most: a gay, intimate, erudite and philosophical society." He also became a friend of the two most influential of the Physiocrats, the Marquis of Mirabeau and Turgot; thus, says Bernard Faÿ, Franklin "turned the enormous influence of this famous school in favor of America, which was a big step toward the control of [French] public opinion."

Franklin also borrowed, from the Physiocrats, some of their

ideas. "He reduced them," Faÿ writes, "to their simplest elements, saw how they could be utilized in the Anglo-American discussion, and to what point they supported the claims of the American farmers against the English merchants . . . This was a real revolution in his mind. The old English Whig system of Thomas Gordon, and the mercantile theories of William Petty, by which he had been guided since 1720, suddenly seemed old-fashioned. The constitutional discussion between England and America had already tired him, and he thought it was missing the main issue . . . the Physiocrats furnished him with a doctrine, which he made use of in his writings in these stormy years."

Jefferson too was greatly interested in the ideas of the Physiocrats, and seems to have been considerably influenced by them, although he could not accept the idea of a benevolent despotism. One of Jefferson's letters appears to imply that he was aware of the connection between Physiocracy and China, but neither he nor Franklin ever seems to have been moved to make any considerable investigation of Chinese philosophy itself.

Although there can be little question of any influence, in any but a very indirect sense, it is interesting to compare the thought of Thomas Jefferson with that of Confucius. They were alike in their impatience with metaphysics, in their concern for the poor as against the rich, in their insistence on basic human equality, in their belief in the essential decency of all men (including savages), and in their appeal not to authority but to "the head and heart of every honest man." [12] Jefferson's statement that "the whole art of government consists in the art of being honest" is amazingly similar to *Analects* 12.17, and other such examples could be cited.

Although they were vigorous champions of the cause of the common man, neither Confucius nor Jefferson minimized (as some advocates of democracy appear to do) the fact that men are by no means equal in their capacities. In 1813 Jefferson wrote to John Adams: "I agree with you that there is a natural aristocracy among men. The grounds of this are virtue and talents. . . . There is also an artificial aristocracy, founded on wealth and birth . . . The natural aristocracy I consider as the most precious gift of nature, for the instruction, the trusts, and government of society. . . . May we not even say, that that form of government is the best, which provides most effectually for a pure selection of these natural aristoi into the offices of government?"

It would be difficult to epitomize the theory of the Chinese examination system more neatly. Jefferson believed it to be so urgent that the talented youth of the nation be selected and educated for the tasks of government, that in 1779 he introduced into the Virginia House of Representatives a measure designed to accomplish this purpose, entitled A Bill for the More General Diffusion of Knowledge. This bill declared general education to be the best safeguard of democracy. It also asserted that the government should be administered by the "wise and honest," and that "those persons, whom nature hath endowed with genius and virtue, should be rendered by liberal education worthy to receive, and able to guard the sacred deposit of the rights and liberties of their fellow citizens, and that they should be called to that charge without regard to wealth, birth or other accidental condition or circumstance." Since, however, the poor could not afford to educate their children, the talented among them "should be sought for and educated at the common expence of all," for the public good.

Jefferson's bill sought to establish a system of education having three levels. In the local schools, all children were to be taught gratis for three years. Periodically "the boy of best genius in the school, of those whose parents are too poor to give them further education" was to be selected "after the most diligent and impartial examination and inquiry," and sent forward to one of twenty grammar schools, to be educated "at the public expence." There the students would be subjected to frequent examination, and only the best retained. Finally, a small number of these were "to be sent and continued three years in the study of such sciences as they shall chuse, at William and Mary College." Jefferson explained that "By that part of our plan which prescribes the selection of youths of genius from among the classes of the poor, we hope to avail the state of those talents which nature has sown as liberally among the poor as the rich, but which perish without use, if not sought for and cultivated." [13]

Jefferson's plan had three principles in common with the

Chinese examination system: (1) Education was to be considered a principal concern of the state. (2) Students of outstanding ability were to be selected, by means of competitive examinations, at three levels; students at the lowest level were to be selected from small districts, and at the highest from the whole state (corresponding to the Chinese district, provincial, and national examinations). (3) A major purpose was to "avail the state" of the services, as officials, of the most talented of its citizens, whether they might be rich or poor and regardless of pedigree. It differed from the Chinese system in that it provided some free education for all, it called for the education of the talented wholly at public expense, and Jefferson would have required that his "natural aristocrats" must not only pass examinations but also be elected to office, not appointed as in China.

These similarities do not, of course, prove that Jefferson's ideas were influenced by the Chinese examination system. There is, however, a distinct possibility of such influence. It seems certain that Jefferson knew of the existence of the Chinese system before he introduced his bill of 1779. It has been demonstrated that not later than 1776 he had read, and made extensive notes on, a work in which Voltaire declared that "the mind of man could not imagine a better government" than that of China at the beginning of the seventeenth century, where virtually all power lay in the hands of a bureaucracy "whose members were admitted only after several severe examinations." [14] The Chinese examination system was described in detail in numerous early European books,[15] of which at least one is known to have been in Jefferson's library.[16]

Jefferson considered his educational program to be of fundamental importance. Only in some such manner, he was convinced, could democracy fortify itself against being slowly perverted into tyranny. His bill of 1779 was so amended as to defeat its purpose. In 1806, as President, he proposed to the Congress that the Constitution be amended to permit the setting up of "a national establishment for education." In 1813 he wrote John Adams that he still hoped that the principle of his original bill might be made "the keystone of the arch of our government." In 1817 he wrote that he was "now entirely absorbed" in the promotion of a plan for education which embodied it. He continued to work and write on its behalf until his latest years.

Although no such educational program as Jefferson advocated was adopted, the principle that men should be selected for office on the basis of their capacity, rather than their popularity, has received recognition in Western democracies in the institution of a civil service recruited through competitive examinations. As to the origin of this system in the British Empire, we need no longer speculate. In 1943 Têng Ssŭ-yü published a carefully documented study showing that the British system was inspired by that of China. Among other evidence, he showed that such examinations were first held by the East India Company, at its Indian establishments which were in touch with China, and that when the adoption of the system was being debated in Parliament its supporters and opponents alike made reference to the Chinese system.

In the United States of America, the institution of civil service examinations was adopted subsequently, chiefly under British influence. It is worthy of remark, however, that while the measure was pending before Congress, Ralph Waldo Emerson observed that in the matter of "requiring that candidates for public office shall first pass examinations" to show themselves qualified, "China has preceded us, as well as England and France, in this essential correction of a reckless usage."

CHAPTER XVI

CONFUCIUS AND THE REPUBLIC OF CHINA

THE view that Confucius was a political reactionary even in his own day, that he had given strong support to monarchical despotism, and that Confucianism was in large part a tool for propaganda by means of which the emperors kept their subjects in submission, has of course made the name of Confucius anathema in some circles under the Republic of China. The undeniable fact that during the first half of the twentieth century the name of Confucius has often been exploited by war lords and other persons who were, at best, but dubious friends of democracy, has not contributed to his popularity. It is quite understandable, therefore, that there has grown up an impression that the relation between Confucius and the Republic of China is chiefly a negative one, and that the Chinese Revolution was a process in which Confucianism was supplanted by democracy, which was imported from the West.

There is some truth to this, if Confucianism is limited to mean only the rigid state orthodoxy that was sponsored by the Manchu dynasty. We have seen, however, that the philosophy of Confucius himself was something quite different, and that during the last centuries of the empire there was developing a movement among many of the more able and independent scholars which sought to revive this earlier Confucianism. In the last chapter we saw that early Confucian ideas, taken to Europe by the Jesuits, contributed something to the development of democracy in the West. They also played a role in connection with the Republic of China.

Obviously, Confucianism did not by itself bring into being the Republic of China. That was done chiefly by Western pressure, which made it evident that China could not continue her prevailing ways and remain a sovereign state. But with the form of the Constitution of the Republic, and perhaps even with the fact that China became a republic at all, Confucianism did have something to do. Western pressure on Japan caused that nation to alter its government profoundly in 1868, but instead of instituting a republic the Japanese set up a strongly centralized monarchy. The different responses, by Japan and by China, to what was essentially the same stimulus were determined in large part by the difference in their traditional philosophies.

If many Chinese of the twentieth century have failed to distinguish adequately between the orthodox state Confucianism and the early thought of which it was a perversion, this is by no means true of all of them. Hu Shih has pointed out that this recent orthodoxy "failed to grasp the democratic spirit of classical Confucianism." Of the greatest practical importance is the fact that Sun Yat-sen, "father of the Republic of China," was fully aware of it.

In an analysis of the background of Sun's philosophy Leonard Shihlien Hsü, formerly an official of the Chinese Ministry of Foreign Affairs, has written, "The Movement of Higher Criticism during the Tsing [Manchu] dynasty had also tremendous influence upon Dr. Sun's thinking. . . . About two hundred and fifty years ago a group of scholars began to agitate for emancipation and criticism. Some had even denied the authenticity of all Confucian Classics excepting the first part of *The Analects* . . . they wanted to go back to Confucius. Dr. Sun, according to Mr. Tai Chi-tao [a fellow revolutionist with Sun], a recognized authority on Sunyatsenism, not infrequently assumed himself to be the modern successor of the Confucian school of philosophy."

In his lectures, which in their printed form had tremendous circulation and influence, Sun repeatedly hailed Confucius as a democrat. He asserted that "both Confucius and Mencius were exponents of democracy. . . . Confucius always quoted the words of Yao and Shun, because they did not hold the empire as a hereditary possession. While their government was monarchical in name, it was in fact democratic, and this is why Confucius honored them." [1]

Although Sun recognized that he had borrowed much from the West, he did not consider himself to be a mere importer of Western democracy. In fact he declared that "China anticipated Europe and America by developing a democratic philosophy thousands of years ago." And again, "Europe surpasses China, not in political philosophy, but only in material civilization. . . . What we need to learn from Europe is science, not political philosophy. As for the true principles of political philosophy, the Europeans need to learn them from China."

In his famous work called *The Three Principles of the People,* Sun declared that if China were to be restored to her rightful position in the world it was essential "to revive our ancient morality." He then enumerated the virtues that are usually called Confucian as those which must be practiced. Still more surprising, he asserted that it was also necessary to revive China's ancient learning and quoted a passage from one of the classics produced by the Confucian school, the *Great Learning,* as illustrating the sort of ancient political philosophy that must be guarded as a "national treasure," the like of which no foreign nation possessed.

Undoubtedly, one of the reasons why Sun made such statements was his desire that the Chinese should regain their self-confidence. But it would be a great mistake to interpret them as nothing but empty patriotic gestures, or to suppose that he was not profoundly influenced by China's own philosophy. Paul M. A. Linebarger has said of Sun's thinking that "the form was Western but the content was still Chinese." That this is true is evident from even casual study of his utterances. It is well known that Sun was influenced by Karl Marx, but when Marx and Confucianism clashed Marx sometimes emerged the loser.

This is clear in connection with the doctrine of class struggle. Sun pointed out that in the years since Marx wrote there had been very considerable advances in the direction of economic justice. "What," he asked, "is the cause of this social evolution? If we judge on the basis of the doctrines of Marx, we must say that it has been caused by the class struggle, and that the class struggle is caused by the capitalist oppression of the workers; and that since the interests of capitalists and workers are opposed and cannot be harmonized the class struggle is the result and this makes for progress." In fact, however, this has not proved to be the case. Better conditions for the workers have meant greater profits for capital, which in turn has meant higher wages for the workers. "Thus the interests of capital and labor have proved to be not in conflict, but in harmony. And social progress is caused by this harmony between the economic interests of men in general, not by conflict." Thus the class struggle is not a cause of progress but a symptom of disease in the social process, Sun concludes, and "we should call Marx not a social physiologist but a social pathologist." Here it is apparent that Sun was influenced by the Chinese, and Confucian, emphasis upon the necessity for cooperation between all the members of society. The same influence was at work when he repudiated the Marxian doctrine of surplus value.

The Chinese Constitution is based, not on the threefold division of powers that we know in Western democracies, but on a fivefold division devised by Sun Yat-sen. Arthur N. Holcombe has written of Sun's total plan for the government of China, "Whatever may be thought of some details of Dr. Sun's program, his plan is based upon a political philosophy comparing favorably with that of any other modern revolutionary leader." Sun himself made it clear that that plan was based on a blend of ideas both Western and Chinese, and on a philosophy indebted both to Montesquieu and to Confucius. He once went so far as to say that his plan for a five-power constitution was essentially the constitution of the Chinese Empire turned upside down.

In studying the constitutions of various democracies and the way they worked out in practice, Sun decided that two functions were lacking. He further concluded that these were precisely functions which had been performed in the Chinese Empire under Confucian auspices, and by officials who enjoyed a large measure of independence from interference by the emperor. The results had been so good that Sun made these two functions independent powers, vesting them in two of the five Yüan.

It will be recalled that the duty of a minister to reprove error on the part of his ruler, which Confucius stressed, came to be vested, under imperial rule, in particular officials. These censors also had the duty of searching out and denouncing corruption anywhere in the government. Although Sun recognized that the functions of criticism are performed in Western governments by legislative bodies and by the courts, he believed that there is great virtue in having in the government such a body of elder statesmen, whose explicit function it is to criticize without fear or favor, and to impeach officials guilty of corruption. He therefore incorporated the institution of the censorate in his five-power constitution, as the Control Yüan.

The examination system, upon which Sun's fifth power is based, was not devised by Confucius. Its foundation, however, was clearly laid by Confucius, who repeatedly urged the necessity of "promoting the upright" and of putting the administration of the government into the hands of the virtuous and capable. He also urged that such persons, having been prepared for administrative responsibilities by suitable education, should be selected for government posts without regard to any qualifications except character and capacity. The examination system was an attempt to put these principles into practice.

Sun Yat-sen did not wish to continue the examination system exactly as it had been administered under the empire. He (like Confucius) was much too sensible to suppose that a mere knowledge of ancient books could qualify a man for governmental office. But he was convinced that the practice of democracy in Europe and America had fallen far short of what might be expected of it, and he laid a large share of the blame upon a false conception of human equality. He did not believe, any more than did Confucius or Jefferson, in a hereditary aristocracy, but like both Confucius and Jefferson he believed that in fact "men are not naturally equal." The only kind of equality that can be realized is equality of opportunity. He said, "If we pay no attention to the differences of intelligence and ability between individuals, but push down those who distinguish themselves in order to insist upon absolute equality among men, humanity will not advance but retrogress. Thus when we speak of democracy and equality, yet wish the world to advance, we are speaking only of political equality. For equality is not a thing given in nature, but is created by men; and the only equality which men can bring about is equality of political status."

Sun therefore believed that while every man should have equal power to control the government, through suffrage, only those possessing the requisite knowledge and ability should hold office. All men should be given equal opportunity to become qualified, but their qualifications should be tested by a system of examinations. He planned, therefore, that "all candidates for office, whether elective or appointive, national or local, must first pass examinations administered by the Central Government in order to insure that they possess the necessary qualifications."

The possibility for political manipulation in such a system is obvious. Sun hoped, however, to minimize this by vesting the control of examinations in a separate organ of the government, the Examination Yüan, modeled to some extent after the corps of officials who administered this function under the empire.

By adding to the three powers of government recognized in the West these further two derived from Confucianism, Sun believed that it would be possible to correct the deficiencies of democratic government as it is practiced in the West, and to establish "the most complete and the finest government in the world." It should be noted that, whatever the merits of this hope, they cannot be judged upon the basis of the functioning of the Chinese government up to this time. For while it includes both a Control Yüan and an Examination Yüan, these organs have never, in this transitional period, been given the scope or the powers which Sun Yat-sen desired for them.

In what esteem the Chinese of the future will hold Confucius, only the future can tell. Yet it seems clear that, whether they praise his name or forget it, all Chinese will continue to be influenced by him, for a long time to come. Linebarger wrote, in 1938, that Confucianism was still "the greatest single intellectual force in the country." In 1943 Lin Yutang asserted that "Confucianism, as a live force in the Chinese people, is still going to shape our national conduct of affairs . . ."

That there is at least a measure of truth in this was perhaps demonstrated in 1945, when the Foreign Minister of the Republic of China surprised the conference called to organize the United Nations by announcing that China was "prepared, in conjunction with other nations, to yield if necessary a part of our sovereignty to the new international organization." Twenty-one years earlier Sun Yat-sen had pointed out that "Cosmopolitanism, which has only recently been propounded in Europe, was being discussed in China more than two thousand years ago." As evidence of that fact, he referred to one of the Confucian Classics.

POSTSCRIPT

WE have considered the story of Confucius, a man of Lu of obscure origin, who never accomplished very much while he was alive. We have watched his influence grow after his death until men who were enemies of his principles were compelled to try to pervert them in self-defense. In this effort they were partially, but only partially, successful.

We have seen his name acclaimed by men of many centuries and many nations. We have traced, though only in outline, the manner in which his ideas (though often considerably transformed) have played varied roles of some importance in the history of diverse civilizations. Reflecting upon these facts, it is impossible not to ask what is the reason for the extraordinary persistence of his influence. Since Confucius was primarily concerned with social and political philosophy, the reason will probably be found in that sphere.

The organization of states may be divided, in the broadest possible manner, into two types: authoritarian and democratic. It goes without saying that there are many varieties of each and combinations of the two. In authoritarian states power is ultimately vested in one or more individuals, while a large proportion of the people have no effective share of power. In democratic states power is ultimately vested in the people as a whole. Under authoritarian government the end is commonly conceived to be "the good of the state," which may sacrifice to itself the welfare of a great many of its citizens. A true democracy, on the other hand, must be concerned with the welfare and the happiness of each of its citizens, since each one is fully a member of the state.

History has shown that true and effective democracy is a political condition difficult to bring about, and still harder to perpetuate. By comparison, authoritarianism is a hardy growth. There are a number of reasons for this. Under authoritarian rule the philosophy of the state and the duty of the individual are prescribed by the government, with relative clarity. In a democracy, however, the state has no philosophy (except democracy in the broadest sense), and the duty of the individual is not at all clear. It may be his duty either to support or to oppose the government, and no tribunal save his own conscience can tell him which it is.

There are many, however, who are eager to tell the citizen of a democracy what is his duty, with every artifice of oratory. Quite rightly, the citizen regards with scepticism those who are so zealous to do his thinking for him. He is faced by a difficult choice. Shall he entrust the fortunes of the state to professional politicians, who may be of questionable integrity, or to the well-meaning but unskilled efforts of amateurs?

There is an even greater dilemma. In a democracy, the ultimate authority lies with the whole body of the people, who, as regards the political sphere, are too often not even amateurs. For an amateur is a "lover," and the citizens of democracies are not always fond of participating in the processes of politics. The more satisfactory their government is, the less interest they will take in it. Thus a good democratic government is, in a sense, its own greatest foe. For when its citizens are not vigilant, there is always the danger that enemies of democracy may be able to take over the state.

Democracy is also faced by a more subtle intellectual dilemma. Political philosophers are agreed with Confucius that in a cooperative state the people must have faith in their government. Furthermore, since all must take some part in determining

the ends and even the methods of the government, they must be
in some measure of agreement upon a basic philosophy of government. Yet no democracy can prescribe such a philosophy to
its citizens, nor can it declare that any belief whatsoever is beyond criticism and not subject to discussion, without placing
itself on questionable ground. It is for this reason that democracies always have been, and always must be, somewhat vulner-
able to authoritarian propaganda. Against this they must defend
themselves, yet without prohibiting the reasonable exercise of
free speech.

Not every thinker who has approved of democracy as an abstract principle has been able to provide for it a consistent
philosophy fulfilling its rather difficult requirements. The philosophy of Confucius did this to an unusual degree, and it is
suggested that it is for this reason that his ideas have met with
such widespread sympathy. To say that the philosophy of Confucius was democratic in the full modern sense of that term
would be going too far. On the other hand, it does not go too
far to say that Confucius was a forerunner of democracy, a
voice crying in the wilderness, preparing the way. Furthermore
—and this is the heart of our story—he had an appreciation of
some of the basic principles underlying successful cooperation
between men that has seldom been surpassed, and not frequently equaled, by other philosophers. He did not merely approve of the cooperative state; he was passionately devoted to its
realization. He provided for democracy not merely a philosophy
but a battle cry. Still more remarkable, he was able to combine
the utmost zeal with a thoroughly judicious temper, and to call
for sacrifice in the name of the democratic cause without ever
making excessive claims which would have undermined the
logical integrity of its position.

Confucius seems to have been aware that the greatest battle
of democracy is not a dramatic contest against evil, but the quiet
struggle that goes on within the heart of the individual against
boredom. Authoritarianism tempts him with pageantry and
with final solutions to all the problems; democracy offers only
simple human dignity and a chance to work unceasingly for
human happiness, with no reward save the opportunity to go
on working. The last battle of democracy can never be fought.

Nor can the supreme goal of democracy be a perfect state or a perfect system of government, in the sense of static perfection, for it is an illusion to suppose that things will ever cease to change. Democracy can hope only to produce men and women who are capable of meeting new situations effectively.

Confucius seems to have recognized the threefold danger that is risked by him who lays down, for the guidance of society, any unalterable standard, whether it be a system of metaphysics, or books, or laws, or merely principles. First, it stifles initiative. Second, it may do harm, when conditions arise that were not foreseen by the lawgiver. Finally, if criticism (which cannot be stifled in a cooperative society) destroys the people's faith in the standard, they may be left completely without guidance. Confucius did not seek to impose any absolute authority.

Yet some authority there must be if the state is not to lapse into anarchy. That authority Confucius was willing to confide to men. Not to just any men, but to men imbued with the Way. The Way was not, however, a fixed code; still less was it concerned with metaphysics. It was a body of ideals which men had made and which men must continue to develop. "Men can enlarge the Way; the Way cannot [of itself] enlarge the man." It resembled what is today called the "democratic way of life," except that Confucius advocated it with more zeal and enthusiasm than is often associated with modern democracy. He knew that without such enthusiasm the cooperative society is impossible.

Confucius put his faith in men. Not in all men, he was not so naïve. But he believed that most men were honest. He did not think that all men were capable of taking part in the government. He did advocate, however, that all of them should be given some education, to make them truly members of the cooperative state, and he proposed that those among them who showed themselves able and virtuous should be given further education and placed in positions of authority. Once there, he was willing to permit them to govern according to their own best judgment. And he believed that in the long run the people in general would be able to distinguish the good official from the bad.

He trusted the human race.

APPENDIX

The Authenticity of the *Analects*

ALL scholars seem to be agreed that, while some parts of the *Analects* are subject to question, the book in general is our best single source for Confucius. This unanimity is remarkable, since the *Analects* seems not to have been mentioned by name in any work older than the Han dynasty. Passages found in it also appear, however, in works from a period earlier than Han,[1] and it is evident that these sayings were handed down in the Confucian group for some time without having any particular name attached to them.

It seems impossible to be certain when the sayings of Confucius and his disciples were first gathered into a book. The first collection was probably made, not by Confucius' disciples, but by some of their disciples. It may be, as has been argued, that the first ten chapters of our present *Analects* were the original book, while the next five were added somewhat later. It seems certain that Ts'ui Shu was correct in his hypothesis that Chapters 16–20 represent a still later addition. In these chapters Confucius is commonly called "Master K'ung" instead of "the Master," and other differences set them apart.[2] Nevertheless, the fact that the last five chapters were

---

[1] Such occurrences are listed in Legge I. 17–18.

[2] Ts'ui's criticism of the *Analects*, which is the most important contribution made to the subject by a single scholar, is contained in the works listed in the bibliography under Ts'ui, Ts'ui(2), and Ts'ui(3). His conclusions are summarized in Ts'ui(3) 24–35. I have outlined the history of the text in some detail in Creel(5) II. 9–20. See also Ch'ien Mu(2).

joined to the text late does not mean that none of their materials existed early. Analects 1.3 is repeated verbatim as 17.17, which seems to prove that some early materials were included in the last chapters. Chapter 19, which in general concerns the disciples rather than Confucius, seems to be just as authentic as any of the earliest chapters. However, as will be discussed below, the proportion of doubtful materials in the last five chapters is much higher.

In the Former Han dynasty there are said to have been three versions of the *Analects*. Around the end of that period a scholar named Chang Yü, on the basis of two of them, made a new version which became so popular that the others disappeared.[3] About 175 A.D. the text of the *Analects* was carved on stone tablets, and a number of the fragments of this text still exist. Although they show some differences from the text now current, most of these are negligible and do not seriously affect its meaning.[4]

Internal evidence shows the *Analects* to be an early book. Bernhard Karlgren found it to have "quite the same grammatical system" as the *Mencius*, with minor differences which he explained on the ground that the *Analects* was the older text.[5] It lacks certain concepts, such as that of *Ti*, "Earth" (in its metaphysical sense), *yin* and *yang*, and the "five elements," which would almost certainly appear in it if it were a very late Chou or Han work.[6] The Confucius depicted in the *Analects* is not a superhuman sage, but a simple and understandable human being. He is not exalted, as in later legend, nor is it claimed that he ever held any governmental post of great importance. He has doubts and weaknesses, as well as convictions and strength.

One of the best evidences of its authenticity is the fact that, while the *Analects* is obviously a Confucian book, it contains much that Confucians would have preferred that it did not include. Chapter 19 details squabbles between the disciples, and 19.25 tells us that one of them said Confucius was no better than the disciple Tzŭ-kung. In 6.26 it is related that Confucius had an interview with a notorious duchess; this has embarrassed countless prudish Confucians, and was used by their enemies to mock them in Han times.[7] Yet these things

---

[3] See *Han Shu* 30.20b–21a; Ts'ui 2.18; Ts'ui(2) 3.33–39.
[4] The text of these recovered fragments has been published in Chang Kuo-kan 44–46, and in Lo(3) hsia 29a–34a.
[5] Karlgren 34–35.
[6] For the late date of these concepts see Chap. XII, notes 22, 26 and 36.
[7] *Yen T'ieh Lun*(2) 72–73.

were not deleted from the text, which must increase our respect for it.

Nevertheless, the *Analects* contains questionable passages, ranging from the slightly dubious to the clearly false. Chapter 10 poses a special problem. Henri Maspero and Arthur Waley have considered it to be a ritual treatise telling what the ideal gentleman should do, which was incorporated into the *Analects* with certain adaptations.[8] This may well be true; certainly one can not safely use all parts of this chapter as describing the conduct of Confucius. However, 10.2, 10.11.2, and 10.12 concern a specific individual, presumably Confucius.

A number of passages have nothing to do either with Confucius or with his disciples, and seem to be irrelevant intrusions into the text; these are 16.14, 18.2, 18.9–11, and 20.1. The *Analects* carved on stone in Han times apparently lacked 20.3, and this passage is also said not to have appeared in the Lu version,[9] which is believed to have been the best early text. I have recorded my doubts about 2.4 (see Chap. IX, note 9) and 9.8 (p. 202). Ts'ui Shu has questioned 15.1.1 on the ground that it is improbable, with good reason.[10] Waley suspects 16.1,[11] and the doubt may be well founded. Here we find both Tzŭ-lu and Jan Ch'iu in the service of the Chi family, and Confucius speaks as if Jan Ch'iu held the chief power. It appears, however, that Tzŭ-lu was steward before Jan Ch'iu, and it seems questionable that a man of Tzŭ-lu's temper would have remained in the service of the Chi after demotion. The following passages seem to reflect Taoist thinking, and must therefore be regarded with some reservation: 14.39–42, 16.11.2, 17.19 (see Chap. XII, note 21), 18.5–8.

In nine sections in the last five chapters, Confucius is quoted as using numbers in a very pedantic fashion, speaking of the three errors, the nine cares, the four bad qualities, etc.; these are: 16.4–8, 16.10, 17.6, 17.8, 20.2. Confucius is not quoted as speaking in this manner in the first fifteen chapters—5.15 and 14.30 are only apparent analogies, for the principle is somewhat different—nor in the *Mencius*. Although the content of some of these passages may come from Confucius, it is probable that they have been cast in the didactic style of later Confucianism.

[8] Maspero 459; Waley 55.
[9] *Lun Yü* 20 *Chiao K'an Chi* 3b.
[10] Ts'ui 3.28–29.
[11] Waley 204 n. 6.

Finally, there are six sections that appear to controvert the ascertainable facts, about the circumstances or the philosophy of Confucius, to such a degree that they must be considered false additions to the text. The evidence against these passages has been stated elsewhere; they are: 7.16 (see p. 201), 13.3 (Chap. XIII, note 13), 16.2 (p. 220), 16.9 (p. 221), 18.3 (Chap. IV, note 29), and 18.4 (Chap. IV, note 28).

NOTES

The works corresponding to bibliographical abbreviations are listed in the Bibliography.

Chapter I

1. Since this chapter summarizes much of the content of the entire book, little evidence will be presented for its statements. The same points will be developed fully later.

Chapter II

1. See *An.* 6.4. The fact that the *Tso Chuan* seems to include no reference to any ruling family named Jan appears to eliminate the possibility that he could have been the heir of a ruler. Nowhere, to my knowledge, is there any statement that he was.

2. Heredity was not, of course, the basis on which the emperors Yao and Shun are supposed to have passed on their thrones. But recent research has made it clear, not only that these emperors were legendary, but that the works which relate that they transmitted their offices on the basis of virtue were written after the time of Confucius. See pages 186–189.

3. That is to say the original text of the *I Ching*, but not the so-called Ten Wings or appendices, which come from a time later than that of Confucius; these will be discussed later.

4. For detailed criticism of some of the books of the *Shu* see Creel 55–89 and 111 n. 7. The following are the books that I believe are undoubtedly pre-Confucian: *T'ang Shih, Hsi Po K'an Li, Wei Tzŭ, Ta Kao, K'ang Kao, Chiu Kao, Tzŭ Ts'ai, Shao Kao, Lo Kao, To Shih,*

Chün Shih, To Fang, Ku Ming, Pi Shih, Wên Hou chih Ming, and *Ch'in Shih.*

In addition to these there are several books that may have been composed as early as the time of Confucius, but which must be left in the doubtful class. The remainder, which make up a considerable portion of the *chin wên* text of the *Shu,* are definitely late forgeries.

No mention has been made of the *ku wên* text, because it is generally agreed that, as Chinese scholars showed long ago, it is false.

5. See pages 202–204.

6. See Chap. XII note 3.

7. Gustav Haloun has published three brief texts, which he calls "Frühkonfuzianische Fragmente." They are interesting, but none of them appears, on the ground of its date and content, to warrant inclusion among our basic materials for Confucius. See Haloun and Haloun (2).

Chapter III

1. For fuller discussion of this propaganda campaign, and of the revised version of the early history, see Creel 47–95, and Creel (4) 367–375. It must be noted, however, that there is more evidence than I formerly supposed to indicate that the Chou were subject to the Shang, though not in precisely the manner depicted in the orthodox histories.

2. Duke Chuang was the second son. The Mêng family was at first known as Chung, Legge says because of descent from a concubine (*Tso* 74).

Chapter IV

1. *Tso* 618–619. This speech is entered in the *Tso Chuan* ahead of its proper chronological place; this misled the author of the *Historical Records* (see *Mem. Hist.* V.294 n.3). The conversation that includes the genealogy is supposed to have taken place when Confucius was thirty-three and before he was known, yet it predicts his future greatness. Ts'ui Shu has pointed out that the genealogy involves considerable difficulties (Ts'ui 1.1–5).

This genealogy makes Confucius the descendant of the dukes of Sung, who in turn were heirs of the deposed Shang kings. It was probably based, not on fact, but on the idea that Confucius ought to have been emperor. As early as the *Mo Tzŭ* we find a Confucian asserting that if a sage had been on the throne in his lifetime, Confucius would have been made emperor (*Mo Tzŭ* 12.11b), and Mencius felt called upon to explain why it was that Confucius had not occupied the throne (*Mencius* 5[1]6.3).

2. The *Kung-Yang Chuan* and the *Ku-Liang Chuan* both date his birth in 552 B.C., while the *Historical Records* gives 551. Scholars have long debated which of these dates is correct, without settling the quest-

tion. The year 551 is more generally used, and for that reason is employed in this book.

Henri Maspero believed it possible that Confucius might have been born, and died, as much as twenty-five years later than the accepted dates, 551–479 (Maspero 455 n. 1). This seems unlikely, however. The date of his birth might well have been in doubt, but since the disciples of Confucius carried on an uninterrupted tradition there is no reason why the date of his death should not be well known. In fact, there is good evidence for at least the approximate accuracy of the 479 date. The latest event in his life that can be fixed by comparing the *Analects* with the *Spring and Autumn Annals* is 481 (see *An.* 14.22 and *Tso* 838), and no events or persons which would force us to extend his life past 479 seem to occur in any of the valid materials concerning his life. The *Mencius* (3[1]4.13) indicates that after Confucius' death a number of his disciples mourned near his tomb for three years. And the disciple Jan Ch'iu, who enjoyed high favor with the Chi family, is not mentioned as having taken part in public life after 481 until 472 (see *Tso* 824–825, 826, 838, 854). Tzŭ-kung, who Mencius says mourned for six years, was a principal figure in the diplomacy of Lu up to and including the year 480; thereafter he is not mentioned as taking part in public life, though it is clear that he was still highly regarded and his services were desired (see *Tso* 791, 813, 825, 828–829, 842–843, 859–860, 861). These facts support the date of 479. If it be said that the *Tso Chuan* has been tampered with, to delete any instances of disciples taking part in affairs during the mourning period, there is evidence to the contrary in the fact that it is recorded that Tzŭ-kao participated in a diplomatic conference in 478 (*Tso* 851). Tzŭ-kao, it will be recalled, had not been in high favor as a disciple (*An.* 11.17, 11.24), nor was he a very thorough Confucian (*Tso* 843).

If Confucius died in 479 and was born in 551 he lived to be seventy-two. For various reasons it is probable that he lived to be about this old. As early as 498 his disciple Tzŭ-lu held the important office of steward of the Chi family (*Tso* 781). *Analects* 2.4 (which may not be genuine, however) refers to Confucius as having attained the age of at least seventy, and the *Analects* in general paints him as a venerable figure. It is probable, therefore, that he was born in the neighborhood of 551 B.C.

3. Both the *Discourses of the Confucian School* (*K'ung Tzŭ Chia Yü*) and the *Historical Records* identify Confucius' father as one Shu Liang Hê (*Chia Yü* 9.10, *Mem. Hist.* V.287 and n.1). He is evidently supposed to be the same person as the Shu Hê mentioned in the *Tso Chuan* (446, 474). It is very remarkable, however, that on neither occasion does the *Tso Chuan*, which usually brings in the name of Confucius on the slightest pretext, say that Shu Hê was his father. Why, then, was the identification made later?

The probable reason is absurdly simple. The only description of Confucius' father given in the *Analects* is that he was a *Tsou jên*, a "man of

Tsou" (*An.* 3.15). The only "man of Tsou" mentioned in the *Tso Chuan* is Shu Hê. This was no doubt quite enough for those who scanned the early literature in search of every scrap of data on Confucius.

4. Not only do we not know that Shu Hê was his father (see preceding note), but the statement of the *Discourses of the Confucian School* that Shu Hê was the *tai fu* of Tsou, which would presumably mean that he was its governor, appears to have no adequate foundation (*Chia Yü* 9.10b). The T'ang dynasty commentator K'ung Ying-ta explained that since the *Tso Chuan* called Shu Hê *Tsou jên* (man of Tsou), this meant that he was the *tai fu* of Tsou (*Tso Chuan Chu Su* 31.3b). His argument is not convincing.

5. *An.* 19.22. The story told in the *Tso Chuan* (667–668), to the effect that when he was twenty-six Confucius studied with a certain Viscount of T'an, is unworthy of serious consideration. This individual is not mentioned either in the *Analects* or in *Mencius*, where we should certainly expect a teacher of the Master to appear; and the mention in connection with him of phoenixes, dragons, various sorts of "cloud officers," "fire officers," "water officers," "bird officers," and so forth, and the groupings in nines and fives, are all characteristic of the mythology of a later day.

6. See page 106.

7. The *Tso Chuan* (618–619) tells us that when Confucius was thirty-three the dying head of the Mêng family told his heir and another of his sons to study with Confucius, and they did so. These are sometimes supposed to have been Confucius' first disciples. But there are several suspicious aspects to this story. In giving his command Mêng Hsi Tzŭ foretells Confucius' greatness and outlines a genealogy that would make him the descendant if not the heir of kings. Furthermore, if the head of the powerful Mêng family, and his brother, had been Confucius' disciples at an early date, this should have powerfully aided him, and we would expect the fact to be chronicled in the *Analects*. Yet each of them is named only once in that work, and there is no evidence that either was a disciple (*An.* 2.5, 14.6; the identification of Nan-Kung Kuo with Nan Jung is most dubious).

8. According to the *Tso Chuan* (781), in 498 B.C. Tzŭ-lu, as steward of the Chi family, was playing a decisive role in domestic policy in the state of Lu. At this time Confucius was fifty-three; tradition makes Tzŭ-lu nine years younger, or forty-four at this time, which accords with the circumstances. Tsêng Hsi, another disciple, was the father of the disciple Tsêng Shên (*Mencius* 4[1]19.3) and must therefore have belonged to the older group. *Mencius* (7[2]37.4) mentions Tsêng Hsi together with two other disciples who do not appear in the *Analects*, and Tsêng Hsi himself appears there only once (*An.* 11.25). It is quite possible that the *Analects* omits mention of a number of Confucius' earlier students.

9. *I.e., Chi Shih Tsai.* For evidence that the office of *tsai* to a particular family was unique, see *Tso* 404 and 622.

10. Tzŭ-lu, Jan Ch'iu, and Kung-Hsi Hua studied with Confucius at a time when they were unemployed and felt their abilities to be unrecognized (*An.* 11.25). Confucius recommended Tzŭ-lu and Jan Ch'iu to the Chi family (*An.* 6.6) and both of them held (successively, in all probability) the office of its steward. Kung-Hsi Hua was sent as an envoy to Ch'i (*An.* 6.3). Jan Yung came from a family on which there was some blot that threatened to hamper his official career (*An.* 6.4); nevertheless Confucius had a high opinion of his abilities (*An.* 6.1.1), and he too is said to have held the office of steward of the Chi family (*An* 13.2), which he could hardly have obtained without the Master's help.

11. *Tso* 760–770. On the basis of *An.* 17.1 Maspero says that Confucius "seems to have accepted" a post with Yang Hu, and to have felt himself compromised after the failure of the plot (Maspero 456–457). This is most improbable. First, both the *Analects* and *Mencius* (3[2]7.3) speak of Yang Huo, not Yang Hu; they may be the same, but this is not certain. Second, the *Mencius* makes no mention of the question of taking office, and the *Analects* merely quotes Confucius as saying, "I am going to take office"; it does not even say that he did so at all, to say nothing of under Yang Hu. Third, the whole career of Yang Hu as described in the *Tso Chuan* makes it evident that he was not the sort of person Confucius would have liked; he was a violent swashbuckling intriguer, and both the *Analects* and *Mencius* make it clear that Confucius wanted nothing to do with Yang Huo. It is most unlikely, therefore, that he was a partisan of Yang Hu.

12. In *Analects* 6.6 he asks whether Tzŭ-lu should be given a governmental post; this must be prior to the date when Tzŭ-lu became steward of the Chi family, and thus not later than 498 (*Tso* 781).

13. *An.* 17.5. Some Chinese scholars have found this incident shocking, and have spent a great deal of effort in trying to prove it could not have happened. One of these is Ts'ui Shu, who points out among other arguments that when Confucius was minister of crime of Lu he could scarcely have been "summoned" by a rebel against its government (Ts'ui 2.14-17). This is true, but since it is very doubtful that Confucius ever held that office, this very occurrence becomes further evidence against the theory that he did hold it, at this time at any rate. Fung Yu-lan believes that the incident described in *Analects* 17.5 did occur (Fung[3] 37-38); Ch'ien Mu thinks that it took place probably in 502 or 501, which agrees precisely with the present reconstruction (Ch'ien Mu 14-16).

14. The speech ascribed to Confucius, with its contempt for barbarians and its reference to what is "unlucky as regards the spirits," does not sound at all like the *Analects.* The idea that, as here represented, the mere turn of a word could cause the strong and warlike state of Ch'i to

disgorge lands she did not wish to, is absurd. The scholars who prepared an imperial edition of commentaries on the *Ch'un Ch'iu* for the K'ang Hsi emperor omitted this passage, and quoted the opinions of a number of scholars who have denounced it as false (*Ch'in Ting Ch'un Ch'iu* 35.11a–12a). Surprisingly, the *Tso Chuan* relates very few episodes in the life of Confucius, and no others at any such length or in such detail as this one. It is clearly an anecdote that was made up and inserted into the text, in order, as the work just cited points out, to give Confucius credit for the return of lands mentioned in the *Ch'un Ch'iu*.

15. *Mo Tzŭ*(2) 209. Of this *Fei Ju* chapter Mei Yi-pao writes that "the composition and style show remarkable variations from the other books [of the *Mo Tzŭ*]. And the confused dates and facts of the historical allusions show this chapter to be written at a much later date" (*Ibid.* 200 n.1). Hu Shih has indicated scepticism concerning this chapter (Hu 151). Especially dubious is the reference to Confucius as "K'ung Mou", that is, "a certain Mr. K'ung." This is a form employed by pious Confucians to avoid using either of Confucius' personal names. Yet it was not used as early as the *Mencius,* although Mencius was a good Confucian. Its curious occurrence here, in an attack on Confucius, clearly shows that the passage is a late addition to the text.

16. These stories occur in *Chia Yü* 1.4b–7a, 7.10a–12b; and *Hsün Tzŭ* 389–390. The latter reference occurs in a part of the *Hsün Tzŭ* which is clearly late; Liang Ch'i-ch'ao believed it had been put together in Han times. See Liang 115. For genuine Confucian sayings about punishments, see *An.* 2.3, 12.18, 12.19, 13.11. For refutation of the story that Confucius executed one Shao Chêng Mao, see Ts'ui 2.22–24.

17. See Maspero, 457 n.2. The *Tso Chuan* gives the name of the minister of crime of Lu only once, where it is mentioned that Tsêng Wu-chung held the office in 552 (*Tso* 490). Although heads of the family twice had to flee the state thereafter, successors to them were appointed and the family continued extremely important (*Tso* 502-503, 710-712, 817, 855). In the absence of any evidence to the contrary, it is likely that its chief continued to be minister of crime.

18. Prior to 498 Chi K'ang Tzŭ asked Confucius about the suitability for official posts of these three disciples (*An.* 6.6). Subsequently, Tzŭ-lu was steward of the Chi family in 498, and Tzŭ-kung was present at a diplomatic conference in 495 and later served the Chi family in important posts (*Tso* 781 and 791). The *Tso Chuan* states that Jan Ch'iu was steward of the Chi family in 484 (*Tso* 824). *An.* 11.23 and 16.1 seem to indicate that Tzŭ-lu and Jan Ch'iu were simultaneously in the service of the Chi family; this was probably before Tzŭ-lu went with Confucius on his travels, not later than about 493. It must be noted, however, that the authenticity of 16.1 is uncertain.

19. The incident of Kung-Shan Fu-jao inviting Confucius presumably occurred between 502, when the revolt of Yang Hu took place, and 498 when Kung-Shan had to flee from Lu. Confucius was almost cer-

tainly not in any considerable office when that invitation was tendered. Mencius says that he took office under Chi Huan Tzŭ, who died in 492 (*Mencius* 5[2]4.7); furthermore, the *Tso Chuan* (802) says that by 492 Confucius was in Ch'ên, presumably having started on his travels.

Other less reliable accounts also indicate him to have been in office around 500. That is the year in which Confucius is said, in the very dubious anecdote incorporated in the *Tso Chuan*, to have assisted Duke Ting at the meeting at Chia-ku (*Tso* 776-777). The *Ku-Liang Chuan* (19.12b-13b) has another version of the same story. The *Kung-Yang Chuan*, which omits this story in a manner that seems to constitute a denial of it, speaks of Confucius as being "successful with the Chi family," which perhaps means that he was in its service, in 500 and again in 498 (*Kung-Yang Chuan* 26.8, 26.11a).

20. *An.* 10.2. Since this passage occurs in Chapter 10, Waley and some others would have us suppose that it refers to the manner of "the gentleman," not of Confucius personally. But it would seem that this passage, like certain others in that chapter, must refer to a particular individual.

21. Compare *ts'ung pi tai fu*, which is interpreted as "to be one of the *pi tai fu*," in *Tso* 618 and *Tso Chuan Chu Su* 44.15a.

22. If we suppose that, as is improbable, he first took office under Duke Ai, the situation is not changed. Except for *An.* 14.22, which we can definitely date in 481 (*Tso* 840), which is too late for the present purpose, the only two conversations this duke held with Confucius are not what we should have expected him to say to a familiar minister (*An.* 2.19, 6.2).

23. The *Analects* does not record any interview between Confucius and Chi Huan Tzŭ.

24. The *Kung-Yang Chuan* (26.11a) says that Confucius advised this move.

25. The *Tso Chuan* (781) says that on one occasion Confucius caused the duke and the heads of the three families to be rescued by ordering soldiers to their assistance when they were besieged. This is doubtful. The name of Confucius turns up here with suspicious abruptness, and this is the only occasion on which he is ever depicted as commanding troops.

26. This interpretation of *shih* seems preferable to the common one of "private business." Tai Wang understood it in this way; see Tai 13.3a.

27. *An.* 13.14. This translation is rather free, but I believe that it correctly conveys the meaning. The passage is commonly supposed to date from the period after Confucius' return to Lu from his travels. But Confucius left Lu because he had become disillusioned, and after he returned his advice was deliberately disregarded. It hardly seems probable, therefore, that at that late date he would still have expected to be consulted on any important matter that arose.

28. *An.* 18.4, which seems to imply that Ch'i sent female musicians to divert the Duke of Lu and cause Confucius to resign, because Ch'i was afraid he would make Lu too powerful, is like much of the rest of Chapter 18 almost certainly false. It is part of the legend of Confucius. Ts'ui Shu points out that Mencius does not mention this incident where we should expect him to, and questions it (Ts'ui 2.25-26).

29. The *Mo Tzŭ* includes two such stories; see *Mo Tzŭ*(2) 206-208. Not only do they occur in a section of that work which is clearly interpolated (see note 15 above); one of them has Yen Tzŭ telling Duke Ching, who died in 490, about a rebellion in Ch'u which did not take place until 479 (*Tso* 847). A somewhat different version of one of these stories is given in the *Yen Tzŭ Ch'un Ch'iu*, which also contains several others which confront Yen Tzŭ and Confucius, or represent them as contemporaries; see *Yen Tzŭ* 7.25b–26a, 28b–29b, 30b–33a, 34. This is chronologically difficult. While the *Tso Chuan* mentions Yen Tzŭ frequently he last appears there in 516, when Confucius was only thirty-five (*Tso* 718-719). The references in the *Yen Tzŭ Ch'un Ch'iu*, on the other hand, depict Confucius as having established his reputation at the time of these events; in fact, by that time Yen Tzŭ was probably dead. For these and other reasons, these anecdotes cannot be considered historical. The date of the *Yen Tzŭ Ch'un Ch'iu* as a whole is difficult to determine; it is generally agreed that it must date from a time considerably later than that of Confucius. See *Wei Shu* 607-609.

An. 18.3 scarcely merits mention. Confucius never ranked with the heads of the three families of Lu, and in any case the Duke of Ch'i would scarcely have cited them for his example. Like much of the rest of chapter 18, this is undoubtedly legend.

30. Because of *An.* 11.2 it has been supposed that at least ten disciples, including most of the very prominent ones, traveled with him; but it seems clear that two unrelated sayings have been erroneously interpreted as referring to each other. Both the *Analects* (5.21) and *Mencius* (7[2]37) indicate that while Confucius was in Ch'ên he had a sizeable group of disciples still in Lu. Both Tzŭ-kung and Jan Ch'iu were in the service of the Chi family in Lu for some and possibly for all of the time he was away. The *Tso Chuan* (791, 813, 825) mentions Tzŭ-kung as in public service in Lu in 495, 488, and 484; there is no indication of any break. Jan Ch'iu is first mentioned in 484, but by that time he was already steward of the Chi family and commander of an army; it must have taken him some time to reach this position (*Tso* 824-826). It is true that *An.* 13.9 says that "when Confucius went to Wei, Jan Ch'iu drove for him." But we have no way of knowing when this trip was made; if it was at the time when Confucius set off on his travels, Jan Ch'iu might still have performed this service as a courtesy and then returned to Lu.

31. *An.* 13.3 suggests that Confucius was about to be put in charge

of the government of Wei, but this passage appears to be clearly false; see Chapter XIII, note 13.

32. *An.* 15.1.1, in which Confucius leaves Wei because he is offended at being asked about strategy, is implausible; see Ts'ui 3.28–29 and Ch'ien Mu 38–40.

33. To this it may be objected that Tzŭ-hsia speaks with him, in *Analects* 12.5. The *Historical Records* makes Tzŭ-hsia forty-four years younger than Confucius (*Shih Chi* 67.28); if this is true he cannot have been older than fourteen, at the very most, when Confucius began his travels. It is possible, however, that Ssŭ-Ma may have studied with Confucius before his travels, while the conversation with Tzŭ-hsia took place later.

34. *Mencius* 5(1)8.3. The ruler is called Ch'ên Hou Chou, but this must refer to Duke Min, who reigned 501-479; see *Mêng Tzŭ* 9 hsia 10a and Yen Jo-chü 4.38a.

35. The commentary attributed to K'ung An-kuo states that the Duke of Shê "usurped" the title of *kung*, and it is probably for this reason that he has sometimes been called an adventurer. Hsing Ping explains that the ruler of Ch'u usurped the title of king and "all his governors of districts" thereupon called themselves dukes (*Lun Yü* 7.6b-7a). This is of course mere Chou chauvinism since there is no good evidence that Ch'u was ever subject to the Chou house. For a more accurate view, see Tai 7.3a.

36. *Tso* 805, 847. We know that Confucius did visit Ts'ai (*An.* 11.2.1; *Mencius* 7[2]18), and it was probably there that the two men met, as Ts'ui Shu has pointed out (Ts'ui 3.11-14). Ts'ui has shown that it is most unlikely that Confucius ever, as later tradition asserted, visited Ch'u, except in so far as Ts'ai was at that time part of Ch'u. None of the early sources say he did. The portion of the *Mo Tzŭ* in which this statement is made, and an absurd story is told about Confucius' actions in Ch'u (*Mo Tzŭ*[2] 206), is an obviously interpolated and false passage. See note 15 above and *Mo Tzŭ*(2) 206 n.3.

37. The circumstances and the date of this affair are much debated. I follow the explanation of Liu Kung-mien, which makes Pi Hsi a subordinate of the Fan and Chung-Hang families rather than, as Hsing Ping would have it, of Chao Chien Tzŭ; see Liu Pao-nan 20.8a, and *Lun Yü* 17.4a. Liu's version of this occurrence places it in 490.

38. Ts'ui Shu hotly denies that this could have happened. His concern is chiefly with Confucius' reputation; his arguments are weak (see Ts'ui 2.36-39 and note 39 below). Fung Yu-lan believes it did occur (Fung[3] 37-38). It is mentioned in *Mo Tzŭ*, but in a garbled form and in the dubious Fei Ju section (*Mo Tzŭ*[2] 211).

39. Even Ts'ui Shu, who was certainly one of the greatest of scholars and for whose integrity I have the highest respect, was betrayed by his overeagerness to discredit *Analects* 17.7. He declared that in Confucius' day the term *fu tzŭ* was never used to denote the person to whom one

was directly speaking, as it is used in this passage (Ts'ui 2.38-39). In fact, however, this mode of address also appears in *Analects* 11.25.9, 12.8.2, 14.30, and 17.4.3. Ts'ui takes care of 11.25 and 17.4 by saying that they are probably false, but he appears to ignore the other two passages.

40. *Mencius* 5(2)4.7. He mentions a Duke Hsiao, but no such duke of Wei is known. This must be Ch'u; see Ts'ui 3.29.

41. The *Tso Chuan* quotes Confucius as saying at this point, "The bird chooses the tree; how can the tree choose the bird?" (*Tso* 826). In its tacit assumption that the traveling philosopher is a bird of passage and in its arrogance, this statement does not sound like Confucius but reflects the conditions of a later day. For Mencius, for instance, it would be totally in character.

42. Both the *Tso Chuan* and the *Discourses of the States* say that Confucius refused to answer, and only made known his opinion privately to Jan Ch'iu (*Tso* 826; *Kuo Yü* 5.16a-17a). But this is incredible in view of Confucius' usual forthrightness in the *Analects*, the caustic candor of his statements to Chi K'ang Tzŭ, and his repudiation of Jan Ch'iu as a result of this incident.

43. *An.* 7.14. This passage is usually interpreted as dating from the time when Confucius was in Wei; see Ts'ui 3.26. This would mean that Jan Ch'iu and Tzŭ-kung were with Confucius in Wei at a time when in fact they were probably both in Lu. Ts'ui Shu recognizes the awkwardness of this but tries to resolve it in a rather forced manner. The whole incident is much more in place if we understand it as taking place in Lu in 479, at the time when Duke Ch'u fled to Lu for refuge (*Tso* 846). At that time both Jan Ch'iu and Tzŭ-kung, as responsible officials, were vitally concerned with the question of how the exile should be treated, which was important to the political fortunes of Lu.

44. I have combined the accounts of the *Tso Chuan* (840) and the *Analects* (14.22). The *Tso Chuan* disagrees with the *Analects*, saying that Confucius refused to present the matter to the head of the Chi family, but it is unlikely that he would have been so naïve as to expect the powerless Duke to take independent action.

45. The account given in the *Li Chi* (1.138–139) and copied in the *Historical Records* (*Mem. Hist.* V.423–425) is utterly inconsistent with his character, as Ts'ui Shu has recognized (Ts'ui 4.12).

46. See note 2 above.

Chapter V

1. For reasons explained in the Appendix I have used only a few passages of *Analects* 10 in writing this chapter; see p. 293.

2. *An.* 16.11.2, which appears to praise those who "live in retirement to seek the fulfillment of their aims" is very possibly a Taoist interpolation into the *Analects*; much of Chapter 16 is dubious. In any case

Confucius' idea about retirement from the world, as we see it for instance in *An.* 7.10.1 and 15.6.2, is not that it is a course which is good in itself, but that it is the only thing which a self-respecting man can do when the evil are firmly in power. But always he is waiting for his chance to take an active and effective part in the government.

3. *Lao Tzŭ*, chapters 3, 19, 37, 80. It should be noted, however, that the *Chuang Tzŭ* condemned this aspect of the Moist philosophy as "too barren" and "contrary to human nature" (*Chuang Tzŭ* II.219).

Chapter VI

1. Not only is there no indication that he did, but his poverty, persisting to the time of his death, seems to show that he did not; see *An.* 6.9, 11.7, 11.10, and *Mencius* 4(2)29.2.

2. Ts'ui Shu has completely refuted the story of the *Han Shih Wai Chuan* to the effect that Yen Hui attended upon and conversed with Duke Ai of Lu; see Ts'ui(2) 1.2–3.

3. *An.* 5.9; see also 3.21. Ch'ien Mu believes that these censures are incompatible with the manner in which Tsai Yü's opinion is quoted in *Mencius* 2(1)2.25-26. He thinks them to have been falsely inserted into the *Analects*, for reasons that are somewhat involved and not wholly convincing; see Ch'ien Mu 50–53.

4. See note 2 above.

5. The *Han Fei Tzŭ* says that after Confucius' death there were eight groups of Confucians, stemming from eight teachers; three of these are disciples of Confucius, namely Tzŭ-chang, Yen (Hui, presumably), and Ch'i-Tiao K'ai (*Han Fei* 19.12.). The exclusion of Tzŭ-hsia and the inclusion of Yen Hui and Ch'i-Tiao K'ai seem equally surprising. Yen Hui died young and before Confucius' death; it is unlikely that he founded a distinct school. Ch'i-Tiao K'ai is mentioned only once in the *Analects* (5.5), and very little elsewhere; the *Mo Tzŭ* mentions him only to blame Confucius for his "ferocious appearance" (*Mo Tzŭ*[2] 211).

The *Historical Records* states that "after the death of Confucius the seventy disciples scattered and traveled among the feudal lords" (*Shih Chi* 121.3).

6. This passage, *An.* 17.4, is doubted by Ts'ui Shu, but his objections are weak; see Ts'ui(2) 2.19.

7. Mencius compares Tzŭ-hsia and Tsêng Shên to certain fearless bravos (*Mencius* 2[1]2.6-8). Careful examination of the passage reveals, however, that Mencius is attributing to them moral rather than physical courage.

8. More correctly called Tsêng Ts'an (see *Shih Chi* 67.32), but in this book the more common usage is followed.

9. The authorship of the *Classic of Filial Piety* (*Hsiao Ching*) has frequently but erroneously been attributed to him; see Creel(5) I.35.

Chapter VII

1. For the doubts expressed by an able French Sinologist a century ago, see Biot 10-72.

2. See Kuo 16b–17b. Legge translated a passage in the *Bamboo Books* as stating that an imperial college was built at the beginning of the Chou dynasty, but in fact this seems to have been what one bronze inscription calls a "hall for the study of archery." Certain later works assert that other arts were also studied there, but there seems to be no early evidence for this. See *loc. cit.*; *Shu*, Prolegomena 140; and *Shih* 458 n.

3. Maspero attributed such ideas to Confucius, and said that he derived them from the *Hung Fan* of the *Shu Ching*; see Maspero 463 n. 2. But that text contains frequent references to the so-called five elements (*wu hsing*) and is shot through with the use of mystical numbers; neither of these, nor the whole make-up of the text, is characteristic of a time as early as that of Confucius (see Chapter XII, note 36) and it is certainly later. Arthur Waley also ascribes a kind of magical thinking to Confucius, but he recognizes that the type of cosmological magic mentioned above "does not belong to the teaching of Confucius in the *Analects*"; see Waley 18 and 64-66.

4. See Creel, H. G., *Sinism: A Study of the Evolution of the Chinese World-View* (Chicago, 1929), p. 65. A major presupposition of this book was that the metaphysical system of Han times was of quite early origin; this was, of course, wholly erroneous. There are probably few important propositions in this book, which was written twenty years ago, to which I should subscribe today.

5. For fairly clear instances of the efficacy of example in the early literature, see: *Shih* 405, 447, 459, 493, 511, 618; compare *Shih*(2) 297, 260, 265, 183, 300, 268. See also *Shu* 498. There are, certainly, passages in the *Analects* that may be interpreted as referring to magical influence, such as *An.* 2.1, 13.6 and 15.4. But they may also be explained as depending upon the force of example, and when we consider Confucius' thought as a whole, as well as the intellectual climate of the time, this is much more probable; see *An.* 4.1, 5.2, 15.9.

6. This statement is based upon examination of the *Shu*, the *Shih*, and the original text of the *I*. There are some passages in which the context does not make definition possible. One case in which the sense may be similar to that in which the term is used by Confucius occurs in *Shu* 628; this is in the *Ch'in Shih*, which is plausibly ascribed to a date not very much earlier than that of Confucius. It is possible that this sense is present in *I Ching* 106 and 130.

7. There is no conclusive evidence on this point. This seems to have been the practice a little later, however, with Mo Tzŭ and with Mencius (see Mo *Tzŭ*[2] 252 and *Mencius* 2[2]10.3); and it is probable in view of the economic conditions of the time.

8. Tzǔ-hsia states this point specifically in *An.* 19.12.

9. The character *li* does not occur in the original text of the *Book of Changes (I Ching)* nor does Jung Kêng list it as occurring in any of the many bronze inscriptions analyzed in his *Chin Wên Pien*. In books of the *Shu* which are probably pre-Confucian it occurs with the broader sense only in the *Chin T'êng*, concerning the date of which there is some question (*Shu* 360). In the *Shih* it has the broader sense twice (*Shih* 85, 323).

10. Arthur Waley holds this only in a limited sense; he writes, "I do not think that Confucius attributed this magic power to any rites save those practised by the divinely appointed ruler" (Waley 66). But the whole idea of magical efficacy is foreign to the pattern of Confucius' thought in general, as we see it in the *Analects*. It is true that *An.* 12.1 is sometimes interpreted as meaning that if one (presumably the ruler) would practice *jên* (virtue) for only one day, all in the world would become *jên*. If that is what the passage means it does, indeed, speak of magic. But if the passage is genuine it can hardly mean that; compare *An.* 13.11 and 13.12 where it is said that good rulers would need a century in one case and a generation in another to right the ills of the world.

11. That is, relatively speaking; from our point of view the Confucian prescription of three years' mourning was, of course, excessive. See *Li Chi* I.131, 176-178.

12. Although the first section of this passage, *Analects* 15.1, is dubious (see Ts'ui 3.28-29), the point of the portion quoted is also expressed in *An.* 4.2 and 8.10.

13. *An.* 2.22. I have slightly abbreviated this passage by simplifying the figure.

14. This seems, for instance, to be the only sense in which it is used in the *Book of Changes (I Ching* 117, 182). The evidence concerning the history of this character is manifold, but it would take us too far afield to detail it here.

15. *An.* 15.40. *Cf. I Li* I.233-234. Waley would limit the meaning of *tz'ǔ* to "pleas, messages, excuses for being unable to attend to one's duties, etc." (Waley 201, n. 2). For the sense of "language," however, see *Shu* 628, *An.* 8.4, and *Mencius* 2(1)2.18 and 5(1)4.2.

16. See Waley's discussion of this practice in *Shih* (2) 335–337.

17. The *Li Chi* was edited in Former Han times by Tai Shêng, who used materials of various date. How old its oldest materials are is debatable; certainly some of them must, because of their style and content, stem from times much later than that of Confucius.

The *Chou Li* describes an ideal system of orderly centralized government, supposed to have existed at the beginning of Western Chou times, which was not possible in the circumstances and is refuted by all the testimony of genuinely early books and bronze inscriptions. Maspero believed it to date from the fourth century B.C., but to have been edited and interpolated in Han times (Maspero XII). Hu Shih has considered it a Han work (Hu[2] 222).

18. Here I am referring, of course, only to the *chin wên* text, which itself includes a certain number of forgeries; see Creel 55–93, 97 n. 1, 2. The fact that the text of *Mo Tzŭ* includes the term *shang shu* does not prove the existence of a corpus in Mo Tzŭ's time. The character 尚 *shang* is used in the sense of "to preserve" in several bronze inscriptions (see Jung Kêng 2.2b-3a); thus it seems probable that *shang shu* originally meant nothing more than "archives." Furthermore, Sun I-jang has quite correctly pointed out that the expression *shang shu* makes no sense in the text of the *Mo Tzŭ*, and so emends the text that it is eliminated; see *Mo Tzŭ* 8.15a.

19. *An.* 2.21, 7.17, 14.43. This omits 11.24, which seems merely to refer to books in general.

Chapter VIII

1. *Analects* 1.1.1. Huang Shih-san has pointed out that *yüeh* in this passage has the sense of "joy arising from thorough understanding," which is related to the sense in which the same character is pronounced *shuo* (see Huang 1.1b).

2. *An.* 2.18. Here *tai* is rendered in the sense of "what is only probable." This fits the passage better, and a similar usage occurs in *Shu* 548 and in *Mencius* 1(1)7.17. The usual reading, "what is dangerous," conflicts squarely with *An.* 2.24, 14.13.3, and 15.8.

3. K'ang 10.1b. This did not mean that Confucius wrote all of the Classics that now circulate. K'ang believed that a large part of them was forged by Liu Hsin.

4. *Mem. Hist.* V.398-400. Our present *Book of Poetry* includes three hundred and five pieces; in addition, there are the names of six more, which have been lost.

5. The orthodox theory, that Confucius composed the *Spring and Autumn Annals*, was followed by George A. Kennedy in a recent study. He prepared a map showing the relative amount of data on various states, and concluded that "everything else being equal, the states in the path of Confucius' travels . . . seem better represented than others" (Kennedy 48). The valuable data he assembled admit of another interpretation, however. His map and tables assume more significance if we read them as indicating the political relationships of the state of Lu. For instance, his tables on p. 45 show that before 580 B.C. the deaths of *no* rulers of Wu were recorded, but after that *all* were. It was precisely in 584 B.C. that the northern states, including Lu, began to have relations with Wu (*Tso* 364).

Kennedy's main thesis, that the work does not contain an esoteric doctrine, seems unquestionable, and he has marshaled impressive evidence for it.

6. *Mencius* 4(2)21.2 refers to "the *Spring and Autumn Annals* of Lu," but the very next section says that it recorded "the affairs of Duke Huan of Ch'i and Duke Wên of Chin." The work we know is a chronicle of Lu, and mentions these persons only incidentally. A similar objection exists where Mencius says that the work he describes is a record of "the affairs of the Son of Heaven" (*Mencius* 3[2]9.8). Many scholars have questioned that Mencius was speaking of our *Spring and Autumn Annals.* See Ku 42 and *Tso,* Prolegomena 4 n.

7. *Li Chi* II.166-167. The treatise here referred to is a section of the *Book of Etiquette and Ceremonial (I Li).*

8. *An.* 9.14 quotes Confucius as saying that after his return from Wei to Lu "the music was correct," which may indicate some work of revision on his part; however, it may also indicate only that he instructed the musicians of the Lu court (see *An.* 3.23, 8.15).

9. Bones apparently used for divination were found in two sites of the "black pottery" Neolithic culture that preceded the Shang at Anyang; see Creel 176-177.

10. Waley, *Shih*(2) 275. Legge translates the poem according to tradition (*Shih* 611-613), but the rendering of *ssŭ* as "he thinks" shows its absurdity especially at the end of the first stanza.

11. *An.* 2.21.2. This passage occurs, in slightly different form, in *Shu* 535. It is here in a *ku wên* document, which is undoubtedly, as scholarly opinion generally holds, forged. It is not unlikely that the forger embodied in his work this quotation that is found in the *Analects.* Even though we cannot, therefore, be quite certain of the original, it seems clear that Confucius is twisting the meaning, for *yu chêng* would seem to indicate that the person in question has an official position. Confucius is evading the question, probably because he is embarrassed for his disciples, who have failed to get him a position even equal to theirs.

12. Compare *I Li* I.119 and *An.* 3.16; *Li Chi* I.147 and *An.* 7.9.1; *Li Chi* I.89 and *An.* 7.9.2; *Li Chi* I.153 and *An.* 10.6.10; *Li Chi* II.363 and *An.* 13.22.1.

13. *An.* 13.22. Compare *I Ching* 126, and *Li Chi* II.363-364.

Chapter IX

1. See Plato(2) 65–66; Taylor 164–171; and Rogers 156–157.

2. See *Tso* 549-551. Elsewhere, Tzŭ-ch'an of Chêng is quoted as predicting that Ch'ên would be destroyed in "not more than ten years"; nine years and five months later this event occurred (*Tso* 557, 623). There are scores of such prophecies in the *Tso Chuan.*

3. See *An.* 14.43, 17.21; *Mencius* 3(1)2.4. The date of origin of the practice of mourning for three years has been much debated; if we may judge from the passage in *Mencius* 3(1)2.3, it was far from universal in Confucius' day.

4. See Creel(2) 82–90. My more general conclusions in that article require considerable modification.

5. As stated above, T'ien and Ti were originally different, but were merged into one before Confucius' time.

6. See *Mencius* 1(1)4.6 and *Li Chi* I.173. Chinese scholars seem to have believed that the use of images was first, and real human sacrifice was derived from it; the actual history seems clearly to have been the reverse.

7. See *An.* 6.4. It has been held that this should be read "said *to* Chung Kung," but *An.* 9.20 makes clear that it may properly be read "of."

8. Weber 293. It would. be pleasant to be able to say that Weber's comments on Confucius and Confucianism were all equally penetrating, but unfortunately this is not the case. Nevertheless, he did make some keen observations, which are quite remarkable in view of the fact that he worked with translations and secondary materials.

9. It is attributed to him in only two passages, *An.* 2.4 and 16.8. The extremely regular form of 2.4, and its utterly smug content, render it suspect. 16.8 is also dubious, because of its manner of using the number three and its authoritarian cast.

10. *An.* 12.5.3-4. This is to cut off the quotation, but not, I believe, in a manner that does violence to its sense.

11. It is not listed by Sun Hai-po in the *Chia Ku Wên Pien*, and Tung Tso-pin tells me that he has never encountered the character in his twenty years of research on the oracle bones (verbal communication of 18 November 1947).

12. *Tao* has the sense of "road" or "path" in: *I Ching* 79; *Shih* 52, 55, 151, 155, 156, 160 (thrice), 161, 185 (twice), 196 (twice), 197, 206, 218 (twice), 247, 261, 331, 332, 336, 349, 353, 418, 424, 441, 546, 617 (cf. *Shih Chu Su* 20 chih 1.15b, columns 6-7). It means "conducted" in: *Shu* 99, 102, 113, 119. It means "to tell" or "to state" in: *Shu* 388, 558; and *Shih* 74 (twice). It means "course of action" in: *I Ching* 76, 93, 108; *Shu* 477, 567; *Shih* 469.

13. See *Li Chi* I.140 and *Chia Yü* 10.11; these are not two accounts, but the same one with only negligible differences. Blood revenge is not mentioned in the *Analects*; to advocate it seems opposed to Confucius' temper. Hsün Tzŭ seems to have deplored it (*Hsün Tzŭ* 343).

14. I am not forgetting *An.* 8.9, "The Master said, 'The people can be caused to follow it, but they cannot be made to understand it.' " But the passage is not wholly clear, and we do not know its circumstances or particular reference.

15. *An.* 13.30. This does not refer to merely military training; see *An.* 13.29.

16. Many scholars have written at great length about the virtue called 仁 *jên*. But after one has read their discussions and considered the many passages in which it occurs in the *Analects*, it is still hard to see how it can be defined more closely than as "virtue" or "complete virtue." The character 德 *tê* also has the sense of "virtue"; sometimes it rather

denotes the qualities of a person or thing, whether good or bad, as we may speak of the "evil virtues" of a poison. In the *Analects*, however, the characters *tê* and *jên* sometimes seem quite interchangeable; this is especially clear in 14.5, and when we compare 6.20 with 12.21.3. Waley almost always interprets *tê* as meaning "inner power"; this seems to me, however, to be a conception more common in a period much later than that of Confucius. This translation seems clearly to break down when applied to *An.* 14.36.

17. It is true that *An.* 16.9 begins, "Confucius said, 'Those born with knowledge compose the highest class.' " But this section is almost certainly false; see p. 221.

18. Even Mencius said of the *Book of History* that "rather than believe all of it, it would be better to be without it" (*Mencius* 7[2]3). It is Hsün Tzŭ, the authoritarian, who declared that the method of study "begins with reciting the Classics, and ends in learning *li*" (*Hsün Tzŭ*[2] 36).

19. This translation is peculiarly inappropriate in *An.* 6.20.

20. An especially clear instance is in *An.* 9.3.

21. *An.* 7.19. The rendering of *ku* as "the past" is that of Waley, and it seems definitely better here than the more usual "antiquity." Although only a century separated Confucius and Mencius, the latter referred to Confucius as among the "*ku* sages" (*Mencius* 2[1]2.22).

22. *An.* 3.9. This translation is based on comparison of this passage with variant versions that occur in *Li Chi* II.324 and *Chia Yü* 1.20b–21a. These latter works are not cited as reliable sources for the utterances of Confucius, but as indications of the way in which this saying was understood at a relatively early date. No translation is given for *wên hsien* because I simply do not know how it should be translated.

23. *An.* 2.18. This translation of *tai* was explained in Chapter VIII, note 2.

24. *An.* 7.27. Literally, "These are the stages by which . . ." All of the commentators and translators known to me take *tz'ŭ* here in the sense of "next" or "second," so that we get, "This is the second-best kind of knowledge," next, that is, to innate knowledge. But it is most doubtful that Confucius believed in innate knowledge. Furthermore, this comment is a meaningless appendage to the passage, distinctly anticlimactic.

It is probable that the original meaning of *tz'ŭ* was that of a lodging place, a stage in a journey; it has this sense in the original text of the *Book of Changes* (*I Ching* 188) and possibly in *An.* 4.5. Here Confucius speaks of the stages in the journey to knowledge or wisdom.

25. As for instance in his naïve belief that it was possible to predict changes in ceremonial usages even a hundred generations in the future; see *An.* 2.23.

Chapter X

1. *An.* 3.16 reads, "The Master said, 'In archery it is not piercing the leather [of the target] that counts, because men's strength is not equal. This was the old way.'" But this shift of emphasis from strength to skill alone is not what we should expect among the old military aristocracy; rather it sounds like a part of the general Confucian attempt to supplant the purely military attitudes. Support is given to this view by the fact that the text of the *I Li* (I.95) states: "The arrow that does not pierce the target, although it should hit it, is not to score." A later note to the same work uses the very words of the *Analects*, however, saying, "In ceremonial shooting it is not piercing the leather that counts" (*I Li* I.119).

2. The only section of the *Book of History* in which Yü is mentioned, which appears to be pre-Confucian, is the *Tribute of Yü.*

3. It is evident that the "model emperor" lore was embryonic in Confucius' day from the fact, for instance, that Hou Chi, mythical remote ancestor of the Chou house, is mentioned in *An.* 14.6 as having "possessed the empire." Viewed in the light of the developed legends of the emperors, this is anachronistic nonsense.

4. *An.* 16.2 speaks of a feudal order, but at the same time advocates a centralization greater than that which ordinarily characterizes feudalism. This passage is almost certainly a late addition to the text; see pages 220–221.

5. It is possible that all of Confucius' disciples were men of some aristocratic lineage, though a number of them were in depressed circumstances. But Confucius never set up a qualification of birth, and the result was that, if not in his own day then soon after, the Confucians came to include men of thoroughly plebeian origin.

6. See Chapter XII, note 17.

7. Kuo(3) 63–70. Kuo states, among other arguments, that while the *Analects* indicates that Confucius was not a fomenter of disorder, the *Mo Tzŭ* and the *Chuang Tzŭ* say he was, and that when there are three authorities, one should follow the two which agree. But such mathematical use of evidence, without due investigation and weighting, is scarcely admissible. Such investigation immediately discredits much of the evidence which Kuo takes most seriously.

Kuo's essay on Confucius (*ibid.* 63–92) is an important work. Like many of his other writings, it combines brilliant insight and broad scholarship with a frequently disappointing lack of critical care in the assembling and use of materials. On several major points Kuo has stated a view essentially similar to that given in this volume. In order not to be accused of plagiarism I should like to point out that most of this book had been written, in first draft, before I read Kuo's essay, and that I had stated many of these points in my teaching before Kuo's work was published. I am very glad to have his concurrence in these views, which confirms my confidence in their correctness.

8. *An.* 13.13. See also 2.20, 4.13, 12.17, 12.18, 13.6.

9. Confucius was not the first to emphasize the importance of good and able ministers. It is mentioned in sections of the *Book of Poetry* and the *Book of History* dating from the beginning of the Chou period; the Duke of Chou, especially, insisted upon the necessity of good ministers. Yet it is probably through Confucius that this idea attained its authority in later times. Hsün Tzŭ, who flourished around 300 B.C. and greatly influenced the theory of Chinese government, elaborated this point with historical illustrations, but concluded his argument with a quotation ascribed to Confucius (*Hsün Tzŭ* 154-155).

10. *An.* 3.1, 3.2, 3.22, 7.35, 14.15. From *An.* 8.14 (identical with 14.27) and 14.28 it has been argued that Confucius condemned criticism of government policies by those not in office. But it is inconceivable that one who criticized so freely as he did could have meant this; the statements must have been made with special references now lost to us.

11. *An.* 12.11.2. On the basis of this, and of *An.* 13.3, there has been fathered upon Confucius an elaborate doctrine of "the rectification of names." There are many difficulties with *An.* 13.3; it seems to be clearly a late interpolation, probably made under Legalist influence. See Chap. XIII, note 13.

An. 12.11 (quoted in the text) has no necessary connection with the doctrine of "rectification of names." Since the only passage in the *Analects* that does is 13.3, and it is evidently false, there seems to be no indication that Confucius knew this doctrine.

12. Plato(3) 496–497. Compare *An.* 14.4, 15.6.2, 19.25.4.

13. Opinion on Confucius' views concerning law has been colored by a passage in the *Tso Chuan* where he is quoted as opposing the publication of laws, chiefly on the ground that this would undermine the stratification of society, and as asking, "When there is no distinction between the noble and the humble, how can the state be governed?" (*Tso* 732). This does not sound at all like Confucius. On the other hand, its content is remarkably similar to that of a letter which Shu-hsiang of Chin is alleged to have written fifteen years before Confucius was born (*Tso* 609-610). The attribution to Confucius is highly questionable.

14. Merriam 11–12. He points out that the first of these statements is in part adapted from Durkheim.

15. For instance, "Mo Tzŭ said to Lo Hua-li, 'I hear that you love valor.' Lo Hua-li replied, 'Yes, whenever I hear that there is a brave knight somewhere I always go and kill him.' " *Mo Tzŭ(2)* 221.

16. Two different theories as to the origin of the term *ju* are developed at length in Hu(5) 3-81 and Fung(3) 1-61. My own conclusions are in partial, but only partial, agreement with each. Both Hu and Fung agree that the character *ju* had the sense of "weak"; and Fung thinks, as I do, that it was applied to the scholars because they were not warlike.

There are only slight traces of the probable fact that *ju* was once a term of derision, but since it soon came to be the name of the most honored class in the community this is not remarkable. How many

Christians realize that in the Roman Empire the cross was symbolic of horror and degradation? In the *Tso Chuan*, *ju* is used as a term of disapprobation (*Tso* 853), and Waley (239) suggests that *ju* was a contemptuous nickname applied to the people of Lu because of their "pacific" nature. In the *Li Chi* (II.409-410) Confucius is quoted as saying that the name *ju* is wrongly used as one of reproach, and Duke Ai tells him, "Never, so long as I live, will I use *ju* as a term of derision." This conversation is wholly apocryphal, but there would seem to be no adequate explanation for the presence of these statements, in such a respectable Confucian work as the *Li Chi*, except that *ju* must have been, at one time, a term of derision.

17. In the *Analects* it occurs only in 6.11. In the *Mencius* it occurs only twice (3[1]5.3 and 7[2]26.1), only once in the mouth of Mencius himself. Although Mo Tzŭ lived before Mencius, he seems to have made more use of the term and to have considered Confucius as a *ju* (*Mo Tzŭ(2)* 238); whether this is because he was critical of the Confucian group is not clear. The *Fei* ju chapter in Mo Tzŭ is, however, of later date; see Chap. XII, note 3.

Chapter XI

1. *Li Chi* II.409. This statement is attributed to Confucius, but the whole of this *Ju Hsing* chapter is clearly later and apocryphal; see Chap. XIV, note 20.

2. See Chap. XII, note 3.

3. *Mencius* 7(1)18. See also *Kuo Yü* 5.10b, and *Shu* 466–468. The latter reference resembles the passage quoted above from Plato. It is from the *Wu I*, a book that is not (as it pretends) as old as the time of the Duke of Chou, but is probably pre-Han.

4. I do not forget, of course, that much of the *Records on Ceremonial* was copied from the *Hsün Tzŭ*. But here I am speaking of "the more pedestrian portions."

Chapter XII

1. The criticism of this text by Hu Shih, in Hu 151–152, seems to me excellent. See also Fung 80–81.

2. See *An.* 3.4, 9.11, 11.7, 11.10. Mo Tzŭ said that in his own day many *shih* and *chün tzŭ* were doubtful about the suitability of lavish burial and long mourning (*Mo Tzŭ[2]* 125). Mo Tzŭ also attacked the practice of three years' mourning which, as we have seen, Confucius apparently did advocate.

3. *Mo Tzŭ(2)* 201 n.1. See also Hu 151. Many things betray the false character of this *Fei Ju* chapter. In it, and apparently in it alone in the book, Confucius is referred to as "K'ung Mou," *i.e.*, "So-and-so K'ung." This is a manner of reference to Confucius that came into vogue in the Confucian school because extreme piety forbade pronouncing the personal name of the Master. Its use seems to have begun late, however; it

does not occur in the *Analects* nor even in the *Mencius*, although Mencius lived later than Mo Tzŭ and was a good Confucian. In this chapter, which attacks Confucius, it is most incongruous.

4. This principle is found repeatedly in the *Analects*, as we have noted; see especially 2.19 and 12.22. Ku Chieh-kang says that the latter passage is a late interpolation in the *Analects*, and that it "shows Moist influence"(Ku[6] 55). But since Confucius lived before Mo Tzŭ, this statement can stand only if it is true that Confucius did not advocate that men should be promoted on the basis of their ability; in fact, this idea pervades the *Analects*. The argument that An. 12.22 is suspect because it is "at the end of the chapter," is not quite accurate; two sections follow it, and these look all right. An. 12.22 looks, not late, but early. If it were as late as the *Mencius*, or as An. 20.1.2, it would probably refer to Shun's promoting Yü, rather than Kao Yao.

5. See Ku(6). In my opinion this study makes the error of assuming that Confucianism had a character more homogeneous than could be expected in the circumstances, based consistently on the principle of "treating relatives with special affection and honoring those ˙of exalted rank" (*ch'in ch'in kuei kuei*, p. 31). But it is very doubtful that these, especially *kuei kuei*, may properly be called the basic principles of Confucianism, particularly as we find it in Confucius himself. Furthermore, Mo Tzŭ bitterly criticized the Confucians, and Mencius returned the compliment; if the idea of the selection of ancient rulers on the basis of virtue had been an invention of the Moists, that fact alone would probably have prevented the Confucians from regarding it with favor. Yet they did; see for instance *Mencius* 5(1)5, 5(1)6. Moreover, as Fung Yu-lan has pointed out, the Moist Canon section of the *Mo Tzŭ*, which is generally regarded as representing the thought of the later Moist school, criticizes the use of Yao and Shun as models, which clearly seems to be "an attack upon the Confucian reverence for such Sages" (Fung 274–275). This does not support the view that the legends concerning Yao and Shun were inventions of the Moist school.

6. If Confucius had believed, much less originated this idea, it should be mentioned in the *Analects*, which it is not (except in 20.1, which is a late addition to the text). Furthermore *Analects* 12.22.6 seems to prove that Tzŭ-hsia did not know this doctrine; he would hardly have spoken of ministers if he could have adduced the far more striking illustration of the selection of kings. There is a passage in the *Mencius* (5[1]7.7) that quotes Confucius as referring to the abdication of Yao and Shun, but Ku Chieh-kang says that the language used here is anachronistic and that the passage is a later interpolation; see Ku(6) 56. In any case, it is doubtful that Confucius made this statement.

7. *Chan Kuo Ts'ê* 9.11b-13a. The *Han Fei Tzŭ* has several versions of this story, of which the latter indicate that this was a willing abdication (*Han Fei* 14.7a-9a).

8. In fact, he went so far as at least to acquiesce in an attack on Yen,

by Ch'i, after it fell into disorder; see *Mencius* 2(2)8. The *Chan Kuo Ts'ê* (9.13a) says that Mencius deliberately provoked this attack.

9. *Mencius* (5[1]7 and 9) does, it is true, mention traditions to the effect that this happened, but it is uncertain to what extent they were elaborated under the influence of Confucian doctrine.

10. This is my conclusion on the basis of examination of the literature and inscriptions. Ku Chieh-kang makes the same point and cites manifold evidence for it, in Ku(6) 33-42.

The *Mencius* (6[2]7.3) includes a statement to the effect that when Duke Huan assembled the feudal lords one of the articles of the covenant was, "*shih* shall not hold office hereditarily." This whole passage is very curious. From the later specific mention of *tai fu* it looks as if this was intended to refer only to lower offices; this would seem probable in view of Mencius' advocacy elsewhere of hereditary tenure for high officials (*Mencius* 1[2]5.3, 1[2]7.1-4, 3[1]3.8). Ku Chieh-kang points out that in the *Kung-Yang Chuan* and the *Ku-Liang Chuan* the terms of this covenant are given quite differently, and suggests that Mencius had no authority for his statement (Ku[6]4.1). Certainly it does look very strange, considered as history.

11. It is fairly clear that Confucius did not know the content of this work, yet Mencius named and quoted from it (*Mencius* 5[1]4.1). Ku Chieh-kang believes that the present *Yao Tien* was completed only in Han times (Ku[6] 98-99).

12. Creel, Lorraine 72-74. It may be significant that although the *Mencius* is more than twice as long as the *Analects*, the character *hsüeh*, "study," occurs more than twice as frequently in the *Analects* as in *Mencius*.

13. For instance, in the *Mencius* we do not find Confucius speaking in numbers, of "the three so-and-so," "the nine so-and-so," etc., as he is made to do in the latter portion of the *Analects*. On these later chapters, see the Appendix.

14. Although the *Mo Tzŭ* says that Confucius was minister of crime of Lu (*Mo Tzŭ*[2] 209), this statement is in the *Fei Ju* chapter, and this part of that chapter, at least, is probably later than the *Mencius*; see note 3 above.

15. Compare, for instance, the *Lao Tzŭ*, chap. 80 and elsewhere. It is not impossible that this is, in fact, a Taoist interpolation in the *Mencius*; it is interesting to note that all three of the passages last cited are in the first section of Chapter 7, and that nowhere else are "Heaven and Earth" mentioned together in this way.

16. See Waley (3) 49-50.

17. The literature of this debate is most voluminous. Ts'ui Shu attacked the validity of the *Lao Tzŭ* long ago; see Ts'ui 1.21–22. Hu Shih has been the principal defender among critical scholars of the traditional dating of the work; see Hu(5) 103–134. Waley has ventured the most definite dating; he says that it was produced by "an anonymous Quietist," "about 240 B.C." (Waley[3] 86).

Lorraine Creel (27–35) has shown that the *Lao Tzŭ* attacks certain doctrines that do not appear to have existed prior to Confucius and repeatedly uses expressions that do not occur in the literaturé earlier than the *Mo Tzŭ* or the *Mencius*.

18. A number of these stories involve Yen Hui, but the *Analects* mentions the death of Yen Hui several times.

19. *Chuang Tzŭ* I.211 puts the term *yin yang* into the mouth of Confucius; for its late date see note 22 below.

20. *Chuang Tzŭ* II.166-176. This passage refers to the death of Tzŭ-lu, which did not take place until Confucius was seventy-one.

21. It has long been recognized that certain passages dealing with recluses show Taoist influence. I suspect, on this score, *An.* 16.11, 12; 18.5, 6, 7, 8. Compare *Chuang Tzŭ* I.319; II.120-121, 135-136, 153, 192-201.

An. 17.19 is probably a Taoist intrusion. The self-conscious reference by Tzŭ-kung to transmission of Confucius' doctrines looks late. The sentiment ascribed to Confucius and the language look Taoist. The expression *pai wu* does not fit with Confucius' thought; in fact, the character *wu* occurs nowhere else in the *Analects*. Compare *Lao Tzŭ* chaps. 1, 43, and *Chuang Tzŭ* I.335-336, 338, II.3-5, 104-105, 121, 128.

22. It is necessary to discriminate between the occasional use of one of the characters *yin* and *yang* in another sense, and the presence of the philosophic concept. The concept is not present in the text of the *Book of Changes*, the *chin wên* text of the *Book of History*, the *Book of Poetry*, the *Analects*, nor even in so late a Confucian text as the *Mencius*. Not even the characters seem to appear in the Shang oracle bones; the identification of the character *yang* by Sun Hai-po in his *Chia Ku Wên Pien* (14.5a), appears to be a very natural error in reading a not very legible inscription; see Yeh 5.47a. Tung Tso-pin assures me that in his twenty years of research on the oracle bones he has never encountered either character (verbal communication of 21 October 1947). The concept seems also to be absent from bronze inscriptions of pre-Confucian date.

It is present in every one of the appendices to the *Book of Changes* except the last two, occurring as follows: *I Ching* 223, 224, 267, 355, 357, 359, 388, 395, 414, 420-424, 426.

23. This is probably why so many of the dubious passages in the last five chapters of the *Analects* involve numbers. Although sayings of this type are not attributed to Confucius in the *Mencius*, Confucius is quoted by the *Chuang Tzŭ* (II.209) as enumerating "nine tests" for the inferior man.

24. This reference is made almost certain by the apparent reference to Yen Hui in *I Ching* 392.

25. See note 22 above.

26. The character *ti* is rare in the early literature, where "earth" is usually denoted by *t'u*. Sun Hai-po does not list *ti* in his *Chia Ku Wên Pien*, and Tung Tso-pin assures me that he has never encountered the

character in Shang oracle bone inscriptions (verbal communication of
21 October 1947). Jung Kêng does not give *ti* as occurring in any of the
bronze inscriptions analyzed in his *Chin Wên Pien*, and Kuo Mo-jo
wrote in 1932 that the character as the counterpart of Heaven "had not
been seen" in early bronze inscriptions (Kuo 31b). In the original text
of the *Book of Changes* it occurs only once (*I Ching* 135), but with
no metaphysical sense. In the *chin wên* text of the *Book of History* it
appears only three times (*Shu* 245, 354, 593); all of the documents in
which it is found have been held to have been written or edited at a
relatively late date, yet even here *ti* does not have its metaphysical sense.
In the *Book of Poetry* it occurs only twice, both times with the meaning
of the physical earth (*Shih* 307, 317). Its three occurrences in the *Analects* (9.18, 14.39, 19.22) have no metaphysical sense. In *Mencius* the
character is frequent, but it is still not clear that it is a metaphysical
concept (the sense of the occurrence in *Mencius* 7(1)13.3 is debatable).

The character *ti* occurs many times in the appendices, though it is
absent from the last two. In the others it appears as a definitely metaphysical concept as follows: *I Ching* 226, 227, 233, 235, 238, 239, 242,
243, 257, 268, 281, 353, 354, 359, 362, 374, 380, 381, 393, 417, 420,
421, 423, 429.

27. See p. 201.

28. Statements to this effect are included in the following works:
Fung 381 and n. 4; Fung(2) 198–201; Fu *chung* 61–62; Honda 50–53;
Dubs.

29. *An.* 13.22; cf. *Li Chi* II.363. I would translate this passage as
follows: "The Master said, 'The people of the south have a saying, "A
man without constancy will not make even a good wizard or physician."
Good! Inconstant in his virtue, he is likely to incur disgrace. It is not
sufficient merely to divine.' "

The quoted saying is part of the original text of the *Book of Changes*
(*I Ching* 126), but Confucius seems to have known it merely as a
proverb. The above translation is in part similar to that of Waley.

30. For some specific passages in the appendices to the *Book of
Changes* that closely resemble passages in Taoist works, compare: *I
Ching* 213 with *Chuang Tzŭ* I.171; *I Ching* 226 with *Lao Tzŭ* chaps.
24, 34, 36; *I Ching* 335 with *Lao Tzŭ* chap. 42 and *Chuang Tzŭ* II.47;
I Ching 362–363 with *Lao Tzŭ* chaps. 7, 38; *I Ching* 365–366 with
Lao Tzŭ chap. 42; *I Ching* 382–383 with *Chuang Tzŭ* I.193, 210, 244–
245; *I Ching* 385 with *Lao Tzŭ* chap. 80 and *Chuang Tzŭ* I.287–288;
I Ching 411 with *Chuang Tzŭ* II.194.

31. The *Ching Tien Shih Wên* (24.8a) says 魯 讀 易 為 亦 . Many
scholars think that this means that the Lu text had a different character
here, but Chang Hsin-ch'êng argues that this refers only to pronuncia-
tion; see *Wei Shu* 71–72.

Homer H. Dubs has suggested that the entirety of *Analects* 7.16 was
interpolated; see Dubs.

32. It occurs only in a fragment of the *Chuang Tzŭ* that is now lost,

but is quoted by the *T'ai P'ing Yü Lan* 849.2a. This variant has Tzŭ-lu
wishing to divine for Confucius, who responds, "My divining was done
long ago." For this reference I am indebted to Waley 131 n. 3.

33. Ku(5) 9. The only other time the phoenix is referred to in the
Analects it is mentioned by a recluse of Taoist type in *An.* 18.5. That
this passage is undoubtedly a late addition under Taoist influence has
already been noted; in fact the same incident is related, in language
which is at some points identical, in *Chuang Tzŭ* I.221. The river chart
is mentioned in one of the appendices to the *Book of Changes*; see *I
Ching* 374. The fact that a river chart is mentioned in an early section
of the *Book of History* (*Shu* 554) has no necessary significance in this
connection. Nothing is said there about it; it may have been just a map.

34. With a possible variation, according to different scholars, of a
century or more either way. Maspero's data on predictions would seem to
make it difficult for the date to be earlier than about 300 B.C., but of
course interpolated passages are always possible. See Maspero(2) and
Karlgren.

35. The frequency of these predictions is astonishing. I have counted
them for only one five-year period, 541–537 B.C. inclusive; there are
twenty-five (*Tso* 575–606), and they are probably more frequent in some
other periods. I have not been able to check the accuracy of all of these
predictions.

Some of the predictions in the *Tso Chuan* do not bear fruit. But for
some remarkable ones that do see *Tso* 103, 187 (fulfilled 209), 397,
486 (fulfilled 500), 503, 509 (fulfilled 517), 527, 532 (fulfilled 542
and 598), 843.

36. The date of origin of the *wu hsing* is not wholly clear. Waley has
written, "In common with most scholars in China and Japan I see no
reason to place the Five Element theory earlier than the 4th century"
(Waley[3] 109 n. 1). There is at least one occurence of *wu hsing* in the
Mo Tzŭ (10.8a), but this is in the *Ching* section which is generally
recognized to be relatively late.

It has been held that the *wu hsing* theory existed in Mencius' time
(see Ch'ên Mêng-chia). The evidence Ch'ên cites on p. 46 shows that
the kind of thinking with which the theory was associated was beginning
to be developed in Mencius' day, but does not necessarily prove that the
concept of *wu hsing* existed at that time. The reference he quotes from
the *Hsün Tzŭ* is not conclusive, since there is evidence that this particular part of the *Fei Shih Êr Shih* chapter is an interpolation; see *Hsün
Tzŭ*(3) 3.12b. The fact that the *wu hsing* are never mentioned in *Mencius* makes this all the more probable.

37. *Tso* 310. He later restored the state, after taking many hostages,
probably because of fear of reprisals by other states.

38. *Tso* 619. Since Confucius could give his elder brother's daughter
in marriage (*An.* 5.1.2), he was apparently the head of his family.

39. *Tso* 305, 403-404. The attribution of the first of these sayings to
Confucius is condemned by the *Ch'in Ting Ch'un Ch'iu* 20.16b–17a. Of

the second Legge notes that "the critics unanimously agree in protesting against the ascription of it to him" (*Tso* 404).

40. See Karlgren 58–64.

41. In defense of an earlier date, see Waley(3) 137 and Haloun 456–460. Paul Pelliot, like many other scholars, believed that our present *Chia Yü* is a forgery by Wang Su, who died 256 A.D.; see Pelliot 421 n. 430.

42. Compare the first sentence of *Lao Tzŭ* chap. 47 with *Chia Yü* 2.18a. Ts'ui Shu pointed out that this work also borrows extensively from *Chuang Tzŭ* and *Lieh Tzŭ*; see Ts'ui 3.18. The *Discourses* scrambles texts with broad catholicity. Four pages after the plagiarism from *Lao Tzŭ* noted above it lifts a large part of *Mencius* 1(2)15.1 and quotes it as having been spoken by Confucius (*Chia Yü* 2.22b–23a).

43. For this point I am indebted to Creel, Lorraine 136–137.

44. *An.* 7.27. As evidencing the broad interpretation of the term study by Confucius and his immediate disciples, and the fact that for them mere book learning did not receive prior emphasis, see *An.* 1.7, 1.14, 6.6, 13.5.

45. *Hsün Tzŭ*(2) 184, 264. For his rejection of Taoist metaphysics see *ibid.* 96.

46. See Liang 115.

Chapter XIII

1. On the criticism of the *Han Fei Tzŭ* I have chiefly followed Ch'ên Ch'i-t'ien and Jung Chao-tsu (see Bibliography).

2. *Shang Chün Shu* 291–292. It seems improbable that any of this book is actually by Shang Yang, and this passage is probably not from its oldest part, but it is quite Legalist. Cf. *Han Fei* 2.10a; this section of the book may not be by Han Fei Tzŭ, but it seems to be clearly Legalist.

3. See *Shang Chün Shu* 1–40. Ch'i Ssŭ-hê maintains that a considerable portion of the reforms of Shang Yang consisted in transplanting to Ch'in practices that were already known in the state of Wei (魏), where he had previously held office; see Ch'i(2).

4. *Shih Chi* 63.28. This is questioned by Ch'ien Mu (442–443). I agree with Bodde (77) that it is likely. I agree with Ch'ien, however, that the story of the means by which Ch'in got Han Fei Tzŭ sent to Ch'in is absurd.

5. So that all roads would have ruts at the same distance apart and vehicles, especially the imperial war chariots, could move everywhere without difficulty.

6. *Mem. Hist.* II.180–182. On "buried alive" see Bodde 117 n.3.

7. See *Han Fei* 3.7a, 11.19b–20a, 14.12b–13.

8. In *Han Fei* 9.9b–10a there are two versions of a story that states that under the Yin dynasty anyone who threw ashes in the street was heavily punished; one version says his hand was cut off. Confucius

praised this, saying that "to cause people to do what is easy [not throwing ashes] in order to avoid involvement in what they dislike [punishment] is the proper way to govern." This latter statement epitomizes Legalism, and in fact we find it credited one page later (with the negligible alteration of a few characters) to the Legalist Shang Yang. As for punishment for throwing ashes in the street, this was said by Li Ssŭ to have been a law that Shang Yang established in Ch'in (*Shih Chi* 87.30). The whole idea directly contradicts what Confucius says in *An.* 13.2.1.

These anecdotes are translated by W. K. Liao, but in both cases the concluding and crucial sentences are incorrectly rendered (*Han Fei*[2] 293–294).

9. On unification of weights and measures see *Shu* 36. The entire book called the *Lü Hsing* (*Shu* 588–611) is very Legalistic.

10. *Li Chi* II.323–324. The paragraph which follows this reads, "Although one may occupy the throne, if he does not have the necessary virtue he may not venture to establish [literally, make] *li* and music. Although one may have the virtue, if he does not occupy the throne he also may not venture to establish *li* and music." Here, in the first sentence, the Legalist ideas that precede are softened by a Confucian modification, while the second sentence again swings back toward Legalism.

11. The chain-like form of this passage is not characteristic of genuine sayings in the *Analects*. The term "Son of Heaven" was not part of Confucius' vocabulary as we find it in the *Analects*; he refers merely to the "king." Except for this passage, "Son of Heaven" occurs only once in the *Analects*, in 3.2, as part of a quotation from the *Book of Poetry*. The term *p'ei ch'ên* occurs nowhere in the *Analects* except in this passage. Furthermore, this expression seems to occur in no other work as early as the *Analects*, and is not found even in the *Mencius*; it would appear to be a late term.

12. For instance, Ku Chieh-kang, one of China's most brilliant and critical scholars, in a brief essay on "Confucius' Governmental Policies and their Background" published in 1941, based his discussion chiefly on *Analects* 16.2. He recognized that other parts of the *Analects* appear to disagree with it, but treated the ideas of 16.2 as fundamental. See Ku(6) 45–47.

13. Concerning *An.* 13.3 Waley has pointed out that "the whole of this highly elaborate, literary paragraph bears the stamp of comparatively late date. . . . Later Confucian literature supplies many examples of such rhetorical 'chains.'" (Waley 172 n. 1). He notes that the idea of "rectification of names" was not mentioned by Mencius, and considers it characteristic of the latter part of the fourth century B.C.; Waley thinks this passage may be "an interpolation on the part of Hsün Tzŭ or his school" (*ibid.* 21–22).

This is quite possible. Hsün Tzŭ himself wrote a brilliant treatise entitled *Chêng Ming*, "The Rectification of Names" (or better, as Duyvendak has suggested, "The Correct Use of Terminology"); this is the very term that is discussed in *An.* 13.3. But in this work, which makes up the twenty-second section of the *Hsün Tzŭ*, there is no reference to Confucius or to *An.* 13.3, which would seem to indicate that Hsün Tzŭ himself did not know it; the *Book of Poetry* is repeatedly quoted as evidence, and so good a proof text from the *Analects* would hardly have been omitted. Furthermore, this would seem to absolve Hsün Tzŭ personally of the suspicion of interpolating section 13.3; if he took so much trouble, one would expect him to have used the quotation he inserted.

However, there are resemblances to *An.* 13.3 in section 22 of *Hsün Tzŭ*. Punishment is mentioned prominently (*Hsün Tzŭ* 318), and Duyvendak has pointed out the similar use of the character *kou*; see *Hsün Tzŭ* 321 and Duyvendak 245 n. 1. But in *An.* 13.3 there is a more prominent and exclusive emphasis on punishments than in *Hsün Tzŭ*. It would seem, therefore, to have been written in the light of the *Hsün Tzŭ*, but by a more Legalistic individual.

There are two Legalist works in which the "rectification of names" is mentioned. At the very end of *The Book of Lord Shang* there is a passage which has almost the same purport as that of *An.* 13.3 (*Shang Chün Shu* 334–335). And in the *Han Fei Tzŭ* it is stated that "when names are rectified things are settled" (*Han Fei* 2.10b). In both of these works the term *chêng ming* occurs in inverted form, as *ming chêng*. There is another parallel with the *Han Fei Tzŭ*. *An.* 13.3 begins, "Tzŭ-lu ˋsaid, 'The ruler of Wei is waiting for you to administer the government.' " Neither history nor early tradition makes Confucius prime minister of Wei, but an anecdote in the *Han Fei Tzŭ* begins, "Confucius was Prime Minister of Wei" (*Han Fei* 12.3b).

It seems not at all improbable that *An.* 13.3 is, as Waley has suggested, an interpolation made under the influence of Hsün Tzŭ. But that philosopher's two most famous students were Legalists, and the passage seems to show definite Legalist influence.

14. This passage influenced the interpretation of *An.* 7.27. See Chap. IX, note 24.

Chapter XIV

1. Chavannes notes one expression from the *Book of Poetry* and one from the *Book of History; Mem. Hist.* II.142 n. 2, 145 n. 5. In addition *chao hsi pu hsieh* (*Mem. Hist.* 146) is too similar to the wording of the *Book of Poetry* for accident; there we have *chao hsi pu hsia* (*Shih* 424). The *hsieh* was substituted, possibly for reasons of rhyme, probably by analogy with the similar phrase *su yeh fei hsieh* which occurs twice in the same work (*Shih* 543, 546).

The first two characters of the sentence *chü ts'o pi tang*, which Chavannes translated as, "Il a enlevé l'erreur; il a fixé ce qu'il fallait faire" (*Mem. Hist.* II.147), evidently allude to *An.* 2.19 and 12.22.3. The sentence should therefore be translated, "In promoting and setting aside

officials, he always hit the mark," which fits into the context much better. It is not remarkable, of course, that Chavannes failed to note this
allusion; in a work of the magnitude of the *Historical Records* it is utterly
impossible to catch them all.

2. *Mem. Hist.* II.182. It is quite possible, of course, that this whole
conversation is apocryphal. Nevertheless, in the light of the events which
followed, it is clear that there was at least a tradition linking the name
of Fu Su with Confucianism.

3. *Han Shu(2)* I.104. Wilbur (137) believes that this manumission
could not have been, and perhaps was never even meant to be, enforced.
This does not destroy its effectiveness as propaganda, however, and it is
with this that we are here concerned.

4. *Han Shu(2)* I.118. I have slightly altered this translation, in one
respect, from that of Dubs.

5. This showed, for instance, when he lost patience with his faithful
counselor Li I-chi and called him a "stupid Confucian"; see *Han Shu(2)*
I.84.

6. In the reign of Han Wu Ti the financial circumstances of many
Confucians were greatly improved. Nevertheless in a debate that took
place just after that reign a Legalist high official repeatedly characterized
them as men from "farms and poverty-stricken alleys," too poor even to
afford proper clothing. See *Yen T'ieh Lun(2)* 77, 103, 121.

7. Compare *Han Shu(2)* I.236–237 with *Mencius* 1(2)5.3 and
7(1)22.3; *Han Shu(2)* I.266 and *Mencius* 1(1)3.5, 1(2)2, 1(2)5.3.

8. *Han Shu(2)* I.265. People became slaves to the government for
crime, and the status was apparently hereditary. Wilbur (134) questions that all government slaves were freed at this time, on the ground
of probability.

9. A friend has warned me that I will incur the serious displeasure
of Sinologists by referring to Han Wu Ti merely as "Wu." As precedent
I should like to point out, therefore, that Wu Wang of Chou is thus
referred to in *An.* 19.22; additional instances could be cited.

10. See *An.* 2.19, 11.23, 12.22, 14.20, 14.23; *Mencius* 1(2)8, 1(2)9,
4(1)20; *Hsün Tzŭ(2)* 85, 125; *Hsün Tzŭ* 155, 181. Two further passages in this vein occur in portions of the *Hsün Tzŭ* that have been said
to be additions to the text by Han Confucians; if this is true they are all
the more interesting in the present connection. See *Hsün Tzŭ* 397,
413–414.

11. *I.e.*, a pun on the fact that *chêng*, used to mean "first" in "first
month," also means "correct"; see *Han Shu* 56.5a.

12. A paraphrase of *An.* 20.2.3. This section is almost certainly a late
addition to the *Analects*, but Confucius may well have made this statement.

13. He stated (*Han Shu* 56.9a) that punishments were used a great
deal by the Yin dynasty. But Tung Tso-pin, who has specialized on that
period for many years, knows of no such tradition (verbal communica-

tion of 13 March 1948). However, severe punishments under Yin are mentioned in two versions of an anecdote in the *Han Fei Tzŭ*; see *Han Fei* 9.9b–10a.

14. *Han Fei* 1.19. This chapter of the work has been suspected to be an addition of early Han date, but for our present purpose this does not invalidate it.

15. For additional evidence of this, see *Mem. Hist.* III.557–558.

16. *Shih Chi* 112.4. This translation of this passage (which has been differently rendered by others) is in essential agreement with the Japanese version of Makino Kenjiro; see Makino 315.

17. See *Yen T'ieh Lun*(2) 63–65, where even the scholars do not contend that Kung-Sun Hung accomplished anything.

18. See *Yen T'ieh Lun*(2) 38, 40–43, 66–67, 70–73, 112, 122–123; *Yen T'ieh Lun* 5.2a, 5b–6a.

This work is well known not to be an exact transcript of the debate, but a literary work by Huan K'uan based on it (*Han Shu* 66.16b); it must therefore be used with some caution. Nevertheless it was written within a few decades of the event and seems on the whole to ring true when compared with other materials of the period; no serious question of its general authenticity seems ever to have been raised (see *Yen T'ieh Lun*[2] xxxix–xli). When we bear in mind the Legalistic phraseology in the examination paper of the "Confucian" Kung-Sun Hung, it seems quite reasonable to suppose that an official like Sang Hung-yang might well have been, as he is represented in this work, an openly avowed Legalist.

19. See *Wei Shu* 442–445; Fung 361–369; Kuo(3) 119–121.

20. This is certainly true of the *Ju Hsing*, *Li Chi* II.402–410, which pretends to be a dialogue between Confucius and Duke Ai of Lu. The occurrence of the term *ju* in only one passage of the *Analects*, 6.11, makes it evident that in Confucius' day it had not the sense in which it is constantly used here. The statements put in Confucius' mouth to the effect that the faults of a *ju* may not be enumerated to his face, and that he sometimes refuses to take office preferring to live in retirement (*Li Chi* II.405, 408), reflect the Confucianism of a later day.

21. Compare *Li Chi* I.138–139 with *An.* 7.34 and 9.11.

22. Compare *Li Chi* I.136–137 with *An.* 11.7; see Ts'ui 3.28.

23. Compare *An.* 7.20 with *Mem. Hist.* V.310–315, 330, 349–351, 352–353.

24. *Mem. Hist.* V.345; this story occurs with some variation in *Chia Yü* 5.23b–24a. The version in the *Historical Records* has two flaws. First, it violates the principle of good faith which Confucius seems to have practiced as well as preached. Second, it places an emphasis on supernatural sanction that is not in accord with what we know of Confucius.

25. See Duyvendak(3) 333. On the problem of interpolation in the *Historical Records* as a whole, see Jäger.

26. Dubs, whose labors in translating the *Ch'ien Han Shu* make him exceedingly well versed in the period, has stated flatly that Ssŭ-Ma Ch'ien was a Taoist (*Han Shu*[2] II.346). Chavannes, while opposing this position, cites early opinions upholding this view that weigh heavily in its favor. Against it he opposes only the fact that Ssŭ-Ma Ch'ien paid overt honor to Confucius (*Mem. Hist.* I.xlix–l). It may be pertinent to note, however, that Chavannes states two pages later that Ssŭ-Ma Ch'ien wrote "un livre satirique."

27. Even if, as Chavannes maintained, the final passage of the chapter is by Ssŭ-Ma Ch'ien (*Mem. Hist.* I.l, and n. 1) this does not prove that the bulk of the chapter itself may not have been written by his father.

28. See *Mem. Hist.* V.299–301 and 299 n. 4; *Chuang Tzŭ* I.338–340, 357–358, II.46–49, 63–66. For criticism of this purported meeting, see Ts'ui 1.19–22; Ch'ien Mu 4–8; Dubs(3) 216.

29. See *Yen T'ieh Lun, passim*; *Han Shu* 66.16b. Note also how Pan Ku damns with faint praise in his summary of Wu's achievements, *Han Shu*(2) II.120.

Chapter XV

1. So called because, instead of accepting the commentaries of the Sung scholars as its standard, it went back to those of the Han dynasty.

2. For such reports by Jesuit writers of this period see, for instance, Trigault 136–175, and Du Halde III.14–63. See also Dunne 89–91. Burton reported in his *Anatomy of Melancholy* that "Matthew Riccius the Jesuit informeth us" that "of all Nations they [the Chinese] are the most superstitious" (Burton 310).

3. See Voltaire XVI.330–333 and Montesquieu I.142–144. E. Carcassone made an excellent analysis of Montesquieu's treatment of China, showing that he was largely concerned with maintaining certain preconceived principles to which China did not conform, and discussing the whole problem of the doubt of the Jesuits' reports; see Carcassone.

4. Under another title; see Bibliography under Fénelon.

5. See Lach 4–5, 140, Reichwein 20, and the bibliographies in Pinot 458–466.

6. See especially Chu, Reichwein, Pinot, Maverick, Hudson, Lovejoy, and Rowbotham(2).

7. Compare *An.* 13.16; Le Comte 125; and Diderot in *Encyclopédie* IX.357.

8. See *Shih*(2) 255; *Shu* 454–458, 495–502; *An.* 13.13, 14.20, 17.5; *Mencius* 1(2)8.

9. See for instance the astonishment with which the prosperity of the region of Canton was noted by Poivre (138–140). Such observations were common.

10. Pierre Bayle (1647–1706) was an extremely important figure

among the thinkers who paved the way for the French Revolution, who greatly influenced both Voltaire and the editor of the great *Encyclopédie,* Diderot. He was educated in a Jesuit college. His important *Dictionnaire Historique et Critique* includes a number of references to China. Lanson wrote, "If Bayle was able to hold, not without scandal but without absurdity, that a society of atheists could maintain itself, and be as well regulated as any Christian society, it was because this paradox was authorized by one fact: the missionaries had observed or believed they had observed, in China, a society, the best governed and the most virtuous of all, where the governing group, the literati, were atheists" (Lanson 18).

11. See, for instance, Le Comte 241-311; Du Halde II.115-123; and Voltaire XVI.330-333, XXI.211-214. See also Reichwein 102-103.

12. For convenience of comparison these points will be numbered. For the views of Confucius see the following passages in the *Analects:* (1) 7.20, (2) 11.16, (3) 6.1.1, 7.7, (4) 6.17, 9.13, 13.19, (5) 17.21. For those of Jefferson see Koch, as follows: (1) 114, (2) 174, (3) 133, (4) 116–119, (5) 145.

13. This summary has been made in part from the original bill, and in part from a description of it contained in Jefferson's *Notes on Virginia;* see Jefferson II.220-229 and III.251-255.

14. Voltaire XXI.212. Voltaire adds that these officials were "elected by suffrage," which of course is erroneous but might have heightened Jefferson's interest. For the date at which Jefferson read and made notes on this work *(Essai sur les Moeurs)* see Jefferson(2) 14.

15. Têng Ssŭ-yü includes eleven works in English and three in French, published prior to 1775, in his "Bibliography of Western Books or Articles Describing the Chinese Examination System"; see Têng 308-312. This list did not pretend to be exhaustive.

16. After the old Library of Congress was burned, Jefferson sold his personal library to Congress in 1815. It is catalogued in *Catalogue of the Library of the United States,* printed by Jonathan Eliot (Washington, 1815). This list includes two works (but without specifying editions, *ibid.* 10, 120) that give fairly full accounts of the examination system; these are Du Halde (III.1–14), and Le Comte (280–283). Jefferson had the French edition of the latter work. Of the former, only the first volume was in his library when it was sold, so that it is uncertain whether he had once had the third volume.

Chapter XVI

1. Sun Yat-sen I. *Min Ch'üan Chu I* 10; (2) 169; (3) 232–234. Translations from the *Three Principles of the People* are based on consultation of these three works; I have not been able to follow any single translation. Much of the published translations from Sun's works is unsatisfactory, and sometimes misleading. One reason for this is that much

of this material, originally delivered as lectures, can hardly be translated both literally and intelligibly.

For other passages in which Sun refers to Confucius as holding democratic ideas see: Sun Yat-sen I. *Min Shêng Chu I* 44, (2) 444, (3) 476; Sun Yat-sen II. *Min Ch'üan Ch'u Pu* 104.

REFERENCES

The works corresponding to bibliographical abbreviations are listed in the Bibliography.

Page 1 line 7: *An.* 9.6.3. P. 5 l. 32: Jefferson IX. 428. P. 6 l. 1: Sun Yat-sen I, *Min Ch'üan Chu I* 10; Sun Yat-sen(2) 169; Sun Yat-sen(3) 232. P. 6 l. 27: Lecky I.310. P. 7 l. 7: Han Yü 11.1b. P. 7 l. 11: Wilhelm 71. P. 7 l. 14: Ts'ui 1.4. P. 7 l. 18: Ch'ien Mu 37.38. P. 8 l. 19: Pick 96-97. P. 9 l. 29: *An.* 6.1.1. P. 17 l. 12: *Tso* 453. P. 17 l. 20: *Tso* 440-441. P. 18 l. 8: *Tso* 825. P. 20 l. 27: *Tso* 388. P. 20 l. 31: *Tso* 832. P. 20 l. 32: *Tso* 142. P. 20 l. 33: *Tso* 698. P. 20 l. 37: *Tso* 290. P. 21 l. 4: *Tso* 589. P. 21 l. 26: *Tso* 722. P. 21 l. 34: *Tso* 629. P. 22 l. 11: Mei 176-177. P. 22 l. 15: *Tso* 551, 576, 829. P. 22 l. 21: *Tso* 748. P. 23 l. 1: *Tso* 610. P. 23 l. 7: *Tso* 328. P. 23 l. 27: Ch'i 178-179. P. 25 l. 6: *An.* 3.15. P. 25 l. 14: *An.* 5.1, 11.5, 11.7, 16.13. P. 25 l. 15: *An.* 11.7. P. 25 l. 17: Ts'ui 4.22-23. P. 25 l. 20: *An.* 9.6. P. 25 l. 21: *An.* 11.7. P. 26 l. 9: *Kuo Yü* 15.8a. P. 26 l. 23: *Mencius* 5(2)5.4. P. 26 l. 25: *An.* 9.6. P. 26 l. 34: *An.* 7.7. P. 26 l. 36: *An.* 9.22. P. 27 l. 25: *An.* 5.4, 6.14, 11.24.4, 15.10.6. P. 29 l. 10: *An.* 11.24, 12.17, 12.18, 12.19, 14.13.2, 19.1. P. 29 l. 13: *An.* 9.5. P. 29 l. 17: Fung 48-49. P. 30 l. 5: Ch'ien Mu 56-62. P. 30 l. 7: *Tso* 825. P. 30 l. 14: *Tso* 840. P. 30 l. 18: *An.* 12.3, 12.4, 12.5. P. 30 l. 19: *An.* 6.9, 11.7, 11.10, 11.18; *Mencius* 4(2)29.2. P. 30 l. 29: *An.* 6.4, 7.7. P. 31 l. 9: *Mo Tzŭ*(2) 238-239. P. 31 l. 13: *An.* 4.9, 8.13, 14.1, 15.31. P. 31 l. 15: *An.* 2.18. P. 31 l. 17: *An.* 8.12. P. 32 l. 8: Gibbon 564. P. 32 l. 37: *Tso* 861. P. 33 l. 4: *Tso* 825. P. 33 l. 6: *An.* 11.24. P. 33 l. 7: *Tso* 851. P. 34 l. 9: *Tso* 802. P. 34 l. 28: *An.* 10.11.2. P. 34 l. 33: *An.* 12.18. P. 34 l. 35: *An.* 12.17. P. 35 l. 2: *An.* 6.6. P. 35 l. 6: *Tso* 781. P. 35 l. 24: *Tso* 760. P. 35 l. 31: *Tso* 773, 816-817. P. 36 l. 2: *An.* 17.5. P. 36 l. 34: *An.* 7.7.

P. 37 l. 8: *Tso* 776-777. P. 37 l. 29: *Tso* 745. P. 37 l. 33: *Mencius* 6(2)
6.6. P. 38 l. 9: *An.* 9.11. P. 38 l. 23: *An.* 2.21. P. 38 l. 32: *An.* 9.12.
P. 39 l. 6: *An.* 12.18. P. 39 l. 23: *An.* 13.14. P. 39 l. 27: *An.* 11.7, 14.22.
See also *Tso* 840. P. 40 l. 25: *An.* 3.19, 13.15. P. 40 l. 28: *Mencius*
5(2)4.7. P. 41 l. 5: *Mencius* 5(2)4.7. P. 41 l. 16: *Tso* 640, 655, 770,
778. P. 41 l. 21: *Tso* 781. P. 41 l. 30: *An.* 14.38. P. 42 l. 10: *Mencius*
6(2)6.6. P. 42 l. 22: *Chuang Tzŭ* II.172. P. 42 l. 26: *An.* 7.13, 12.11;
Mencius 5(2)1.4, 7(2)17; *Mo Tzŭ*(2) 206-209. P. 42 l. 29: *Mem. Hist.*
V. 304-310. P. 42 l. 36: *Shih Chi* 14.148; *Mem. Hist.* IV.205, V.331.
P. 42 l. 37: *An.* 15.1; *Mencius* 5(2)4.7. P. 43 l. 5: *Mencius* 3(2)4.1.
P. 43 l. 16: *Mencius* 5(1)8.2; *Tso* 762, 857. P. 43 l. 17: *Mencius*
5(2)5.7. P. 43 l. 21: *Mencius* 5(2)4.3 and 7. P. 43 l. 32: *Tso* 785, 788-
789. P. 44 l. 2: *Tso* 802. P. 44 l. 3: *An.* 15.1; *Mencius* 5(1)8.3. P. 44
l. 5: *An.* 7.22; *Mencius* 5(1)8.3. P. 44 l. 19: *Tso* 778, 779, 826, 831,
839-40. P. 44 l. 28: *Tso* 840. P. 44 l. 29: *An.* 12.5. P. 44 l. 30: *Tso* 840.
P. 44 l. 36: *An.* 12.5. P. 45 l. 6: *An.* 12.4. P. 45 l. 18: *An.* 7.22;
Mencius 5(1)8.3. P. 45 l. 21: *An.* 9.5, 11.22; see also Ts'ui 3.3-6. P. 45
l. 27: *An.* 15.1.2; *Mencius* 5(1).8.3. P. 45 l. 30: *Tso* 802. P. 45 l. 37:
Tso 794. P. 45 l. 38: *Tso* 795. P. 46 l. 4 *Tso* 809-810. P. 46 l. 9: *An.*
7.30. P. 46 l. 10: *Mencius* 7(2)18. P. 46 l. 13: *An.* 5.21; *Mencius*
7(2)37.1. P. 46 l. 32: see pages 203-204. P. 47 l. 2: *Tso* 675, 700, 703,
721, 723, 734, 737, 805, 846-847. P. 47 l. 12: *An.* 13.16. P. 47 l. 18:
An. 13.18. P. 47 l. 26: *An.* 7.18. P. 47 l. 37: *Tso* 784-785. P. 48 l. 10:
An. 17.7. P. 49 l. 5: *Tso* 788-789. P. 49 l. 9: *Tso* 798-799. P. 49 l. 14:
Ts'ui 3.29-30 and *Tso* 843. P. 49 l. 17: *Mem. Hist.* V.377, n.2. P. 49
l. 38: *An.* 7.28. P. 50 l. 10: *An.* 5.14. P. 50 l. 12: *Tso* 843. P. 50 l. 23:
Tso 826. P. 50 l. 31: *Tso* 791, 813, 825. P. 51 l. 2: *Tso* 824-825. P. 51
l. 12: *Tso* 826. P. 52 l. 30: *An.* 11.23.3. P. 52 l. 34: *An.* 11.16; *Mencius*
4(1)14.1. P. 53 l. 6: *An.* 9.14. P. 53 l. 14: *Tso* 828-829. P. 53 l. 36:
Tso 103, 542, 589, 623, 629, 718, 809-811, 821, 838-840. P. 54 l. 16:
An. 11.7. P. 54 l. 17: *An.* 11.8. P. 54 l. 19: *Tso* 840. P. 54 l. 21: *Tso* 843.
P. 54 l. 31: *An.* 14.37. P. 54 l. 38: *An.* 19.24. P. 54 l. 39: *Mencius*
7(2)19.3. P. 55 l. 16: *An.* 9.11. P. 55 l. 20: *An.* 7.34. P. 55 l. 23:
Mencius 3(1)4.13. P. 56 l. 3: *An.* 19.24. P. 56 l. 4: *Mencius* 2(1)2.28.
P. 57 l. 21: *An.* 7.4. P. 58 l. 2: *An.* 7.37. P. 58 l. 4: *An.* 1.8.1, 11.7. P. 58
l. 7: *An.* 7.28, 9.7. P. 58 l. 14: *An.* 5.24. P. 58 l. 16: *An.* 14.6. P. 58
l. 20: *An.* 11.7, 16.13, 17.10. P. 58 l. 30: *Mencius* 2(1)2.18. P. 58
l. 34: *An.* 6.14, 12.20, 14.25, 17.18. P. 58 l. 36: *An.* 1.14, 4.9, 7.15,
8.13, 14.3, 15.31. P. 59 l. 2: *An.* 7.11. P. 59 l. 12: *An.* 1.1.1, 7.13, 8.15.
P. 59 l. 14: *An.* 7.31, 17.20. P. 59 l. 23: *Mo Tzŭ*(2) 117-122, 175-181, 224.
P. 59 l. 29: *Han Fei* 17.20b; *Shang Chün Shu*(2) 197, 208. P. 59 l. 31:
An. 13.16. P. 59 l. 33: *An.* 7.6.; see also 17.4. P. 60 l. 4: *Li Chi* II.167.
P. 60 l. 13: *An.* 9.5. P. 60 l. 15: *An.* 7.30. P. 60 l. 17: *An.* 3.11, 9.7.
P. 60 l. 19: *An.* 1.10, 3.15; see also 5.14. P. 60 l. 21: *An.* 6.1, 17.4,
17.21. P. 60 l. 23: *An.* 5.27, 7.2, 7.32, 7.33, 9.6, 14.30. P. 60 l. 27: *An.*
14.37; see also 15.19. P. 60 l. 35: *An.* 15.41. P. 61 l. 1: *An.* 10.12. P. 61
l. 2: *An.* 7.26. P. 61 l. 9: *An.* 9.22. P. 61 l. 26: *An.* 9.2. P. 61 l. 30: *Lun*

Yü Shih 493-494. P. 61 l. 34: *Ibid.* 1032, on *An.* 17.4.4; Ts'ui(2) 2.19. P. 62 l. 5: *An.* 17.20. P. 62 l. 12: *An.* 11.9; see also 11.8. P. 62 l. 15: *An.* 14.46. P. 63 l. 6: *Mencius* 2(1)3.2; see also Ch'ien Mu 56-62. P. 63 l. 12: *Shih Chi* 67.41-42; *An.* 14.38. P. 64 l. 1: Ch'ien Mu 75-76. P. 64 l. 8: Ts'ui(2) 3.32. P. 64 l. 16: *An.* 12.12.2. P. 64 l. 18: *Mencius* 2(1)8.1. P. 64 l. 23: *An.* 5.7, 11.12. P. 64 l. 36: *An.* 7.10. P. 65 l. 3: *An.* 5.6. P. 65 l. 8: *An.* 11.14. P. 65 l. 17: *An.* 14.8. P. 65 l. 35: *Tso* 838. P. 66 l. 4: *Tso* 843. P. 66 l. 8: *An.* 11.21. P. 66 l. 12: *An.* 6.10. P. 66 l. 15: *An.* 5.7.3, 6.6. P. 66 l. 26: *An.* 11.16, 11.23. P. 66 l. 32: *Tso* 854. P. 67 l. 6: *An.* 11.2, 11.18, 19.23, 19.25; *Mencius* 2(1)2.18; *Tso* 859-861. P. 67 l. 20: *Mencius* 3(1)4.13. P. 67 l. 17: *An.* 19.23, 19.25. P. 67 l. 18: *Mencius* 2(1)2.27. P. 67 l. 20: *An.* 1.15, 6.6. P. 67 l. 27: *An.* 5.3, 5.11, 14.31. P. 67 l. 33: *An.* 5.8, 11.18. P. 67 l. 38: *An.* 4.7. P. 68 l. 14: *An.* 5.25; for "fur clothing" see Liu Paonan 6.26b. P. 68 l. 24: *An.* 2.9. P. 68 l. 26: *An.* 5.8, 11.2.2; *Mencius* 2(1)2.18. P. 68 l. 28: *An.* 6.2, 6.5, 9.19, 9.20, 11.6. P. 68 l. 34: *An.* 7.10. P. 69 l. 1: *An.* 6.9, 11.7, 11.10; *Mencius* 4(2)29.2. P. 69 l. 11: *An.* 11.10. P. 69 l. 12: *An.* 11.8, 11.9. P. 69 l. 22: *An.* 6.24, 17.21. P. 69 l. 23: *An.* 11.2.2; *Mencius* 2(1)2.18. P. 69 l. 30: *An.* 3.21. P. 70 l. 11: Ts'ui(2) 1.40-41. P. 70 l. 18: *Mencius* 3(1)4.13. P. 70 l. 23: *An.* 11.2.2. P. 70 l. 35: *An.* 11.15. P. 70 l. 36: *An.* 2.18, 12.20. P. 70 l. 39: *An.* 19.1-2. P. 71 l. 3: *An.* 19.15-16. P. 71 l. 8: *Han Fei* 19.12a; *Shih Chi* 121'.3. P. 71 l. 10: *An.* 19.3, 19.12. P. 71 l. 12: *Mo Tzŭ(2)* 215. P. 71 l. 14: *Shih Chi* 121.4. P. 71 l. 15: *Ibid.* 67.29. P. 71 l. 19: *An.* 3.8, 11.2.2. P. 71 l. 21: *An.* 11.15. P. 71 l. 29: *An.* 19.3. P. 71 l. 34: *Han Fei* 19.12b. P. 72 l. 3: *An.* 19.12. P. 72 l. 5: *An.* 13.17. P. 72 l. 11: *An.* 19.11. P. 72 l. 17: *An.* 6.11. P. 72 l. 23: *Han Fei* 13.4b. P. 72 l. 37: *Mencius* 4(2)31. P. 73 l. 8: *Mencius* 2(1)2.6-8, 4(2)31. P. 73 l. 22: *An.* 8.4. P. 73 l. 24: *An.* 8.3; see also 8.7. P. 73 l. 28: *An.* 1.9, 19.17, 19.18; *Mencius* 4(1)19. P. 75 l. 13: *Mencius* 3(1)3.10 P. 76 l. 21: *An.* 2.12. P. 76 l. 23: *An.* 14.13. P. 76 l. 33: *An.* 13.13. P. 77 l. 10: *Li Chi* II.280. P. 77 l. 33: *Shih* 260-261, *Shih(2)* 123. P. 78 l. 17: *An.* 7.7. P. 78 l. 25: *Mencius* 7(2)30. P. 78 l. 30: *An.* 7.8. P. 78 l. 34: *An.* 4.9. P. 78 l. 36: *An.* 8.12. P. 79 l. 18: *An.* 2.10, 4.7, 5.9. P. 79 l. 25: *An.* 11.25; see also 5.25. P. 79 l. 37: *An.* 11.21. P. 80 l. 11: *An.* 1.15, 2.3. P. 80 l. 15: *Mo Tzŭ(2)* 252. P. 80 l. 18: *An.* 9.22. P. 80 l. 21: *An.* 7.23. P. 80 l. 25: *An.* 4.5, 5.7. P. 80 l. 33: *Mo Tzŭ(2)* 229. P. 80 l. 39: *Hsün Tzŭ(2)* 52. P. 81 l. 9: *An.* 6.1, 17.4. P. 81 l. 13: *An.* 17.21. P. 81 l. 16: *An.* 7.8, 8.17, 9.10, 14.8. P. 81 l. 19: *An.* 9.18. P. 81 l. 25: *An.* 11.14. P. 81 l. 29: *An.* 14.31. P. 81 l. 38: *Mencius* 2(1)2.26. P. 82 l. 12: *An.* 9.2. P. 82 l. 38: For examples, see Wu 15.18 and Lo(2) 42. P. 82 l. 39: Bryce 23. P. 83 l. 3: Lo(2) 6.11b-12a. P. 83 l. 6: *I Li* I.229. P. 83 l. 14: Kuo(2) 109b-110a; *Shih* 440, *Shih(2)* 249; *Tso* 33, 81-82, 381-382. P. 83 l. 16: *I Li* I.200-201, 244. P. 83 l. 19: *I Li* I.18. P. 84 l. 5: *Tso* 305. P. 84 l. 16: *An.* 12.2. P. 84 l. 20: *An.* 3.3. P. 84 l. 22: *An.* 3.26. P. 84 l. 24: *An.* 3.4. P. 84 l. 26: *An.* 17.11. P. 84 l. 30: *Li Chi* I.400-401. P. 84 l. 31: *An.* 3.4. P. 84 l. 39: *Li Chi* I.390. P. 85 l. 15: *An.* 9.3. P. 85 l. 22: See *An.*

14.23 and *Mencius* 2(2)2.4. P. 85 l. 39: *Li Chi* I.177. P. 86 l. 18: *An.* 8.2.1. P. 86 l. 25: *An.* 5:16. P. 86 l. 37: Byrnes 138. P. 87 l. 12: *An.* 15.17; see also 3.8.3. P. 87 l. 17: *An.* 6.16. P. 87 l. 19: *An.* 8.8, 14.13, 16.13. P. 87 l. 22: *An.* 19.12. P. 87 l. 32: *An.* 6.25; see also 9.10. P. 88 l. 5: Lin 107. P. 88 l. 18: Lang 13. P. 88 l. 21: Aristotle 1340. P. 88 l. 23: Plato(3) 401; see also Plato(4) 672. P. 88 l. 24: *An.* 3.23, 3.25, 7.13, 8.15, 17.11. P. 88 l. 27: *An.* 9.14. P. 88 l. 28: *An.* 7.31, 17.20. P. 88 l. 34: Plato(3) 398-400, 424; Plato(4) 700-701, 802; *An.* 15.10. P. 88 l. 36: *Mencius* 2(1)2.27. P. 88 l. 39: *An.* 11.14.1, 11.25.7. P. 89 l. 5: *An.* 14.13.1. P. 89 l. 8: *An.* 8.8. P. 89 l. 19: Altshuler 79-80. P. 89 l. 22: *Ibid.* 77. P. 89 l. 30: See La Master. P. 90 l. 3: *An.* 15.5. P. 90 l. 6: *An.* 5.14, 14.19, 15.13. P. 90 l. 8: *An.* 5.24. P. 90 l. 10: *An.* 17.12. P. 90 l. 16: *An.* 13.20.3. P. 90 l. 17: *An.* 1.8.4, 9.24, 19.21. P. 90 l. 22: *An.* 6.20, 12.21.3, 15.37. P. 90 l. 24: *An.* 2.24. P. 90 l. 25: *An.* 14.13, 15.8. P. 90 l. 36: Hearnshaw 437. P. 91 l. 12: *An.* 14.3; this is based on the translation of Arthur Waley. P. 91 l. 16: *An.* 8.7. P. 91 l. 36: *An.* 9.18. P. 91 l. 38: *An.* 9.25. P. 92 l. 1: *An.* 15.20. P. 92 l. 4: *An.* 4.14. P. 92 l. 6: *An.* 12.21.3. P. 92 l. 7: *An.* 15.14. P. 92 l. 10: *An.* 7.21. P. 92 l. 12: *An.* 4.17. P. 92 l. 18: *An.* 6.13. Cf. *Tso* 825. P. 92 l. 19: *An.* 14.29. Cf. *Lun Yü* 14; *Chiao K'an Chi* 7a. P. 92 l. 20: *An.* 2.13. P. 92 l. 24: *An.* 14.9. P. 92 l. 29: *An.* 17.14. P. 92 l. 30: *An.* 4.24. P. 92 l. 34: *An.* 15.10. P. 93 l. 14: *An.* 6.14. P. 93 l. 17: *An.* 17.18. P. 93 l. 21: *An.* 13.17. P. 93 l. 22: *An.* 14.38. P. 93 l. 30: *An.* 1.8. P. 93 l. 31: *An.* 3.7, 15.21. P. 93 l. 33: *An.* 2.18, 13.17. P. 93 l. 36: *An.* 1.14. P. 93 l. 37: *An.* 4.16. P. 93 l. 39: *An.* 12.20, 15.18. P. 94 l. 5: *An.* 13.24. P. 94 l. 8: *An.* 15.19. P. 94 l. 22: *An.* 8.11, 13.26. P. 94 l. 25: *An.* 13.25. P. 94 l. 27: *An.* 2.14, 13.23. P. 94 l. 28: *An.* 4.5.3, 7.36, 8.6. P. 94 l. 32: *An.* 12.4, 14.30. P. 95 l. 1: *An.* 5.2; see also 4.1, 4.25, 9.13. P. 95 l. 5: *An.* 1.14, 15.9. P. 95 l. 7: *An.* 1.6. P. 95 l. 9: *An.* 1.8, 9.24, 12.23. P. 95 l. 18: *An.* 17.5, 17.7. P. 95 l. 30: Williamson I.61. P. 95 l. 35: *An.* 1.6, 1.7. P. 96 l. 1: *An.* 13.5. P. 96 l. 4: *An.* 7.24. P. 96 l. 14: *An.* 2.2, 13.5. P. 96 l. 16: Cf. *An.* 3.8.1 and *Shih* 95. P. 96 l. 21: *An.* 17.10. P. 96 l. 28: *An.* 17.9; 8.8. P. 97 l. 7: *An.* 16.13.2; see Tai 16.4a. P. 97 l. 12: *An.* 13.5. P. 97 l. 20: Ch'ien Hsüan-t'ung; Ku(4); *Shih*(2) 335-337. P. 97 l. 28: *Shih*(2) 37. P. 97 l. 31: *Shih* 150-151. P. 97 l. 36: *An.* 1.15, 3.8. P. 97 l. 39: Ku(4) 347. P. 98 l. 19: *Wei Shu* I.269-280. P. 98 l. 25: *Tso* 455, 802. P. 100 l. 8: *An.* 1.10, 3.15. P. 100 l. 15: *An.* 15.25. P. 100 l. 18: *An.* 17.8.3. P. 100 l. 20: *An.* 2.4. P. 101 l. 1: *An.* 5.27. P. 101 l. 8: *Kuo Yü* 5.8b-9a, 13b-15a. P. 101 l. 15: *An.* 1.7, 17.4, 19.22. P. 101 l. 21: *Mo Tzŭ*(2) 233. P. 101 l. 36: K'ang 11.1a. P. 102 l. 7: *Ibid.* 10.2b-3a. P. 102 l. 31: *An.* 7.1. P. 103 l. 3: Ts'ui 3.34-36. P. 103 l. 5: *An.* 2.2, 13.5. P. 103 l. 7: *An.* 9.30. P. 103 l. 8: *An.* 15.10.6, 17.18. P. 103 l. 12: *An.* 9.14. P. 103 l. 18: *Mem. Hist.* V.316, 390, n.4, 390-391; Ts'ui 3.36-38. P. 103 l. 24: *Mencius* 7(2)3.1. P. 103 l. 31: *Tso* 539. P. 103 l. 32: *Tso* 707. P. 103 l. 33: *Tso* 170. P. 103 l. 39: *Mencius* 3(2)9.11; see also 3(2)9.8 and 4(2)21.3. P. 104 l. 13: Kennedy. P. 104 l. 15: *Tso*,

Prolegomena 5-6. P. 104 l. 26: *Mencius* 3(2)9.8. P. 104 l. 31: *Mencius* 5(1)6.3. P. 105 l. 2: An. 2.23, 3.9. P. 105 l. 4: *Mem. Hist.* V.316. P. 106 l. 10: Fung(2) 202; Maspero 459. P. 106 l. 21: An. 3.2, 7.10.3, 9.26. P. 106 l. 23: An. 1.15, 2.2, 3.8, 12.10.3. P. 106 l. 25: An. 2.2. P. 106 l. 31: An. 2.21.2 and 14.43.1. P. 107 l. 35: An. 13.4. P. 108 l. 2: An. 13.5. P. 109 l. 15: Wilson 100-101. P. 110 l. 2: Windelband 24. P. 110 l. 33: Wilson 100-113. P. 111 l. 33: An. 19.22.2. P. 111 l. 34: *Mencius* 7(2)38. P. 111 l. 39: Mei 185. P. 112 l. 21: Karlgren(2) 4. P. 112 l. 34: Compare An. 12.2 with *Tso* 226, and An. 13.29-30 with *Tso* 201-202. P. 112 l. 36: Mei 181-185. P. 113 l. 37: Lo 1.25.1, 6.58.4; Liu Ê 190.2. P. 114 l. 16: Creel(3). P. 114 l. 36: *Mo Tzŭ* 12.15a. P. 115 l. 10: An. 3.9, 3.15, 3.17, 11.25.7. P. 115 l. 20: An. 7.20. P. 115 l. 21: An. 8.21. P. 115 l. 25: An. 11.11. P. 115 l. 29: An. 6.20. P. 115 l. 37: Kant IX.308. P. 116 l. 7: An. 2.24, 3.10, 3.11, 3.12. P. 116 l. 12: An. 7.34. P. 116 l. 26: An. 6.26, 7.22, 9.5, 11.8, 14.37. P. 116 l. 36: *Shu* 369, 374, 385, 457-459, 495-502; *Shih* 432-436, 598-599; Kuo(2) 33b-34a. P. 116 l. 38: *Shu* 500; Kuo(2) 139a; *Shih* 501. P. 117 l. 1: *Shu* 548. P. 117 l. 8: An. 5.12. P. 117 l. 29: An. 15.31. P. 117 l. 37: *Shih* 528-529. P. 117 l. 39: *Shu* 433; *Shih* 375, 397, 445, 479-481, 579, 590, etc. P. 118 l. 8: Kuo(2) 202b-203b. P. 118 l. 12: *Mo Tzŭ*(2) 129, 252-253. P. 118 l. 16: *Shu* 409, 431; Kuo(2) 140b-141a. P. 118 l. 22: Creel 214-218. P. 118 l. 24: *Shih* 198-200; *Shih*(2) 268; *Tso* 177, 225, 244, 352, 374, 606, 635, 649. P. 118 l. 29: *Mo Tzŭ*(2) 125. P. 118 l. 32: *Mem. Hist.* II.195. P. 118 l. 35: Wilbur 154, 393. P. 119 l. 3: *Li Chi* I.181-182. P. 119 l. 28: *Shih*(2) 265. P. 119 l. 30: Kuo(2) 133a. P. 119 l. 37: An. 6.1. P. 120 l. 9: Wilson 106, Jacobsen 213, Irwin 338-341. P. 120 l. 31: An. 3.11; cf. *Li Chi* II.272, 311. P. 121 l. 2: *Mo Tzŭ*(2) 202, 234. P. 121 l. 5: An. 6.2, 11.6. P. 121 l. 8: An. 14.13. P. 121 l. 19: An. 14.38. P. 121 l. 34: An. 6.10, 9.18. P. 122 l. 12: An. 15.31. P. 122 l. 33: Jung Kêng (2.23) lists *luo* as occurring in four inscriptions: Kuo(2) 59b, 129a, 186a, 198b. See also Kuo(2) 140b. P. 123 l. 7: An. 9.26, 15.39. P. 123 l. 12: An. 11.23.3. P. 123 l. 24: An. 4.15, 15.2.3. P. 125 l. 5: Creel, Lorraine 22-25. P. 125 l. 13: An. 6.15. P. 125 l. 16: An. 4.8. P. 125 l. 38: Creel(4) 127-131. P. 126 l. 24: *Shu* 392-395. P. 126 l. 33: An. 4.18. P. 127 l. 1: An. 13.18. P. 127 l. 12: An. 1.6, 2.21 (cf. 1.2), 1.6, 12.11, 17.9. P. 127 l. 15: *Shih* 273, 489. P. 128 l. 11: An. 12.5.4. P. 128 l. 14: An. 9.13, 13.19, 15.5; Waley 108 n.1. P. 128 l. 19: Hummel 350. P. 128 l. 26: An. 13.16. P. 128 l. 36: An. 12.9. P. 129 l. 5: An. 4.17, 5.26, 12.4, 15.14. P. 129 l. 10: An. 13.9, 13.29, 13.30, 17.4.3; cf. 2.3. P. 129 l. 13: An. 17.4. P. 129 l. 28: An. 14.17, 14.18, 15.36. P. 129 l. 31: An. 11.23.3. P. 130 l. 11: An. 4.5, 4.12, 4.16, 6.20, 7.11, 14.13.2. P. 130 l. 14: An. 14.13, 19.1. P. 130 l. 20: An. 7.15. P. 130 l. 27: An. 4.14. P. 130 l. 29: An. 14.41. P. 130 l. 33: *Mencius* 2(1)2.7. P. 130 l. 38: An. 12.4.3. P. 131 l. 2: An. 7.29. P. 131 l. 6: An. 9.25. P. 131 l. 9: An. 15.6.2. P. 131 l. 16: An. 9.24; see also 1.8. P. 131 l. 27: Kant IX.339. P. 131 l. 29: An. 1.6. P. 131

l. 33: *An.* 4.15. P. 131 l. 39: *An.* 15.23. P. 132 l. 7: *An.* 6.28. P. 132
l. 10: Kant VIII.47. P. 132 l. 21: Kant IX.230. P. 132 l. 31: *An.*
9.13. P. 132 l. 34: *An.* 12.19. P. 133 l. 2: *An.* 13.11. P. 133 l. 5:
An. 6.17. P. 133 l. 11: *An.* 17.3. P. 133 l. 13: *An.* 5.9. P. 133 l. 16: *An.*
17.2. P. 133 l. 29: *Mencius* 4(1)2.2. P. 134 l. 8: *An.* 17.21. P. 134
l. 13: *An.* 9.4. P. 134 l. 13: *An.* 14.34. P. 134 l. 17: *Mencius* 5(2)1.5.
P. 134 l. 20: *An.* 4.10. P. 134 l. 26: *An.* 1.13. P. 134 l. 31: *An.* 14.13.
P. 135 l. 8: *An.* 15.30. P. 135 l. 11: *An.* 2.15. P. 135 l. 37: *An.*
15.25. P. 136 l. 10: *An.* 15.2. P. 136 l. 29: Kant IX.231. P. 137 l. 9:
An. 13.24, 15.27. P. 137 l. 37: Jacobsen 203; cf. 177. P. 138 l. 8:
An. 1.8, 7.3, 7.21, 9.23, 9.24, 15.29, 19.21. P. 138 l. 37: *An.* 2.17. P.
139 l. 6: *Mencius* 4(2)10. P. 139 l. 9: *An.* 13.21; cf. *Mencius* 7(2)37.2-7.
P. 139 l. 11: *An.* 11.15. P. 139 l. 13: *An.* 6.27. P. 140 l. 9: Weber
121. P. 140 l. 24: Escarra 74. P. 140 l. 36: *An.* 6.16. P. 141 l. 4: *An.*
6.24. P. 141 l. 9: *An.* 8.17. P. 141 l. 20: *An.* 15.15. P. 142 l. 15:
Plato(4) 740. P. 143 l. 30: *An.* 7.1, 7.19. P. 144 l. 1: Plato(3) 464,
(4) 739, (4) 797-798. P. 144 l. 5: Tung I.2-4. P. 144 l. 10: *Shu* 386,
390, 391; *Shih* 509. P. 144 l. 12: *Kuo*(2) 34a, 132a, 133a, 134b-135a. P.
144 l. 19: *An.* 2.23, 3.14, 9.3; cf. *Yen T'ieh Lun*(2) 79. P. 144 l. 21:
An. 3.14; cf. *Li Chi* II.324. P. 144 l. 27: *An.* 15.10. P. 145 l. 5:
Mencius 7(2)38. P. 145 l. 18: *Ku*(2) 135. P. 145 l. 22: *Kuo*(2)
203b, 247a. P. 145 l. 25: *Shih* 622; *An.* 14.6. P. 145 l. 38: *An.* 9.5;
cf. 19.22. P. 146 l. 2: *An.* 7.5; cf. 8.11. P. 146 l. 5: *Mencius* 3(1)4.2;
Shryock 103, 110 n. 36, 134. P. 147 l. 6: *Shu* 368, 385, 482. P. 147
l. 11: *Shu* 496-497. P. 147 l. 16: Cicero 25. P. 147 l. 19: Plutarch 344.
P. 147 l. 28: *Shu* 368, 383, 389-391, 395, 409, 414, 431, 498-501.
P. 147 l. 33: Bryce 66. P. 148 l. 20: *Mem. Hist.* II.170. P. 149 l. 15:
An. 12.7. P. 150 l. 8: *Han Fei* 4.5b, 16.5b-6a, 16.10b-11a, 18.3b, 18.10b-
11a, 18.12b, 19.17b. P. 150 l. 14: *An.* 12.5.4. P. 150 l. 24: *An.* 2.3.
P. 150 l. 33: Lindsay 240. P. 150 l. 39: Plato(3) 557-558, (4) 710;
Aristotle 1279. P. 151 l. 8: *An.* 12.17, 12.18, 12.19. P. 151 l. 13: *An.*
19.19. P. 151 l. 16: Plato(4) 803. P. 151 l. 21: *An.* 12.22.1. P. 151
l. 25: *An.* 5.15, 6.28, 14.45; *Mencius* 4(2)29.1. P. 151 l. 29: *An.* 13.9.
P. 151 l. 30: *An.* 4.5, 4.9, 7.11, 7.15, 8.13, 11.16, 14.11. P. 151 l.
33: *An.* 6.3.2. P. 151 l. 39: Plato(4) 744, 756; Aristotle 1318. P. 152
l. 11: *An.* 8.13. P. 152 l. 13: *An.* 13.9. P. 152 l. 21: *An.* 7.7, 9.7, 15.38.
P. 152 l. 24: Burns 176. P. 153 l. 2: Quoted in Lindsay 135. P. 153 l.
11: *Lao Tzŭ* chap. 65. P. 153 l. 15: *Han Fei* 18.8b, 19.8b-9a. P. 153
l. 20: *Mencius* 1(2)8, 4(2)32, 6(2)2. P. 153 l. 29: *An.* 14.4. P. 153
l. 35: *An.* 9.26.1. P. 153 l. 39: *Mencius* 2(1)2.7. P. 154 l. 2: *An.*
11.23.3; cf. 14.23. P. 154 l. 15: *An.* 6.1.1, 6.4, 11.2.2. P. 154 l. 25:
Cicero 137. P. 154 l. 30: *An.* 13.24, 15.27. P. 154 l. 35: *An.* 8.9,
17.4.3. P. 155 l. 14: *An.* 15.24. P. 155 l. 25: *Mem. Hist.* II.142. P. 155
l. 28: *Han Fei* 19.17b-18a. P. 155 l. 36: *An.* 13.4, 13.16; cf. 14.45.
P. 156 l. 10: Plato(4) 776-778; Aristotle 1253-1255, 1268-1269, 1279.
P. 156 l. 25: Wilbur 11, 237, 241. P. 156 l. 37: *Tso* 589, cf. *Mencius*
4(2)3.4; *Kuo Yü* 1.6b-9a, 4.9b-11a, 5.10a-11b, 6.3a-7a. P. 157 l. 30:

Tso 500, 857. P. 158 l. 13: Mem. Hist. I.298. P. 158 l. 15: An. 3.5.
P. 158 l. 17: Mencius 1(2)5. P. 158 l. 20: An. 17.5.3. P. 158 l. 27:
Mencius 1(2)8. P. 159 l. 5: Plato(3) 473, 499-502. P. 159 l. 13: An.
15.4; cf. 2.1. P. 159 l. 21: An. 12.22. P. 159 l. 24: An. 2.19, 2.20,
12.22, 13.2. P. 159 l. 34: Linebarger 130. P. 160 l. 2: Han Fei 16.10b-
11a, 18.7b-8a, 18.12b, 19.7b-8a. P. 160 l. 12: An. 14.20. P. 160 l.
15: An. 11.24. P. 160 l. 18: An. 3.19, 14.8. P. 160 l. 24: An. 13.15.5,
14.23. P. 160 l. 36: Lindsay 284. P. 161 l. 27: An. 2.12. P. 161 l. 33:
An. 15.6.2; cf. 7.10, 8.13. P. 162 l. 1: An. 2.24.2, 14.13.2, 15.8, 19.1.
P. 162 l. 3: T'ang 159-161. P. 162 l. 27: Hsün Tzŭ 165. P. 163 l. 4:
Aristotle 1287. P. 163 l. 9: Han Fei 18.7b-8a, 18.12b, 19.7b-8a. P. 163
l. 25: Linebarger 5. P. 163 l. 30: Aristotle 1287. P. 163 l. 38: Lindsay
54-55. P. 164 l. 3: Radin 502. P. 164 l. 4: Windelband 171-173. P.
164 l. 17: Merriam 50-70. P. 164 l. 24: Aristotle 1289. P. 165 l. 19:
Hattersley 154. P. 166 l. 30: Kant(2) 24, 27. P. 167 l. 3: Hattersley
240. P. 167 l. 10: Lindsay 281. P. 167 l. 13: Merriam 19. P. 167 l. 20:
Holcombe 171-172. P. 168 l. 9: Burns(2) 187. P. 168 l. 14: Finer
22-23. P. 168 l. 23: An. 15.28. P. 168 l. 31: An. 12.19, 13.11. P. 168
l. 37: Finer 35. P. 169 l. 2: An. 15.15. P. 169 l. 6: Lindsay 121. P.
169 l. 9: Quoted in ibid. 124. P. 169 l. 12: An. 12.13; cf. 2.3, 13.11.
P. 169 l. 31: An. 4.8. P. 169 l. 35: An. 6.18. P. 170 l. 10: Lindsay 60.
P. 170 l. 14: Burns(2) 234. P. 170 l. 26: Mencius 2(1)3.2. P. 171 l. 5:
Kuo Yü 15.4. P. 171 l. 6: An. 12.7, 13.29, 13.30, 14.22; Tso 840. P. 171
l. 9: An. 3.7, 7.26; Shryock 71. P. 171 l. 17: An. 3.16, 5.6, 7.10, 7.20,
14.5, 14.6, 14.35, 17.23, 17.24; Mencius 2(1)2.7. P. 174 l. 14: An.
17.5. P. 174 l. 28: Shih Chi 63.27. P. 174 l. 38: Mencius 1(1)6,
1(1)7, 2(2)12, 4(1)9; Hsün Tzŭ(2) 112. P. 175 l. 22: Hu 151. P.
176 l. 3: Mencius 3(1)4.13. P. 176 l. 5: Han Fei 19.12ab. P. 176 l. 12:
Shih Chi 67.29, 121.3-4. P. 176 l. 15: Mencius 4(2)31.3, 6(2)6.3. P.
176 l. 21: Ibid. 5(2)7.4, 7(2)34.1. P. 176 l. 24: Hsün Tzŭ(2) 109,
135. P. 176 l. 26: See Mencius 2(2)13, 5(1)6.3. P. 176 l. 29: Ibid.
7(1)20. P. 176 l. 38: Ibid. 1(2)8. P. 177 l. 21: Ibid. 2(2)3, 3(2)4.1,
7(2)30.1. P. 177 l. 27: Yen T'ieh Lun(2) 66. P. 177 l. 30: Shih Chi
74.12. P. 178 l. 32: Han Fei 18.1ab, 19.8b-9a, 19.14b. P. 178 l. 10:
Ibid. 19.8b-9a. P. 178 l. 12: Chuang Tzŭ I.288. P. 178 l. 21: Mencius
6(1)16. P. 178 l. 28: Hsün Tzŭ 89-90. P. 179 l. 13: Mo Tzŭ(2) 202-
203. P. 179 l. 30: An. 3.4; cf. 19.14. P. 180 l. 6: An. 9.6. P. 180 l. 10:
Plato(4) 695. P. 180 l. 18: An. 2.12, 9.6, 13.4. P. 182 l. 22: Mo
Tzŭ(2) 82, 189, 239. P. 183 l. 6: Huai Nan Tzŭ 21.7a. P. 183 l. 13:
Mo Tzŭ(2) 237-238. P. 183 l. 19: Ibid.(2) 125. P. 183 l. 25: Hsün
Tzŭ(2) 204-206. P. 183 l. 30: Mo Tzŭ(2) 219, 230-233. P. 184 l. 7:
Ibid.(2) 238. P. 184 l. 14: Ibid.(2) 229. P. 184 l. 18: Fung 84. P. 184
l. 26: Mo Tzŭ(2) 56. P. 184 l. 30: Quoted in Finer 19. P. 185 l. 4: Mo
Tzŭ(2) 62-63, 111, 137. P. 185 l. 12: Ibid.(2) 160-174, 236-237. P. 185
l. 31: Ibid.(2) 224. P. 186 l. 6: Kallen 310. P. 186 l. 18: An. 8.21, 14.6.
P. 187 l. 4: Mo Tzŭ 12.11b. P. 187 l. 5: Mencius 5(1)6.3. P. 187 l. 18:
Mem. Hist. IV.142. P. 187 l. 31: Mencius 5(1)5, 5(1)6. P. 187 l. 36:

Hsün Tzŭ(2) 198-200. P. 187 l. 38: *Han Shu*(2) I.218. P. 188 l. 6: *Ibid.*
I.233-236; *Mem. Hist.* II.455-457. P. 189 l. 2: Creel 55-89. P. 189 l.
7: *Mencius* 7(2)3.1. P. 189 l. 32: *Shih Chi* 74.3. P. 189 l. 36: Ts'ui
4.29-30. P. 189 l. 37: *Mencius* 2(2)10.1, 6(2)6.1. P. 190 l. 4: *Mencius*
5(1)5, 5(1)6, 7(2)14.1-2. P. 190 l. 6: *Ibid.* 1(2)7.5. P. 190 l. 9: *Ibid.*
1(2)9, 2(1)4-5. P. 190 l. 11: *Ibid.* 1(1)7.20-22, 1(2)5.3, 2(1)5, 2-5,
3(2)8. P. 190 l. 13: *Ibid.* 1(1)1, 6(2)4; *An.* 4.12, 4.16, 13.17, 14.13.2;
Kant(2) 66. P. 190 l. 15: *An.* 13.13. P. 190 l. 17: *Mencius* 1(2)6,
1(2)8, 2(2)4, 5(2)9.1. P. 190 l. 19: *Ibid.* 2(2)5, 5(2)9, 7(1)31. P. 190
l. 23: *Ibid.* 5(2)6.4-6. P. 190 l. 26: *Ibid.* 5(2)7, 7(1)8. P. 190 l. 29:
Ibid. 4(2)31.3. P. 191 l. 3: *Ibid.* 2(2)13, cf. 5(1)6.3, 7(1)36. P. 191
l. 5: *Ibid.* 7(1)20. P. 191 l. 11: *Ibid.* 4(1)6. P. 191 l. 16: *Ibid.* 1(2)7.3.
P. 191 l. 18: *Ibid.* 1(2)9, 2(1)4-5. P. 191 l. 29: *Ibid.* 3(1)1, 4(2)32,
6(2)2.1-5. P. 191 l. 35: *Ibid.* 1(2)1, 2(1)2, 2(1)6, 4(2)12, 4(2)19,
6(1)1-8, 7(2)33.1. P. 192 l. 19: *Ibid.* 7(1)4.1. P. 192 l. 21: *Ibid.* 7(1)
1.1. P. 192 l. 35: *An.* 2.10. P. 193 l. 3: *Mencius* 4(1)15. P. 193 l. 16:
Ibid. 4(1)1.4. P. 193 l. 17: *Ibid.* 4(1)2.2. P. 193 l. 20: *Ibid.* 6(2)10.7.
P. 193 l. 23: Fung 108. P. 193 l. 37: *Mencius* 2(1)2.23-24, 5(1)6.3,
5(2)1.6. P. 194 l. 4: *Ibid.* 5(1)4.1, 5(1)8.1. P. 194 l. 6: *Ibid.* 3(2)3.1,
6(2)6.6. P. 194 l. 18: *Ibid.* 5(2)2. P. 194 l. 24: *Ibid.* 7(1)4.1. P. 194
l. 28: *Ibid.* 7(1)5. P. 194 l. 35: *Ibid.* 7(1)13. P. 195 l. 31: *Chuang
Tzŭ* I.191. P. 195 l. 38: *Ibid.* I.197. P. 196 l. 8: *Lao Tzŭ* chaps. 18, 38.
P. 196 l. 9: *Ibid.* chaps. 19, 48, 80; *Chuang Tzŭ* I.198, 255-256, 288-290.
P. 196 l. 10: *Lao Tzŭ* chap. 81. P. 196 l. 11: *Ibid.* chap. 20. P. 196 l. 13:
Chuang Tzŭ II.177. P. 196 l. 15: *Lao Tzŭ* chaps. 30, 31, 57, 69, 74, 75.
P. 196 l. 17: *Ibid.* chap. 44; *Chuang Tzŭ* I.169-170, 390, II.149-165.
P. 196 l. 20: *Ibid.* II.153-154. P. 196 l. 24: *Ibid.* I.261. P. 197 l. 1: *Lao
Tzŭ* chap. 56. P. 197 l. 5: *Ibid.* chap. 5; *Chuang Tzŭ* I.332-333. P. 197
l. 11: *Lao Tzŭ* chaps. 37, 48. P. 197 l. 15: *Ibid.* chap. 3. P. 197 l. 16:
Chuang Tzŭ I.305. P. 197 l. 25: *Ibid.* I.228-229, 252, II.135-136, 166-
176, 180. P. 198 l. 3: *Ibid.* I.354-362, II.144. P. 198 l. 5: *Ibid.* II.192-
201. P. 198 l. 30: *Lao Tzŭ* chap. 47. P. 199 l. 4: Ku(3); Waley(3) 141.
P. 200 l. 4: *An.* 7.20. P. 200 l. 6: *I Ching* 411. P. 200 l. 13: *Ibid.* 354,
366. P. 200 l. 22: *Shu* 367, 421, 437, etc. P. 200 l. 25: The references
are too numerous to list completely; for examples see *Tso* 711, 790, 793,
810. P. 200 l. 27: *I Ching* 351, 369. P. 200 l. 38: Fu *chung* 61b. P. 201
l. 2: *Hsün Tzŭ*(2) 104. P. 201 l. 9: Gibbon 389. P. 201 l. 18: *I Ching*
359. P. 201 l. 20: *Ibid.* 389. P. 201 l. 21: *Chuang Tzŭ* II.57-58. P. 201 l. 25:
An. 15.11. P. 201 l. 27: *Chuang Tzŭ* I.355, 360. P. 202 l. 30: Chang
Hsin-hai 5. P. 203 l. 3: Maspero(2) 191. P. 203 l. 8: *Tso* 221, 302, 599,
618, 622, 675, 731. P. 203 l. 10: For examples see *Tso* 103, 397. P. 203
l. 37: *Tso* 282-283, 335. P. 204 l. 7: *Tso* 324, 327-328, 347. P. 204 l. 11:
Tso 316, 320-321. P. 204 l. 23: Macaulay 352-353. P. 204 l. 29: *Tso*
667-668, 802, 843. P. 205 l. 10: *Ch'in Ting Ch'un Ch'iu* 35.11a-12a.
P. 205 l. 22: *Kuo Yü* 5.8b-9a, 11a-15a, 16a-17a. P. 206 l. 4: *Chia
Yü* 2.19, 3.20b, 10.17a, 10.19b-20a. P. 206 l. 12: *Ibid.* 7.8b-10a. P.
206 l. 16: *Ibid.* 8.14a-17b. P. 206 l. 19: *Ibid.* 4.16b, 7.11b-12a;

cf. *An.* 12.19, 13.19. P. 206 l. 25: *Chia Yü* 1.21a, 2.17b-18a. P. 206
l. 31: *Ibid.* 3.1a-2b. P. 206 l. 35: *Mem. Hist.* V.299 n. 4. P. 207 l. 9:
Duyvendak(2) 95; Ch'ien Mu, *T'ung Piao* 101. P. 207 l. 20: See Duy-
vendak 221. P. 207 l. 35: *Hsün Tzŭ*(2) 175-181, 275. P. 208 l. 20: *Ibid.*
301. P. 208 l. 22: *Ibid.* 302. P. 208 l. 27: *Ibid.* 65. P. 208 l. 34: *Ibid.*
52. P. 209 l. 15: *Chuang Tzŭ* I.198. P. 209 l. 16: *Hsün Tzŭ*(2) 49-50.
P. 209 l. 18: *Ibid.* 49-50, 96-97, 119, 276-277. P. 209 l. 21: *Ibid.* 36.
P. 209 l. 23: Dubs(2) 108. P. 209 l. 30: *Hsün Tzŭ*(2) 289. P. 209 l. 33:
Fung 311. P. 209 l. 38: *Hsün Tzŭ*(2) 121. P. 210 l. 4: *An.* 13.9.3; *Hsün
Tzŭ*(2) 124. P. 210 l. 7: *Hsün Tzŭ* 121. P. 210 l. 15: *Ibid.* 77. P. 212
l. 22: *Han Fei* 16.7a, 18.6a; *Shih Chi* 63.14. P. 213 l. 1: Bodde 112-
119. P. 213 l. 9: *Han Fei* 19.1, 3, 17. P. 213 l. 13: Ch'i(2) 182-187.
P. 213 l. 27: *Han Fei* 19.7a. P. 213 l. 34: *Shang Chün Shu* 181, 186,
303; *Han Fei* 18.8b, 19.8b. Cf. *Lao Tzŭ* chaps. 3, 19, 65. P. 213 l. 36:
Lao Tzŭ chap. 65. P. 214 l. 9: Ch'i(2) 166. P. 214 l. 16: *Shang Chün
Shu* 125; cf. 24. See also *Mem. Hist.* II.44-45, 62, V.179; *Hsün Tzŭ*(2)
311-312; Bodde 2-3, 7, 19-20. P. 214 l. 28: *Hsün Tzŭ* 222-223. P. 215
l. 12: *Shih Chi* 87.5, 41; Bodde 14-15, 50. P. 215 l. 14: *Hsün Tzŭ*(2)
169-170. P. 216 l. 7: *Han Fei* 17.5a, 9, 20b; 18.3b, 7, 10-11a, 12b,
19.3b, 7b-8a, 13b-14a, 17b. P. 216 l. 16: *Shih Chi* 63.14. P. 216 l. 22:
Mem. Hist. II.91. P. 216 l. 24: *Ibid.* II.135. P. 216 l. 33: *Ibid.* II.128.
P. 216 l. 37: *Ibid.* II.155-156. P. 217 l. 5: *Ibid.* II.178. P. 217 l. 10:
Aristotle 1312-1313. P. 217 l. 20: *Han Fei* 18.8b, 19.8b-9a. P. 217 l. 24:
Mem. Hist. II.128. P. 217 l. 27: *Ibid.* II.170-173. P. 217 l. 38: *Ibid.*
II.171-174. P. 218 l. 5: *Ibid.* II.182. P. 218 l. 7: Bodde 163-165. P. 218
l. 24: *Han Fei* 9.9b-10a, 11, 13.4b. P. 218 l. 29: *Ibid.* 12.3b-4a. P. 219
l. 1: *Hsün Tzŭ* 389-390; Ts'ui 2.23; Ch'ien Mu 22-23. P. 219 l. 9:
Ts'ui(2) 3.9-13; Fung 369-371; Hughes 86-87. P. 219 l. 29: *Mem. Hist.*
II.135. P. 220 l. 1: *An.* 9.6.3, 11.23.3. P. 220 l. 4: *Han Fei* 19.3b, 17a;
Mem. Hist. II.171. P. 220 l. 8: *Chia Yü* 1.22b. P. 220 l. 34: *An.* 13.9.4,
13.29, 13.30, 17.4.3. P. 221 l. 20: *Han Fei* 19.16b. P. 223 l. 5: *Ibid.*
19.17b. P. 223 l. 20: *Mem. Hist.* II.108; cf. Bodde(2) 21. P. 223 l. 22:
Mem. Hist. II.106. P. 223 l. 26: *Ibid.* II.108-113. P. 224 l. 3: *Ibid.*
II.142, 158, 166. P. 224 l. 8: *Ibid.* II.179-180, 222-223, 232. P. 224
l. 25: *Ibid.* II.134, 137. P. 224 l. 28: *Ibid.* II.157, 182, 330. P. 225 l. 4:
Ibid. II.171, 180; *Shih Chi* 99.11. P. 225 l. 17: *Mem. Hist.* II.171-174.
P. 226 l. 4: *Shih Chi* 48.4. P. 226 l. 9: *Mem. Hist.* V.432; *Shih Chi*
121.5. P. 226 l. 10: *Yen T'ieh Lun* 4.11b; *Shih Chi* 121.5. P. 226 l. 15:
Shih Chi 121.4. P. 226 l. 20: *Han Shu* 36.1a. P. 226 l. 30: *Mem. Hist.*
V.432; *Shih Chi* 121.5. P. 227 l.5: *Mem. Hist.* II.268. P. 227 l. 8: *Ibid.*
II.308, 318. P. 227 l. 11: *Ibid.* II.273. P. 227 l. 15: *Ibid.* II.305. P. 227
l. 17: *Ibid.* II.310. P. 227 l. 21: *Ibid.* II.317. P. 227 l. 26: *Ibid.* II.323.
P. 228 l. 36: *Han Shu*(2) I.109-111, 113-114. P. 229 l. 6: *Ibid.* I.58.
P. 229 l. 16: *Ibid.* I.16, 75. P. 229 l. 19: *Ibid.* I.106-107. P. 229 l. 28:
Linebarger 130. P. 229 l. 35: *Han Shu*(2) I.115. P. 229 l. 38: *Ibid.*
I.15-22. P. 230 l. 6: *Han Shu* 43.7. P. 230 l. 16: *Han Shu*(2) I.75-77.
P. 230 l. 20: *Ibid.* I.100-102. P. 230 l. 32: *Ibid.* I.22; cf. *Han Shu*

43.16b-17a. P. 232 l. 7: *Han Shu*(2) I.206. P. 232 l. 23: *Ibid.* I.223-224. P. 232 l. 38: *Ibid.* I.216. P. 233 l. 9: *Ibid.* I.218, 244-245, 255. P. 233 l. 11: *Ibid.* I.233-236. P. 233 l. 15: *Ibid.* I.267-268. P. 233 l. 31: *Han Shu* 49.8a-9a. P. 234 l. 8: *Han Shu*(2) II.46, 49-50, 54, 69-70, 72-73, 77-79. P. 234 l. 13: *Ibid.* II.28. P. 235 l. 2: *Shih Chi* 130.9. P. 235 l. 20: *Ibid.* 121.13-15. P. 236 l. 3: *Ibid.* 121.16-19. P. 236 l. 16: *An.* 13.5. P. 236 l. 22: *Yen T'ieh Lun*(2) 59-61, 70-71, 77, 87-88; *Han Shu*(2) II.196-198, 301. P. 236 l. 27: *Yen T'ieh Lun*(2) 39, 76; *Shih Chi* 112.3-5. P. 237 l. 10: *Han Shu* 56.1b-3a. P. 238 l. 2: *Ibid.* 56.8b-9b. P. 238 l. 11: *Ibid.* 56.13b-14a. P. 238 l. 18: *Ibid.* 56.14a-19a. P. 238 l. 26: *Ibid.* 53.4b-5a. P. 238 l. 31: *Ibid.* 56.19a-20a. P. 238 l. 37: *Ibid.* 56.20b. P. 239 l. 5: *Ibid.* 56.20a. P. 239 l. 20: *Ibid.* 58.1b-2b. P. 239 l. 32: *Han Fei* 18.13a. P. 239 l. 37: *Han Shu* 58.2b-4a. P. 240 l. 3: *Han Shu*(2) II.55-56, and notes 12.3, 12.4, 12.6; *Mem. Hist.* II.171; *Han Fei* 16.3b. P. 240 l. 22: *Yen T'ieh Lun*(2) xxiv. P. 240 l. 26: *Shih Chi* 112.5-6. P. 240 l. 35: *Ibid.* 112.7. P. 240 l. 38: *Shih Chi* 121.19; *Han Shu* 56.20b. P. 241 l. 3: *Shih Chi* 112.4-8. P. 241 l. 10: *Ibid.* 121.9-12. P. 241 l. 39: *Mem. Hist.* III.568-569. P. 242 l. 4: *Ibid.* III.558. P. 242 l. 8: *Han Shu*(2) II.16, 106. P. 242 l. 14: *Ibid.* II.51, 58-60. P. 242 l. 22: *Han Shu* 88.25b. P. 242 l. 37: *Mem. Hist.* I.cvi. P. 243 l. 12: Hu(3) 28, 34-35. P. 244 l. 1: Waley 241; Fung 370. P. 244 l. 35: Fung 43; Mei 182; *Mem. Hist.* V.436. P. 245 l. 3: Chang Hsin-hai 8. P. 245 l. 16: *Mem. Hist.* V.333 n. 3. P. 245 l. 19: Ts'ui 1.18-19. P. 245 l. 22: *Mem. Hist.* V.347 n. 1, 351 n. 5, 371 n. 2. P. 245 l. 24: Ts'ui 2.27-28; Ch'ien Mu 42-45; Wilhelm 76-84. P. 245 l. 28: *Mem. Hist.* V.336-337. P. 246 l. 5: *Ibid.* V.353-354, 385-386, 388. P. 246 l. 10: Ts'ui 2.35-36. P. 246 l. 15: *Mem. Hist.* V.411. P. 246 l. 21: Ch'ien Mu 37-38, 42. P. 246 l. 25: Ts'ui 1.4; cf. 4.23. P. 246 l. 30: *Shih Chi* 130.7-10. P. 247 l. 13: *Ibid.* 121.19. P. 247 l. 26: *Mem. Hist.* III.558-559. P. 247 l. 28: *Ibid.* I.lii. P. 248 l. 4: *Ibid.* I.xlix-l. P. 248 l. 5: *Ibid.* I.lii. P. 248 l. 13: Cf. *Ibid.* I.l, V.434-435 and 435 n. 1. P. 250 l. 2: *Han Shu* 75.3b-4a; *Han Shu*(2) II.210. P. 250 l. 9: *Yen T'ieh Lun*(2) 124; *An.* 17.5.3. P. 250 l. 36: *Ch'in Ting Ch'un Ch'iu*, Preface by the Emperor, 1b-4b. P. 250 l. 39: *Ch'in Ting Ch'un Ch'iu* 26.21b-22a, 27.30a. P. 251 l. 36: Wittfogel 27-28, 39; Kracke 121. P. 252 l. 18: See Wittfogel. P. 252 l. 18: See Kracke. P. 254 l. 19: Chu 295. P. 255 l. 8: Macaulay 333-334. P. 255 l. 18: Brunetière 199. P. 255 l. 23: Lefebvre vi. P. 255 l. 29: Lefebvre 50. P. 256 l. 4: Lefebvre 215. P. 256 l. 17: Lovejoy 108. P. 256 l. 24: Leibniz, *praefatio* (3). P. 256 l. 30: Voltaire XLIX.284-285. P. 256 l. 38: Budgell, Introduction 95-96. P. 257 l. 8: Quesnay 636. P. 257 l. 25: See Dunne and Rowbotham. P. 257 l. 33: Pinot 9. P. 257 l. 36: Quoted in Reichwein 78. P. 258 l. 13: Voltaire XXI.220-221. P. 258 l. 35: Quoted from Ricci's *Commentaries* in Dunne 125. See also Trigault 157. P. 258 l. 37: Bernard I.324; cf. Bernard(2) 101-108. P. 259 l. 7: Bernard I.325. Cf. Rowbotham 64-65. P. 259 l. 10: Hu(6) 30. P. 259 l. 14: Chu 113, 135. P. 259 l. 16: *Ibid.* 110. P. 259 l. 31: Dunne 154-159; Bernard I.325; *Eminent Chinese* I.422-423; *Chu* 99-153, 166-

168; Chang Yin-lin 62-66. P. 259 l. 34: Hu(6) 70. P. 259 l. 36: Hsü 30-31. P. 260 l. 8: Pinot 183-185. P. 260 l. 19: Bernard I.334. P. 260 l. 23: Dunne 92. P. 260 l. 35: Reichwein 78. P. 261 l. 2: *An.* 15.40. P. 261 l. 5: Reichwein 77. P. 261 l. 11: Voltaire XLIX.271. P. 261 l. 13: *Ibid.* XVI.335. P. 261 l. 23: Reichwein 80. P. 261 l. 24: Voltaire XLIX.272. P. 261 l. 32: Fénelon 43. P. 261 l. 36: Montesquieu I.142. P. 262 l. 11: *Encyclopédie* III.347. P. 262 l. 25: Le Comte 242. P. 262 l. 34: See Goodrich. P. 263 l. 3: Lach 96-97. P. 263 l. 38: Hattersley 143. P. 264 l. 6: Bédé 286. P. 264 l. 16: Lanson 413. P. 264 l. 20: *Loc. cit.* P. 266 l. 27: Lanson 5-28. P. 266 l. 34: *Ibid.* 24-25. P. 267 l. 11: Pinot 15-16, 141-142. P. 267 l. 23: Lanson 411-412. P. 267 l. 30: *Ibid.* 420. P. 268 l. 3: See for instance Purchas 387. P. 268 l. 14: Lach(2) 440-441 and n. 17; Reichwein 85. P. 268 l. 18: Pinot(2) 213-214; Maverick 44-58. P. 268 l. 24: Montesquieu I.346-350. P. 268 l. 32: Lindsay 128. P. 269 l. 9: Du Halde II.18; Quesnay 572-573; Goldsmith I.181. P. 269 l. 11: Montesquieu I.144. P. 269 l. 23: Le Comte 284. P. 269 l. 28: Laski 80. P. 270 l. 4: Pinot 395. P. 270 l. 5: Purchas 387. P. 270 l. 10: Du Halde III.12. P. 270 l. 13: Burton 503. P. 270 l. 27: Budgell 91-97. P. 270 l. 29: Goldsmith I.137-141. P. 270 l. 34: Voltaire XVI.335; Maverick 30, 49, 201, 235; Poivre 160-161. P. 272 l. 2: Lovejoy 135. P. 272 l. 10: Chinard 75. P. 272 l. 31: Voltaire XVI.111. P. 272 l. 37: Budgell 91. P. 273 l. 9: Quoted in Reichwein 81. P. 273 l. 26: Koch 44. P. 273 l. 37: Weulersse 351. P. 273 l. 38: Pinot(2). P. 274 l. 10: Maverick 127. P. 274 l. 17: Quesnay 564. P. 274 l. 27: Quesnay 656. P. 274 l. 32: Faÿ 343. P. 274 l. 34: Faÿ 342. P. 274 l. 38: Faÿ 415. P. 275 l. 12: Faÿ 343-344. P. 275 l. 14: Koch 178-185. P. 275 l. 15: Parrington II.11. P. 275 l. 17: Koch 172. P. 275 l. 29: Jefferson I.446. P. 276 l. 4: Jefferson IX.425. P. 277 l. 14: *Ibid.* IX.426. P. 277 l. 32: *Ibid.* II.221, IX.425-427. P. 277 l. 35: *Ibid.* VIII.494. P. 277 l. 38: *Ibid.* IX.428. P. 278 l. 1: *Ibid.* X.95. P. 278 l. 2: *Ibid.* IX.501, X.51; Arrowood 129-131; Jefferson(3) 49-52. P. 278 l. 16: See Têng. P. 278 l. 24: *Ibid.* 306. P. 280 l. 25: Hu(4) 200. P. 281 l. 2: Hsü 30-31. P. 281 l. 15: Sun Yat-sen I. *Min Ch'üan Chu I* 10-11; (2) 170; (3) 236. P. 281 l. 19: Sun Yat-sen I. *Min Tsu Chu I* 52; (2) 98; (3) 158-159. P. 281 l. 30: Sun Yat-sen I. *Min Tsu Chu I* 66, 70; (2) 125-126, 133-134; (3) 186, 194-195. P. 281 l. 37: Linebarger 193. P. 282 l. 20: Sun Yat-sen I. *Min Shêng Chu I* 15-16; (2) 390-391; (3) 429-430. P. 282 l. 24: Sun Yat-sen I. *Min Shêng Chu I* 16; (2) 391-392; (3) 430. P. 282 l. 32: Holcombe(2) 435. P. 282 l. 34: Sun Yat-sen II. *Min Ch'üan Ch'u Pu* 99-112. P. 282 l. 37: *Ibid.* II. *Min Ch'üan Ch'u Pu* 106-107. P. 283 l. 7: Sun Yat-sen I. *Min Ch'üan Chu I* 100-112; (2) 340-360; (3) 383-400. P. 283 l. 19: Sun Yat-sen I. *Min Ch'üan Chu I* 109-110; (2) 356-358; (3) 397-398. P. 283 l. 28: *An.* 2.19, 6.1.1, 7.7, 11.24, 12.22, 14.19, 14.20, 15.13. P. 284 l. 1: Sun Yat-sen I. *Min Ch'üan Chu I* 35; (2) 220; (3) 281. P. 284 l. 10: Sun Yat-sen I. *Min Ch'üan Chu I* 36; (2) 221; (3) 282. P. 284 l. 19: Sun Yat-sen II. *Chien Kuo Fang Lüeh* 3. P. 284 l. 30: Sun Yat-sen I. *Min Ch'üan Chu I* 110;

(2) 358; (3) 398. P. 285 l. 3: Linebarger 24. P. 285 l. 5: Lin(2) 2. P. 285 l. 11: *The New York Times* (New York), April 27, 1945, p. 12. P. 285 l. 16: Sun Yat-sen I. *Min Tsu Chu I* 52-53; (2) 98-99; (3) 159-160. The passage quoted is evidently one which occurs in the *Great Learning* (*Li Chi* II.411), although Sun here substituted the character *p'ing* for *ming ming tê yü.* P. 287 l. 39: *An.* 12.7. P. 289 l. 21: *An.* 15.28.

BIBLIOGRAPHY

THE works listed here are those cited in the notes and references. They are arranged alphabetically under their bibliographical abbreviations.

Abbreviation	*Work*
Altshuler	Ira M. Altshuler, M. D., "The Part of Music in the Resocialization of Mental Patients," in *Occupational Therapy and Rehabilitation* XX (Baltimore, 1941), 75–86.
An.	The *Lun Yü* 論語 commonly called the *Analects of Confucius*. The sections are numbered as in the translations by Legge, Waley, and others.
Aristotle	*Aristotle's Politics*, tr. by Benjamin Jowett (1905; reprinted Oxford, 1931) (Pagination given as in Bekker).
Arrowood	Charles Flinn Arrowood, *Thomas Jefferson and Education in a Republic* (New York and London, 1930).
Bédé	Jean-Albert Bédé, "Gustave Lanson," in *The American Scholar* IV (New York, 1935), 286–291.
Bernard	Henri Bernard, S.J., *Le Père Matthieu Ricci et la Société Chinoise de son temps (1552–1610)* 2 vols. (Tientsin, 1937).
Bernard(2)	Henri Bernard, S.J., *Sagesse Chinoise et Philosophie Chrétienne* (Tientsin, 1935).
Biot	Édouard Biot, *Essai sur l'Histoire de l'Instruction Publique en Chine, et de la Corporation des Lettrés* (Paris, 1847).

Abbreviation	*Work*
Bodde	Derk Bodde, *China's First Unifier* (Leyden, 1938).
Bodde(2)	Derk Bodde, *Statesman, Patriot and General in Ancient China* (New Haven, 1940).
Brunetière	Ferdinand Brunetière, *Études Critiques sur l'Histoire de la Litterature Française*, 8e série (Paris, 1907).
Bryce	James Bryce, *The Holy Roman Empire*, 8th ed., rev. (London and New York, 1897).
Budgell	Eustace Budgell, *A Letter to Cleomenes King of Sparta* (London, no date but Library of Congress catalogue gives 1731).
Burns	C. Delisle Burns, *Democracy, Its Defects and Advantages* (New York, 1929).
Burns(2)	C. Delisle Burns, *Challenge to Democracy* (New York, 1935).
Burton	Robert Burton, *The Anatomy of Melancholy* (1621; reprinted New York, 1938).
Byrnes	James F. Byrnes, *Speaking Frankly* (New York, 1947).
Carcassone	E. Carcassone, "La Chine dans l'Esprit des Lois," in *Revue d'Histoire Littéraire de la France*, 31e Année (Paris, 1924), 193–205.
Cassirer	Ernst Cassirer, "Kant, Immanuel," in *ESS* VIII, 538–542.
Chan Kuo Ts'ê	*Chan Kuo Ts'ê* 戰國策 (*Ssŭ Pu Ts'ung K'an* ed.).
Chang Hsin-hai	Chang Hsin-hai, "Some Types of Chinese Historical Thought," in *Journal of the North China Branch of the Royal Asiatic Society* LX (Shanghai, 1929), 1–19.
Chang Kuo-kan	Chang Kuo-kan, ed., *Han Shih Ching Pei T'u* 漢石經碑圖 (Peiping, 1931).
Chang Yin-lin	Chang Yin-lin, "Ming Ch'ing chih Chi Hsi Hsüeh Shu Ju Chung Kuo K'ao Lüeh" 明清之際西學輸入中國考略, in *Ch'ing Hua Hsüeh Pao* I (Peking, 1924), 38–69.
Ch'ên Ch'i-t'ien	Ch'ên Ch'i-t'ien, *Han Fei Tzŭ Chiao Shih* 韓非子校釋 (Shanghai, 1940).
Ch'ên Mêng-chia	Ch'ên Mêng-chia, "Wu Hsing chih Ch'i Yüan" 五行之起源, in *Yenching Hsüeh Pao* XXIV (Peking, 1938), 35–53.
Ch'i	Ch'i Ssŭ-hê, "Chan Kuo Chih Tu K'ao" 戰國制度考, in *Yenching Hsüeh Pao* XXIV (Peking, 1938), 159–219.

Abbreviation	Work

Ch'i(2) — Ch'i Ssŭ-hê, "Shang Yang Pien Fa K'ao" 商鞅變法考, in *Yenching Hsüeh Pao* XXXIII (Peiping, 1947), 163–194.

Chia Yü — *K'ung Tzŭ Chia Yü* 孔子家語 (*Ssŭ Pu Ts'ung K'an* ed.).

Ch'ien Hsüan-t'ung — Ch'ien Hsüan-t'ung, "Lun *Shih Ching* Chên Hsiang Shu" 論詩經真相書, in KSP I, 46–47.

Ch'ien Mu — Ch'ien Mu, *Hsien Ch'in Chu Tzŭ Hsi Nien* 先秦諸子繫年, 2nd ed. (Shanghai, 1936).

Ch'ien Mu(2) — Ch'ien Mu, *Lun Yü Yao Lüeh* 論語要略 (1925; reprinted Shanghai, 1934).

Ch'in Ting Ch'un Ch'iu — *Ch'in Ting Ch'un Ch'iu Chuan Shuo Hui Tsuan* 欽定春秋傳說索纂 (1721; Kiangnan Shu Chü reprint of 1888).

Chinard — Gilbert Chinard, *Thomas Jefferson, the Apostle of Americanism*, 2nd ed., rev. (Boston, 1946).

Chinard(2) — Gilbert Chinard, "Jefferson and the Physiocrats" in *University of California Chronicle* XXXIII (Berkeley, 1931), 18–31.

Ching Tien Shih Wên — Lu Tê-ming, *Ching Tien Shih Wên* 經典釋文 (*Ssŭ Pu Ts'ung K'an* ed.).

Chu — Chu Ch'ien-chih, *Chung Kuo Ssŭ Hsiang Tui Yü Ou Chou Wên Hua chih Ying Hsiang* 中國思想對於歐洲文化之影響 (Changsha, 1940).

Chuang Tzŭ — *The Writings of Kwang-zze*, tr. by James Legge, in *Sacred Books of the East* XXXIX, 125–392 and XL, 1–232 (1891; reprinted London, 1927).

Cicero — Cicero, *The Speeches*, tr. by N. H. Watts (London and New York, 1923).

Creel — H. G. Creel, *Studies in Early Chinese Culture*, First Series (Baltimore, 1937).

Creel(2) — H. G. Creel, "Was Confucius Agnostic?" in *T'oung Pao* XXIX (Leyden, 1935), 55–99.

Creel(3) — H. G. Creel, "Shih T'ien" 釋天, in *Yenching Hsüeh Pao* XVIII (Peiping, 1935), 59–71.

Creel(4) — H. G. Creel, *The Birth of China* (London, 1936; New York, 1937).

Creel(5) — H. G. Creel, T. C. Chang, and R. C. Rudolph, *Literary Chinese by the Inductive Method*, 2 vols. (Chicago, 1938–1939).

Abbreviation	*Work*

Creel, Lorraine — Lorraine Creel, *The Concept of Social Order in Early Confucianism* (unpublished Ph.D. dissertation, University of Chicago, 1943).

Dubs — Homer H. Dubs, "Did Confucius Study the 'Book of Changes'?" in *T'oung Pao* XXV (Leyden, 1928), 82–90.

Dubs(2) — Homer H. Dubs, "The Failure of the Chinese to Produce Philosophical Systems," in *T'oung Pao* XXVI (Leyden, 1929), 98–109.

Dubs(3) — Homer H. Dubs, "The Date and Circumstances of the Philosopher Lao-dz," in Journal of the American Oriental Society LXI (Baltimore, 1941), 215–221.

Du Halde — J. B. Du Halde, S.J., *The General History of China*, tr. by R. Brookes, Vol. I (London, 1736), Vols. II–IV, 3rd ed. rev. (London, 1741).

Dunne — George H. Dunne, S.J., *The Jesuits in China in the Last Days of the Ming Dynasty* (unpublished Ph.D. dissertation, University of Chicago, 1944).

Duyvendak — J. J. L. Duyvendak, "Hsün-tzŭ on the Rectification of Names," in *T'oung Pao* XXIII (Leyden, 1924), 221–254.

Duyvendak(2) — J. J. L. Duyvendak, "The Chronology of Hsün-tzŭ," in *T'oung Pao* XXVI (Leyden, 1929), 73–95.

Duyvendak(3) — J. J. L. Duyvendak, "*The Origin and Development of the State Cult of Confucius.* By John K. Shryock." Review in *Journal of the American Oriental Society* LV (New Haven, 1935), 330–338.

Eminent Chinese — Arthur W. Hummel, ed., *Eminent Chinese of the Ch'ing Period*, 2 vols. (Washington, 1943–1944).

Encyclopédie — *Encyclopédie, ou Dictionnaire Raisonné des Sciences, des Arts et des Métiers*, ed. by Denis Diderot and J. L. d'Alembert, Vols. III and IX (Paris, 1753 and Neufchastel, 1765).

Escarra — Jean Escarra, *Le Droit Chinois* (Peking and Paris, 1936).

ESS — *Encyclopaedia of the Social Sciences*, ed. by Edwin R. A. Seligman and Alvin Johnson, 15 vols. (1930–1935; reprinted New York, 1937).

Faÿ — Bernard Faÿ, *Franklin, the Apostle of Modern Times* (Boston, 1929).

Fénelon — François de Salignac de La Mothe Fénelon, *Dialogues des Morts*, first published at Cologne in

Abbreviation	Work
	1700 as *Dialogues divers entre les cardinaux Richelieu et Mazarin et autres* (Paris, 1819).
Finer	Herman Finer, *The Future of Government* (London, 1946).
Fu	Fu Ssŭ-nien, *Hsing Ming Ku Shun Pien Chêng* 性命古訓辨證 (Changsha, 1940).
Fung	Fung Yu-lan, A *History of Chinese Philosophy, the Period of the Philosophers*, tr. by Derk Bodde (Peiping, 1937).
Fung(2)	Fung Yu-lan, "K'ung Tzŭ Ts'ai Chung Kuo Li Shih Chung chih Ti Wei" 孔子在中國歷史中之地位, in *KSP* II, 194–210.
Fung(3)	Fung Yu-lan, *Chung Kuo Chê Hsüeh Shih Pu* 中國哲學史補 (Shanghai, 1936).
Gibbon	Edward Gibbon, *The History of the Decline and Fall of the Roman Empire*, 3 vols. (1776–1788; reprinted New York, 1946).
Goldsmith	Oliver Goldsmith, *The Citizen of the World*, 2 vols. (1762; reprinted London, 1790).
Goodrich	Luther Carrington Goodrich, *The Literary Inquisition of Ch'ien-lung* (Baltimore, 1935).
Haloun	Gustav Haloun, "Fragmente des Fu-tsï und des Tsïn-tsï. Frühkonfuzianische Fragmente I," in *Asia Major* VIII (Leipzig, 1933), 437–509.
Haloun(2)	Gustav Haloun, "Das Ti-tsï-tsï. Frühkonfuzianische Fragmente II," in *Asia Major* IX (Leipzig, 1933), 467–502.
Han Fei	Wang Hsien-shên, *Han Fei Tzŭ Chi Chieh* 韓非子集解 (1896).
Han Fei(2)	*The Complete Works of Han Fei Tzŭ*, tr. by W. K. Liao, Vol. I (London, 1939).
Han Shu	Wang Hsien-ch'ien, *Ch'ien Han Shu Pu Chu* 前漢書補註 (1900).
Han Shu(2)	Pan Ku, *The History of the Former Han Dynasty*, tr. by Homer H. Dubs, Vols. I and II (Baltimore, 1938 and 1944).
Han Yü	*Chu Wên Kung Chiao Han Ch'ang Li Hsien Shêng Chi* 朱文公校韓昌黎先生集 (*Ssŭ Pu Ts'ung K'an* ed.).
Hattersley	Alan F. Hattersley, *A Short History of Democracy* (Cambridge, 1930).
Hearnshaw	F. J. C. Hearnshaw, "Chivalry, European," in *ESS* III, 436–441.

Abbreviation	Work
Höffding	Harald Höffding, *A History of Modern Philosophy*, tr. by B. E. Meyer, Vol. II (1900; reprinted London, 1920).
Holcombe	A. N. Holcombe, *Government in a Planned Democracy* (New York, 1935).
Holcombe(2)	A. N. Holcombe, "Chinese Problem," in ESS III, 431–436.
Honda	Honda Seishi, "Tso I Nien Tai K'ao" 作易年代考, in *Hsien Ch'in Ching Chi K'ao* 先秦經籍考, tr. by Chiang Chia-an (Shanghai, 1933) shang 39–66.
Hsü	Leonard Shihlien Hsü, *Sun Yat-sen; His Political and Social Ideals* (Los Angeles, 1933).
Hsün Tzŭ	Liang Ch'i-hsiung, *Hsün Tzŭ Chien Shih* 荀子柬釋 (Shanghai, 1936).
Hsün Tzŭ(2)	*The Works of Hsüntze*, tr. by Homer H. Dubs (London, 1928).
Hsün Tzŭ(3)	Wang Hsien-ch'ien, *Hsün Tzŭ Chi Chieh* 荀子集解 (1891).
Hu	Hu Shih, *Chung Kuo Chê Hsüeh Shih Ta Kang* 中國哲學史大綱, Shang Chüan, 15th ed. (Shanghai, 1930).
Hu(2)	Hu Shih, "Wang Mang, the Socialist Emperor of Nineteen Centuries Ago," in *Journal of the North China Branch of the Royal Asiatic Society* LIX (Shanghai, 1928), 218–230.
Hu(3)	Hu Shih, "The Establishment of Confucianism as a State Religion During the Han Dynasty," in *Journal of the North China Branch of the Royal Asiatic Society* LX (Shanghai, 1929), 20–41.
Hu(4)	Hu Shih, "Confucianism," in ESS IV, 198–201.
Hu(5)	*Hu Shih Lun Hsüeh Chin Chu* 胡適論學近著, Vol. I (Shanghai, 1935).
Hu(6)	Hu Shih, *The Chinese Renaissance* (Chicago, 1934).
Huai Nan Tzŭ	*Huai Nan Tzŭ* 淮南子 (Ssŭ Pu Ts'ung K'an ed.).
Huang	Huang Shih-san, *Lun Yü Hou An* 論語後案 (1844).
Hudson	G. F. Hudson, *Europe and China* (London, 1931).
Hughes	E. R. Hughes, *The Great Learning and the Mean-in-action* (New York, 1943).
Hummel	William F. Hummel, "K'ang Yu-wei, Historical Critic and Social Philosopher, 1858–1927," in

Bibliography 347

Abbreviation	Work
	Pacific Historical Review IV (Glendale, Calif., 1935), 343–355.
I Ching	The *Yi King*, tr. by James Legge, in *Sacred Books of the East* XVI, 2nd ed. (Oxford, 1899).
I Li	The *I-li*, tr. by John Steele, 2 vols. (London, 1917).
Intellectual Adventure	H. and H. A. Frankfort, John A. Wilson, Thorkild Jacobsen, William A. Irwin, *The Intellectual Adventure of Ancient Man* (Chicago, 1946).
Irwin	William A. Irwin, "The Hebrews," in *Intellectual Adventure*, 223–360.
Jacobsen	Thorkild Jacobsen, "Mesopotamia," in *Intellectual Adventure*, 125–219.
Jäger	Fritz Jäger, "Der heutige Stand der Schï-ki-Forschung," in *Asia Major* IX (Leipzig, 1933), 21–37.
Jefferson	The *Writings of Thomas Jefferson*, ed. by Paul Leicester Ford, 10 vols. (New York and London, 1892–1899).
Jefferson(2)	The *Commonplace Book of Thomas Jefferson*, ed. by Gilbert Chinard (Baltimore and Paris, 1926).
Jefferson(3)	The *Life and Selected Writings of Thomas Jefferson*, ed. by Adrienne Koch and William Peden (New York, 1944).
Jung Chao-tsu	Jung Chao-tsu, *Han Fei Tzŭ K'ao Chêng* 韓非子考證 (Shanghai, 1936).
Jung Kêng	Jung Kêng, *Chin Wên Pien* 金文編, rev. ed. (Changsha, 1939).
Kallen	Horace M. Kallen, "Pragmatism," in *ESS* XII, 307–311.
K'ang	K'ang Yu-wei, *K'ung Tzŭ Kai Chih K'ao* 孔子改制考 (1897; reprinted Peking, 1922).
Kant	*Immanuel Kant's Sämmtliche Werke*, ed. by K. Rosenkranz and F. W. Schubert, 14 vols. (Leipzig, 1838–1842).
Kant(2)	Immanuel Kant, *Perpetual Peace*, reprint of translation published in London in 1796, translator unnamed (Los Angeles, 1932).
Karlgren	Bernhard Karlgren, *On the Authenticity and Nature of the Tso Chuan* (Göteborg, 1926).
Karlgren(2)	Bernhard Karlgren, "Huai and Han," in *Bulletin of the Museum of Far Eastern Antiquities* XIII (Stockholm, 1941).
Kennedy	George A. Kennedy, "Interpretation of the Ch'un-

Abbreviation	*Work*
	Ch'iu," in *Journal of the American Oriental Society* LXII (Baltimore, 1942), 40–48.
Koch	Adrienne Koch, *The Philosophy of Thomas Jefferson* (New York, 1943).
Kracke	E. A. Kracke, Jr., "Family vs. Merit in Chinese Civil Service Examinations under the Empire," in *Harvard Journal of Asiatic Studies* X (Cambridge, 1947), 103–123.
KSP	*Ku Shih Pien* 古史辨, ed. by Ku Chieh-kang et al., 7 vols. Vols. I–V (Peiping, 1926–1935), Vols. VI–VII (Shanghai, 1938–1941).
Ku	Ku Chieh-kang, "Lun K'ung Tzŭ Shan Shu *Liu Ching* Shuo chi Chan Kuo Chu Tso Wei Shu Shu" 論孔子删述六經說及戰國著作偽書書, in *KSP* I, 41–43.
Ku(2)	Ku Chieh-kang, "Ch'un Ch'iu Shih ti K'ung Tzŭ hê Han Tai ti K'ung Tzŭ"春秋時的孔子和漢代的孔子, in *KSP* II, 130–139.
Ku(3)	Ku Chieh-kang, "*Chou I* Kua Yao Tz'ŭ Chung ti Ku Shih" 周易卦爻辭中的故事, in *KSP* III, 1–44.
Ku(4)	Ku Chieh-kang, "*Shih Ching* Tsai Ch'un Ch'iu Chan Kuo Chien ti Ti Wei"詩經在春秋戰國間的地位, in *KSP* III, 309–367.
Ku(5)	Ku Chieh-kang, "Chan Kuo Ch'in Han Chien Jên ti Tsao Wei yü Pien Wei"戰國秦漢間人的造偽與辨偽, in *KSP* VII (1), 1–64.
Ku(6)	Ku Chieh-kang, "Shan Jang Ch'uan Shuo Ch'i Yü Mo Chia K'ao" 禪讓傳說起於墨家考, in *KSP* VII(3), 30–107.
Ku-Liang Chuan	*Shih San Ching Chu Su* 十三經注疏, *Ch'un Ch'iu Ku-Liang Chuan Chu Su* 春秋穀梁傳注疏 (Nanchang, 1815).
Kung-Yang Chuan	*Shih San Ching Chu Su* 十三經注疏, *Ch'un Ch'iu Kung-Yang Chu Su* 春秋公羊注疏 (Nanchang, 1815).
Kuo	Kuo Mo-jo, *Chin Wên Ts'ung K'ao* 金文叢考 (Tokyo, 1932).
Kuo(2)	Kuo Mo-jo, *Liang Chou Chin Wên Tz'ŭ Ta Hsi K'ao Shih* 兩周金文辭大系考釋 (Tokyo, 1935).

Abbreviation	Work
Kuo(3)	Kuo Mo-jo, *Shih P'i P'an Shu* 十批判書 (Chung-king, 1945).
Kuo Yü	*Kuo Yü* 國語 (*Ssŭ Pu Ts'ung K'an* ed.).
Lach	Donald F. Lach, *Contributions of China to German Civilization, 1648–1740* (unpublished Ph.D. dissertation, University of Chicago, 1941).
Lach(2)	Donald F. Lach, "Leibniz and China," in *Journal of the History of Ideas* VI (New York, 1945), 436–455.
La Master	Robert J. La Master, "Music Therapy as a Tool for Treatment of Mental Patients in the Hospital," in *Hospital Management* LXII.6 (Chicago, 1946), 110–114, LXIII.1 (1947), 110–114.
Lang	Paul Henry Lang, *Music in Western Civilization* (New York, 1941).
Lanson	Gustave Lanson, "Le Rôle de l'Experience dans la Formation de la Philosophie du XVIIIe Siècle en France," in *La Revue du Mois* IX (Paris, 1910): I. "La Transformation des Idées Morales et la Naissance des Morales Rationelles de 1680 à 1715," 5–28; II. "L'Éveil de la Conscience Sociale et les Premières Idées de Réformes Politiques," 409–429.
Lao Tzŭ	The Taoist work 老子, also known as the *Tao Tê Ching* 道德經.
Laski	Harold J. Laski, "Democracy," in ESS V, 76–85.
Lecky	W. E. H. Lecky, *History of the Rise and Influence of the Spirit of Rationalism in Europe*, 2 vols. (New York, 1866).
Le Comte	Louis Daniel Le Comte, *Memoirs and Observations . . . Made in a Late Journey Through the Empire of China*, tr. from the Paris ed. (London, 1697).
Lefebvre	Georges Lefebvre, *The Coming of the French Revolution*, tr. by R. R. Palmer (Princeton, 1947). First published as *Quatre-vingt-neuf* (Paris, 1939).
Legge	*The Chinese Classics*, tr. by James Legge, Vols. I–II, 2nd ed. rev. (Oxford, 1893–1895), Vols. III–V (London, 1865–1872).
Leibniz	Gottfried Wilhelm, freiherr von Leibniz, *Novissima Sinica*, 2nd ed. (Leipzig? 1699).
Li Chi	*The Lî Kî*, tr. by James Legge, in *Sacred Books of the East* XXVII and XXVIII (1885; reprinted London, 1926).

Abbreviation	*Work*
Liang	Liang Ch'i-ch'ao, "Hsün Ch'ing chi Hsün Tzŭ" 荀卿及荀子, in *KSP* IV, 104–115.
Lin	Lin Yutang, "Li: the Chinese Principle of Social Control and Organization," in *Chinese Social and Political Science Review* II, No. 1 (Peking, 1917), 106–118.
Lin(2)	Lin Yutang, *The Wisdom of Confucius* (New York, 1943).
Lindsay	A. D. Lindsay, *The Modern Democratic State*, Vol. I (New York and London, 1947).
Linebarger	Paul M. A. Linebarger, *Government in Republican China* (New York and London, 1938).
Liu Ê	Liu Ê, ed., *T'ieh-yün Ts'ang Kuei* 鐵雲藏龜, reprinted with transcriptions by Pao Ting (1931).
Liu Pao-nan	Liu Pao-nan and Liu Kung-mien, *Lun Yü Chêng I* 論語正義 (first pub. 1866) in *Huang Ch'ing Ching Chieh Hsü Pien* (Chiangyin, 1886–1888) 1051–1074.
Lo	Lo Chên-yü, ed., *Yin Hsü Shu Ch'i Ch'ien Pien* 殷盧書契前編 (1912).
Lo(2)	Lo Chên-yü, *Chên Sung T'ang Chi Ku I Wên* 貞松堂集古遺文 (1931).
Lo(3)	Lo Chên-yü, *Han Hsi P'ing Shih Ching Ts'an Tzŭ Chi Lu* 漢熹平石經殘字集錄, rev. ed. (1938).
Lovejoy	Arthur O. Lovejoy, "The Chinese Origin of a Romanticism," in *Essays in the History of Ideas* (Baltimore, 1948) 99–135.
Lun Yü	*Shih San Ching Chu Su* 十三經注疏, *Lun Yü Chu Su* 論語注疏 (Nanchang, 1815).
Lun Yü Shih	Ch'êng Shu-tê, *Lun Yü Chi Shih* 論語集釋 (Peking, 1943).
Macaulay	Thomas Babington Macaulay, "*The Romance of History. England.* By Henry Neele." Unsigned review in *The Edinburgh Review* XLVII (Edinburgh, 1828), 331–367.
Makino	Makino Kenjiro, *Shiki Kokujikai* 史記國字解 VII (Waseda University; Tokyo, 1919).
Maspero	Henri Maspero, *La Chine Antique* (Paris, 1927).
Maspero(2)	Henri Maspero, "La composition et la date du Tso tchouan," in *Mélanges Chinois et bouddhiques* I (Brussels, 1932), 137–215.

Abbreviation	*Work*
Maverick	Lewis A. Maverick, *China, a Model for Europe* (San Antonio, 1946).
Mei	Mei Ssŭ-p'ing, "Ch'un Ch'iu Shih Tai ti Chêng Chih hê K'ung Tzŭ ti Chêng Chih Ssŭ Hsiang" 春秋時代的政治和孔子的政治思想 in *KSP* II, 161–194.
Mem. Hist.	Se-ma Ts'ien, *Les Memoires Historiques*, tr. by Édouard Chavannes, 5 vols. (Paris, 1895–1905).
Mencius	*Mencius*, the book named after the philosopher Mêng Tzŭ 孟子. The sections are numbered as in Legge's translation.
Mêng Tzŭ	*Shih San Ching Chu Su* 十三經注疏, *Mêng Tzŭ Chu Su* 孟子注疏 (Nanchang, 1815).
Merriam	Charles E. Merriam, *The New Democracy and the New Despotism* (New York and London, 1939).
Mo Tzŭ	Sun I-jang, *Mo Tzŭ Chien Ku* 墨子閒詁 (1895).
Mo Tzŭ(2)	*The Ethical and Political Works of Mo Tzŭ*, tr. by Mei Yi-pao (London, 1929).
Montesquieu	Charles de Secondat, Baron de Montesquieu, *The Spirit of Laws*, tr. by Thomas Nugent, 2 vols. (Cincinnati, 1873).
Morley	John Viscount Morley, *Diderot and the Encyclopaedists*, Vol. I (London, 1923).
Parrington	Vernon Louis Parrington, *Main Currents in American Thought*, 3 vols. (New York, 1930).
Pelliot	Paul Pelliot, "Meou-tseu ou les doutes levés," in *T'oung Pao* XIX (Leyden, 1920), 255–433.
Pick	Bernhard Pick, *The Extra-Canonical Life of Christ* (New York, 1903).
Pinot	Virgile Pinot, *La Chine et la Formation de l'Esprit Philosophique en France (1640–1740)* (Paris, 1932).
Pinot(2)	Virgile Pinot, "Les Physiocrates et la Chine au XVIIIe siècle," in *Revue d'Histoire Modern et Contemporaine* VIII (Paris, 1906–1907), 200–214.
Plato	*Cratylus*, in *The Dialogues of Plato*, tr. by Benjamin Jowett, 2 vols. (1892; reprinted New York, 1937) I, 173–229. (Pagination given, for this and the following dialogues, as in Stephens).
Plato(2)	*Phaedo*, in *ibid.* I, 441–501.
Plato(3)	*The Republic*, in *ibid.* I, 591–879.
Plato(4)	*Laws*, in *ibid.* II, 407–703.

Abbreviation	Work
Plutarch	*Plutarch's Lives*, "the translation called Dryden's," rev. by A. H. Clough, Vol. II (Boston, 1864).
Poivre	Pierre Poivre, *Travels of a Philosopher*, tr. from French, translator unnamed (Dublin, 1770).
Purchas	Samuel Purchas, *Hakluytus Posthumous or Purchas His Pilgrims*, Vol. XII (1625; reprinted Glasgow, 1906).
Quesnay	François Quesnay, "Despotisme de la Chine," in *Oeuvres Économiques et Philosophiques de F. Quesnay*, ed. by Auguste Oncken (Frankfort and Paris, 1888), 563–660. First published serially in the *Éphémérides du Citoyen* (Paris, 1767); translated in Maverick 141–304.
Radin	Max Radin, "Jus Gentium," in *ESS* VIII, 502–504.
Reichwein	Adolf Reichwein, *China and Europe; Intellectual and Artistic Contacts in the Eighteenth Century* (New York, 1925).
Rogers	A. K. Rogers, *The Socratic Problem* (New Haven, 1933).
Rowbotham	Arnold H. Rowbotham, *Missionary and Mandarin, the Jesuits at the Court of China* (Berkeley and Los Angeles, 1942).
Rowbotham(2)	Arnold H. Rowbotham, "The Impact of Confucianism on Seventeenth Century Europe," in *Far Eastern Quarterly* IV (1945), 224–242.
Shang Chün Shu	*The Book of Lord Shang*, tr. by J. J. L. Duyvendak (London, 1928).
Shih	*The Chinese Classics*, tr. by James Legge, Vol. IV, *The She King*, 2 pts. (London, 1871).
Shih(2)	*The Book of Songs*, tr. by Arthur Waley (Boston and New York, 1937).
Shih Chi	Takigawa Kametaro, *Shih Chi Hui Chu K'ao Chêng* 史記會注考證, 10 vols. (Tokyo, 1932–1934).
Shih Chu Su	*Shih San Ching Chu Su* 十三經注疏, *Mao Shih Chu Su* 毛詩注疏 (Nanchang, 1815).
Shryock	John K. Shryock, *The Origin and Development of the State Cult of Confucius* (New York and London, 1932).
Shu	*The Chinese Classics*, tr. by James Legge, Vol. III, *The Shoo King*, 2 pts. (London, 1865).
Sun Hai-po	Sun Hai-po, *Chia Ku Wên Pien* 甲骨文編 (Peiping, 1934).

Abbreviation	Work
Sun Yat-sen	Sun Chung-shan, *Chung-shan Ts'ung Shu* 中山叢書, 3rd ed., 4 vols. (Shanghai, 1927).
Sun Yat-sen(2)	Sun Yat-sen, *San Min Chu I, the Three Principles of the People,* tr. by Frank W. Price (Shanghai, 1929).
Sun Yat-sen(3)	Sun Yat-sen, *The Triple Demism of Sun Yat-sen,* tr. by Paschal M. D'Elia (Wuchang, 1931).
Tai	Tai Wang, *Tai Shih Chu Lun Yü* 戴氏注論語 (1871).
T'ai P'ing Yü Lan	*T'ai P'ing Yü Lan* 太平御覽 (Yangchow, 1806).
T'ang	T'ang Yung-t'ung, "Wang Pi's New Interpretation of the *I ching* and *Lun-yü*," tr. by Walter Liebenthal, in *Harvard Journal of Asiatic Studies* X (Cambridge, 1947), 124–161.
Taylor	A. E. Taylor, *Socrates* (1932; reprinted Edinburgh, 1933).
Têng	Têng Ssŭ-yü, "Chinese Influence on the Western Examination System," in *Harvard Journal of Asiatic Studies* VII (Cambridge, 1943), 267–312.
Trigault	Nicholas Trigault, *The China That Was,* tr. by L. J. Gallagher, from work published in 1615 (Milwaukee, 1942).
Tso	*The Chinese Classics,* tr. by James Legge, Vol. V, *The Ch'un Ts'ew, with the Tso Chuen,* 2 pts., (London, 1872).
Tso Chuan Chu Su	*Shih San Ching Chu Su* 十三經注疏, *Ch'un Ch'iu Tso Chuan Chu Su* 春秋左傳注疏 (Nanchang, 1815).
Ts'ui	Ts'ui Shu, *Chu Ssŭ K'ao Hsin Lu* 洙泗考信錄, in *Ts'ui Tung-pi I Shu* 崔東壁遺書, ed. by Ku Chieh-kang, 8 vols. (Shanghai, 1936) III.
Ts'ui(2)	Ts'ui Shu, *Chu Ssŭ K'ao Hsin Yü Lu* 洙泗考信餘錄, in *Ts'ui Tung-pi I Shu* IV.
Ts'ui(3)	Ts'ui Shu, *Lun Yü Yü Shuo* 論語餘說, in *Ts'ui Tung-pi I Shu* V.
Tung	Tung Tso-pin, *Yin Li P'u* 殷曆譜 (Li-chuang, Szechwan, 1945).
Voltaire	*Oeuvres Complètes de Voltaire,* 92 vols. (Impr. de la Société Littéraire-typographique, 1785–1789).
Waley	*The Analects of Confucius,* tr. by Arthur Waley (1938; reprinted London, 1945).

Abbreviation	Work
Waley(2)	Arthur Waley, "The Book of Changes," in *Bulletin of the Museum of Far Eastern Antiquities* V (Stockholm, 1933), 121–142.
Waley(3)	Arthur Waley, *The Way and Its Power* (London, 1934).
Weber	*From Max Weber: Essays in Sociology*, tr. and ed. by H. H. Gerth and C. Wright Mills (New York, 1946).
Wei Shu	*Wei Shu T'ung K'ao* 偽書通考, ed. by Chiang Hsin-ch'êng (Changsha, 1939).
Weulersse	G. Weulersse, "The Physiocrats," in *ESS* V, 348–351.
Wilbur	C. Martin Wilbur, *Slavery in China During the Former Han Dynasty* (Chicago, 1943).
Wilhelm	Richard Wilhelm, *Confucius and Confucianism*, tr. by G. H. and A. P. Danton (London, 1931).
Williamson	H. R. Williamson, *Wang An Shih*, 2 vols. (London, 1935–1937).
Wilson	John A. Wilson, "Egypt," in *Intellectual Adventure* 31–121.
Windelband	Wilhelm Windelband, *A History of Philosophy*, tr. by James H. Tufts (New York, 1923).
Wittfogel	Karl August Wittfogel, "Public Office in the Liao and the Chinese Examination System," in *Harvard Journal of Asiatic Studies* X (Cambridge, 1947), 13–40.
Wu	Wu Ta-ch'êng, *K'ê Chai Chi Ku Lu* 愙齋集古錄 (1896).
Yeh	Yeh Yü-shên, *Yin Hsü Shu Ch'i Ch'ien Pien Chi Shih* 殷虛書契前編集釋 (Shanghai, 1934).
Yen Jo-chü	Yen Jo-chü, *Chiao Chêng Ssŭ Shu Shih Ti* 校正四書釋地, revised by Ku Wên (1803).
Yen T'ieh Lun	Huan K'uan, *Yen T'ieh Lun* 鹽鐵論 (*Ssŭ Pu Ts'ung K'an* ed.).
Yen T'ieh Lun(2)	Huan K'uan, *Discourses on Salt and Iron*, tr. by Esson M. Gale (Leyden, 1931).
Yen Tzŭ	*Yen Tzŭ Ch'un Ch'iu* 晏子春秋 (*Ssŭ Pu Ts'ung K'an* ed.).

INDEX

Index